Praise from Job Seekers for the
Knock 'em Dead Books

"I was sending out hordes of resumes and hardly getting a nibble—and I have top-notch skills and experience in my field. I wasn't prepared for this tough job market. When I read your book, however, I immediately began applying some of your techniques. My few nibbles increased to so many job interviews I could hardly keep up with them!"

—C.S., Chicago, Illinois

"Every time I've used your book, I've gotten an offer! This book is incredible. Thanks for publishing such a great tool."

—W.Z., Columbia, Maryland

"I read and used your book, *Resumes That Knock 'em Dead*, as I searched for a job. I was called for an interview and was up against ten applicants. To make a long story short, I interviewed on Monday morning, and by Monday afternoon knew I had the job."

—E.H. (no address given)

"I've used *Knock 'em Dead* since 1994 when I graduated. It's the reason I've made it to VP—thank you!"

—P.L., Norfolk, Virginia

"After reading your book, *Resumes That Knock 'em Dead*, I rewrote my resume and mailed it to about eight companies. The results were beyond belief. I was employed by one of the companies that got my new resume, and received offers of employment or requests for interviews from every company. The entire job search took only five weeks."

—J.V., Dayton, Ohio

"My son called me from college last night, desperate to help a friend on her first interview. My advice? Tell her to drop everything and head to the nearest bookstore to get *Knock 'em Dead*. The book is a godsend and helped me obtain the job of my dreams eight years ago. It is by far THE best book on interviewing out there. I highly recommend it to everyone I know who asks me for help. As a Director of HR now, I know. No one should go to an interview without reading, re-reading, and re-re-reading this informative, absorbing, tremendously helpful book. It is utterly amazing. Thank you!"

—S.D., Philadelphia, Pennsylvania

"I am very grateful for your *Knock 'em Dead* series. I have read the trio and adopted the methods. In the end, I got a dream job with a salary that is almost double of my previous! By adopting your methods, I got four job offers and had a hard time deciding!"

—C.Y., Singapore

"I rejigged my resume exactly as you outlined in your book and one employer said, 'You can tell this person has a real love of PR from his resume.' Within three weeks I had three job offers and was able to pick and choose the perfect job for myself."

—M.W., Detroit, Michigan

"Your book is simply fantastic. This one book improved my yearly income by several thousand dollars, and my future income by untold amounts. Your work has made my family and myself very happy."

—M.Z., St. Clair Shores, Michigan

"I cannot tell you what a fabulous response I have been getting due to the techniques you describe in your books. Besides giving me the tools I needed to 'get my foot in the door,' they gave me confidence. I never thought I could secure an excellent position within a month!"

—B.G., Mountainview, California

"My job search began a few months ago when I found out that I would be laid off because of a corporate buyout. By following your advice, I have had dozens of interviews and have received three very good job offers. Your excellent advice made my job hunt much easier."

—K.C., St. Louis, Missouri

"I heard of your book right after I bombed out on three interviews. I read it. I went on two interviews after reading it. I have been told by both of those last two interviewers that I am the strongest candidate. I may have two job offers!"

—B.V., Albuquerque, New Mexico

"I read your book and studied your answers to tough questions. The first interview that I went on after doing this ended up in a job being offered to me! The interviewer told me that I was the best interviewee she'd seen! Thanks a million for writing your book. I am so thankful that I had heard about you!"

—K.P., Houston, Texas

"I just finished writing the letter I have dreamed of writing for three years: my letter of resignation from the Company from Hell. Thanks to you and the book *Knock 'em Dead*, I have been offered and have accepted an excellent position with a major international service corporation."

—C.C., Atlanta, Georgia

"After having seen you on television, I decided to order the *Knock 'em Dead* books. Your insights into selling myself helped me find opportunities in my field that would not have been attainable otherwise."

—E.M., Short Hills, New Jersey

"I just received the offer of my dreams with an outstanding company. Thank you for your insight. I was prepared!"

—T.C., San Francisco, California

"I got the position! I was interviewed by three people and the third person asked me all the questions in *Knock 'em Dead*. I had all the right answers!"

—D.J., Scottsdale, Arizona

"Thank you for all the wonderfully helpful information you provided in your book. I lost my job almost one year ago. I spent almost eight months looking for a comparable position. Then I had the good sense to buy your book. Two months later, I accepted a new position. You helped me turn one of the worst experiences of my life into a blessing in disguise."

—L.G., Watervliet, New York

"I was out of work for four months—within five weeks of reading your book, I had four job offers."

—S.K., Dallas, Texas

"I followed the advice in *Knock 'em Dead* religiously and got more money, less hours, a better hospital plan, and negotiated to keep my three weeks vacation. I start my new job immediately!"

—A.B., St. Louis, Missouri

KnOCK 'em DEaD

RESUMES

9TH EDITION

Standout advice from America's
leading job search authority

MARTIN YATE, CPC
New York Times bestselling author

Aadamsmedia
Avon, Massachusetts

Published by Adams Media, a division of F+W Media, Inc.
57 Littlefield Street
Avon, MA 02322
www·adamsmedia·com

ISBN 10: 1-4405-0587-X
ISBN 13: 978-1-4405-0587-4
eISBN 10: 1-4405-0882-8
eISBN 13: 978-1-4405-0882-0

Printed in the United States of America.

10 9 8 7 6 5 4 3 2 1

Library of Congress Cataloging-in-Publication Data
available from the publisher.

This publication is designed to provide accurate and authoritative information with regard to the subject matter covered. It is sold with the understanding that the publisher is not engaged in rendering legal, accounting, or other professional advice. If legal advice or other expert assistance is required, the services of a competent professional person should be sought.

— From a *Declaration of Principles* jointly adopted by a Committee of the American Bar Association and a Committee of Publishers and Associations

Many of the designations used by manufacturers and sellers to distinguish their product are claimed as trademarks. Where those designations appear in this book and Adams Media was aware of a trademark claim, the designations have been printed with initial capital letters.

This book is available at quantity discounts for bulk purchases.
For information, please call 1-800-289-0963.

CONTENTS

ACKNOWLEDGMENTS

In twenty-five years of publication around the world, the *Knock 'em Dead* books owe their success to millions of satisfied readers who spread the word, and four generations of dedicated professionals at Adams Media. Thank you for all of your support, and through it that greatest of honors: making a difference in someone's life every day.

INTRODUCTION

The Facts of Your Professional Life

On the list of things you want to do in life, writing your resume is right up there with hitting yourself in the head with a hammer. Your resume is the most financially important document you will ever own. If it works, you work, if it doesn't you won't.

A killer resume is the foundation of every successful career; what you learn in these pages will guide your success for years to come.

CHAPTER 1

WHY YOUR RESUME SUCKS AND HOW TO MAKE IT SHINE

> *Read this book with a highlighter—*
> *it will save time as you refer back to important passages.*

YOUR RESUME IS the most financially important document you will ever own.

When it works, the doors of opportunity open for you. When it doesn't work, they won't. No one enjoys writing a resume, but it has such a major impact on the money you earn during your work life, and consequently on the quality of your whole life outside of work, that you know this is something that needs to be done right.

You didn't come to this book for a good read. You came because you are facing serious challenges in your professional life. Whatever your situation, upper-level executive, seasoned pro, or fresh out of school and wondering how it's done, you realize a new approach is demanded.

The way the professional world works has changed dramatically in the last fifteen years, and nothing has changed as much as the way companies recruit and the ways we find jobs. Because everything related to corporate recruitment and selection has changed almost beyond recognition, in turn everything to do with your approach to the job search needs to be re-thought. At the foundation of things that have to be examined is your resume: if it works, you will, if it doesn't, you won't.

In these pages you are going to learn very quickly how to build a resume that works. Because the approach is based on the end game of a successful life, everything I teach you about developing a kick-ass resume will also give you a firmer grasp on critical job-search, interview, and career-management skills.

What you'll learn here goes way beyond writing a resume. When you are done, you will walk away with a killer resume, one that will land you that new job, plus an incredible bonus of some key strategies and tactics for your job search, interviews, and even some amazing insights into winning raises and promotions.

Self-Awareness Gives You an Edge

Employers always favor self-aware candidates—and this is exactly what you are about to become. Beyond opening doors of opportunity, the way you build your resume will give you an understanding of what employers need, how they think about and prioritize those needs, and what you have to do in response to get their attention and that job offer.

Your employer just wants to make a buck

Staff only gets added to the payroll to enhance profitability. Think about this: If you owned a company, there just isn't any other reason you would add workers to your payroll. So it is implicit in the employment contract that we all contribute to profitability in some way.

If you're not solving problems, "you ain't doin' squat."

No resume gets read, no one gets interviewed, and no one gets hired unless someone somewhere is trying to solve a problem. That problem may be finding a quicker way to manufacture silicon chips, speed up accounts receivable, leverage social networking for brand management, or any one of a million other profit challenges.

The only reason a job ever comes into existence is because the employer needs to hire someone who knows and can handle the problems that occur in a specific area of professional responsibility. Not having someone is costing them revenue and profits. Problem solving, the application of critical thinking within your area of expertise is what you are paid to do. It is why every job opening exists, and why every job gets filled with the person who seems to have the firmest grip on how to identify, prevent, and solve problems related to that job.

Why No One Wants to Read Your Resume

You may think that resume writing is a tough job, but what about the resume readers? Go to the resume samples section and try to read and understand six resumes in a row. Then you'll know why no one wants to read your resume.

The reality is that no one ever reads resumes unless they have to, which means that when your resume does get read, a job exists—a job has been carefully defined and titled, a salary range has been authorized, the position has been budgeted, and the funds have been released. *Whenever a recruiter searches a resume database or reads a resume, s/he is doing it with a specific job and the language and priorities of that job description in mind.*

Why They May Never Get the Chance

The impact of technology on the workplace causes the nature of all jobs to change almost as rapidly as the pages on a calendar. In the not-so-distant past, someone would have immediately reviewed your resume, but today resumes no longer go straight to a recruiter or manager's desk; they are more likely to go to a resume database.

This means that before a human being reads your resume, it must be chosen from that database as worth reviewing. Keep in mind that some of those databases contain over 35 million resumes.

Can you see that if your resume's a gumbo of everything you've ever done, *everything you happen to think is important*, it is never going to work?

The Resume That Kicks Butt and Takes Names

Your resume works when it focuses on your strengths as they are related to the responsibilities and deliverables of a specific target job. This requires that your resume focus on how employers—your customers—think about, prioritize, and describe this job's deliverables.

Deliverables refer to what you are expected to deliver by way of results as you execute your assigned responsibilities.

You know that phrases like "the customer is always right," "the customer comes first," and "understand your customer" underlie successful businesses. When you apply this thinking to a resume, you create a document tailored to your customers' needs, in the same way that corporations tailor products to be appealing to their customers. Focused on a specific target job and built from the ground up with the customer's needs in mind, your resume will perform better in the recruiters' resume database searches and it will be far more attractive to human eyes already glazed from the tedium of resume reading.

Get smart: this is not your last job change

You live and work in a far less secure professional world than anyone has ever known. No longer is there any such thing as job security. You are somewhere in the throes of a half-century worklife, a career in which you are likely to have three or more distinct careers and statistically likely to change jobs about every four years. This is a world where economic recessions come around every seven to ten years and age discrimination is going to begin to kick in around age fifty.

This is a wake-up call: You need a tougher, more pragmatic approach to your professional life. You need to survive and prosper. You need to find a better way.

When I started to talk about these issues twenty-five years ago, I was called a communist and asked how I could suggest that Americans be disloyal to their employers. History has shown it is the corporations that broke the employment contract, yet even today I still hear that companies demand the unblinking loyalty and blind fidelity of their employees. I'm sorry, but if you believe these sorry myths, your life and the lives of your loved ones will suffer.

Start to think of yourself as a corporation, MeInc, a financial entity that must always plan and act in the best interests of its economic survival. Like any corporation, MeInc has products and services that are constantly under development. These are the ever-evolving skill bundles that define the professional you. Again just like any corporation, these products and services are branded and sold to your targeted customer base: employers who hire people like you.

The success of MeInc depends on how well you run your company, and like every successful company you'll need initiatives for Research and Development, Strategic Planning, Marketing, Public Relations, and Sales. Research and Development. Every company is continually involved in identification and development of products and services that will appeal to their customers. You must likewise have the same ongoing initiatives. This translates to skill building in response to market trends, which you do by being connected to your profession and by monitoring the changing market demands for your job on an ongoing basis.

- **Strategic Planning:** The development of career management strategies. You'll begin to think of your career over the long term, where you want to be and how you are going to get there—how you will stay on top of skill development, how you will develop and maintain a desirable professional brand.

- **Marketing and PR:** The effective branding of MeInc. as a desirable product requires establishing credibility for the services you deliver. You must position these services so your professional credibility becomes visible to an ever-widening circle, within your company to encourage professional growth and within your profession to encourage your employability elsewhere.
- **Sales:** MeInc. needs a state-of-the-art sales program to sell your products and services.

Your new resume is the primary sales tool for MeInc., the company you embody. It is the most financially important document you will ever own, you can learn how to do it right, starting right now.

CHAPTER 2
GET INSIDE YOUR CUSTOMER'S HEAD

"THE CUSTOMER IS always right" is probably the first business lesson you ever learned. If you are on the front lines of your company, interacting daily with customers, vendors, and others, you completely understand the importance of "getting inside your customer's head."

Yet when it comes to creating resumes, no one ever seems to do this. As I've stressed, and will continue to do so, your resume is the primary marketing device for every job change throughout your worklife. More than anything else, your resume determines your professional success.

Your current resume is probably a straightforward and honest recitation of all you have done. It lists everything that you *think* is important, but despite all your efforts this resume isn't working. That's because a simple recitation of all your accomplishments and activities results in a hodgepodge of what *you* think is important, *not what your customers believe is important.* You're building a resume that tries to have the widest possible appeal, but your customers—the people who can hire you—ignore it because it isn't built with their needs in mind.

Have you ever looked at a Swiss army knife? It's got knife blades, bottle openers, screwdrivers . . . it does practically everything. But companies aren't hiring human Swiss army knives. They are hiring human lasers, with exceptional skills focused in a specific area. *You need a resume that speaks to the priorities of your customer.*

The most productive resumes start with a clear focus on the target job and its responsibilities, and do so from the point of view of the recruitment process and the selection committee, the customer comes first, so let's get inside the customer's head.

Target Job Deconstruction

There's a practical and easy way to get inside the employer's head. It's called a Target Job Deconstruction (TJD). It's a way to get a tight focus on what your customers are buying and what will sell before you even start writing your resume. Take half a day to do a TJD and your investment will yield:

- A template for the story your resume *must* tell to be successful
- An objective tool against which you can evaluate your resume's likely performance
- A complete understanding of where the focus will be during interviews
- A very good idea of the interview questions that will be heading your way and why
- Relevant examples with which to illustrate your answers
- A behavioral profile for getting hired and for professional success throughout your career
- A behavioral profile for *not* getting hired and for ongoing professional failure

Building a TJD
Step #1: Collect postings

Collect six to ten job postings of a job you can do and jobs you would enjoy. If you are interested in more than one job, you must prioritize them. The most productive resumes focus on a single job. I'll show you a very fast and effective editing technique a little later in the chapter to develop a custom resume for each job. Save the postings in a folder and also print them out.

Not sure where to start? Try *these* job aggregators (or spider, robots, or bots) that run around thousands of job sites looking for jobs with your chosen keywords.

www.indeed.com
www.simplyhired.com
www.WorkTree.com
www.JobBankUSA.com
www.Job-Search-Engine.com
www.JobSniper.com
www.SourceTool.com
www.jobster.com

Step #2: Create the document

Create a new document and title it "TJD for (your chosen target job title)."

Step #3: Identify target job titles

Start by inserting in your document the subhead: "Target job titles." Then copy and paste in all the variations from your samples. Looking at the result you can say, "When employers are hiring people like this, they tend to describe the job title with these words." From this you can come up with a suitable target job title for your resume, coming right after your name and contact information. This will help your resume's database performance and also act as a headline, giving the reader's eyes an immediate focus.

Step #4: Identify skills and responsibilities

Add a second subhead titled "Skills/Responsibilities/Requirements/Deliverables etc." Look through the job postings—it might be easier to spread printouts across your desk. You are looking for a requirement that is common to all of your job postings. Take the most complete description and copy and paste it (with a #6 beside it, signifying it is common to all six of your samples) into your document. Underneath this, add additional words and phrases from the other job postings used to describe this same requirement. Repeat this exercise for any other requirements common to all six of your job postings.

The greater the number of keywords in your resume that are directly relevant to your target job, the higher the ranking your resume will achieve in recruiters' database searches. The higher your ranking, the greater the likelihood that your resume will be rescued from the avalanche and passed along to human eyes for further screening. This has led directly to the denser resumes we are seeing today and the increasing prevalence of Core Competency sections that capture all relevant keywords in one place. (More about this important section later.)

Repeat the exercise for requirements common to five of the jobs, then four, and so on, all the way down to those requirements mentioned in only one job posting.

Step #5: Identify problems to solve

At their most elemental level, all jobs are the same—they focus on problem identification, avoidance, and solution in that particular area of expertise; this is what we all get paid for, no matter what we do for a living.

Go back to your TJD and start with the first requirement. Think about and note the problems you will typically need to identify, solve, and/or prevent in the course of a normal workday as you deliver on this requirement of the job. List specific examples, big and small, of your successful identification, prevention, and/or solution to the problems. Quantify your results when possible.

Repeat this with each of the TJD's other requirements by identifying the problems inherent to that particular responsibility. Some examples may appear in your resume as significant professional achievements. Others will provide you with the ammunition to answer all those interview questions that begin, "Tell me about a time when . . . ." because interviewers are concerned with your practical problem identification and solution abilities.

Step #6: Identify behavioral profile for success

Think of the *best* person you have ever seen doing this job and what made her stand out. Describe her performance, professional behavior, interaction with others, and appearance: "That would be Carole Jenkins, superior communication skills, a fine analytical mind, great professional appearance, and a nice person to work with." You are describing the person all employers want to hire. Do this for each and every requirement listed on your TJD.

This is your behavioral profile for professional success. Apply what you learn from this to your professional life. It will increase your job security by opening doors to the inner circles that exist in every department and company, and by leading to the plum assignments, raises, and promotions that over time add up to professional success.

Step #7 Identify behavioral profile for failure

Now think of the *worst* person you have ever seen doing this job and what made that person stand out in such a negative way. Describe his performance, professional behaviors, interaction with others, and appearance: "That would be Jack Hartzenberger, morose, critical, passive aggressive, always looked like he slept in his suit, and smelled like it too." You are describing the person that all employers want to avoid and, incidentally, a behavioral profile for professional suicide.

Now your resume can focus on what the customers wants to hear

Once you complete and review your TJD, you will have a clear idea of exactly the way employers think about, prioritize, and express their needs when they hire someone for the job you want.

Now you know the story your resume needs to tell to be maximally productive in the resume databases, and when it gets retrieved for human review. You now have the proper focus for a killer resume.

Here is a simple before and after example that will illustrate how powerful this process can be. The resume is for a young graduate with a computer science degree looking for her first position in the professional world. When we first spoke, she had been out of school for nearly three months and had had a couple of telephone interviews and one face-to-face interview. Her search was complicated by the fact that she is a foreign national and needed to find a company that would sponsor her. This is not easy at the best of times, but in today's tough job environment, it is a significant additional challenge. The first resume is the one she was using; the second she created after completing the Target Job Deconstruction process.

KNOCK 'EM DEAD TIP

As a rule of thumb, you need about 70 percent of a job's requirements to pursue that job with reasonable hope of success, especially in a down economy when competition is more fierce. If you complete the TJD process and realize you don't make the grade, you have probably saved yourself a good deal of frustration pursuing a job you had no real chance of landing. What you need to do in this instance is pull your title goals back one level. Use this TJD and the missing skills it identifies as a professional development tool: To warrant that next promotion, you'll need to develop these abilities.

For samples of real Target Job Deconstructions, check out *www.knockemdead.com* on the resume advice pages.

I have taken professionals from entry level through C-suite executives in Fortune 25 companies through this process. They all say a couple of things: it was a pain but it was a logical, sensible thing to do and worth it, and they almost all get job offers surprisingly quickly. I can't guarantee that of course, but unless you have rocks for brains you have to see the logic in this approach.

JYATITI MOKUBE

10611 ABERCORN STREET, APT 85
SAVANNAH, GA 31419
SOFTWAREGAL@GMAIL.COM
(401) 241-3703

Education

- Armstrong Atlantic State University, Savannah, GA
- MSc. Computer Science (3.5 GPA), December 2007
- University of Technology, Kingston, Jamaica
- BSc. Computing & Information Technology, November 2005
- Graduated Magna Cum Laude (3.7 GPA)

Key Skills

- Programming
- Programming Languages: C, C++, Java, VB.Net
- Database Programming: SQL
- Website Design
- Design Languages/Tools: HTML, CSS, JavaScript, Dreamweaver.
- Problem Solving and Leadership
- Honed an analytical, logical, and determined approach to problem solving and applied this as group leader for my final year (undergraduate) research project.
- Team Player
- Demonstrated the ability to work effectively within a team while developing a Point-of-Sale system over the course of three semesters.
- Communication
- Demonstrated excellent written and oral communication skills through reports and presentations while pursuing my degrees, and as Public Relations Officer for the University of Technology's Association of Student Computer Engineers (UTASCE).

Work Experience

January 2006–December 2007
- Armstrong Atlantic State University, Savannah, GA
- Graduate Research Assistant, School of Computing
- Developed a haptic application to demonstrate human-computer interaction using Python and H3D API.
- Developed an application to organize text documents using the Self-Organizing Map algorithm and MATLAB.

July–November 2005
- Cable & Wireless Jamaica Ltd, Kingston, Jamaica
- Internet Helpdesk Analyst
- Assisted customers with installing and troubleshooting modems and Internet service-related issues via telephone.

July–August 2003
- National Commercial Bank Ja. Ltd, Kingston, Jamaica
- Change Management Team Member
- Generated process diagrams and documentation for systems under development using MS Visio, MS Word, and MS Excel.

Awards/Honors

- President's Pin for graduating with a GPA above 3.75   November 2005
- Latchman Foundation Award for Academic Excellence & Outstanding Character   March 2005
- Nominated School of Computing student of the year   March 2005
- Recognized by Jamaica Gleaner as top student in School of Computing & IT   February 2005
- Nominated for Derrick Dunn (community service) Award   March 2004
- Honor roll/Dean's List   2002–2005

Languages

- French (fluent), Italian (basic)

Extracurricular Activities

- Singing, acting, chess, reading
- Member of Association for Computing Machinery, AASU student chapter

References

- Available upon request.

JYATITI MOKUBE

10611 Abercorn Street, Apt 85
Savannah, GA 31419
softwaregal@gmail.com, (401) 241-3703

Talented, analytical, and dedicated Software Engineer with strong academic background in object-oriented analysis and design, comfort with a variety of technologies, and interest in learning new ones.

SUMMARY OF QUALIFICATIONS

- Excellent academic record. Achieved 3.55 GPA (Master's) and 3.77 GPA (Bachelor's, Dean's List for all eight semesters)
- Familiarity with the software development lifecycle, from identifying requirements to design, implementation, integration, and testing.
- Familiarity with agile software development processes.
- Strong technical skills in Java development and Object-Oriented Analysis and Design (OOA/D).
- Strong understanding of multiple programming languages, including C, C++, JavaScript, Visual Basic, and HTML.
- Familiar with CVS version control software.
- Excellent communications skills with an aptitude for building strong working relationships with teammates.
- Proven background leading teams in stressful, deadline-oriented environments.

TECHNICAL SKILLS

Languages:	Java, JavaScript, C, C++, Visual Basic, HTML, SQL, VB.Net, ASP.Net, CSS
Software:	Eclipse, NetBeans, JBuilder, Microsoft Visual Studio, Microsoft Office Suite (Word, PowerPoint, Excel, Access), MATLAB
Databases:	MySQL, Oracle
Operating Systems:	Windows (NT/2000/XP Professional)
Servers:	Apache Server

EDUCATION

MS in Computer Science, Armstrong Atlantic State University, Savannah GA, December 2007[AU: degree listed as "MSc" in first resume]
- Completed a thesis in the area of Computer Security (Digital Forensics: Forensic Analysis of an iPod Shuffle)

BS in Computing & IT, University of Technology, Kingston, Jamaica, November 2005[AU: degree listed as "BSc" in first resume]

LANGUAGES

Fluent in English, French, and Italian

PROFESSIONAL EXPERIENCE

Armstrong Atlantic State University, Savannah, GA 01/2006–12/2007

14

Graduate Research Assistant, School of Computing
- Developed a haptic application to demonstrate human-computer interaction using Python and H3D API.
- Developed an application to organize text documents using the Self-Organizing Map algorithm and MATLAB.

Cable & Wireless Jamaica Ltd, Kingston, Jamaica   07/2005–11/2005

Internet Helpdesk Analyst
- Assisted customers with installing and troubleshooting modems and Internet service-related issues via telephone.

National Commercial Bank Ja. Ltd, Kingston, Jamaica   07/2003–08/2003

Change Management Team Member
- Generated process diagrams and documentation for systems under development using MS Visio, MS Word, and MS Excel.

AWARDS/HONORS
- President's Pin for graduating with a GPA above 3.75 11/2005
- Latchman Foundation Award for Academic Excellence & Outstanding Character 03/2005
- Nominated School of Computing student of the year 03/2005
- Recognized by Jamaica Gleaner as top student in School of Computing & IT 02/2005
- Nominated for Derrick Dunn (community service) Award 03/2004

PROFESSIONAL AFFILIATIONS

Association for Computing Machinery (ACM)

REFERENCES

Available upon request.

Now, what was the result of this resume revamping? She started using the new resume at the beginning of March 2008 and almost immediately got an invitation to interview. She subsequently relocated out of state and started work at this company on April 14.

The target-job focused resume opened doors, positioned her professionally, told her what the employer would want to talk about, and was a powerful spokesperson after she left. The end result was a great start to a new career. It all came about because she took the time to understand how her customer—the employer—was thinking about and expressing the job she wanted to do!

Here is another example: the original resume, the third version, followed by the final (eighth) version of the resume. The final version generated eight interviews in the first week at the beginning of recessionary 2010. I hope you'll see the enormous difference TJD makes in the resume writing process and also recognize that a really kick-ass resume takes time and effort.

First resume:

Nancy Wright

123 Main Street
Anywhere, VA 22652

(555) 555-5555
nancywright@yahoo.com

Public Relations Experience

Nancy Wright has more than thirteen years of public relations experience, primarily focused on high-tech and start-up companies. An Olympic gold medalist in swimming, Wright also spent twelve years serving as a free-lance color commentator for sports/news outlets including NBC and ESPN.

Wright & Company Public Relations, *Founder and Principal*   **2003 – present**
Provide the professional work of a large public relations agency along with the personal service available from a smaller company. Develop and execute PR campaigns that meet the specialized needs of each client. Programs and services include corporate and product positioning, ongoing PR strategy and tactics, leadership branding, media training, speaker placement, and ongoing media contact. Clients have included: *AirPlay Networks, ReligiousSite.com, PanJet Aviation.*

Three Boys Public Relations, *Co-Founder and Principal*   **2001 – 2003**
Established a Silicon Valley PR firm that helped high-tech companies accomplish objectives by managing leadership positioning, strategic branding and publicity. Clients included:
- *ABC Systems* – Project work included managing all annual Sales Conference communications for Charles Smith, Group Vice President, U.S. Service Provider group. Helped launch Smith's new fiscal year strategy, objectives, and goals to his 1,000+ employees.
- *NextLink Technologies* – Successfully positioned the start-up as an industry leader by leveraging the market's widespread use of NextLink's industry-standard GreatD networking software. Rapidly expanded the company's leadership position by garnering positive coverage in all targeted publications.

ABC Systems, *Marketing Manager*   **2000 – 2001**
Directed internal marketing activities for the iProduct after ABC acquired InfoGame and its technology. Shortly after the acquisition, ABC reorganized InfoGame and later licensed the iProduct trademark to Apple.

InfoGame Technology Corporation, *Public Relations Manager*   **1998 – 2000**
Designed and executed all company and product strategy. Placed hundreds of stories with news and feature media including the Today Show, Regis & Kathie Lee, ABC's Y2K special hosted by Peter Jennings, The Wall Street Journal, The New York Times and Fast Company. Within eighteen months of launching InfoGame's PR, the company was acquired by ABC Systems.

XYZ Public Relations, *Account Manager; Senior Account Executive; Account Executive*   **1996 – 1998**
Designed and managed all PR strategy and activities for start-up and unknown software, Internet and networking companies. Managed teams of up to 10 PR professionals. Promoted annually for delivering results for the following clients:
- *InfoGame Technology Corporation* – Repositioned InfoGame from fledgling company to a leader in the Internet appliance space. Introduced the new management team, the iProduct and the back-end software. Garnered positive coverage in hundreds of media outlets including The Wall Street Journal, The New York Times and USA Today. InfoGame was acquired by ABC Systems within 18 months of PR campaign.
- *Triiliux Digital Systems* – Accelerated Triiliux and its CEO out of obscurity and into a position of undisputed leadership. Successfully positioned CEO as an industry expert with ongoing speaker placement and quotes in all of Triiliux's top publications. Placed CEO on the magazine cover of the company's topmost publication. Triiliux was acquired by Intel after the two year PR campaign.
- *LinkExchange* – Transformed unknown company into a "player" in the Internet advertising arena. Placed hundreds of stories in both business and industry media including the The Wall Street Journal, CNNfn, and AdWeek. LinkExchange was acquired by Microsoft after an eighteen month PR campaign.

- *The Internet Mall* – Launched this obscure company to the press, landing continual coverage in all top Internet and business publications including The New York Times and Internet World. Within a year of the campaign, the company was acquired by TechWave, now Network commerce.

Other Relevant Experience

Motivational Speaker/ Guest Celebrity   1989 – present
Coach audiences at corporations, business forums, schools, and functions how to effectively set and achieve goals, using the road to the Olympics as a model. Travel the country making guest appearances at events, functions and parades. Past or present clients include: IBM, Hardees, Speedo America, Busch Gardens, Alamo Rent-A-Car, and others.

Television Color Commentator   1988 – 2000
- Provided expert commentary for swimming events, including the Olympics in this town for NBC.
- Provided half-time interviews and feature packages for the Miami Heat.
- Work included NBC, ESPN, FoxSports, SportsChannel, Turner Sports, SportSouth, and others.

The College Conference, Associate Commissioner   1991 – 1993
- Managed all aspects of Conference television and marketing packages.
- Increased marketing revenue by 33% in the first year.

International Swimming Hall of Fame, Assistant Director   1989 – 1991
- Helped drive fund raising efforts for new building.
- Served as one of three spokespeople for the Hall of Fame, delivering speeches at community events.
- Successfully managed and completed all fund raising aspects for the NCAA Wall of Fame.
- Developed community affairs programs.

Awards and Honors
- Two Olympic gold medals (1984 Los Angeles USA), and a silver and bronze (1988 Seoul, Korea).
- Two-time NCAA Champion.
- 26-time NCAA All American.
- Hall of Fame Inductee: International Swimming Hall of Fame, University of Florida Athletic HOF, Region Swimming HOF, Anywhere High School HOF.
- Wikipedia: http://en.wikipedia.org/wiki/NancyWright

Education
University of Florida, Bachelor of Science, Journalism   1989

Third resume:

Nancy Wright, Account Supervisor

801 Spring Mountain Way, Fort Valley, VA 22652 • mwbradburne@yahoo.com • Tel: 540.933.6828 Cell: 540.333.6828

Performance Profile

High tech public relations professional with 11 years experience – including seven in Silicon Valley – in a variety of sectors including software, Internet, networking and consumer electronics. Substantial experience in PR campaigns that lead to company acquisitions. Expertise in all aspects of strategic and tactical communications, from developing and managing PR campaigns, multiple accounts and results-oriented teams, to writing materials and placing stories. Twenty years experience as a motivational speaker and twelve as a free-lance TV color commentator. Two-time Olympic gold medalist.

Core Competencies

High Tech Public Relations • Strategic Communications • Counsel Executives • Manage Teams • Manage Budgets • Multiple Accounts • Multiple Projects • Leadership Positioning • PR Messaging • Client Satisfaction • Media Training • Media Relations • Pitch Media • Craft Stories • Place Stories • PR Tactics • Press Releases • Collateral Materials • Research • Edit • Manage Budgets • Manage Teams • Mentor • Strong Writing Skills • Detail Oriented • Organizational Skills • Motivated • Team Player • New Business

Strategic Public Relations Leadership

Position companies as both industry leaders and sound investments. The following four companies were acquired within two years of commencing the PR campaigns: InfoGear Technologies (acquired by Cisco), Trillium Digital Systems (acquired by Intel), LinkExchange (acquired by Microsoft), and The Internet Mall (acquired by TechWave, now Network Commerce).

Executive Communications Manager

Develop executive communications. Created positioning for Charles Smith, Group VP, and launched it to his 1,000+ employees at the ABC Sales Conference. Refined Smith's public speaking delivery and style.

Media Coverage

Pro-actively place stories. Samplings of past placements include: ABC World News Tonight, CNN, The Today Show, Associated Press, Baltimore Sun, Boston Globe, Business Week, Fast Company, Financial Times, Forbes, Fortune Magazine, Inc., MSNBC.com, New York Times, Parade, San Jose Mercury News, SJ Business Journal, SF Chronicle, USA Today, Wired, Wall Street Journal, AdWeek, CommsDesign, Computer Reseller News, Computer Retail Week, Computer Shopper, Computer World, CRN, CNET, EE Times, Embedded.com, Internet. com, InformationWeek, Internet.com, Internet Telephony Magazine, Light Reading, Network World, Phone+, PC Magazine, Red Herring, TMCnet, VoIP News, VON and ZDNet, Dataquest, Forrester Research, Frost and Sullivan, Jupiter Communications and Yankee Group.

PROFESSIONAL EXPERIENCE

Wright & Associates Public Relations, Anywhere, VA   **2006-present**

Develop and deliver strategic communications that meet the specific needs of each client. Drive all PR strategy and tactics, messaging, media training, media relations, budget management, story creation and placement. Sampling of past or present clients include AirTight Networks (also a former InfoGear, Cisco, NextHop client), JesusCentral.com (eHealthInsurance.com founder), and ProJet Aviation.

Co-Founder and Principal, Three Boys Public Relations, Redwood City, CA   **2001-2003**

Silicon Valley PR firm that partnered with high tech clients to meet their corporate objectives. In charge of developing and managing all strategic and tactical aspects of public relations including thought leadership, leadership branding, press materials, stories, media relations and publicity.
- Cisco Systems – Acting Executive Communications Manager to Carlos Dominguez, VP.
- NextHop Technologies – Company's first PR counsel. Repositioned obscure company, impaired by trademark dilution, into an industry leader. (Acquired by U4EA Technologies in 2008.)

Marketing Manager, ABC Network Systems, San Jose, CA   **2000-2001**

Directed internal, cross-functional marketing activities for the iProduct® after Cisco acquired InfoGear and its technology. Shortly after the acquisition, Cisco dissolved the InfoGear/Managed Appliances Business Unit (MASBU) and later licensed the iProduct trademark to Apple.

Public Relations Manager, InfoGame Technology Corporation, Redwood City, CA   **1998-2000**

Company's first PR counsel. Advised CEO and VP of marketing on all aspects of PR. Developed and implemented ongoing PR campaign, strategies and tactics.
- Established "iProduct Reviews" program, garnering hundreds of additional positive stories.
- Managed and inspired cross-functional teams of marketing, operations and customer service.

Account Supervisor, Senior Account Executive, Account Executive, XYZ Advertising & Public Relations (Acquired by FLEISHMAN-HILLARD in 2000), Mountain View, CA   **1996-1998**

Promoted annually for successful track record of positioning unknown start-up companies into industry leaders. Designed and managed all PR strategy and activities for start-up, software, Internet and networking companies. Managed teams of up to ten PR professionals.
- Accelerated Trillium and its CEO out of obscurity and into undisputed leadership. Continually landed top speaking placements and media coverage.
- Transformed the unknown LinkExchange into a highly publicized leader in the Internet advertising arena. Placed hundreds of stories in both business and industry media.
- Designed and managed InfoGear Technology's repositioning from fledgling company to a leader in the Internet appliance space.
- Launched newcomer The Internet Mall, landing continual coverage in all top Internet and business publications.

OTHER RELEVANT EXPERIENCE

Motivational Speaker/ Guest Celebrity

Representative clients: IBM, Hardees, Speedo America, Busch Gardens, Alamo Rent-A-Ca   **1989-present**
- Coach audiences on how to use the Olympic model to set and achieve goals, and succeed in business and life.

Television Sports Commentator

Swimming analyst for NBC, ESPN, FoxSports, SportsChannel, Turner Sports and others   **1988-2000**
- Covered the Barcelona Olympics. Half-time reporter for Miami Heat and Southern Conference games.

AWARDS & ACHIEVEMENTS

Four Olympic swimming medals: two gold, one silver, one bronze
- Southland Corporation's Olympia Award for academic and athletic leadership.
- Southeastern Conference, NCAA and USA Swimming Champion.
- Hall of Fame Inductee: International Swimming Hall of Fame, University of Florida, Pacific Northwest Swimming, Washington State Swimming Coaches Assoc., Mercer Island H.S.

EDUCATION

University of Florida, Gainesville, FL
- Bachelor of Science in Journalism.
- Minor in Speech.

123 Main Street
Anywhere, VA 22222

Nancy Wright

Home (555) 555-5555
Mobile (555) 333-5555
nancywright@yahoo.com

Group Manager • Account Director • PR Manager

Performance Profile
High tech public relations professional with 13 years experience, including nine in Silicon Valley, in the software, Internet, networking, consumer electronics and wireless industries. Substantial experience in PR and strategic communications campaigns that lead to company acquisitions. Experienced in all aspects of strategic and tactical communications from developing and managing multiple campaigns, accounts and results-oriented teams to developing and placing stories. Seasoned motivational speaker and freelance TV color commentator. Two-time Olympic gold medalist.

Core Competencies

High Tech Public Relations	Craft & Place Stories	Budget Management	Client Satisfaction
Strategic Communications	Strong Writing Skills	Account Management	Organizational Skills
Executive Communications	Media Training	Project Management	Thought Leadership
PR Messaging & Tactics	Multiple Projects	Detail Oriented	PR Counsel
Story Telling	Story Placement	Acquisition Positioning	Social Media
Collateral Materials	Counsel Executives	Pitch Media	
Leadership Branding	Strong Editing Skills	Market Research	
Analyst Relations	New Business Development	Build & Lead Teams	
Media Relations	Team Management	Mentor	

Strategic Public Relations Leadership
Orchestrated PR campaigns that positioned companies as both industry leaders and sound investments. Developed and directed PR campaigns for four companies that were subsequently acquired within two years of the campaigns: *InfoGame Technologies* (creator of the first iProduct®, acquired by *ABC Network*), *Triiliux Digital Systems* (acquired by *Intel*), *LinkExchange* (acquired by *Microsoft*), and *The Internet Mall* (acquired by *TechWave*). Proven client satisfaction demonstrated in repeat business and account growth: over a span of ten years, contracted by former *InfoGame* execs to serve as communications counsel for *NextLink Technologies, ABC Network Systems* and *AirPlay Networks*.

Executive Communications Management
Executive Communications Manager for iconic executive and public speaker, *Charles Smith, Group VP, Service Provider Sales, ABC Network Systems* (currently *senior VP* and *technology evangelist* for *ABC Network*). Developed communication messaging, strategy and platform skills for VP, Group VP and C-level executives.

Media Coverage
ABC World News Tonight, CNN, The Today Show, Associated Press, Baltimore Sun, Boston Globe, Business Times, Business Week, CNN.com, Fast Company, Financial Times, Forbes, Fortune Magazine, Inc., MSNBC.com, New York Times, Parade, San Jose Mercury News, SF Chronicle, USA Today, Wired, Wall Street Journal, AdWeek, CommsDesign, Computer Reseller News, Computer Retail Week, Computer Shopper, Computer World, CRN, CNET, EE Times, Embedded Systems Design, Internet.com, InfoWorld, InformationWeek, Internet.com, Internet Telephony, LightReading, Network World, Phone+, PC Magazine, Red Herring, TMCnet, VoIP News, VON and ZDNet, Dataquest, Forrester Research, Frost and Sullivan, Jupiter Communications, Yankee Group.

—— **Professional Experience** ——

Principal   2003 to Present
Wright & Associates Public Relations, Anywhere, VA
Develop and deliver strategic communications. Drive all PR strategy and tactics, messaging, media training, media relations, budget management, story creation and placement for technology clients.
- Representative clients include *AirPlay Networks* (former *InfoGame* and *NextLink client*), *ReligiousSite.com* (founded by *eCompany.com* founder), and *PanJet Aviation*.

Principal   **2001-2003**
Three Kids Public Relations, Redwood City, CA
Developed and implemented all strategic and tactical aspects of public relations for Silicon Valley clients, including thought leadership, leadership branding, story creation and telling, media materials, stories, media relations and publicity.
- *ABC Network Systems*—Executive Communications Manager to Charles Smith, Group VP at *ABC Network,* a highly pursued public speaker.
- *NextLink Technologies*—Company's first PR counsel. Repositioned obscure company, impaired by trademark dilution, into an industry leader by leveraging market's widespread knowledge and use of *NextLink's* industry-standard *GreatD* networking software.

Marketing Manager   **2000 to 2001**
ABC Network Systems, San Jose, CA
Directed internal, cross-functional marketing for iProduct, following ABC Network acquisition of *InfoGame* and its technology.
- Shortly after acquisition, ABC Network dissolved *InfoGame/Managed Appliances Business Unit (MASBU)*.

Public Relations Manager   **1998 to 2000**
InfoGame Technology Corporation, Redwood City, CA
Advised CEO and VP of marketing on all aspects of PR. Developed and implemented all strategies, tactics and stories.
- Revamped the start-up's teetering image that was ruining *iProduct* sales. After two press tours, garnered hundreds of additional stories in all top trade and consumer media with the *iProduct Reviews* program. Catapulted company into a leadership position in the Internet appliance industry, setting it up for acquisition. *iProduct* is now a household name.
- Managed and inspired cross-functional teams of marketing, operations and customer service to work outside their job responsibilities to deliver excellent service to hundreds of editors beta testing the *iProduct 2.0.*

Account Supervisor; Senior Account Executive; Account Executive   **1996 to 1998**
XYZ Advertising & Public Relations (Acquired by FLEISHMAN-HILLARD in 2000), Mountain View, CA
Promoted annually for successful track record of positioning unknown companies as both industry leaders and solid investments/acquisitions. Designed and managed all PR strategy and activities for start-up, software, Internet and networking companies. Managed teams of up to ten PR professionals.
- Re-positioned, re-branded, re-launched, and re-introduced *InfoGame*, the *iProduct 1.0* and *2.0*, positioning them collectively as leading the nascent Internet appliance space.
- Accelerated *Triiliux* and its CEO out of obscurity and into undisputed leadership through media placement and top speaking engagements.
- Transformed unknown *LinkExchange* into a highly publicized leader in the Internet advertising arena. Placed hundreds of stories in both business and industry media.
- Launched *The Internet Mall,* landing continual coverage in all top Internet and business publications.

—— **Complementary Experience** ——

Motivational Speaker/ Guest Celebrity   **1989 to Present**
Coach audiences on how to use the Olympic model to set and achieve goals, and succeed in business and life. Representative clients: IBM, Hardees, Speedo America, Busch Gardens, Alamo Rent-A-Car.

Television Sports Commentator   **1987 to 2000**
Swimming analyst for NBC, ESPN, FoxSports, SportsChannel, Turner Sports and others. Covered the Olympics. Half-time reporter for Miami Heat and The College Conference.

Awards & Achievements
Winner—Two Olympic swimming gold medals plus one silver and one bronze.
Recipient Southland Corporation's Olympia Award for academic and athletic leadership.
NCAA, USA, Southeastern Conference swimming champion and 26-time NCAA All American.
Hall of Fame Inductee: International Swimming Hall of Fame, University of Florida, Pacific Northwest Swimming, Washington State Swimming Coaches Association, Mercer Island High School.

EDUCATION—University of Florida, Gainesville, FL; B.S. in Journalism, Minor in Speech.

CHAPTER 3
GARBAGE IN, GARBAGE OUT

HOW WELL THIS most important document you are ever going to own comes out depends on what goes in. So if you don't want a garbage resume, you need a logical way to gather the right information to tell that story.

When you got inside your customer's head, you gained a clear understanding for the story your resume needs to tell. Now with requirements and deliverables of your target job in front of you, work backwards through your professional life, methodically pulling out the skills and experiences that will help your resume tell the story of someone who can nail this target job.

Examine your work history through the lens of your target job

There are different ways to look at any experience, and how you tell a story depends on your point of view. Examine your work history through the lens of your TJD, and gather all the information with the greatest relevance to your target job. This is the raw material for the story your resume will tell and for the way you define who you are as a professional: your professional brand. The more notes you have, the better. Even if some of information you gather doesn't make it into your resume, it will still have immense value preparing you for the interviews your resume will generate and the insights it will give you into yourself as a professional entity, commodity, and brand. More on this later.

Fifty Percent of the Success of Any Project Is in the Preparation

Here's the information-gathering questionnaire we use at *www.knockemdead.com* for our professional resume writing service. It will help you gather all the resume-relevant information about your professional life in one place. To help you get the most out of this not-the-most-exciting task, you'll find a lot of "how to and why to" advice as you work through it. The process is going to take a few hours so it may be best to promise yourself that you'll see it through and intersperse doing it with reading the rest of the book. It's best to do the work on your computer: you never run out of space and all the information will be collected in an MS Word document, ready to be molded into a finished resume. Go to the resume advice pages on *www.knockemdead.com*, and download the "Resume Questionnaire."

Half the success of any project depends on the preparation. The work you do here is also going to have a real impact on your career and the quality of your life outside of work for years to come. So bite the bullet and do it right.

Resume Questionnaire

Please Note: An electronic document is expandable, so if you need additional space, don't limit yourself to the lines/pages provided.

Your first step is to complete the Critical Target Job Deconstruction exercise. This will create a composite Job Description and brings focus to the story your resume needs to tell.

Name (exactly as wanted on resume): _____

Address: _____

City: _____ **State:** _____ **Zip:** _____

Home Phone: _____ **Mobile:** _____

E-mail: _____

Are you willing to relocate?   Yes ( ) No ( )

Are you willing to travel?   Yes ( ) No ( )

Please answer the following questions as completely and accurately as possible. Not all questions may apply to you. If they do not apply, mark them N/A.

Position/Career Objective: List top three job title choices in order of preference.

If the titles are for related positions (*e.g. 1–Sales; 2–Marketing; 3–Business Development*) your resume will be developed to reflect the cross-functional target(s). If the goals are not related (*e.g. 1–Rocket Scientist; 2–Pastry Chef; 3–Landscape Designer*), the resume will be written to fit your first selection. (We will discuss creating additional versions of your resume.)

1. _____

2. _____

3. _____

Desired Industry Segment _____

Is this a career change for you? Yes ( ) No ( )

Purpose of Resume (e.g. job change, career change, promotion, business development/marketing tool) _____

Summarize your experience in this field in a couple of sentences. *Do not provide details of positions here—We just want to get the big picture; just a sentence or two about your background.* For example: I have been in the accounting field for twelve years and received three promotions to the current position which I've held for two years.)

_____

_____

_____

What are some terms (keywords) specific to your line of work? (If you're not sure, you can find these showing up consistently on job postings.)

_____

_____

What are your key strengths that you want to highlight on your resume? What makes you stand out from your competitors? Drill down to the essence of what differentiates your candidacy.

_____

_____

Current Salary: _____ **Expected Salary:** _____

Education

List all degrees, certificates, diplomas received, dates received, school or college, and location of school or college. Begin with the most recent and work backwards.

Name of College/Univ: _____
City/State: _____
Degree Obtained (i.e, BS, BA, MBA, AA) _____ Year Completed _____
Major: _____ Minor: _____
Overall GPA _____ GPA in Major _____
Honors (include scholarships):

_____

_____

_____

Extracurricular Activities (include leadership, sports, study abroad, etc.):

_____

_____

_____

Name of College/Univ: _____
City/State: _____
Degree Obtained (i.e., BS, BA, MBA, AA) _____ Year Completed _____
Major: _____ Minor: _____
Overall GPA _____ GPA in Major _____
Honors (include scholarships):

_____

_____

Extracurricular Activities (include leadership, sports, etc., study abroad, etc.):

_____

_____

_____

_____

High School (only if no college):

Name:_____ City/State: _____ Year: _____

Professional Development (training courses/seminars/workshops, etc.)

Ongoing professional education signals commitment to success. If you attended numerous courses, list the most recent and/or relevant to your career and indicate that additional course information is available. Those courses that have been rendered obsolete by technology and the passage of time can be ignored.

Course Name: _____
Completion Date: _____ Duration: _____
Certification Obtained: _____ Location of Training: _____
Sponsoring Organization: _____

Course Name: _____
Completion Date: _____ Duration:_____
Certification Obtained: _____ Location of Training: _____
Sponsoring Organization: _____

Course Name: _____
Completion Date: _____ Duration:_____
Certification Obtained: _____ Location of Training:_____
Sponsoring Organization: _____

Professional Certifications:

_____

_____

Professional Licenses:

_____

_____

Military (include branch of service, locations, position, rank achieved, years of service, honorable discharge, key accomplishments, special recognition, awards, etc.)

_____

_____

_____

Professional Organizations/Affiliations
Active membership in a professional association is a key tool for career resiliency and success.

Name of Organization: (include city/state or chapter): _____
_____

Leadership Roles Held: _____

Name of Organization: (include city/state or chapter): _____
_____

Leadership Roles Held: _____

Name of Organization: (include city/state or chapter): _____
_____

Leadership Roles Held: _____

Name of Organization: (include city/state or chapter): _____
_____

Leadership Roles Held: _____

Name of Organization: (include city/state or chapter): ———————————

Leadership Roles Held: ————————————————————————

Name of Organization: (include city/state or chapter): ———————————

Leadership Roles Held: ————————————————————————

Publications/Presentations: Title/Periodical/Location/Date (Begin each on a new line)

————————————————————————————————
————————————————————————————————
————————————————————————————————

Patents and Copyrights

You can also include here your work on projects that resulted in copyrights and patents, so long as you make clear your real contribution.

————————————————————————————————
————————————————————————————————
————————————————————————————————

Computer Skills (include hardware, operating systems, software, Internet, e-mail, etc.)

Maybe it's just MS Word and Excel or maybe it runs to languages and protocols. Nobody today gets ahead without technological adeptness. Capture your fluency here and update regularly; that alphabet soup of technology just might help your resume in database searches.

Hardware:

————————————————————————————————
————————————————————————————————

Operating Systems:

_____

_____

_____

_____

_____

Software Applications:

_____

_____

_____

_____

_____

Other if relevant:

_____

_____

_____

_____

_____

Foreign Languages (indicate level of fluency and if verbal/written)

_____

_____

_____

Global Experience/Cultural Diversity Awareness

In our global economy any exposure here is relevant, and it doesn't have to be professional in nature. If you've traveled extensively or you were an Army brat and grew up in ten different countries, that can be a big plus. Just name the countries not the circumstances.

Corporate Awards/Recognition (indicate where and when received):

_____

_____

_____

_____

Community/Volunteer Activities (name of organization, years involved, positions held):

_____

_____

_____

_____

Hobbies/Interests/Avocations

Include activities with which you fill your out-of-work hours. Your resume may include those activities that can say something positive about the professional you. For example, in sales and marketing just about all group activities show a desirable mindset. Bridge might argue strong analytical skills, and the senior exec who still plays competitive lacrosse and runs marathons is crazy not to let the world know.

_____

_____

_____

_____

Action Verbs

In describing your work experience at each position you have held, it might be helpful to select from the following list the action verbs that best characterize your daily work, duties, responsibilities, and level of authority. Select from the following list or use other "action verbs" when completing the sections. Briefly describe your routine duties, responsibilities, and level of authority.

Do not provide the information here; instead, use it as a guide in completing the information for each position you've held.

These are just suggestions. Please don't limit yourself to the use of these verbs only.

accepted	conceptualized	evaluated	interviewed
accomplished	conducted	examined	introduced
achieved	consolidated	executed	invented
acted	contained	expanded	launched
adapted	contracted	expedited	lectured
addressed	contributed	explained	led
administered	controlled	extracted	maintained
advanced	coordinated	fabricated	managed
advised	corresponded	facilitated	marketed
allocated	counseled	familiarized	mediated
analyzed	created	fashioned	moderated
appraised	critiqued	focused	monitored
approved	cut	forecast	motivated
arranged	decreased	formulated	negotiated
assembled	defined	founded	operated
assigned	delegated	generated	organized
assisted	demonstrated	guided	originated
attained	designed	headed up	overhauled
audited	developed	identified	oversaw
authored	devised	illustrated	performed
automated	diagnosed	implemented	persuaded
balanced	directed	improved	planned
budgeted	dispatched	increased	prepared
built	distinguished	indoctrinated	presented
calculated	diversified	influenced	prioritized
cataloged	drafted	informed	processed
chaired	edited	initiated	produced
clarified	educated	innovated	programmed
classified	eliminated	inspected	projected
coached	emended	installed	promoted
collected	enabled	instigated	proposed
compiled	encouraged	instituted	provided
completed	engineered	instructed	publicized
composed	enlisted	integrated	published
computed	established	interpreted	purchased

recommended	resolved	solidified	trained
reconciled	restored	solved	translated
recorded	restructured	specified	traveled
recruited	retrieved	stimulated	trimmed
reduced	revamped	streamlined	upgraded
referred	revitalized	strengthened	validated
regulated	saved	summarized	worked
rehabilitated	scheduled	supervised	wrote
remodeled	schooled	surveyed	
repaired	screened	systemized	
represented	set	tabulated	
researched	shaped	taught	

Accomplishments/Achievements/Successes

When completing the next few pages of the questionnaire, refer to the following questions to refresh your memory regarding accomplishments and achievements (regarding professional experience) for each position. Remember: people hire results (accomplishments and achievements) and look to past performance as an indication of the value you offer. You don't need to provide answers to all these questions here. Rather, consider the various positions you've held and come up with four to six of the strongest contributions you made in each position. As you think about this, read through these questions to help stimulate your thinking. Above all, ask yourself how your current employer is better off now than when the company hired you.

1. Did you increase sales / productivity / volume? Provide percentage or amount.
2. Did you generate new business or increase client base? How? What were the circumstances?
3. Did you forge affiliations, partnerships, or strategic alliances that impacted company success? With whom and what were the results?
4. Did you save your company money? If so, how and by how much?
5. Did you design and/or institute any new system or process? If so, what were the results?
6. Did you meet an impossible deadline through extra effort? If so what difference did this make to your company?
7. Did you bring a major project in under budget? If so, how did you make this happen? What was the budget? What were you responsible for saving in terms of time and/or money?
8. Did you suggest and/or help launch a new product or program? If so, did you take the lead or provide support? How successful was the effort? What were the results?
9. Did you assume new responsibilities that weren't part of your job? Were they assigned or did you do so proactively? Why were you selected?

10. Did you introduce any new or more effective systems, processes, or techniques for increasing productivity? What was the result?
11. Did you improve communication in your firm? If so, with whom and what was the outcome?
12. How did your company benefit from your performance?
13. Did you complete any special projects? What were they and what was the result?

When describing your accomplishments / achievements use the following three-step CAR format:

C = Challenge (think of a challenge you faced or problem you had to resolve)
A = Action (what action did you take?)
R = Results (what was the result of the action you took? What was the value to the company?

Professional Experience

All right, now you're ready to assemble information about your work history and experience. Begin with your present employer / project. Include self-employment, contract, and volunteer or unpaid work if it applies to your career target. Be sure to list different positions at the same company as separate jobs. Repeat the section below as many times as you need to in order to encompass all the professional positions you've held.

Name of company: _____

City/State: _____ Dates of employment: _____

Your actual job title: _____

Your functional /working job title if different from actual title: _____

Title of person you report to _____

Number of people you supervise: _____

Their titles or functions: _____

_____

Briefly describe the size of the organization (volume produced; revenues; number of employees; local, national, or international; etc.) _____

_____

_____

What it is that they do, make, or sell? _____

_____

_____

Where do they rank in their industry in terms of their competitors?

_____

_____

_____

_____

_____

What were you hired to do? Briefly describe your routine duties, responsibilities, and level of authority. Use numbers (size) and percentages, quantify budgets, state with whom you interacted, etc. Provide two to three brief sentences about your major overall area of responsibility and list them in order of importance. Refer back to the list of action verbs to help you brainstorm.

Example:

Selected to re-engineer and revitalize this $65 million business unit with accountability for thirty-two direct reports in four cities across the United States. Established strategic vision and developed operational infrastructure. Managed Supply Chain, Logistics/Distribution, Forecasting, System Integration, Project Management, Contracts Administration and Third-Party Site Operations.

Or more simply:

Drove production for world's largest wallboard plant, with 258 employees working in multiple shifts.

1. _____

_____

_____

_____

_____

_____

_____

_____

_____

Briefly describe three to five of your accomplishments in this position. Use the most significant achievements or contributions that best support your career target and describe them in a brief statement, referring to the accomplishments guidelines. Use numbers wherever possible.

Give facts and figures. Please note: Distill the accomplishments into their essence. How did your accomplishment contribute to bottom line performance/ROI?

_____
_____
_____
_____
_____
_____
_____
_____
_____
_____
_____
_____
_____
_____

Be sure to take your time on this exercise. It may be tempting to rush through it or look for shortcuts, but avoid that pitfall. You're assembling the information that's going to be the mortar and bricks of your resume, and you need it to be as complete and well thought out as possible.

Now that you've collected all the bits and pieces, it's time to start putting them together.

CHAPTER 4
KEEP IT SIMPLE, STUPID

I'VE BEEN WRITING about resumes for twenty-five years and writing them for longer, longer than most. No one likes writing a resume, but you have to trust me when I tell you that there is no easier way than the way I am showing you. That shortcut you're thinking of? It won't work. If it did we'd be talking about it.

This is the most streamlined way I know to give you a premium, powerful resume for a professional job in the shortest time with the least hassle.

Kill the Big Myth

No good written communication is ever completed in a single draft, and your resume is no exception. Your resume is a sales document: It is short and has to capture a lot of very carefully focused and worded information. To come up with a great finished product you will need to go through five steps:

1.   A first draft to capture all the essentials on a basic resume template
2.   A second draft to give the resume the right professional brand
3.   A third draft when you paste it into different templates and choose the one(s) best for you
4.   As many more drafts over a week or so, until you cannot possibly improve it further
5.   A final draft for your formatted resume, where you complete the editing and polishing process
6.   An ASCII version of your resume for specific online applications

Putting Together Your First Draft

With your TJD and completed Resume Questionnaire from the previous chapter, you know what the customer wants and what you have to offer. All that remains is to start assembling the pieces in a way that tells your story effectively.

To help you do this most efficiently, I've created a resume *Layout Template* for you. This is intended as a means to graphically capture and review the components your resume will contain. It is not intended as a template for your finished resume. It's just a gathering place for all the components of your finished document in a resume-like format. By using it you'll become familiar with all the resume building blocks, and when the time comes to decide on a layout and template, everything will be ready to cut and paste.

Why can't you choose a template right now? Because you select a template based on its layout and suitability to tell a particular story. This means you first have to determine all the components that will be in your story, and you don't know that till you've collected all the relevant information in one place. It's too soon to choose final templates at this point.

You can find an MS Word version at *www.knockemdead.com*. Go to the resume advice pages and download the Resume Layout Template. You can delete my commentary as you start to fill it out with your real-world experiences and information.

(Name)
Mailing address (if appropriate) • Telephone & Cell phone • email address

(Target Job Title & Brand Statement)
Pharmaceutical Sales Management Profession
Poised to outperform in pharmaceutical software sales repeating records of achievement with major pharmaceutical companies
Helps database visibility and gives focus to human eye and mind, followed by a one sentence career-branding statement of the value proposition you bring to the job

Performance Profile/ Career Summary
No more than five lines of unbroken text can be followed by a second similar paragraph or short list of bullets. Your intent is to capture your ability to do the target job. What goes in here? Take the most common requirements from your TJD exercise Step#?? and re-write as your performance profile. This will help your resume's database visibility and will create immediate resonance with the recruiter's eyes. Always note bi-lingual skills here, we live in a global economy.

Core Competencies
<u>This should be a bulleted</u> ~ List ~ Of all the keywords ~ You identified In step # ?? ~ Of the TJD ~ Exercise~this list can be ~ As long as ~ You like ~ A Core Competency section ~ increases database visibility ~ And for the reader ~ Gives them immediate focus ~ "Oh she can talk about this and this and this" ` and each word you use here ~ can be repeated in the context ~ of the jobs where~ it was applied

Technical Competencies
[An optional category depending on your experience]

Performance Highlights
[An optional category depending on your experience]

Professional Experience

Company name & location
Job title • employment dates

Company name & location
Job title • employment dates

Company name & location
Job title • employment dates

Education
(May come at front of resume if these are critical professional credentials, especially relevant or highlight an important strength)
Licenses/Professional accreditations
 (May come at front of resume if these credentials are critical credentials, especially relevant or highlight an important strength)
Ongoing Professional Education
Professional Organizations/Affiliations
Publications, Patents, Speaking
Languages
Military service
Extra curricular interests
(If they relate to the job)

Closing brand statement

"I believe that leadership by example and conscientious performance management underlies my department's consistent customer satisfaction ratings."

References Available On Request

(Employers assume that your references are available, only end your resume with this if there is

The Parts of the Template

Name

Give your first and last name only. It isn't necessary to include your middle name(s). My name is Martin John Yate, but my resume says simply Martin Yate, because that is the way I would introduce myself in person. Notice also that it isn't M.J. Yate, because I answer to Martin and not M.J.; unless you are known by your initials don't put them on your resume.

It is not required to place Mr., Ms., Miss, or Mrs. before your name, unless yours is a unisex name like Gayle, Carroll, and Leslie, in which case it is acceptable to write Mr. Gayle Jones or Ms. Gayle Jackson.

If you always add Jr. or III when you sign your name and that is the way you are addressed to avoid confusion, go ahead and use it.

Address

If you abbreviate—such as with *St.* or *Apt.*—be consistent. The state of your residence, however, is always abbreviated, for example: MN, WV, LA. The accepted format for laying out your address looks like this:

Maxwell Krieger
9 Central Avenue, Apartment 38
New York, NY 23456

But with a resume, if space is an issue, you can put your contact information on a single line as you will see in the example resumes and the resume templates available on the website.

It is acceptable to omit both name and address if you are creating a sanitized resume. Your name would be replaced by a target job title and followed by e-mail and telephone contact information.

Telephone Number

Always include your area code because they are no longer unique to geographical locations. Never use a work telephone number on your resume or at any time during your job search.

Most telephone companies now have a master-ring feature allowing you, at no extra charge, to have two or three different numbers, each with a distinctive ring. It might not be a bad idea to use one of these available alternate numbers as your permanent career-management number. Then whenever it rings, you can be sure to finish chewing the Doritos before picking up.

It is a good idea to include your cell number, and if you don't have a master-ring system through your telephone provider, you might decide to use the cell number as your primary contact.

E-Mail

Your e-mail address is an integral part of your contact information, but never use your work e-mail address. Companies can and do monitor Internet and e-mail usage. Besides, it sends the wrong message to potential employers.

Your ISP will allow you to have a number of different e-mail addresses. Take advantage of this and create one that you will only use for career-management initiatives, and try to come up with something that speaks to your profession: *finebiochemist@earthlink.net* or *confidentcloser@ aol.com*. This protects your identity and acts as a focusing headline to a potential reader.

Target Job Title

Every book, blog, or article ever written and every song, TV show, and movie ever made has a title; it gives the audience a focus and draws them in. Makes sense doesn't it? But more than 70 percent of resumes lack a Target Job Title.

The first thing any resume reader looks for is focus. A target job title explains what the resume is about. Start by identifying what your target job title might be by taking all the title variations you collected in the TJD process and coming up with a target job title that works for you. You can always change it if you decide on a better one. Here are some examples taken from finished resumes:

- Certified Occupational Health Nurse Specialist
- Global Operations Executive
- Campaign Field Director
- Marketing Management
- Operations/Human Resources/Labor Relations/Staff Development
- Career Services Professional
- Operations Management
- Healthcare Review—Clinical Consultant
- Agricultural/Environmental Manager
- Horticultural Buying—International Experience

Brand Statement

A short personal brand statement following the target job title introduces the value proposition you bring to the job. More on this shortly and an example that blends the target job title and the brand statement.

Use Subheads to Guide the Reader

Headlines/subheads help guide a jaded and distracted reader through your resume. There are people in the resume writing business who say that any headline like this has "gone out of fashion" and it is "understood by the reader." I completely disagree.

Your resume's job is to open as many doors for you as it can. It does this by making the information as accessible as possible to the target customer. Using headlines in your resume helps the reader absorb your message. Look at these headlines and the way they guide a tired and bored reader:

Target Job Title
(Here's the job I'm after)

Performance Profile
(This is a snapshot of what I can do)

Core Competencies
(Here are all the key professional skills that help me do my job well)

Technical Competencies
(Optional: here are all the technical skills that help me do my job well)

Performance Highlights
(Optional: Outstanding achievements)

Professional Experience
(Where and when everything happened)

In little more than half a page these headlines help the reader get fast access to what you have to offer. These headlines have tested extremely well with headhunters and hiring managers because of the clarity and understanding they deliver.

Performance Profile

The essence of every manager's (read: hiring authority's) job is performance management, and they spend a portion of every year thinking about and giving performance reviews. For that reason, this new and powerful headline will resonate with every manager. Take the major requirements from your TJD and turn them into 2–4 sentences or no more than 5 lines without a paragraph break. It speaks to your grasp of the customer's priorities.

Career/Professional/Executive Summary

These traditional headings encourage you to think about everything you've done rather than focus on customer needs and the reader expects the same. If you use this heading, remember your TJD keep your focus on what you bring to the target job.

Job Objective

Stay away from Job Objective (or Career Objective) if you can, for these reasons:

1. Your wants will not help your performance in database searches, so you are wasting valuable selling space.
2. At this stage no one cares what you want. The only issue is, can you do the job?

If you must use a Job Objective, for example if you are at the start of your career and have no experience to offer, that's okay. Your competitors are in the same boat. Tilt the game in your favor by starting your objective with "The opportunity to" and then, referring to your TJD exercise, rewrite the target job's major priorities as your job objective. This will make a big difference in your resume's productivity. Of the three major options for this important section of your resume, I like the "Performance Profile" headline the most. It's action oriented, captures the essence of the professional you, and brings an immediate focus to who you are and what you bring to the job. Plus, the recruiters respond very positively.

Performance Profiles Keywords & Core Competencies

The words employers use in job postings will be used as search terms, so *use the words you know are important* immediately. You can use them again in the Core Competency section, where they will again be valid. Then use them a third time in the context of the jobs in which those skills were applied and developed.

Here's a performance profile for a Corporate Communications Management professional:

How to create a performance profile

For what to put in this section, refer to your TJD exercise and *rewrite the major priorities of the job as your performance profile*. This will help your resume's database visibility and will create immediate resonance when read by the recruiter.

1. Write three to six bulleted statements that capture the essential professional you, as they relate to the three to six most common requirements identified in your TJD exercises.
2. Combine all this information into just three to five short sentences. Together they will clearly show what you bring to the target job.
3. Check against your TJD to see that, wherever possible, you use the same words employers are using to describe their jobs
4. Dense blocks of text are hard on the eyes. If you have more than five lines, break the text into two paragraphs.

Your objective with a Performance Profile is to demonstrate that you possess exactly the kinds of skills employers seek when hiring this type of person. It's a powerful way to open your resume, both for its impact with the resume search engines and because it gives the reader a clear, immediate summary of what you bring to the table.

PERFORMANCE PROFILE
Strategic communications professional with nine years experience developing effective, high-impact and cost-efficient media outreach plans for consumer, business, and policy audiences in media, entertainment, and technology practice areas. Experienced in managing corporate and crisis communications. Goal and deadline oriented with five years experience managing internal and external communications team members. Adept at working with multiple teams and stakeholders.

The finished product will be a Performance Profile that captures the professional you in words most likely to have a familiar ring to employers' ears.

Core Competencies

A Core Competencies section in your resume helps you in three ways:

1. It insures your resume contains all the keywords that will help it get pulled out of the resume databases for human review.
2. These keywords act as headlines and a time-saving device, quickly identifying that you possess the skills needed for the job.
3. The section reminds you to use as many of the words as you can in the Professional

Experience part of your resume, showing the context in which they were used.

Recruiters appreciate a Core Competency section as a summary of the resume's focus. Each keyword or phrase acts as an affirmation of a skill area and possible topic of conversation.

Confirming lots of topics to talk about so early in the resume is a big bonus for your candidacy. It acts as a preface to the body copy, in effect, saying, "Hey, here are all the headlines. The stories behind them are immediately below," so the reader will pay closer attention.

There's no need to use definite or indefinite articles or conjunctions. Just list the word, starting with a capital—"Forecasting," for example—or a phrase, such as "Financial modeling."

Here's an example of a Core Competencies section, this one for a PR professional:

- High tech Public Relations
- Strategic Communications
- PR Messaging & Tactics
- Press Releases
- Collateral Materials
- Media Relations
- Leadership
- Branding
- Media Training
- Media Pitch & Relations Story
- Strong Writing Skills
- Executive Counseling
- Acquisition Positioning
- New Business Development
- Team Management
- Budget Management
- Account Management
- Project Management
- Detail Oriented
- PR Counsel
- Research
- Team Building & Leadership
- Mentoring
- Client Management
- Organizational Skills
- Thought Leadership
- Investment Positioning

An example for a technologist:

—Core Competencies—

Strategic Planning ~ Full-Cycle Project Management ~ Technical & Application Standards ~ IT Governance Process ~ Technical Vision & Leadership ~ Architecture Roadmaps ~ Technical Specifications & Project Design Best Practices ~ Teambuilding & Leadership ~ Standards & Process Development

If your profession gives you a whole slate of technology competencies, you might choose to add a Technology Competencies section. It breaks up the page and is easier to absorb when they are separated.

Here's an example of a separate Technology Competencies section:

Technology Competencies

Hardware: Sun Servers; HP-UX; AIX; p-Series, z-Series; Windows Server

Operating Systems: Sun Solaris; AIX; HP-UX; Linux; z/OS; OS/400

Languages: C / C++; COBOL; Visual Basic; Java; Unix Korn Shell Scripting; Perl; Assembler; SQL*Plus; RPG

Databases: Oracle; DB2; SQL Server; Microsoft Access; Informix

Applications: MQSeries; Tuxedo; CICS; Microsoft Project, Word, Excel, Outlook, PowerPoint, SharePoint, and Visio; HP Service Desk; Provision; Tele-logic DOORS; Change Synergy; Rational System Architect; Rational System Developer; Visual Studio; CA Clarity; Livelink Other: Cobit 4.1

Think of your Core Competencies section as an electronic business card that allows you to network with computers.

The focus of the story your resume tells might prevent you from using all your keywords in your resume within their work context. But you can place them within your Core Competencies section. It is the perfect spot to list the technical acronyms and professional jargon that speak to the range of your professional skills even when they won't fit into the professional experience section of your resume.

Your resume is a living document, and its content may well change as your job search progresses. Whenever you come across keywords in job postings that reflect your capabilities, but those words are not in your resume, it is time to add them, and if nowhere else, at least in your Core Competencies section.

Performance Highlights/Career Highlights

In completing the resume questionnaire you gathered evidence of achievements and contributions in your work and quantified them whenever you could. Now is the chance to choose two to four of these (depending on the depth of your experience) standout contributions. Capture them in confident statements as shown in the examples, using action verbs in support of your career brand.

Company Names

Each job needs to be identified with an employer. There is no need to include specific contact information, although it can be useful to include the city and state.

When working for a multidivisional corporation, you may want to list the divisional employer. Bell Industries might not be enough, for example, so you could perhaps add Computer Memory Division. Accepted abbreviations include Corporation (Corp.), Company (Co.), or Division (Div.). Remember to be consistent.

Here is how you might combine a job title, company name, and location:

Design Engineer

Bell Industries, Inc., Computer Memory Div., Mountain View, CA

The information you are supplying is relevant to the reader, but you don't wish it to detract from space to sell yourself. If, for instance, space is at a premium and you live in a nationally known city, such as Dallas, you need not add TX.

Employed professionals are justified in omitting clear identification of employers when their industry has been reduced to a small community of experts who know, or know of each other, and where a confidentiality breach is likely to have damaging repercussions. This usually happens to those on the higher rungs of the ladder, and it is quite acceptable to sanitize current employment. Instead of the employer's name you might substitute:

- A National Retail Chain
- A Leading Software Developer
- A Major Commercial Bank

A company name can be followed by a brief description of the business line, and this can be an asset when it talks to a specific targeted job:

> **_Lara Corporation, Inc., Orlando, FL_**   **_1997 to present_**
> _$500 Million Company—One of Largest Resort and Vacation Development/Sales Companies in U.S. In Rapid Growth Through International Expansion, Strategic M&A, Industry Rollup, and IPO_

This is not necessary if the employer, for example Apple, is a household name.

Employment Dates

A resume without employment dates considerably under-performs a resume that has dates and those dates need to be accurate because they can be checked. With a steady work history and no employment gaps, you can be very specific:

> **_January 2004–July 2008_**

If you had an employment gap of six months in, say, 2008, you can disguise this:

> **_MBO Inc._**   **_2006–2008_**
> **_XYZ Inc._**   **_2008–present_**

I am *not* suggesting that you should lie about your work history, and you must be prepared to answer honestly and without hesitation if you are asked.

If you abbreviate employment dates, be sure to do so consistently. It is quite acceptable to list annual dates rather than month and year. Remember, when references get checked, the first things verified are dates of employment and leaving salary; untruths in either of these areas are grounds for dismissal with cause, and that can dog your footsteps into the future.

Professional Experience

Each section of the resume represents another opportunity to communicate your unique achievements and contributions. Replace timeworn descriptions in the Professional Experience section with strong action statements:

- **Before:** Responsible for identifying and developing new accounts.
- **After:** Drove advances in market share and revitalized stalled business by persistently networking and pursuing forgotten market pockets—lost sales, smaller, untapped businesses, prospects overlooked by the competition.

The area where you address your responsibilities and achievements in each job, *as they relate to the customer's needs you identified during TJD,* is the meat of your resume. When working on this part of your resume, constantly refer to your TJD work to remind yourself of the details target employers are most likely to want to read about and the keywords and phrases that will help your resume perform in recruiters' database searches.

The responsibilities and contributions you identify here are those functions that best relate to the needs of the target job. They do not necessarily correspond with how you spent the majority of your working day, nor are they related to how you might prefer to spend your working day. This can perhaps best be illustrated by showing you part of a resume that came to my desk recently. It is the work of a professional who listed her title and duties for one job like this:

> *Motivated a sales staff of six, recruited, trained, managed. Hired to improve sales. Sales Manager increased sales.*

The writer mistakenly listed everything in the reverse order of importance. She's not focused on the items' relative importance *to a future employer,* who above all will want to hire someone who can increase sales. She also wasted space stating the obvious about the reason she was hired as a sales manager: to improve sales. Let's look at what subsequent restructuring achieved:

> *Sales Manager: Hired to turn around stagnant sales force. Successfully recruited, trained, managed, and motivated sales staff of six. Result: 22 percent sales gain over first year.*

Notice how this is clearly focused on the essentials of any sales manager's job: to increase income for the company.

> *Hired to turn around stagnant sales force.* (Demonstrates her skills and responsibilities.)

Successfully recruited, trained, managed, and motivated a consulting staff of six. Result:
22 percent sales gain over first year. (Shows what she subsequently did with the sales
staff, and just how well she did it.)

By making these changes, her responsibilities and achievements become more important
in the light of the problems they solved. Be sure to match your narrative to employers' needs
and to the priorities of that job. Avoid exaggeration of your accomplishments. It isn't necessary.

Achievements

Business has very limited interests. In fact, those interests can be reduced to a single phrase:
making a profit. This is done in just three ways:

1. By saving money in some fashion for the company
2. By increasing productivity, which in turn saves money and provides the opportunity
   to make more money in the time saved
3. By simply earning money for the company

That does not mean that you should address only those points in your resume and ignore valuable contributions that cannot be quantified. But it does mean that you should *try to quantify your
achievements wherever you can.*

Pick two to four accomplishments for each job title and edit them down to bite-size chunks
that read like a telegram. Write as if you had to pay for each entry by the word—this approach
can help you pack a lot of information into a short space. The resulting abbreviated style will
help convey a sense of immediacy to the reader. I'll use an example we can all relate to:

> *Responsible for new and used car sales. Earned "Salesman of the Year" awards, 2006*
> *and 2007. Record holder: Most Cars Sold in One Year.*

Here's another example from a fundraiser's resume:

- *Created an annual giving program to raise operating funds. Raised $2,000,000.*
- *Targeted, cultivated, and solicited sources including individuals, corporations, founda-*
  tions, and state and federal agencies. Raised $1,650,000.
- *Raised funds for development of the Performing Arts School facility, capital*
  expense, and music and dance programs. Raised $6,356,000.

Now, while you may tell the reader about these achievements, never explain how they were
accomplished; the key phrase here is "specifically vague." The intent of your resume is to pique

interest and to raise as many questions as you answer. Questions mean interest, interest means talking to you, and getting conversations started is the primary goal of your resume!

Prioritize your accomplishments, and quantify them wherever possible and appropriate. You can cite achievements as part of a sentence/paragraph or as bullets, for example:

COLLECTIONS:
Developed excellent rapport with customers while significantly shortening payout terms. Turned impending loss into profit. Personally salvaged and increased sales with two multimillion-dollar accounts by providing remedial action for their sales/financial problems.

COLLECTIONS:
Developed excellent rapport with customers while significantly shortening payout terms:

- *Evaluated sales performance; offered suggestions for financing/merchandising, turned impending loss into profit.*
- *Salvaged two multimillion-dollar problem accounts by providing remedial action for their sales/financial problems. Subsequently increased sales.*

Whenever you can, keep each paragraph to a maximum of four or five lines. This ensures that the finished product has plenty of white space so that it is easy on the reader's eyes. If necessary, split one paragraph into two.

Endorsements and Excerpts from Performance Evaluations

You don't see these on resumes very often, but they can make a powerful addition; they are most effective when supporting quantified achievements. These endorsements are not necessary, though, and while they can make a good addition to your resume, they shouldn't be used to excess. One or two are adequate, although I have seen resumes where each job entry is finished with a complimentary endorsement. Here are a couple of examples of how to do them well:

- *Sales volume increased from $90 million to $175 million. Acknowledged as "the greatest single gain of the year."*

- *Earnings increased from $9 million to $18 million. Review stated, "Always has a view for the company bottom line."*

Charts and Graphs

A picture is worth a thousand words, so if you can use a graphic to make a point, it opens up the page and is infrequent enough to get attention. Here is an example of a graphic insert that shows increasing sales achievements. Compare this statement of achievement:

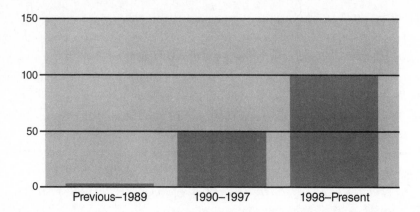

Revenue Growth—Maintained consistent, year-over-year increase through fluctuating economies, from $50,000 to $1.2 million.

With

Revenue Growth—Maintained consistent, year-over-year increases through fluctuating economies, from $50,000 to $1.2 million as illustrated below:

Avoid exaggeration of your accomplishments. It isn't necessary.

Education

Educational history is normally placed wherever it helps your case the most. The exact positioning will vary according to the length of your professional experience and the importance of your academic achievements to the job and your profession.

If you are recently out of school with little practical experience, your educational credentials might constitute your primary asset and should appear near the beginning of the resume.

After two or three years in the professional world, your academic credentials become less important in most professions and move to the end of your resume. The exceptions are in professions where academic qualifications dominate—medicine and law, for example. The highest level of academic attainment always comes first: a doctorate, then a master's, then a bachelor's degree. For degreed professionals, there is no need to go back further into educational history; however, it is optional to list your prestigious prep school.

If you graduated from high school and attended college but didn't graduate, you may be tempted to list your high school diploma first, followed by the name of the college you attended. That would give the wrong emphasis: it says you are a college dropout and identifies you as a high school graduate. In this instance, you would list your college and area of study but omit any reference to earlier educational history.

Employers really appreciate people who invest in their future and there's proof from the U.S. Department of Education to back it up. Of postsecondary students who enrolled in any AA degree program but didn't graduate, 48 percent received better job responsibilities and 29 percent received raises! If they actually graduated, it gets even better: 71 percent gained improved job responsibilities and 63 percent got raises.

Clearly, being enrolled in ongoing education looks good on a resume; you have nothing to lose and everything to gain by committing to your career. Being enrolled in courses toward a degree needn't be expensive, and all other things being equal, when say, a BS is required:

BSc Accounting. (Graduation anticipated Sept 2011)

can help you overcome an otherwise mandatory requirement.

It is normal to abbreviate degrees (PhD, MA, BA, BS, etc). In instances where educational attainment is paramount, it is acceptable to put that degree after your name. Traditionally, this has been the privilege of doctors and lawyers, but there is absolutely no reason that your name shouldn't be followed by, for example, MBA.

List scholarships and awards. More recent graduates will usually also list majors and minors (relevancy permitting—if it helps use it, if it doesn't, don't). The case is a little more complicated for the seasoned professional. Many human resources people say it makes life easier for them if majors and minors are listed, so they can further sift and grade the applicants. That's good for them, but it might not be good for you. The resume needs to get you in the door, not slam it in your face. So, as omitting majors will never stop you from getting an interview, I suggest you err on the side of safety. Leave them off unless they speak directly to the target job.

Don't puff up your educational qualifications. Research has proven that three out of every ten resumes inflate educational qualifications. Consequently, verification of educational claims is quite common. If, after you have been hired, your employer discovers that you exaggerated your educational accomplishments, it could cost you your job.

Ongoing Professional Education

Identify all relevant professional training courses and seminars you've attended. It speaks to professional competency and demonstrates your commitment to your profession. It also shows that an employer thought you worthy of the investment.

Technology is rapidly changing the nature of all work, so if you aren't learning new skills every year, you are being paid for an increasingly obsolescent skill set. Ongoing professional development is a smart career management strategy.

Accreditations, Professional Licenses, and Civil Service Grades

If licenses, accreditations, or civil service grades are mandatory requirements in your profession, you must feature them clearly. If you are close to gaining a particular accreditation or license you should identify it:

Passed all parts of C.P.A. exam, September 2010 (expected certification March 2011)

Civil service grades can be important if you are applying for jobs with government contractors, subcontractors, or any employers who do business with state or federal agencies.

Professional Associations

Membership in associations and societies related to your work demonstrates strong professional commitment, and offers great networking opportunities. See this year's edition of *Knock 'em Dead: The Ultimate Job Search Guide* for strategy and tactics in using these associations to find job opportunities. If you are not currently a member of one of your industry's professional associations, give serious consideration to joining.

Note the emphasis on "professional" in the heading. An employer is almost exclusively interested in your professional associations and societies. Omit references to any religious, political, or otherwise potentially controversial affiliations unless your *certain* knowledge of that company assures that such affiliations will be positively received.

An exception to this rule is found in those jobs where a wide circle of acquaintance is regarded as an asset. Some examples might include jobs in public relations, sales, marketing, real estate, and insurance. In these cases, include your membership/involvement with community/church organizations and the like, as your involvement demonstrates a professional who is also involved in the community and speaks to an outgoing personality with a wide circle of contacts.

By the same token, a seat on the town board, charitable cause involvement, or fundraising work are all activities that show a willingness to involve yourself and can demonstrate organizational abilities through titles held in those endeavors. Space permitting, these are all activities worthy of inclusion because they show you as a force for good in your community.

Companies that take their community responsibilities seriously often look for staff that feels and acts the same way. For instance, you could list yourself as:

American Heart Association: Area Fundraising Chair

If you are a recent entrant into the workplace, your meaningful extracurricular contributions are of even greater importance. List your position on the school newspaper or the student council, memberships in clubs, anything that demonstrates your potential as a productive employee. As your career progresses, however, prospective employers care less about your school life and more about your work life, so once you are a couple or three years into your career the importance of these involvements should be replaced by similar activities in the adult world.

Publications, Patents, and Speaking

These three capabilities are rare and make powerful statements about creativity, organization, determination, and follow-through. They tell the reader that you invest considerable personal time and effort in your career and are therefore a cut above the competition.

Public speaking is respected in every profession because it is such a terrifying thing to do, and I say this as someone who has spoken all over the world for two decades! Publications are always respected but carry more weight in some professions (academia). You will notice in the resume examples in this book that the writers list dates and names of publications but do not often include copyright information or patent numbers; nothing wrong with it, but it isn't necessary. Here's an example of how to cite your publications:

"Radical Treatments for Chronic Pain." 2002. Journal of American Medicine.
"Pain: Is It Imagined or Real?" 2000. Science & Health Magazine.

Patents take years to achieve and cost a fortune in the process (I know; I have two optical patents). They speak to vision, creativity, attention to detail, and considerable tenacity. They are a definite plus in the technology and manufacturing fields.

As you are piecing your resume together, it will almost certainly go beyond the one- and two-page mark. Do not worry about this. Page count considerations are out of date, and besides you haven't gotten to the editing stage yet.

Languages

With the current state of communications technology, all companies can have an international presence. Consequently you should always cite your cultural awareness and language abilities. Hey, there was a benefit to being a military brat and growing up all over the world! If you speak a foreign language, say so.

Fluent in Spanish and French   *Read and write Serbo-Croatian*
Read German   *Understand conversational Mandarin*

If you are targeting companies that have an international presence, I suggest you cite your linguistic abilities at the end of your Performance Profile.

Military

Always list your military experience. Military experience speaks, amongst other things, to your determination, teamwork, goal orientation, and understanding of policies and procedures. There are a number of major international corporations in which the senior ranks are heavily tilted toward men and women with a military background. My experience is not common. The best boss I ever had was Colonel Peter Erbe, an ex-airborne guy and one-time head of officer training at West Point. Everyone respects the commitment and the skills you developed in the military, and this can be a big plus in your career. ("Everyone" includes those of us who don't spend half our waking hours cursing anyone who believes in common courtesy and respect for fellow citizens who hold different political beliefs. Bear this in mind.)

Personal Flexibility, Relocation

If you are open to relocation for the right opportunity, make it clear. It will never, in and of itself, get you an interview, but it won't hurt. Place this information within the first half page so that it is within scanning distance of your address.

Judgment Calls

Here are some areas that do not normally go into your resume, but might. Whether you include them or not will depend on your personal circumstances.

Summer and Part-Time Employment

This should only be included if you are just entering the work force or re-entering it after a substantial absence. The entry-level person can feel comfortable listing dates and places and times. The returnee should include the skills gained but minimize the part-time aspect of the experience.

Reason for Leaving

The topic is always covered during an interview so why raise an issue that could have negative impact? You can usually use the space more productively, so your reason for leaving rarely belongs on a resume.

However, if you have frequently been caught in downsizings or mergers or because you have been recruited for more responsible positions, there can be a sound argument for listing these reasons to counteract the perception of your being a job hopper. You'll see examples in the resume section.

References

Employers assume that your references are available, and if they aren't available, boy, are you in trouble! However there is a case for putting—References Available Upon Request—at the end of your resume. It may not be absolutely necessary to say that references are there for the asking, but those four extra words certainly don't do any harm and may help you stand out from the crowd. Including the phrase sends a little message: "Hey, look, I have no skeletons in my closet."

But only if space allows; if you have to cut a line anywhere this should be one of the first to go.

Never list the names of references on a resume: interviewers very rarely check them before meeting and developing a strong interest in you—it's too time consuming. Additionally, the law forbids employers to check references without your written consent (1970 Fair Credit and Reporting Act), so they have to meet you first in order to obtain your written permission.

FYI, you grant this permission when you fill out an application form. In fact, it is usually the reason you are given an application form to complete when you already have a perfectly good resume. There, at the bottom, just above the space for your signature, is a block of impossibly small type. Your signature below it grants permission for reference and credit checks.

Name Changes and Your References

If you have ever worked under a different surname, you must take this fact into account when giving your references. A recently divorced woman I know wasted a strong interview performance because she was using her maiden name on her resume and at the interview. She forgot to tell the employer that her references would, of course, remember her by a different last name. The results of this oversight were catastrophic: Three prior employers denied ever having heard of anyone by the name supplied by the interviewer.

Marital Status

Some resume authorities think your marital status is important on the basis that it speaks to stability. However, with 50 percent of marriages ending in divorce, the average length of a marriage under fifteen years, and with miserable marriages capable of turning into a raving loonietune, I don't think that argument holds water.

It is also illegal to discriminate against a candidate based on marital status. However, if you think the stability implied by the length of your marriage will enhance your chances, you can include it. There are some areas where this is sometimes considered a valid criteria for consideration: outside sales, trucking, and fundamentalist organizations (the latter perhaps because of their high divorce rates).

Written Testimonials

It is best not to attach written testimonials to your resume. Of course, that doesn't mean that you shouldn't solicit such references. You might consider using them as a basis for those third-party endorsements we talked about earlier; and you have the documents to back up the claims. This way, you get to use them twice to good effect. Testimonials can be helpful to you if you are just entering the work force or are re-entering after a long absence.

Personal Interests

A Korn Ferry study once showed that executives with team sports on their resumes averaged $3,000 a year more than their more sedentary counterparts. Now, that makes giving a line to your hobbies worthwhile, if they fit into certain broad categories. If you participate in team sports, determination activities (running, climbing, bicycling), and "strategy activities" (Bridge, chess, Dungeons & Dragons), consider including something about them. The rule of thumb, as always, is only to include activities that can, in some way, contribute to your chances of being hired.

Occasionally, you will see resumes that include under this heading a candid snapshot of the resume writer as a person. Done well, these can be exciting, effective endings to a resume. Reference to one or two personal activities that speak to a person's ethics or are tied to the job in some way are the most effective.

Fraternities and Sororities

Changing times have altered thinking about listing fraternities and sororities on resumes. In general I recommend leaving them off. However, if your resume is tailored to individuals or companies where membership in such organizations will result in a case of "deep calling to deep," then by all means, list it.

What Never Goes In

Some information just doesn't belong in resumes. Make the mistake of including it, and at best, your resume loses a little power, while at worst, you fail to land the interview.

Personal Flexibility, Relocation

Earlier, I noted that if you are open to relocation for the right opportunity, make it clear, but *conversely, never state that you aren't open to relocation*. Let nothing stand in the way of generating job offers! You can always leverage a job offer you don't want into an offer you do, check out how in Chapter 21 of this year's edition of *Knock 'em Dead: The Ultimate Job Seeker's Guide*.

Titles Such As Resume, Fact Sheet, Curriculum Vitae, Etc.

Their appearance on a properly structured resume is redundant. It makes clear that your resume needs more work. Such titles take up a whole line, one that could be used more productively. Use the space you save for information with greater impact, or buy yourself an extra line of white space to help your reader's eyes.

Availability

All jobs exist because there are problems that need solutions now. For that reason interviewers rarely have time for candidates who aren't readily available. If you are not ready to start work, then why are you wasting everyone's time? As a rule of thumb, let the subject of availability come up at the face-to-face meeting. After meeting you, an employer is more likely to be prepared to wait until you are available, but will usually pass on an interview if you cannot start now or in the reasonably near future, say, two to three weeks.

The only justification for including this (and then only in your cover letter) is if you expect to be finishing a project and moving on at such and such a time, and not before.

For further guidance on this, see Chapter 8 of the latest edition of *Knock 'em Dead Cover Letters*.

Salary

Leave out all references to salary, past and present—it is far too risky. Too high or too low a salary can knock you out of the running even before you hear the starting gun. Even in responding to a job posting that specifically requests salary requirements, don't give the information on your resume. A good resume will still get you the interview, and in the course of the discussions with the company, you'll talk about salary anyway. If you are obliged to give salary requirements, address them in your cover letter—and give a range; you may want to read the section on salary negotiation in the newest edition of *Knock 'em Dead: The Ultimate Job Search Guide*.

Age, Race, Religion, Sex, and National Origin

Government legislation was enacted in the 1960s and 1970s forbidding employment discrimination in these areas under most instances, so it is wisest to avoid reference to them unless they are deemed relevant to the job.

Photographs

In days of old, when men were bold and all our cars had fins, it was the thing to have a photograph in the top right-hand corner of the resume. Today, the fashion is against photographs. Obviously, careers in modeling, acting, and certain aspects of the media require headshots. In these professions, your appearance is an integral part of your product offering.

Health/Physical Description

You are trying to get a job, not a date. Unless your physical appearance (gym instructor, model, actor, media personality) are immediately relevant to the job, leave these issues alone. If you need to demonstrate health, do it with your extracurricular interests.

Early Background

Does not belong. I see resumes that tell about early childhood and circumstances of upbringing. The most generous excuse I can come up with is that the subject's mother prepared the resume.

Expectations and Objectives

No demands, expectations, or objectives. When resumes are being screened no one cares what you want. Stating what you are looking for, apart from squandering the reader's attention and wasting valuable selling space. Your every requirement, narrows your opportunities.

The time for making demands is when the employer extends a job offer. That is when your needs are of interest to your future boss. Until then, concentrate on what you bring to employers.

CHAPTER 5
IF YOU LOOK LIKE A DOG, YOU'LL GET LEFT OUTSIDE

FIRST IMPRESSIONS ARE important. You have the right and the obligation to package your professional experience to its greatest benefit.

Everyone has different work experience: you may have worked for just one employer throughout your career or have worked for five companies in ten years; you may have changed careers entirely, or you may have maintained a predictable career path, changing jobs but staying within one profession or industry.

The look of your resume, the format you choose, depends on what your unique background brings to the target job. While there are three broadly different resume formats to put different work histories in their most exciting light, their goals are constant:

1. To maximize your performance in the resume databases
2. To demonstrate your complete grasp of the job's deliverables
3. To create a professional brand for someone who lives and breathes this work
4. To showcase relevant achievements, attributes, and accumulation of expertise to the best advantage
5. To minimize any possible weaknesses

Resume experts acknowledge three major styles for presenting your credentials to a potential employer: Chronological, Functional, and Combination (Chrono-Functional). Your particular circumstances will determine the right format for you.

The Chronological Resume

The chronological resume is the most widely accepted format. It's what most of us think of when we think of resumes—a chronological listing of job titles and responsibilities. It starts with the current or most recent employment, then works backward to your first job.

This format is good for demonstrating your growth in a single profession. It is suitable for anyone with practical work experience who hasn't suffered prolonged periods of unemployment. It is not always the best choice if you are just out of school or if you are changing careers, where it might draw attention to a lack of specific, relevant experience.

The distinguishing characteristic of the chronological resume is the way it ties your job responsibilities and achievements to specific employers, job titles, and dates.

This is the simplest resume to create:

PARAG GUPTA

104 W. Real Drive • Beaverton, OR 97006 • (503) 123-4286 • parag.gupta@technical.com

SYSTEMS ENGINEER: Motivated and driven IT Professional offering 9+ years of hands-on experience in designing, implementing, and enhancing systems to automate business operations. Demonstrated ability to develop high-performance systems, applications, databases, and interfaces.

- Part of TL9000 CND audit interviews that helped Technical get TL9000 certified, which is significant in Telecom industry. Skilled trainer and proven ability to lead many successful projects, like TSS, EMX, and TOL.
- Strategically manage time and expediently resolve problems for optimal productivity, improvement, and profitability; able to direct multiple tasks effectively.
- Strong technical background with a solid history of delivering outstanding customer service.
- Highly effective liaison and communication skills proven by effective interaction with management, users, team members, and vendors.

Technical Skills

Operating Systems:	Unix, Windows (2000, XP, 7), DOS
Languages:	C, C++, Java, Pascal, Assembly Languages (Z8000, 808x, DSP)
Methodologies:	TL9000, Digital Six Sigma
Software:	MS Office, Adobe FrameMaker, MATLAB
RDBMS:	DOORS, Oracle 7.x
Protocols:	TCP/IP, SS7 ISUP, A1, ANSI, TL1, SNMP
Tools:	Teamplay, ClearCase, ClearQuest, M-Gate keeper, Exceed, Visio, DocExpress, Compass
Other:	CDMA Telecom Standards – 3GPP2 (Including TIA/EIA-2001, TIA/EIA-41, TIA/EIA-664), ITU-T, AMPS

Professional Experience

Technical, Main Network Division, Hillsboro, OR   Jan 1999–Present

Principal Staff Engineer • Products Systems Engineering • Nov 2004–Present

- Known as "go-to" person for CDMA call processing and billing functional areas.
- Created customer requirements documents for Technical SoftSwitch (TSS) and SMS Gateway products. All deliverables done on/ahead schedule with high quality.
- Solely accountable for authoring and allocation, customer reviews, supporting fellow system engineers, development and test, and customer documentation teams.
- Support Product Management in RFPs, customer feature prioritization, impact statements, and budgetary estimates.
- Mentored junior engineers and 1 innovation disclosure [patent] submitted in 2007.
- Resolved deployed customer/internal requirements issues and contributed to Virtual Zero Defect quality goal.
- TOL process champion and part of CND focus group that contributed to reducing CRUD backlog (NPR) by 25% and cycle time (FRT) by 40%.
- Recognized as the TL9000 expert. Triage representative for switching and messaging products.
- Achieved "CND Quality Award" for contribution to quality improvement, May 2007.

Senior Staff Engineer • MSS Systems Engineering • May 2002–Oct 2004

- Led a team of 12 engineers for 3 major software releases of TSS product included around 80 features/enhancements to create T-Gate SE deliverables.
- Led a team of 12 engineers for 3 major software releases of TSS product included around 80 features/enhancements to create T-Gate SE deliverables.

67

The Chronological Resume (page 2)

- Mentored newer engineers to get up to speed on TSS product.
- Created requirements for TSS product, 30 features/enhancements contributing to 5 major software releases. Recognized as overall product expert with specific focus on call processing and billing.
- Played integral role in successfully implementing proprietary commercial TSS billing system.
- Supported PdM organization by creating ROMs, technical support for RFPs (Vivo, Sprint, TELUS, TM, Tata, Inquam, Alaska, Reliance, Pakistan, PBTL, Mauritius, Telefonica, Brasicel and Angola).
- Proactively identified functional areas of improvement for requirements coverage, contributed to resolving several faults, improved customer documentation, and provided reference for future releases as well as other customers.
- Received "Above and Beyond Performance Award" Oct 2003

Senior Software Engineer • EMX Development • Aug 2000–Apr 2002

- Successfully led and coordinated the cross-functional development teams, 30 engineers, to meet the scheduled design, code, and test completion dates ensuring Feature T-Gates are met.
- Feature Technical Lead for Concurrent Voice/Data Services feature, the largest revenue-generating feature for KDDI customer.
- Feature Lead for Paging Channel SMS feature. Created requirements and design; led implementation phase of five engineers' team; supported product, network, and release testing; and created customer reference documentation.
- Performed the role of functional area lead for Trunk Manager and A1 interface functional areas. Provided 2-day Technical Workshops for internal/customer knowledge sharing and functional area transition from Caltel.
- Provided customer site testing and FOA (First Office Application) support for major EMX releases and off-hours CNRC (Customer Networks Resolution Center) support.
- Received "Bravo Award" May 2001, Sep 2001, Jan 2002

Software Engineer • EMX Development • Jan 1999–Jul 2000

- Developed design and code for SMS feature as a Trunk Manager functional area lead for the largest FA impacted by the feature. Supported product, network, and release testing.
- Contributed to customer release documentation. Supported feature-level SMS testing at various internal labs and customer sites resulting in successful deployment at customer sites.
- Designed and coded phases for wiretap and virtual circuits feature development, initial assessment of internal and customer EMX PRs (problem reports) to route/classify issues and providing problem assessments for many of these PRs.
- Created an implementation process to serve as reference for new hires.
- Provided CNRC support during the Y2K transition.
- Received "Above and Beyond Performance Award" Jan 2000, Dec 2000 and "Certificate of Outstanding Achievement" Jun 1999

Education: Master of Science in Computer Engineering • University of Portland, Portland, OR
• 1998
Bachelors of Engineering in Electronics • Technology and Science Institute, India
•1996

Significant Trainings Include
- Open Source Software • WiMAX • Agile Management for Software Engineering
- WSG Requirements Process • Product Security

The Functional Resume

The functional resume format focuses on the professional skills you bring to a specific target job, rather than when, where, or how you acquired them. It also de-emphasizes employers and employment dates by their placement on the second page, which typically gets less attention than your lead page. Because the focus is on the skill rather than the context or time of its acquisition, job titles and employers can likewise play a lesser part with this format.

The functional format is still used, although it is thought less effective than other formats; this may in part be attributable to the more challenging tasks it is chosen for:

- Mature professionals with a storehouse of expertise and jobs pursuing encore careers
- Entry-level professionals whose skimpy experience might not justify a chronological resume
- Those in career transition who want to focus on skills rather than locus of the experience, because that experience was developed in a different professional context
- People returning to the workplace after a long absence

Though functional resumes are more free-form than chronological ones, they should share certain structural features:

Target Job Title

For any resume to be effective, it must be conceived with a specific target job in mind, and this is especially true for a functional resume. Because it focuses so strongly on skills and the ability to contribute in a particular direction, rather than on a directly relevant work history, you really must have an employment objective clearly in mind.

A Performance Profile or Career Summary

Your target job should be followed by a short paragraph that captures your professional capabilities as they address the deliverables of the target job.

Core Competencies

A Core Competencies section in your functional resume will help its performance in databases, and the use of critical keywords early on helps confirm your possession of the essential skills for the job.

Performance Highlights

Based on your target job, this is where you identify the skills, behaviors, and accomplishments that best position you for the job. Notice how clearly these demonstrate competence in the example.

Dates

If your employment history lacks continuity, a functional resume allows you to de-emphasize dates somewhat by their placement, but an absence of employment dates altogether will just draw attention to a potential problem. See Chapter 4, Keep It Simple, Stupid, for more about how to handle employment dates.

Everything else related to Functional resumes follows the rules outlined in Chapter 4.

A Functional Resume That Works

Functional resumes are not as popular as they once were, but in some circumstances, they really are the best choice. On pages 74–75 is a functional resume of someone applying for a job as an art gallery or museum curator whose only prior experience was as an art teacher. Read the first page and then ask yourself if you know what a good gallery or museum curator needs to know. I'll give you a few more interesting insights after you look at the example.

A couple of interesting observations about this functional resume:

- It is more informal in tone than many examples you will see in the book, but as it reflected someone in a profession where personality is a significant part of the job, there is nothing wrong with that. Given these considerations, I decided to give the resume a personal flavor, and the very first words of the Performance Profile immediately draw the reader into a conversation with a passionate and committed professional: "My professional life is focused on art in all it embraces."
- There are professions where a less formal tone is more generally acceptable, usually education, the arts, and the caring professions.
- It is quite clear this person really understands the work of a curator. The first time it was used, this resume resulted in an interview within seventy-two hours, and a job offer was extended at the end of the first hour.
- Now for the kicker: The fact that this person had been the arts department chair of a private elementary through middle school was never an issue, because he so clearly understood the demands of the target job. That was possible because his TJD research allowed the resume to be properly focused and prepared him for exactly the topics that would come up at interview.

• The second time this resume was used, a Core Competencies section was added to increase database visibility. In the middle of the 2008–09 recession he was called by an executive recruiter, had two interviews, and was hired at a 50 percent increase in salary to run one of the nation's blue-chip galleries.

This functional resume was successful because the writer took the time to go through the TJD process and was then able to tell a captivating and believable story, demonstrating that he had exactly the credentials needed.

The Combination Resume

This format an example which appears on pages 78–80, is fast becoming the resume of choice for performance in a database-dominated world. This format has all the flexibility and strength that comes from combining both the chronological and functional formats:

• It allows you maximum flexibility to demonstrate your thorough grasp of the job and its deliverables
• It encourages greater data density and detail of information, which improves database retrieval performance
• It offers more flexibility and scope for establishing a professional brand

This format has all the categories you worked with in creating your first draft in the layout template from Chapter Four:

Target Job Title
(Here's the job I'm after.)

Performance Profile
(This is a snapshot of what I can do.)

Core Competencies
(Here are the key professional skills that help me do my job well.)

Technical Competencies
(Optional: Here are the technical skills that help me do my job well.)

Performance Highlights
(Optional: Outstanding achievements)

Professional Experience
(Where and when everything happened)

This format takes more effort to create, but it is the most productive format in database performance, resonates most powerfully with human eyes, and gives the greatest scope for creating a strong professional brand, which we'll cover in Chapter 7.

Choose a Template

If you haven't already, now is probably a good time to choose a resume template. Look in the samples at the back of the book. You can also get resume and job search letter templates at *www.knockemdead.com*.

When most people look for suitable resume templates they look for ones that reflect someone in their profession. This is *wrong*! Resume templates are *not* designed with particular professions or jobs in mind; they are designed to tell a particular story in a graphically engaging way.

You should *not* choose a particular template because you are an accountant and it's an accountant's resume template, because there is no magically ordained format for resumes by profession. It doesn't matter at all if the accountant chooses the resume template of a geologist. Choose your template based on its ability to accommodate your story in a visually appealing way.

You will find examples of all these styles in the sample section later in the book, and ready-to-use resume templates in MS Word at *www.knockemdead.com*.

If you aren't sure, use the resume layout template from the resume advice pages at the site: your resume will have all the right components and have a perfectly acceptable professional look, until you decide on a final look.

CHAPTER 6
No One Wants To Read Your Resume, So You'd Better Make It Good

THE RECRUITERS AND hiring authorities who need to read your resume hate doing it, they just want to find the right person PDQ (Pretty Damn Quick) and get back to work. In response, resumes must achieve the simultaneous goals of visual accessibility and information density.

You can assume that anyone who reads your resume has an open position to fill and is numb from reading resumes. Understanding exactly what this feels like will help you craft a finished resume that is most readily accessible to the tired eyes and distracted minds of recruiters and hiring authorities.

Charles Chalmers

Manhattan NY 11658 • (212) 232-8269 • fineartist@earthlink.net

Senior Curator

Performance Profile

My professional life is focused on art in all it embraces: drawing, painting, sculpture, photography, cinema, video, audio, performance and digital art, art history and criticism; my personal life is similarly committed. Recently relocated to Manhattan, I intend to make a contribution to the New York arts community that harnesses my knowledge, enthusiasm, and sensibilities.

Core Competencies

Photographer ~ editor ~ drawing ~ painting ~ sculpture ~ photography ~ cinema ~ video ~ audio ~ performance and digital art ~ art history and criticism ~ global artist networks ~ alumni groups ~ first-rank private collectors ~ social networking-themed, resourced, sequenced shows ~ campus & community involvement ~ education & outreach ~ installation-hang, light, and label-media kits ~ artist materials ~ Photoshop-art-staff management ~ curriculum development ~ art handlers-maintenance ~ printers ~ catering ~ graphics ~ portfolio prep-int/ext shows ~ theatre sets ~ streamed video gallery tours

Performance Highlights

ART HISTORY

Thorough knowledge of art history from caves of Lascaux through current artists such as Bruce Nauman, Jessica Stockholder, and Luc Tuymans. Film history from Lumiere Brothers to Almodovar. Current with key critical art and film theory. Ongoing workshops and lectures with the likes of Matthew Barney, Louise Bourgeoise, and Andy Goldsworthy.

RESEARCH NEW ARTISTS

Connected to cutting-edge art and artists through involvement with the art communities and galleries of New York and Boston and the faculty, student, and alumni networks of RISD, Columbia, Boston Museum School, New England School of Art & Design, and now Mass Art. Twenty years of Manhattan gallery openings and networking with artists at MOMA, PS1, Guggenheim, Whitney, Metropolitan, Film Forum, International Center for Photography workshops and lectures.

SOURCING ART WORK

Through local artists, regional and global artist networks, intercultural artist exchanges, alumni groups, first-rank private collectors, personal and family networks, and Internet calls for submissions.

ART AND THE COMMUNITY

Conception and launch of themed, resourced, and sequenced shows that invigorate campus and community involvement. Reconfigure existing art spaces to create dynamic dialogue with visitors. Education and outreach programs.

The Functional Resume (page 2)

ART INSTALLATION

Maintain fluidity of gallery space in preparing exhibitions with recognition of size/time considerations for the art, to insure a sympathetic environment for the presented works. Hang, light, and label shows in sequences that create dialogue between the works.

PUBLIC RELATIONS MATERIALS

Energizing invitations, comprehensive press kits, illustrated press releases, and artist binder materials. Sensitive to placing art in historical/cultural context. Photoshop.

Management experience

Fourteen years art-staff management experience, including curriculum development. Responsible for art instructors, art handlers, maintenance crews, and working with printers, catering, and graphic arts staff.

Professional experience

1994–2005 Chair of Visual Arts, The Green Briar School

Duties: Curriculum development, portfolio preparation, internal and external monthly shows, theatre sets, monthly video news show, taught art history and all the studio arts, managed staff of three.

1989–2004 President Art Workshops

Duties: Private art studio and art history curriculums, staff of four. Private groups to Manhattan museums and gallery tours.

1980–1989 Freelance artist, photographer, and editor

Highlights from the sublime to the ridiculous include: Taught photography at Trinity School, Manhattan; photographer for the Ramones; editor of Pioneer, insurance industry trade magazine; assistant to Claudia Weill, documentary filmmaker, director of "Girlfriends."

Education

MFA. Magna cum laude. Columbia University, 1983
Awards: ****** ***** Prize for film criticism
Taught undergraduate Intro to Film, under ****** ***** and ****** ******.

Subscriptions

Art in America, Art News, Art Forum, New York Times, Parkett, Sight & Sound, Film Comment, Modern Painters.

Memberships

MOMA/PS1, Whitney Museum of American Art, Guggenheim, Metropolitan Museum of Art, DIA.

Recent exhibitions

2004. Corcoran Center Gallery, Southampton, NY
2005. Corsair Gallery, 37 West 33rd St. NY
2006. Fuller Museum, Brockton MA
2002. 2007. Zeitgeist Gallery, Cambridge, MA

Imagine for a moment you are a recruiter. You read resumes for a good part of the day, everyday. Today, you have just completed a resume database search and have twenty resumes to read. Now go read twenty resumes from the sample section without a break. Try to really read and understand each one, but don't spend more than sixty seconds on each.

Three things will happen: first you'll hear a ringing in your ears; next your vision will become fuzzy, and you'll lose the ability to concentrate. After about fifteen minutes, you'll realize why your focus on relevant content and a clear layout for your resume are critical for getting it read and understood . . . one of the reasons those headlines are so appreciated.

Customize the templates you choose

Resume layouts are based on common sense: that which is most valuable in your candidacy comes up front. For example, when you have no experience, your degree is front and center. As experience increases with the passage of time, your education becomes somewhat less important. This is why you will usually see education at the end of a resume, unless your target profession's particular demands require it be emphasized.

However, the resume template you choose isn't sacrosanct. You can customize it to suit your needs. For example, you might decide that moving languages, special training, or other information typically found at the end of the resume to the first page increases the strength of your argument. If that makes sense, go ahead and do it.

There are some professions—medicine, education, and the law, for example—where academic and professional accreditations tend to be kept at the front of the resume. Bear this in mind if you work in one of these professions.

Filling In the Template

Go through your chosen template and transfer the information you developed earlier. Immediately you have a document that is beginning to look like a finished product. But you're not finished yet. Not by any means.

Tighten up sentences

Sentences gain power with verbs that demonstrate an action. For example, a woman with ten years of law firm experience in a clerical position had written in her original resume:

I learned to use a new database.

After she thought about what was really involved, she gave this sentence more punch:

I analyzed and determined the need for a comprehensive upgrade of database, archival, and retrieval systems. Responsible for selection and installation of "in the clouds" archival systems. Within one year, I had an integrated company-wide archival system working.

Notice how verbs show that things happen when you are around the office. The action verbs and phrases we discussed in Chapter 3 give action to a resume. They show things happening. Note that while they tell the reader what you did it and how you did it, they also support the branding statements that can open and close your resume.

Now look at the above example when we add a third party's endorsement:

I analyzed and determined the need for a comprehensive upgrade of database, archival, and retrieval systems. I was responsible for selection and installation of "in the clouds" archival systems. Within one year, I had an integrated company-wide archival system working. A partner stated, "You brought us out of the dark ages, and in the process neither you nor the firm missed a beat!"

Now, while the content is clearly more powerful, the sentences are still clunky and need tightening.

Tight sentences have bigger impact

Space is at a premium, and reader impact is your goal, so keep your sentences to about twenty words. Always aim for simplicity and clarity:

- Shorten sentences by cutting unnecessary words
- Make two sentences out of one

At the same time, you don't want the writing to sound choppy, so vary the length of sentences when you can. You can also start with a short phrase and follow with a colon:

- Followed by bullets of information
- Each one supporting the original phrase

See how these techniques tighten the writing and enliven the reading process:

The Combination Resume (page 1)

John William Wisher, MBA
2541 Bainbridge Blvd.
West Chicago, IL 60185

jwisher@ameritech.net   630.878.2653 630.377.9117

Expert leadership in cost effective supply chain, vendor, and project management within *Fortune* organizations.

EXECUTIVE PROFILE

A visionary, forward-thinking SUPPLY CHAIN AND LOGISTICS LEADER offering 20+ years of progressive growth and outstanding success streamlining operations across a wide range of industries. Excellent negotiation and relationship management skills with ability to inspire teams to outperform expectations. Proven record of delivering a synchronized supply chain approach through strategic models closely mirroring business plan to dramatically optimize ROI and manage risk.

Supply Chain Strategy:—Successfully led over 500 supply chain management initiatives across a wide spectrum of businesses, negotiating agreements from $5K to $27M. Implemented technology solutions and streamlined processes to reduce redundancies and staffing hours, improving both efficiency and productivity. Industries include: automotive and industrial manufacturing, consumer goods, government and defense, healthcare, high tech, and retail.

Industry Knowledge:—Extensive knowledge base developed from hands-on industry experience. Began career in dock operations with experience in Hub and Package Operations, multi-site retail operations management, to custom supply chain strategy development over twenty-one-year career with UPS.

Supply Chain Process Costing:—Built several information packets on total cost of ownership (TCO) and facilitated several C-level negotiations to identify and confirm opportunities. Worked to increase awareness among stakeholders on efficiencies and cost-saving measures ROI. Delivered $3.75M total cost savings to client base over three-year period.

Operations Reorganization:—Designed and implemented new sales force alignment and reporting structure; increased daily sales calls by 20%, reduced travel mileage 23%, and head count by nine; total annual cost savings of $920K.

Logistics:—Experienced across all modes of transportation: ocean, air freight, LTL, TL, mail services, and small package. Performs complex analysis to develop strategy based on cost and delivery requirements.

Project Management:—Implemented complete $1.2M redesign of 11 new UPS Customer Centers. Managed vendor and lease negotiations, developed budgets, training, and sales structure. All 11 centers up and operational on time and on budget.

Cost & Process Improvements

- Implemented complete warehouse redesign for a large optical distributor. Optimized warehouse operations through engineering a new warehouse design, integrating and automating technology, and synchronization of goods movement through ocean, air, ground, and mail services. Reduced transportation expense by 15%, increased production levels by 25%, reduced inventory by 15% and staffing by 20%.

- Built custom supply chain for a nationally recognized golf club manufacturer. Improved service levels by 30%, reduced damage by 45%, and integrated technology to support shipping process automation, reducing billing function staffing hours 50%.

Trust-Based Leadership
Vendor/Client Negotiations
Cross-Functional Collaboration
Supply Chain Mapping
Financial Logistics Analysis
Contingency Planning
Risk Management
Competitive Analysis
Haz Mat Compliance
Inventory Planning, Control, & Distribution
Recruiting/Training/Development
Project Management
Organizational Change Management
Distributive Computing
Budget Management
Labor Relations

78

John William Wisher, MBA

PROFESSIONAL BACKGROUND

United Parcel Service (UPS), Addison, IL   1986 to Present
World's largest package-delivery company and global leader in supply chain services, offering an extensive range of options for synchronizing the movement of goods, information, and funds. Serves more than 200 countries and territories worldwide and operates the largest franchise shipping chain, the UPS Store.

DIRECTOR/AREA MANAGER—SUPPLY CHAIN SALES, 2005–Present

Promoted to lead and develop a cross-functional sales force of 18 in consultative supply chain management services to Chicago-area businesses. Directs development of integrated supply chain management solutions across all modes of transportation, closely mirroring client business plans. Mentors team in Demand Responsive Model, a proven methodology to quickly align internal and external resources with changing market demands, situational requirements, and mission critical conditions. Manages $100M P&L.

Accomplishments:
- Implements over 100 multimillion-dollar supply chain integrations per year with 14% annual growth on 8% plan.
- Develops future organizational leaders; four staff members promoted through effective mentoring and development.
- Choreographed a supply chain movement from the Pacific Rim for a global fast-food chain to deliver 300k cartons to 15k locations all on the same day. Utilized modes of ocean, TL, air, and ground services, allowing for a national release synchronized to all locations on the same release date.
- Designed and implemented an automated reverse logistics program for a nationally recognized health food/supplement distributor. Automated returns process to reduce touches and costly staffing hours. Eliminated front-end phone contact using technology and web automation.

MARKETING MANAGER   2004 to 2005

Fast tracked to streamline sales processes, increasing performance. Performed analysis of sales territory, historical data, operations alignment, reporting structure, and sales trends to devise solutions. Managed and coached area managers in business-plan development and execution of sales strategies. Delivered staff development in cost-reduction strategies and compliance requirements. Accountable for $500M P&L.

Accomplishments:
- Drove $500M+ in local market sales. Grew revenues 2004/2005 revenues 12% and 7% respectively.

RETAIL CHANNEL/OPERATIONS MANAGER   2002 to 2004

Charged with turning around this underperforming business unit. Managed development and implementation of new retail strategy across northern Illinois. Rebranded UPS Customer Centers and the UPS Store. Performed vendor negotiations and collaborated with nine regions to support additional implementations.

Accomplishments:
- Developed key revenue-generating initiatives across multiple channels. Attained 65% growth in discretionary sales. Several strategies adopted across the national organization.
- Re-engineered inventory for over 1,000 dropoff locations, reduced lease expenses by 45% and inventory levels by 40% through weekly measurement, inventory level development by SKU, order process automation, and order consolidation.
- Implemented new retail sales associate structure in 1,100 locations; scored highest national service levels by mystery shoppers.
- Selected as Corporate team member on Mail Boxes Etc. acquisition integration.

PROJECT MANAGER   2001 to 2002

Selected to support several underperforming business areas. Managed key segments of district business initiatives and compliance measures for 1,000 dropoff locations. Reported on status to corporate management. Supervised office staff of 16. Negotiated vendor and lease agreements.

Accomplishments:
- Rolled out and managed ongoing Haz Mat compliance program for all locations.
- Generated $6M in sales through cross-functional lead program and increased participation from 20% to 100%.
- Attained union workforce sponsorship of support-growth program through careful negotiations and persuasion.

SENIOR ACCOUNT MANAGER   1999 to 2001

Delivered $2.8M in growth on $1.1M plan, rated 3rd of 53 managers in revenue generation

ACCOUNT MANAGER   1997 to 1998

Top producer out of 53; $1.3M sales on $500K plan.

John William Wisher, MBA

SERVICE PROVIDER 1994 to 1996
Top producer out of 53; $1.3M sales on $500K plan.

SUPERVISOR OF PACKAGE OPERATIONS 1994
Managed 65 full-time service providers. Performed post-routine analysis, operating strategy development, compliance, payroll, service failure recovery, and new technology implementation. Met 100% DOT and Haz Mat compliance. Reduced post-delivery staffing time by 50% and missed pickups by 65%.

SUPERVISOR OF HUB OPERATIONS 1988 to 1994
Managed up to 100 union employees and staff processing 75K pieces per day involving 40+ outbound bays. Performed complex staff scheduling and maintained low turnover rates. Designed new management reporting format, reducing administrative time by 20% and improved load quality by 30%.

OPERATIONS DOCK WORKER AND TRAINING LEAD 1986 to 1987

EDUCATION
MBA
National Louis University, Wheaton, IL, *4.0 GPA*

BA, Business, Supply Chain Management

Elmhurst College, Elmhurst, IL, *3.84 GPA, Magna cum laude*

Additional Specialized Courses:
• Supply Chain Mapping, 20 Hours
• Financial Logistics Analysis (FLOGAT), 10 Hours
• Hazardous Materials, 20 Hours
• Labor Relations, 30 Hours
• Managers Leadership School, 100 Hours
• Hazardous Materials, 20 Hours
• Managing from the Heart, 30 Hours

Analyzed and determined need for comprehensive upgrade of database, archival, and retrieval systems:

- *Responsible for hardware and software selection.*
- *Responsible for selection and installation of "in the clouds" archival systems.*
- *Responsible for compatible hardware and software upgrades.*
- *Trained users from managing partner through administrators.*
- *Achieved full upgrade, integration and compliance in six months.*
- *Partner stated, "You brought us out of the dark ages, and neither you nor the firm missed a beat!"*

The result is not only easier to read, it also speaks of a professional who knows the importance of *getting to relevant information fast.*

Big words or little words?

Just about anything you think is original in your resume has already been done before a thousand times. One of the biggest mistakes amateur (and professional) resume writers make is using "big words." In an effort to sound professional, they end up sounding pompous and impenetrable. The goal of your resume is to communicate quickly and efficiently, so just as you use short sentences, you should also use common words. They are easy to understand and thus communicate clearly and quickly. Remember:

- Short words in short sentences
- Use them to make short, gripping paragraphs.
- Short words in short sentences in short paragraphs help tired eyes!

Voice and tense

The voice you use in your resume depends on a few important factors: getting a lot said in a small space, being factual, and packaging yourself in the best way.

Sentences can be truncated (up to a point) by omitting pronouns—*I, you, he, she, it, they*—and articles—*a* or *the.* Dropping pronouns is a technique that saves space and allows you to brag about yourself without seeming boastful, because it gives the impression that another party is writing about you.

"*I automated the office*" becomes, "*Automated office.*" It is shorter and more forceful.

At the same time, writing in the first person makes you sound, well, personable.

Use whatever works best for you. If you use personal pronouns, don't use them in every sentence—they get monotonous and take up valuable space on the page. Use a third-person voice through the resume, with a few final words in the first person as a closing brand statement at the end of the document to give an insight into your values. You saw an example of a functional resume with just such a personal tone that works almost magically for its owner.

Many people confuse the need for professionalism with stiff-necked formality. The most effective tone is one that mixes the conversational and the formal, just the way we do in our jobs. The only overriding rule is to make it readable.

Using third person and dropping pronouns throughout the body of the resume helps save space and gives you an authoritative tone. Using an opening and/or using a closing personal brand statement in the first person can provide a very powerful reinforcement of the branding you have striven for throughout the document. For instance, in your closing brand statement you would switch from third person with dropped pronoun to first person:

> *I see performance management as a critical tool to ensure maximum profitability with a sales team; my consistency has always led to motivated, high-performance sales teams.*

The effect is that a third party has been objectively discussing someone's professional background and the first person jumps out at the end with a statement that amplifies the essence of the resume's owner. Integrating brand statements is a new idea and something many resumes do not have. Do it well and you can really stand out.

Resume length

The rule used to be one page for every ten years of experience, and never more than two pages. However, as jobs have gotten more complex, they require more explanation.

The length of your resume is less important than its relevance to the target job. Ideally the first half to two-thirds of the first page of your resume should be tightly focused on a specific target job and include a target job title, performance profile, core competency, and perhaps career highlight sections. Do this and any reader can quickly see that you have the chops for the job. We will discuss branding in detail shortly, but if you realize you cannot make a convincing brand statement right now, better not to make one at all.

If you are seen to be qualified, the reader will stay with you as you tell the story. Given the increasing complexity of jobs, the length and depth of your experience, and the need for data-dense resumes (they are overwhelmingly rewarded in database searches), it is idiotic to limit the length of your resume based on outdated conventions from before the age of computers, let alone the Internet.

The worst, the most heinous crime of all is to cram a seasoned professional's work history into a tiny font sizes in order to get it onto one or two pages. Why? Here's a flash from reality: If you are a seasoned professional with a real track record requiring a complex skill set and you are climbing the ladder of success, it's likely your readers are also successful, seasoned professionals. Now, there is one thing everyone who has been staring at a computer screen for twenty-five years has in common: damaged vision. Let form follow function with your resume, and if it takes three tightly edited pages to tell a properly focused story and keep the document readable, just do it. What's the alternative?

- Leave stuff out? That means you won't get pulled from the resume database. And even if you do, you won't sell yourself to the customer.
- Use tiny fonts? Busy senior people simply won't read your resume because it speaks to a lack of judgment and communication skills, both of which are mandatory for seasoned professionals.

Assuming that your first page clearly demonstrates a thorough grasp of the target job, you can feel comfortable taking that second and third page to tell a concise story. In the resume sample section you'll see examples of justifiably longer executive resumes, requiring greater length to carry a concise message of ability in a complex job.

Worrying too much about length while you write is counterproductive. If the first page makes the right argument, the rest of your resume will be read with serious attention. A longer resume also means that much more space for selling your skills with relevant keywords and more opportunities to establish your brand. However, you should make every effort to maintain focus and take an "if in doubt, cut it out" editing approach. If you have more than twenty years under your belt, many older skills from the first part of your career are now irrelevant. On the whole, the rule of one page for every ten years is still a sensible *guideline*. The bottom line is that your resume can be as long as it needs to be to tell a concise and compelling story.

Does my resume tell the right story

Concentrate on the story your resume needs to tell. You can keep this focus in mind by regularly referring to your TJD and then layering fact and illustration until the story is told. When the story is complete, begin to polish by asking yourself the following questions:

- Are all statements relevant to the target job?
- Where have I repeated myself?
- Can I cut out any paragraphs?
- Can I cut out any sentences?
- Can I condense two sentences into one?

- Can I cut out any words?
- Can I cut out any pronouns?

Remember: If in doubt, cut it out—leave nothing but the focused story and action words!

Resumes evolve in layers

Once your resume is as tight and focused as you can make it—and you can easily go back to it a dozen times, improving it a little at each pass—take a break from it for twenty-four hours to clear your mind. Perform another job search activity, then come back and proof your work.

Resumes are written in layers. They don't spring fully formed in one draft from anyone's keyboard. Earlier, I mentioned my experience working with a marketing professional on her resume. She did a complete resume questionnaire and target job deconstruction and an initial resume layout template. Before we were finished we had completed eight different versions, each evolving until we had a great finished product. It took about two and a half weeks, but then generated eight interviews in a week. Proof again that 50 percent of the success of any project is in the preparation.

Proofreading Your Final Draft

Check your resume against the following points:

Contact Information

- Are your name, address, phone numbers, and e-mail address correct?
- Is your contact information on every page?
- Is the e-mail address hyperlinked, so that a reader of your resume can read it on his or her desktop and reach out to you instantly?

Target Job Title

- Do you have a target job title that echoes the words and intent of the job titles you collected when deconstructing the target job?

- Is this followed by a short one-sentence branding statement that captures the essence of the professional you? Only make brand statements when you really have something to brand.

Performance Profile

- Does it give a concise synopsis of the professional you as it relates to the target job?
- Does the language reflect that of typical job postings for this job?
- Is it prioritized in the same way employers are prioritizing their needs in this job?
- Is it no more than five lines long, so it can be read easily? If more, can you cut it into two paragraphs or use bullets?
- Does it include reference to the transferable skills and learned behaviors that are critical to success? If they don't fit here, make sure they are in the body copy.

Core Competencies

- Is all spelling and capitalization correct? (It's easy to make mistakes here, especially with acronyms.)
- Are there any other keywords you should add?
- Do you have experience in each of the areas you've listed?
- Can you illustrate your experience in conversation?

Career Highlights

- If you included a Career/Performance Highlights section, do the entries support the central arguments of your resume?

Professional Experience

- Is your most relevant and qualifying work experience prioritized throughout the resume to correspond to the employer's needs as they have prioritized them?
- Have you avoided wasting space with unnecessarily detailed employer names and addresses?
- If employed, have you been discreet with the name of your current employer?
- Have you omitted any reference to reasons for leaving a particular job?

- Have you removed all references to past, current, or desired salaries?
- Have you removed references to your date of availability?

Education

- Is education placed in the appropriate position?
- Is your highest educational attainment shown first?
- Have you included professional courses that support your candidacy?

Chronology

- Is your work history in chronological order, with the most recent employment coming first?
- With a chronological or combination resume, does each company history start with details of your most senior position?
- Does your resume emphasize relevant experience, contributions, and achievements?
- Can your body copy include one or more third-party endorsements of your work?
- Can you come up with a strong personal branding statement to end the resume? One that supports the focus and story you have told? Perhaps read your resume and think of the combination transferable skills that are most relevant and come up with a statement of how this selection of transferable skills allows you to perform in the way you do.
- Have you kept punch and focus by eliminating extraneous information?
- Have you included any volunteer, community service, or extracurricular activities that can lend strength to your candidacy?
- Have you left out lists of references and only mentioned the availability of references if there is nothing more valuable to fill up the space?
- Have you avoided treating your reader like a fool by heading your resume, "Resume"?

Writing Style

- Have you substituted short words for long words?
- Have you used one word where previously there were two?
- Is your *average* sentence no more than twenty words? Have you shortened any sentence of more than twenty-five words or broken it into two?

- Have you kept paragraphs under five lines?
- Do your sentences begin, wherever possible, with powerful action verbs and phrases?

Spelling and Grammar

Incorrect spelling and poor grammar are guaranteed to annoy resume readers, besides drawing attention to your poor written-communication skills. This is not a good opening statement in any job search. Spell checkers are not infallible. Check the spelling and send your resume to the most literate person you know for input on grammar and spelling.

At *www.knockemdead.com,* our resume service offers a $19 grammar, syntax, and spell check by a professional editor who also understands resumes. He will vet your resume and return it to you in thirty-six hours with tracked changes and suggestions.

You need some distance from your creative efforts to gain detachment and objectivity. There is no hard-and-fast rule about how long it takes to come up with the finished product. Nevertheless, if you think you have finished, leave it alone at least overnight. Next day start by reading your TJD document before reading the resume. Then you will be able to read your resume with the mindset of a recruiter.

More Than One Resume?

Do you need more than one resume? Probably. With just a few years' experience, most people have a background that qualifies them for more than one job. But this is not an argument for having a general, unfocused, and one-size-fits-all resume. Look at all the jobs you can do (they are all probably closely related in some way) and choose your best shot. Then build a prime resume around this target job.

After you're done, create additional resumes for each of the additional jobs you want to pursue. The process is as simple as changing your target job focus, doing a quick target job deconstruction exercise on the next target job, and then on a duplicate copy of your resume, saved under the name of the second target job, edit out less irrelevant details and replace them with the higher-impact information that is more relevant to the new target job.

Much of your resume is likely to stay exactly as it is, you will already have a layout, and even with a different focus, much of the information will remain the same.

CHAPTER 7
BRANDING YOURSELF ISN'T PAINFUL

LONG-TERM SUCCESS, REWARDING work without layoffs, and professional growth to the degree that fits your goals are much easier to achieve when you are credible and visible within your profession.

I f you create a professional brand as part of an overall career management strategy, it will help you achieve this credibility and visibility because an identifiable brand gives *you* focus and motivation, and *others* an easy way to differentiate you.

Establishing an accepted professional brand takes time. You have to brand something that is good, and spreading the word doesn't happen overnight. But you have to start somewhere and you need to start now. The greater effort you put into working toward credibility and visibility, which translate into the creation of a visible and respected profile in your area of expertise, the quicker you enter the inner circles in your department, your company, and ultimately your profession.

Think of your brand as the formal announcement to the professional community of how you want to be seen in your chosen field, and recognize your resume as the primary branding tool for disseminating the focused and consistent message of your brand. It's the narrative of your resume that captures your capabilities and behavioral profile, and in the process creates a clear image of a unique, consummate professional.

Components of a Desirable Professional Brand

You create an identifiable professional brand by first identifying those skills and behaviors that, combined, make you different and desirable. In other words, your professional brand is the capture and conscious positioning, in your resume, of your best professional qualities. As you might imagine, in order to do this well it helps to understand what employers believe are the most desirable professional qualities.

Transferable skills, learned behaviors, and professional values

There are a selection of transferable skills, values, and behaviors that are admired by employers the world over. Referred to as transferable skills because they can be applied in any job and at any level, they are at the heart of all professional success. These skills are also frequently referred to as *learned behaviors*. In fact, behavioral interviewing techniques predominate in the selection process because of their ability to determine if you possess these very behaviors. (For the skinny on how to ace behavioral interviews, see the latest edition of *Knock 'em Dead: The Ultimate Job Guide*.)

Your experience in the workplace

The transferable skills or learned behaviors that are most desirable to employers are largely developed as a result of experiences in the workplace. Remember that first day on your first job, when you eventually got up the courage to go forage for a cup of coffee?

You found the coffee machine, and there stuck on the wall was a handwritten sign reading:

YOUR MOTHER DOESN'T WORK HERE
PICK UP AFTER YOURSELF

You thought to yourself, "Pick up after myself? Gee, I gotta learn a whole new way of behaving." So you started to observe and emulate the more successful professionals around you, and slowly you developed a whole slate of behaviors/skills that help you succeed in job after job throughout your professional life.

There is a recognized sequence of these inter-related skills/behaviors that are seen as integral to success in every job, at every level, in every profession anywhere in the world. The full list includes:

Application of these skills, behaviors, and values in your work, and your ability to recognize their contributions to what you do, will help:

Communication	Motivation
Critical thinking	Determination
Time management & organization	Integrity
Teamwork	Productivity
Creativity	Procedures
Leadership	

- Your resume stand out in the screening process.
- You stand out as a candidate at job interviews.
- Applied assiduously at work they opens the doors to the inner circle in your department, company, and profession.

With this comes increased credibility and visibility with the accompanying opportunities for new responsibilities and advancement. You can readily understand that the professional recognized as possessing these skills will be known and respected as a consummate professional; which is another way of saying that that person has successfully established a valid professional brand.

Possessing these special skills is one thing. That resume reviewers *know* you are in possession of excellent communication, critical thinking, time management and organization, teamwork, creativity and leadership skills, and that you have integrity and are motivated and determined, well, that is another thing.

Positioning your skills

If development and application of these skills is foundational to establishing a valid professional brand, then part of framing and promoting your brand is the need position them in your resume and in your life. As you read through the breakdown of these skills and values, you'll see, for example, "communication," and think, "Yes, I have good communication skills." When this happens, come up with examples of how your communication skills played an important role in the successful completion of an assignment.

Reading about "time management and organization," you might say, "Now *there's* something I have to work on!" In this instance you have identified a key behavior that needs improvement, and you can immediately set about a personal development program. You'll find links for skill development in these areas on the career success and career management pages at *www.knockemdead.com*.

Understanding the transferable skills, behaviors, and values you possess and how they differentiate you from others is an important step in defining your professional brand. The examples of your application of the these skills or the impact of these values on your work product can be used in your resume, in your cover letters, and as illustrative answers to questions in interviews. But most importantly, if you want to be successful, they need to become part of your life.

KNOCK 'EM DEAD TIP

Transferable skills, behaviors, traits, or values—I've heard them called all of these. Which is right? Behavioral psychologists, management, and career management theorists have been thinking and writing about professional success and behavior for many years. They most commonly refer to these "attributes" as transferable skills, learned behaviors, or developed behaviors. They are just as accurately referred to as values: personal values, professional values, etc. For example, you possess certain communication skills, that when you consider the complexity of subtle skills that make up effective professional communication you will recognize that superior communicators have really worked at it. On the other hand integrity is definitely a value, can be a learned behavior, but is unlikely to be referred to as a transferable skill. I'll break them up in a logical way, but don't get hung up on the nomenclature. Nobody else does.

Critical Attributes

I have broken this list of critical attributes into three sections:

1. Transferable skills
2. Professional values

3. Business values

We'll go through each of them in detail.

Transferable skills

The National Association of Colleges and Employers (NACE), which is made up of major corporation recruiters and university career services professionals, has defined seven transferable skills that every professional entering the workplace must have in order to succeed. These seven include: technical, communication, teamwork, critical thinking, time management and organization, leadership, and creativity skills.

Technical

The technical skills of your profession are the foundation of all success. Without them you won't even land a job, much less succeed in your career.

Technical skills refer to your *ability* to do the job; they are the essentials necessary for success in the day-to-day execution of your duties. You know which skills and tools are needed for a particular task and possess the know-how to use them productively and efficiently. These technical skills vary from profession to profession and do not refer to technology skills or anything technical *per se*.

However, it is a given that one of the technical skills essential to every job is technological adaptivity. You must be proficient in all the computer- and Internet-based applications relevant to your work. Even when you are not working in a technology field, strong technological skills will enhance career stability and help you leverage professional growth.

When people are referred to as "professional," it means they possess the appropriate technical and technology skills necessary for success in their profession and have interwoven them with the other six major transferable skills. Staying current with the essential technical and technology skills of your chosen profession is going to be an integral part of your ongoing professional growth and stability. That's why the continuing education on your resume can be an important tool in developing your professional brand: it reinforces your technical competence and commitment (something we'll address shortly).

You can find useful links for professional development at:

www.knockemdead.com
www.mindtools.com/pages/main/newMN_ISS.htm
www.mindtools.com/page8.html
www.mindtools.com/pages/main/newMN_TED.htm

Communication

As George Bernhard Shaw said: "The greatest problem in communication is the illusion that it has been accomplished." Every professional job today requires communication skills; promotions and professional success are impossible without them. Good verbal communication skills enable you to accurately process incoming information, and considering the interests and sophistication of your audience, present outgoing information persuasively so that it is understood and accepted.

But communication embraces much more than listening and speaking. When the professional world talks about communication skills, they are referring to four primary communication skills and four supportive communication skills.

The primary communication skills are:

- **Verbal skills**—what you say and how you say it.
- **Listening skills**—listening to understand, rather than just waiting your turn to talk.
- **Writing skills**—writing clearly and concisely. Written communication is essential for any professional career. It creates a lasting impression of who you are, and it's an important expression of your professional brand.
- **Technology communication skills**—understanding and being able to use the most up-to-date methods of communication, including computers, cell phones, and social media. Technology has changed the way we communicate, and your ability to navigate the new communication media can and will impact your professional success.

The supportive communication skills are more subtle, but nevertheless, impact every interaction you have with others. They are:

- **Grooming and dress**—dressing appropriately and maintaining cleanliness in everything. Personal grooming and dress tells others who you are and how you feel about yourself, so it's important to manage the message you want others to receive.
- **Social graces**—knowing appropriate behavior in any circumstance. How you behave and how you behave toward others is always noted, and if your table manners are sketchy, odds are you'll never sit at the chairman's table or represent your organization at the higher levels.
- **Body language**—controlling the way in which you physically express yourself. Our bodies subconsciously display how we are feeling, a language of communication humankind learned before speech. For truly effective communication in any aspect of your life, what your mouth says must be in harmony with what your body is saying.
- **Emotional intelligence**—behaving with grace and maturity under all circumstances. Sometimes under stress people retreat emotionally to childhood behaviors. Such behavior is death to your career. For success, understand and manage your emotional intelligence.

Develop effective communication skills in all these areas and you'll gain enormous control over what you can achieve, how you are perceived, and what happens in your life.

You can find assistance with skill development at the following sites or you can go to the career success/management advice pages at *www.knockemdead.com* for active links directly to all the resources:

Verbal skills

www.wordsmith.org/awad/index.html
www.mindtools.com/page8.html
www.latrobe.edu.au/careers/students/employable/toolkit-communication.html
http://stress.about.com/od/relationships/ht/healthycomm.htm

Listening skills

www.mindtools.com/CommSkll/ActiveListening.htm

Writing skills

www.collegeboard.com/student/plan/boost-your-skills/123.html
www.mindtools.com/CommSkll/WritingSkills.htm
www.smashingmagazine.com/2009/06/28/50-free-resources-that-will-improve- your-writing-skills

Grooming and dress

www.tips.learnhub.com/lesson/2800-tips-on-business-dress-etiquette-and- grooming

Social graces

www.menshealth.com/cda/article.do?site=MensHealth&channel=style& category=style.files&co nitem=9d0ade1302eec010VgnVCM10000013281eac

Body language

www.helpguide.org/mental/eq6_nonverbal_communication.htm#improving
www.personadev.com/2008/04/07/10-tips-to-boost-your-body-language-skills/
www.positivityblog.com/index.php/2007/09/10/how-to-improve-your- social-skills/

Emotional intelligence

www.psychology.about.com/lr/emotional_intelligence/337325/1/

To check your Emotional IQ, take the Emotional Intelligence Quiz at this site: *www.psychology.about.com/library/quiz/bl_eq_quiz.htm?questnum=1&cor=3331*

Teamwork

If you become a successful leader one day, it will be because you were first a great team player; that's the way it works.

The professional world revolves around the complex challenges of making money, and such challenges require teams of people to provide ongoing solutions. This in turn requires you to work efficiently and respectfully with others who have totally different responsibilities, backgrounds, objectives, and areas of expertise.

Teamwork demands that you make a commitment to the team and its success. This means you take on a task because it needs to be done, not because it makes you look good. The payback, of course, is that management always recognizes and appreciates a team player, because leaders are almost exclusively chosen from the ranks of team players.

As a team player you are:

1. Always cooperative
2. Always make decisions based on team goals
3. Always keep team members informed
4. Always keep commitments
5. Always share credit, never blame

Teamwork skills are especially important if you intend to be a leader, because all successful leaders need to first understand the critical dynamics of teamwork. It is only by being a team player that you can understand the subtleties of what makes a team pull together and function productively as a unit. Once you learn that, you can discover how to recognize and encourage those who display a team spirit. So if you intend to be a leader, learn to be a team player.

Check out the links below to learn more about developing your teamwork skills.

www.hku.hk/cepc/taccasu/ref/teamwk.htm
www.latrobe.edu.au/careers/students/employable/toolkit-teamwork.html

Critical thinking

You know to come in from the rain, right? Then you know critical thinking impacts everything you do in life. Life and the world of work are full of opportunity, and every one of those opportunities is peppered with problems. With critical thinking skills you can turn those opportunities into achievement, earnings, and fulfillment.

This is the application in the professional world of all those problem-solving skills you've been developing since grade school: a systematic approach to uncovering all the issues related to a particular challenge that will lead to its solution.

Critical thinking, analytical, or problem-solving skills, allow the successful professional to logically think through and clearly define a challenge and its desired solutions, and then evaluate and implement the best solution for that challenge from all available options. Remember, a company hires someone because it has a problem that needs solving.

As a skilled critical thinker and problem solver, you must examine every challenge and ask:

- What's the problem?
- Who is it a problem for?
- Why is it a problem?
- What is causing this problem?
- What are the options for a solution?
- What problems might a given solution create?
- What is the most suitable solution for the situation?

You look through the factors affecting each possible solution and decide which solutions to keep and which to disregard. You look at the solution as a whole and use your judgment as to whether to use the solution or not. Once you have decided on a course of action, you plan out the steps, the timing, and the resources to make it happen, asking yourself:

- How long will it take to implement this solution?
- How much will it cost?
- What resources will I need?
- Can I get these resources?
- Will it really solve the problem to everyone's benefit?
- Will this solution cause its own problems?

Einstein said that if he had one hour to save the world he would spend fifty-five minutes defining the problem. It's a thought worth remembering because a properly defined problem always leads to a better solution. If, as I've said previously, 50 percent of the success of any project is in the prep, critical thinking is an integral part of preparation.

Check out the following links to learn more about developing your critical thinking skills.

www.latrobe.edu.au/careers/students/employable/toolkit-ps.html
www.litemind.com/problem-definition/
www.mindtools.com/pages/main/newMN_TED.htm
www.virtualsalt.com/crebook3.htm

Time Management and Organization

With time management and organization (TM&O) skills you can bring your dreams to life. Without them you will forever spin in underachieving circles.

There are two types of people in the world: the task-oriented, who let tasks expand to fill all the time allotted to them, and the goal-oriented, who organize and prioritize and strive to get all work completed in an orderly manner as quickly and efficiently as quality will allow. One guess as to who has the most successful and fulfilled lives.

The ability to manage time and organize activities increases productivity. The people who do this, often thought of as high achievers and goal-oriented because they get so much done, are just people who learned how to organize themselves and consequently work with more purpose. The result is that they can multitask and seriously outperform their peers.

With TM&O you make a *To Do* list, then ABC prioritize:

- The "A"s absolutely must be done today. "A" priority activities always get your full attention, while the other activities fill in around them. Just remember, your boss's priority is *always* your priority!
- It would be good to get the "B"s done today. These are the first activities to fill in around your "A" priorities.
- "C" goals need to met, but they aren't urgent or are someone else's priority, not yours. These fill in odd moments, until approaching deadlines move them to B status.

Having a *To Do* list handy, means you always have work to do. Referring to it keeps you maximally productive and on track. Make a habit of this for twenty-one days and you will see *big* changes in your productivity.

Plan/Do/Review

Another TM&O technique that encourages productivity without increasing effort is the daily Plan/Do/Review cycle:

Always set aside time at the end of the day to review what happened:

- What went well and why?
- What did not go well, and what can you do about it?
- What new projects have landed on your desk?
- What is their A/B/C priority?

Identify your "A"s for tomorrow. Look at each "A" priority separately and identify exactly where you will jump in on this project tomorrow, what you hope to achieve, and the tools you'll need to do so.

"A" priorities will frequently include large and complex projects, so where do you begin? You break the big task into smaller action steps, things that you can get done tomorrow Because the professional world is full of incredibly complex ongoing activities that demand good organization traits, this skill is at the very heart of your ability to achieve professional success. Developing TM&O skills enables you to do the things you have to do, when they ought to be done, in an organized and professional manner. Check out these links to learn more about developing this skill, and how it relates to resume, job search and other career management issues.

www.latrobe.edu.au/careers/students/employable/toolkit-planning.html
www.mindtools.com/pages/main/newMN_HTE.htm

Leadership

"A leader has two important characteristics: first, he is going somewhere; second, he is able to persuade other people to go with him." The guy who said this, Robespierre, was a principal figure in the French Revolution and literally changed his world.

As you develop teamwork skills, which is a must if you ever hope to lead, notice how you are willing to follow true leaders, but how you refuse to fall in line with people who don't respect you and who don't have your best interests at heart.

When you are credible, when people believe in your competence and believe you have everyone's success as your goal, they will follow you; *you* accept responsibility but *others* gets the credit. When your actions inspire others to think more, learn more, do more and become more, you are on your way to becoming a leader.

Integrating the other transferable skills

Your job as a leader is to make your team function; teamwork skills enable you to pull your team together as a cohesive unit. Your Technical expertise, Critical thinking, and Creativity skills help you correctly define the challenges and their solutions.

Your communication skills enable your team to understand the task and its goals—there's nothing more demoralizing than a leader who can't clearly articulate why the team is doing what it's doing. Your TM&O skills enable you to create a practical blueprint for success so your team can take ownership of the task and deliver the expected results.

Leadership is the most complex of the transferable skills that you will develop in making a success of your professional work life. It is a combination and outgrowth of all the seven transferable skills. Leaders aren't born; they make themselves through hard work. That's the price you pay to achieve this or any other serious goal.

For advice on how to further develop this skill check out these links, which are all live in the site:

www.mindtools.com/pages/main/newMN_LDR.htm
www.mindtools.com/pages/main/newMN_PPM.htm
www.crfonline.org/orc/ca/ca-2.html
www.top7business.com/?id=2113
www.businessballs.com/leadership.htm
www.career-success-for-newbies.com/developing-leadership-skills.html

Creativity

There's a difference between creativity and just having ideas. Ideas are like headaches: we all get them once in awhile, and like headaches they usually disappear as mysteriously as they arrived. Creativity, on the other hand, enables the development of those ideas with the strategic and tactical know-how that brings them to life.

In a professional context, creativity is the generation of new ideas related to a specific situation, challenge, or goal. It is a skill that can be learned and applied to anything you do in life. The ability to bring life to your professional creativity comes from:

- Your critical thinking skills applied within an area of technical expertise.
- Your time management and organization skills combined with your critical thinking skills and technical expertise that enable you to break down a challenge into specific steps, each small enough that some meaningful progress can be made on them daily.
- The communication skills that empower you to persuasively convey your approach and its component building blocks to your target audience, and your teamwork skills come into play whenever others are needed to bring a project to fruition.
- Your leadership skills, which come into play as you lead your new ideas forward through all the challenges they will encounter.

Creative approaches to challenges can take time or can come fully formed in a flash, but the longer you work on developing the supporting skills that bring creativity to life the more often they will become part of your learned behaviors.

Here are five rules for building creativity skills:

1. Whatever you do in life, engage in it fully; commit to developing competence in everything you do, because the wider your frame of reference for the world around you . . . the higher octane fuel you have to propel your ideas to acceptance and reality.
2. Learn something new every day, and treat the pursuit of knowledge as a way of life. Absorb as much as you can about everything. Information exercises your brain and fills your mind with the ever-widening frame of reference that allows you to make creative connections where others won't see them.

3. Ideas are fleeting. Learn to catch them as they occur, whether it's on your PDA or a scrap of paper. Anything will do so long as long as you keep the inspiration.

4. Welcome restrictions in your world. They encourage creativity—ask any successful writer, artist, musician, or business leader.

5. Don't spend your life glued to Facebook or TV because you need to live life, not watch it go by out of the corner of your eye. If you do watch TV, try to learn something or motivate yourself with science, history, or biography programming. If you surf the Internet, do it with purpose.

Building creativity skills enables you to bring your dreams to life; the development of each of these seven interconnected transferable skills will help you do it.

Check this for more insights on creativity:

www.mindtools.com/pages/main/newMN_CT.htm

Professional Values

Successful professionals embody these values everyday in all they do. They'll open doors of opportunity for you from the day you start your first job to the day you retire.

- **Motivation and Energy:** Employers realize that a motivated professional will do a better job on every assignment. Motivation expresses itself in a commitment to the job and the profession, an eagerness to learn and grow professionally, and a willingness to take the rough with the smooth.

Motivation is invariably expressed by the *energy* demonstrated through a person's work. The motivated employee always gives that extra effort to get the job done and to get it done right.

- **Commitment and Reliability:** These qualities embody a dedication to your profession and your job within it, an understanding of the role your function plays in the larger issues of company success, and the empowerment that comes from knowing how your part contributes to the greater good.

Dedication to your professionalism is also an example of enlightened self-interest. The more you are engaged in your career, the more likely you are to join the inner circles that exist in every department and company, enhancing opportunities for advancement. At the same time, this dedication will repay you with better job security and improved professional horizons.

Your dedication will also express itself in your *reliability*: Showing up is half the battle; the other half is your performance on the job. This requires following up on your actions and not relying on anyone else to ensure the job is done and done well.

- **Determination:** This value marks a resilient professional who doesn't get worn down and doesn't back off when a problem or situation gets tough. It's a value that characterizes the individual who chooses to be part of the solution rather than standing idly by and being part of the problem.

The determined professional has decided to make a difference with her presence every day, because it is the right thing to do. She's willing to do whatever it takes to get a job done, even if that includes duties that might not appear in a job description.

- **Pride and Integrity:** Pride in yourself as a professional means always making sure the job is done to the best of your ability. It requires paying attention to the details and to time and cost constraints. Integrity means taking responsibility for your actions, both good and bad. It also means treating others, within and outside of the company, with respect at all times and in all situations. With pride in yourself as a professional with integrity, your actions will always be in the ethical best interests of the company, and your decisions will never be based on whim or personal preference.

Business Values

Companies have very limited interests: making money, saving money (the same as making money), and saving time (which also makes money). Actually, you wouldn't want it any other way, since this keeps those paychecks coming your way. Developing business values that demonstrate sensitivity to the profit imperative of a business endeavor is the mark of a true professional.

- **Productivity:** Always work toward enhanced productivity through efficiencies of time, resources, money, and effort.
- **Economy:** Most problems have two solutions, and the expensive one isn't always the best. Ideas of efficiency and economy should engage your creative mind in ways that others would not consider.
- **Procedures:** You should recognize the need for procedures and understand that they are implemented only after careful thought. Understand and always follow the chain of command. Don't implement your own "improved" procedures or organize others to do so.

As you develop this suite of transferable skills, learned behaviors, and professional values your confidence grows in taking on new challenges. You ask questions, look at challenges calmly and at mistakes squarely, and make changes to eradicate those mistakes. In short, you develop a quiet confidence of the professional who can deliver the goods.

Identifying Your Competitive Difference

The people who will hire you first need to differentiate you from other candidates. The following questionnaire will help you identify all the differentiators that help make you unique. Each of these is a component of your professional brand.

You aren't going to discover anything earth shattering here, just a continuum of behaviors and beliefs you've always had but the value of which you've perhaps never understood. It'll be a series of those, "Of course, I knew that" moments. It will then be logical and natural to integrate them into your resume, giving you "ownership" of your brand; it will feel right, it will fit.

An expandable version of this questionnaire is available in MS Word at *www.knockem dead.com* on the resume advice page under the title "The Competitive Differentiation Questionnaire."

The Competitive Differentiation Questionnaire

Which of the transferable skills, behaviors, and values best captures the essence of the professional you?

_____

_____

_____

Which of the transferable skills, behaviors, and values have you marked for further professional development?

_____

_____

_____

_____

What qualities or characteristics do you share with top performers in your department/ profession?

_____

_____

_____

_____

What have you achieved with these qualities?

_____

_____

_____

_____

What makes you different from others with whom you have worked?

_____

_____

_____

What are the four traits that best define you as a professional and how does each help your performance?

1. _____

2. _____

3. _____

4. _____

How does each help your co-workers?

1. _____
2. _____
3. _____
4. _____

How does each help your department and boss?

1. _____
2. _____
3. _____
4. _____

How does each help your company?

1. _____
2. _____
3. _____
4. _____

Why do you stand out in your job/profession? (If you realize you don't stand out and you want to, examine why the people you admire stand out and use them as a model for development.)

_____
_____
_____

How are you better than others holding the same title? Can you quantify this difference?

_____
_____
_____

What excites you most about your professional responsibilities?

_____
_____
_____

What are your achievements in these areas?

_____

_____

_____

What do your peers say about you?

_____

_____

_____

What does management say about you?

_____

What do your reports say about you?

_____

_____

What are your top four professional skills?

Skill #1: _____
Quantifiable achievements with this skill: _____

Skill #2: _____
Quantifiable achievements with this skill: _____

Skill #3: _____
Quantifiable achievements with this skill: _____

Skill #4: _____
Quantifiable achievements with this skill: _____

What are your top four leadership skills?

Skill #1: _____
Quantifiable achievements with this skill: _____

Skill #2: _____
Quantifiable achievements with this skill: _____

Skill #3: _____
Quantifiable achievements with this skill: _____

Skill #4: _____
Quantifiable achievements with this skill: _____

What do you believe are the three key deliverables of your job?

1. _____
2. _____
3. _____

What gives you greatest satisfaction in the work you do?

_____
_____

What value does this combination of skills, behaviors, values and achievements bring to employers in your target market?

_____
_____

When you identify one of these transferable skills, learned behaviors, and core values as something you possess, it becomes part of your branding signature.

- Ongoing development and consistent application of transferable skills/learned behaviors become an integral part of the professional you.
- They can appear in your resume: in your opening or closing brand statements, performance profile, or performance/career highlights sections or in the body of your resume.
- They will inform the way you approach your work everyday
- And inform the substance of your answers to questions at job interviews
- They become part of you and in return will make you more successful
- When you identify a transferable skill/learned behaviors you *do not* possess, it should immediately become part of your professional development program, because these

attributes go way beyond the branding concept, they underlie your long-term survival and success.

Integrating a Professional Brand into Your Resume

Your professional brand is communicated throughout your resume, but especially with opening and closing brand statements. The first place you begin to establish a professional brand is with your target job title where you consciously decide on the job that best allows you to package your skill-sets and create a professional brand.

Target Job Title and Brand Statement

Your target job title and following brand statement gives the reader a focus on your resume's purpose and goal. The brand statement is a short phrase following the target job title that defines what you will bring to this job. It says in effect, "These are the benefits my presence on your payroll will bring to your team and your company."

Notice the following brand statements focus on the benefits brought to the job, but do not take up space identifying the specifics of how this was done. Professional brand statements often starts with a an action verb such as "Poised to," "Delivering," "Dedicated to," " Bringing," " Positioned to," and "Constructing."

Pharmaceutical Sales Management Professional

Poised to outperform in pharmaceutical software sales repeating records of achievement with major pharmaceutical companies

Senior Operations / Plant Management Professional

Dedicated to continuous improvement ~ Lean Six Sigma ~ Start-up & turnaround operations ~ Mergers & change management ~ Process & productivity optimization ~ Logistics & supply chain

Bank Collections Management

Equipped to continue excellence in loss mitigation / collections / recovery management

Mechanical / Design / Structural Engineer
Delivering high volume of complex structural and design projects for global companies in Manufacturing / Construction / Power Generation

Account Management / Client Communications Manager
Reliably achieving performance improvement and compliance within Financial Services Industry

Consistent Brand Messaging

You will strive to integrate your professional strengths, your brand, into the resume as your write it. When you review and edit your work you want to be sure that the messaging supports the central concepts of your brand.

- Performance Profile
- Performance / Career Highlights
- Professional Experience

Closing brand statement

As we discussed earlier, you will occasionally see a resume closed with a third-party endorsement:

> *"I've never worked with a more ethical and conscientious auditor" Petra Tompkins, Controller.*

Such an endorsement acts as a closing brand statement: a bold statement clarifying the value proposition of the product (that's you, the brand). It's a great way to end a resume. If you have just the right kind of supportable quote, use it.

You can achieve an equally powerful effect with a final comment of your own, a comment that relates to your professional brand and is written in the first person to make it conversational and differentiate it from the voice of the rest of your resume. Most resumes are written in the third person, allowing you to talk about yourself with the semblance of objectivity. Moving into the first person for a final comment at the resume's end acts both as an exclamation point and a matching "bookend" for the brand statement at the beginning. For example:

"I understand customer service to be the company's face to the world and treat every customer interaction as critical to our success; leadership by example and conscientious performance management underlies my department's consistent customer satisfaction ratings."

A True and Truthful Brand

You have to be able to deliver on the brand you create. It must be based on your possession of the technical skills of your profession, those transferable skills and learned behaviors that you take with you from job to job, and the core values that imprint your approach to professional life.

It is all too easy to over-promise, and while the employer might be initially attracted by the pizzazz of your resume, whether or not you live up to its value proposition decides the length and quality of the relationship.

If a box of cereal doesn't live up to the brand's hype, you simply don't buy it again; but sell yourself into the wrong job with exaggerations or outright lies, and it is likely to cost you that job, plus the possibility of collateral career damage that can follow you for years.

Benefits of a defined professional brand

Understanding the skills and attributes demanded for professional success might be your most immediately recognizable benefit. Your professional brand is also extremely valuable for your long-term survival and success. That you know who you are, what you offer, and how you want to be perceived will differentiate you from others. And because you understand yourself and can communicate this understanding you will have a professional presence.

Your professional brand and the long haul

Globalization has made your job less secure than ever, yet you are a financial entity that must survive over what will be at least a half-century work life. During this time you will probably change jobs about every four years and have three or more distinct careers.

In this context you can see that change is fairly constant in everyone's career. While you develop an initial professional brand identity as part of your job search strategy, you don't want to shelve it once you've landed a new job.

In this new, insecure world of work, it makes sense to maintain visibility within your profession. It is nothing more than intelligent market positioning for MeInc. The professional identity/brand built into your new resume is the profile you should keep posted on your professional networking sites on an ongoing basis. This increases your credibility and visibility within your profession as well as the recruitment industry, making you more desirable as an employee and increasing your options.

CHAPTER 8
READY TO LAUNCH

YOU ARE IN the home stretch, giving your resume the final polish before release to a very discriminating public. It has to be a killer to beat the fierce competition in the resume databases, and it has to pack a real visual punch to get serious attention from jaded recruiters and hiring managers.

Your resume will get between five and forty seconds of initial attention. The more accessible it is to the tired and distracted eyes of recruiters and hiring managers, the closer attention it will receive. You'll improve the chances that your resume will receive attention if you:

1. **Make it readable.** You do not have to use 9- and 10-point fonts only a twenty-year-old can read in order to cram everything on one or two pages. (Tip: Twenty-year-olds are almost never in a position to hire you.) Stop worrying about page count. In resumes like everything else, *form follows function*; use the space you need to tell the story you need to tell. Use 11- and 12-point fonts that are easier on adult eyes.

2. **Use headlines.** They help a reader achieve and maintain focus. The first page of your resume always needs to start off strong, and there is no better way of doing that than with a target job title to give the reader focus. For example:

headlines that help accessibility and comprehension:

- Target Job Title (What the resume is about)
- Performance Profit (A snapshot of what I can do)
- Core Competencies (The key professional skills that help me do my job well)
- Technology Competencies (Optional: The technical skills that help me do my job well)
- Performance Highlights (Optional: My outstanding achievements as they relate to the job)
- Professional Experience (Optional: Where and when everything happened)

3. Write a strong Performance Profile, one that customizes your skills to your customers' prioritized needs.
4. **List Core Competencies.** These are the hard skills that enable you to do what you do. Each word or phrase should act as a headline of capability and topic for discussion.
5. **List Technical Competencies.** When you need to separate these from your Core Competencies, clearly define the two competency slates. One list will be too dense for the eye to readily scan.

You should use a Technology Competencies section when:

- Mixing them with other core competencies is confusing
- One list would be too dense for the eye to readily scan
- Technology skills are a critical skill set of an otherwise non-technology job

6. **Write a list of Performance/Career Highlights.** This is an option, provided, of course, that your experience has the depth to support it.

A first page with these headlines and categories in readable fonts will draw the reader in.

Fonts and Font Sizes

You can use one font throughout your resume, but never use more than two fonts: one for head-lines and the other for body copy. The two most popular fonts for business communication are Arial and Times. They probably look boring because you are so used to seeing them, but you see them so much because they are clear and very readable; they work. The biggest criticism of these fonts is their lack of flair and design value. Here are some other fonts that are good for headlines and body copy; because you want your resume to be printed out without problems on the widest range of printers, these fonts also have the advantage that printers almost universally recognize them. I mentioned some acceptable fonts earlier. The nature of each font is unique and the actual size of each is going to vary. Don't be a slave to 12 point; sometimes 11 point might work as a font. Just don't use a smaller font size in order to keep your resume to one or two pages. It must be readable by those tired or distracted eyes.

Avoid or keep capitalized text to a minimum; it's tough on the eyes.

Avoid "script" fonts similar to handwriting. While they look attractive to the occasional reader, they are harder on the eyes of people who read any amount of business correspondence. That said, in the resumes later in this book you will see examples of just this sort of font. For example, the arts, education, and healthcare are areas where the warmer and more personal look of a script font can work and still present a professional-looking resume. Use with discretion.

Avoid typos like the plague!

Resumes that are riddled with misspellings get siht-canned *toute suite*. How annoying is that last sentence? You have a spell checker; use it.

A couple of years back, I counseled an executive vice president in the $400K-per-year range. He was having problems getting in front of the right people. The first paragraph of his resume stated that he was an executive with "superior communication skills." Unfortunately, the other twelve words of the sentence contained a spelling error! Fortunately we caught it. In an age of spell checkers, this sloppiness isn't acceptable at any level.

Remember that spell checkers aren't infallible either and will confuse words and their appropriate usage, so get someone you trust to check it over as well. If you don't know anyone, you can come to our website and for $19 have our in-house editor review and return it in thirty-six hours.

Make every page accessible

Once you decide on fonts, stick with them. More than two fonts will be vaguely disquieting to the reader. You can do plenty to liven up the visual impact of the page and create emphasis with bold, italic, bold italic, underlining, and sizing of words. White space is important; it is easier on the eyes.

Proofing

Even in the age of e-mail and databases your resume is going to be printed out. You should always take printed copies to your interviews. This guarantees each interviewer will have your background laid out in the way you want it. Print it out now to check that onscreen layout matches that of the printed document. Make sure the pagination of the printed copy works the way you intend. Double check the printed copy for:

- Layout and balance
- Typos and grammatical errors
- Punctuation and capitalization
- That everything has been underlined, capitalized, bolded, italicized, and indented, exactly as you intended

Print it out on as many different printers as you reasonably can. Once you have checked the resume, get someone else to review it. A third party will always catch errors you might miss.

Appearance Checklist

Let the resume rest overnight or longer, then pick it up and review it with fresh eyes immediately after you have reread your target job deconstruction.

- What's your immediate reaction to it? Is it clear who and what this document is about? Does it clearly address the needs of your TJD? Are the lines clean?
- Does the copy under each of your headlines tell a convincing story?
- Does the first page of the resume identify you as someone clearly capable of delivering on the job's requirements?
- Have you used only one side of the page?
- Are your fonts readable in the 11- to 12-point range?
- Does the layout accommodate the reader's needs, rather than outmoded concerns on resume length?
- Are your paragraphs no more than five lines long?
- Is there plenty of white space around important areas, such as target job title and your opening and closing brand statements? Recruiters and managers are reviewing resumes on hand-held devices and this helps their readability.

The Final Product

The paper version of your resume should be printed on standard 8½" x 11" (letter-size) paper. Paper comes in different weights and textures; good resume-quality paper has a weight designation of between 20 and 25 pounds. Lighter paper feels flimsy and curls; heavier paper is unwieldy. Most office supply stores carry paper and envelopes packaged as kits for resumes and cover letters.

As for color, white is the prime choice. Cream is also acceptable, and I'm assured that some of the pale pastel shades can be both attractive and effective. Personally, I think that most professionals don't show up in the best light when dressed in pink. White and cream are straightforward, no-nonsense colors. They speak to your professional brand more effectively, assuming you want to be perceived as straightforward and no-nonsense. Cover-letter stationery should have the same contact information as your resume and should *always* match the color and weight of the paper used. Again it's part of the professional branding issue that underlies all the little things you pay attention to in a job search. Set up letterhead for your cover letter stationary, using the same fonts you use with the resume. The coordinated paper size, color, weight, and fonts will give you a cohesive look.

Follow-up

Communication skills are one of the big seven transferable skills and learnable behaviors, and the interview cycle offers you numerous opportunities to use those skills to make your candidacy stand out. After the interview, send follow-up letters that help advance your candidacy. Urgency might require some be sent by e-mail, but whenever you can, a letter sent through traditional mail will really stand out; everyone appreciates the screen break. For more on this, consult the latest edition of *Knock 'em Dead Cover Letters*.

CHAPTER 9
I Lied. Now You Are Ready

YOU STILL HAVE to translate the finished resume into ASCII. Fortunately it is not brain surgery. Here you'll learn about ASCII, MS Word, PDF, and HTML formats and when each is appropriate.

All companies, except the smallest locally owned and focused service/retail operations use online recruitment as their primary staffing strategy. For you, this means a predominantly online job search.

Now you have built a killer resume that says exactly what you want it to say. But there's one last must-do task: you have to decide on the electronic formats to use that will make it visible to your target market. You will need to use different formats to achieve this.

ASCII, MS Word, PDF, and HTML Resumes

The different electronic formats for delivering your resume via the Internet are:

1. Formatted in Microsoft Word or as a PDF file
2. ASCII plain text or with line breaks
3. Web-based/HTML

Formatted resume

A formatted electronic resume is your resume as created in a word-processing document, most often the ubiquitous MS Word. When you attach your resume to an e-mail or print it out for distribution by traditional mail or to take to interviews, you can do it in either MS Word or PDF format.

With PDF, the layout is fixed and will appear exactly as you send it, which can't always be said of MS Word docs. Both ways are acceptable, and there are even people who attach their resume in both formats to give the reader a choice. I lean toward using PDF for electronic distribution because the layout will never change, no matter what.

Plain text or ASCII

This is the simplest and least visually attractive version of the three alternatives. We're talking just the basics: only text, letters, numbers, and a few symbols. ASCII (American Standard Code for Information Interchange) resumes are important because *this is the only format that any and every computer can read*. The reader will not need a word-processing program such as MS Word or WordPerfect, and software or printer compatibility isn't a consideration.

An ASCII resume looks like the average e-mail message you receive. You will see how to create two separate versions of an ASCII resume, one best suited for pasting into the body of an e-mail message, the other for cutting and pasting into resume-bank resume templates. You will need both.

When sending an attached resume in Word or PDF by e-mail, you might also choose to paste an ASCII version of your resume into the body copy of your e-mail message after your signature as some companies have protocols about opening attachments from unknown sources. You would note this at the end of the cover letter/e-mail: "My resume in ASCII format is inserted below, and I have also attached a formatted PDF version."

Web or HTML resume

A web resume is a "nice to have" but is by no means a "must have" for everyone. An HTML, web-based resume, or e-portfolio resume is one that can have additional features such as video and sound and can be uploaded in certain instances to resume banks and social networking sites, or even housed on the Internet at its own URL. There are some advantages to this. For example, if you working in arts, education, certain areas of communications, or technology, the ability to include audio and video clips, music, and pictures can be a plus. Likewise, if you are a web-page design professional or HTML guru, then by all means use the Internet to show your creative and technological abilities. If you are in a creative profession and would typically have a portfolio, a web resume can allow access to your work samples. A web-based/HTML resume is a "nice to have," not a "must have." Don't even think about it until you have properly constructed and branded a resume that portrays you exactly as you wish to be seen.

How to Convert Your Formatted Resume to ASCII

You start this simple process by opening the MS Word formatted version of your resume.

PATRICIA JOHNSON

1234 Murietta Ave. • Palmdale, CA 93550

Residence (661) 555-1234 • Mobile (661) 555-9876 • *PatJohnson@email.com*

FINANCE/ACCOUNTING PROFESSIONAL
Internal Auditor/Financial Analyst/Staff Accountant

Detail oriented, problem solver with excellent analytical strengths and a track record of optimizing productivity, reducing costs, and increasing profit contributions. Well-developed team building and leadership strengths with experience in training and coaching coworkers. Works well with public, clients, vendors, and coworkers at all levels. Highly motivated and goal orientated as demonstrated by completing studies toward B.S. in Finance, graduating with honors concurrent with full-time, progressive business experience.

—*Core Competencies*—

Research & Analysis / Accounts Receivable / Accounts Payable / Journal Entries / Bank Reconciliations
Payroll / Financial Statements / Auditing / General Ledger / Artist Contracts / Royalties / Escalation Clauses

PROFESSIONAL EXPERIENCE

MAJOR HOLLYWOOD STUDIO, Hollywood, CA • 2000 to Present

Achieved fast-track promotion to positions of increasing challenge and responsibility

Royalty Analyst—Music Group, Los Angeles, CA (2005–Present)

Process average of $8–9 million in payments monthly. Review artist contracts, licenses, and rate sheets to determine royalties due to producers and songwriters for leading record label. Ensure accuracy of statements sent to publishers in terms of units sold and rates applied. Research, resolve, and respond to all inquiries.

- Resolved longstanding problems substantially reducing publisher inquiries and complaints.
- Promoted to "Level 1" analyst within only one year and ahead of two staff members with longer tenure.
- Provided superior training to temporary employee that resulted in her being hired for permanent, Level 1 position after only three months.

Accounts Payable Analyst—Music & Video Distribution (2002–2005)

Processed high volume of utility bills, office equipment leases, shipping invoices, and office supplies for 12 regional branches. Assisted branches with proper invoice coding and resolving payment disputes with vendors.

- Identified longstanding duplicate payment that resulted in vendor refund of $12,000.
- Created contract-employment expenses spreadsheet; identified and resolved $24,000 in duplicate payments.
- Gained reputation for thoroughness and promptness in meeting all payment deadlines.
- Set up macro in accounts payable system that streamlined invoice payments.
- Consolidated vendor accounts, increasing productivity and reducing number of checks processed.

Accounts Receivable Analyst—Music & Video Distribution (2000–2002)

Processed incoming payments, received and posted daily check deposits, reviewed applications for vendor accounts, distributed accounting reports, and ordered office supplies. Handled rebillings of international accounts for shipments by various labels.

- Hired as permanent employee from temporary position after only three months.

Additional Experience: Billing Clerk / Accounting Clerk / Bookkeeper (*details available upon request*)

EDUCATION

B.S. in Finance; Graduated with Honors • CALIFORNIA STATE UNIVERSITY, Northridge, CA; 2005
Completed Studies Concurrent with Full-Time Employment
Computer Skills: Windows, Microsoft Office (Word, Excel, PowerPoint), Peachtree, J.D. Edwards, Tracs

Step one

Step one will convert the Word resume to an ASCII (or text) format. It will remove all graphic elements, convert the font to a standardized font, and remove bolding, italics, and underlining. The purpose of doing this step is to produce a document that can be read by all operating systems (Mac, PC, Linux, etc.), all ISPs (Internet service providers), and resume-tracking software systems. You will use it to upload and insert into career and company websites.

1. Save resume using File/Save As feature
2. In "Save As" window, use identifiable name such as NameE-Resume
3. In "File Type," scroll to and select "Plain Text"
4. Make sure that "Insert Line Breaks" is *not* checked
5. Make sure that "Allow Character Substitution" *is* checked
6. Save and close

Step two

The purpose of step two is to make sure that the ASCII document is "clean" and that all information is left justified to optimize readability by resume tracking systems.

When you open the NameE-Resume file, all information will be in simple text and characters will show keyboard characters. Your resume will now look like this:

PATRICIA JOHNSON
1234 MURIETTA AVE. * PALMDALE, CA 93550
RESIDENCE (661) 555–1234 * MOBILE (661) 555–9876 * PATJOHNSON@EMAIL.COM

FINANCE/ACCOUNTING PROFESSIONAL
INTERNAL AUDITOR/FINANCIAL ANALYST/STAFF ACCOUNTANT

DETAIL ORIENTED, PROBLEM SOLVER WITH EXCELLENT ANALYTICAL STRENGTHS AND A TRACK RECORD OF OPTIMIZING PRODUCTIVITY, REDUCING COSTS, AND INCREASING PROFIT CONTRIBUTIONS. WELL-DEVELOPED TEAM BUILDING AND LEADERSHIP STRENGTHS WITH EXPERIENCE IN TRAINING AND COACHING COWORKERS. WORKS WELL WITH PUBLIC, CLIENTS, VENDORS, AND COWORKERS AT ALL LEVELS. HIGHLY MOTIVATED AND GOAL ORIENTATED AS DEMONSTRATED BY COMPLETING STUDIES TOWARD B.S. IN FINANCE, GRADUATING WITH HONORS CONCURRENT WITH FULL-TIME, PROGRESSIVE BUSINESS EXPERIENCE.

-CORE COMPETENCIES-
RESEARCH & ANALYSIS / ACCOUNTS RECEIVABLE / ACCOUNTS PAYABLE / JOURNAL ENTRIES / BANK RECONCILIATIONS
PAYROLL / FINANCIAL STATEMENTS / AUDITING / GENERAL LEDGER / ARTIST CONTRACTS/ROYALTIES/ESCALATION CLAUSES

PROFESSIONAL EXPERIENCE

MAJOR HOLLYWOOD STUDIO, HOLLYWOOD, CA * 2000 TO PRESENT
ACHIEVED FAST-TRACK PROMOTION TO POSITIONS OF INCREASING CHALLENGE AND RESPONSIBILITY
ROYALTY ANALYST-MUSIC GROUP, LOS ANGELES, CA (2005-PRESENT)
PROCESS AVERAGE OF $8-9 MILLION IN PAYMENTS MONTHLY. REVIEW ARTIST CONTRACTS, LICENSES, AND RATE SHEETS TO DETERMINE ROYALTIES DUE TO PRODUCERS AND SONGWRITERS FOR LEADING RECORD LABEL. ENSURE ACCURACY OF STATEMENTS SENT TO PUBLISHERS IN TERMS OF UNITS SOLD AND RATES APPLIED. RESEARCH, RESOLVE, AND RESPOND TO ALL INQUIRIES.
   * RESOLVED LONGSTANDING PROBLEMS SUBSTANTIALLY REDUCING PUBLISHER INQUIRIES AND COMPLAINTS.
   * PROMOTED TO "LEVEL 1" ANALYST WITHIN ONLY ONE YEAR AND AHEAD OF TWO STAFF MEMBERS WITH LONGER TENURE.
   * PROVIDED SUPERIOR TRAINING TO TEMPORARY EMPLOYEE THAT RESULTED IN HER BEING HIRED FOR PERMANENT, LEVEL 1 POSITION AFTER ONLY THREE MONTHS.
ACCOUNTS PAYABLE ANALYST-MUSIC & VIDEO DISTRIBUTION (2002-2005)
PROCESSED HIGH VOLUME OF UTILITY BILLS, OFFICE EQUIPMENT LEASES, SHIPPING INVOICES, AND OFFICE SUPPLIES FOR 12 REGIONAL BRANCHES. ASSISTED BRANCHES WITH PROPER INVOICE CODING AND RESOLVING PAYMENT DISPUTES WITH VENDORS.
   * IDENTIFIED LONGSTANDING DUPLICATE PAYMENT THAT RESULTED IN VENDOR REFUND OF $12,000.
   * CREATED CONTRACT-EMPLOYMENT EXPENSES SPREADSHEET; IDENTIFIED AND RESOLVED $24,000 IN DUPLICATE PAYMENTS.
   * GAINED REPUTATION FOR THOROUGHNESS AND PROMPTNESS IN MEETING ALL PAYMENT DEADLINES.

* SET UP MACRO IN ACCOUNTS PAYABLE SYSTEM THAT STREAMLINED INVOICE PAYMENTS.
* CONSOLIDATED VENDOR ACCOUNTS, INCREASING PRODUCTIVITY AND REDUCING NUMBER OF CHECKS PROCESSED.

ACCOUNTS RECEIVABLE ANALYST–MUSIC & VIDEO DISTRIBUTION (2000–2002)
PROCESSED INCOMING PAYMENTS; RECEIVED AND POSTED DAILY CHECK DEPOSITS, REVIEWED APPLICATIONS FOR VENDOR ACCOUNTS; DISTRIBUTED ACCOUNTING REPORTS, AND ORDERED OFFICE SUPPLIES. HANDLED REBILLINGS OF INTERNATIONAL ACCOUNTS FOR SHIPMENTS BY VARIOUS LABELS.

* HIRED AS PERMANENT EMPLOYEE FROM TEMPORARY POSITION AFTER ONLY THREE MONTHS.

ADDITIONAL EXPERIENCE: BILLING CLERK/ACCOUNTING CLERK/BOOKKEEPER (DETAILS AVAILABLE UPON REQUEST)

EDUCATION
B.S. IN FINANCE; GRADUATED WITH HONORS * CALIFORNIA STATE UNIVERSITY, NORTHRIDGE, CA; 2005
COMPLETED STUDIES CONCURRENT WITH FULL–TIME EMPLOYMENT
COMPUTER SKILLS: WINDOWS, MICROSOFT OFFICE (WORD, EXCEL, POWERPOINT), PEACHTREE, J.D. EDWARDS, TRACS

1. OPEN NAMEE-RESUME FILE. ALL INFORMATION WILL BE IN SIMPLE TEXT AND CHARACTERS WILL SHOW KEYBOARD CHARACTERS.
2. SET MARGINS TO 1" LEFT, 2" RIGHT, 1" TOP AND BOTTOM.
3. ALIGN ALL INFORMATION TO THE LEFT.
4. CHECK FOR STRANGE KEYBOARD-CHARACTER SUBSTITUTIONS SUCH AS DOLLAR SIGNS. USUALLY THE SUBSTITUTION WILL AUTOMATICALLY DEFAULT TO ASTERISKS, WHICH IS FINE. MAKE CHANGES AS APPROPRIATE.
5. CORRECT ANY STRANGE LINE BREAKS.
6. SEPARATE SECTIONS USING ALL CAPS FOR HEADINGS AND LINES COMPOSED OF KEYBOARD CHARACTERS SUCH AS HYPHENS, EQUAL SIGNS, ASTERISKS, TILDES, ETC.
7. SAVE BUT DON'T CLOSE. AGAIN, MAKE SURE THAT "INSERT LINE BREAKS" IS NOT CHECKED AND THAT "ALLOW CHARACTER SUBSTITUTION" IS CHECKED.

Your e-resume will now look like this:

PATRICIA JOHNSON
1234 MURIETTA AVE.
PALMDALE, CA 93550
RESIDENCE (661) 555-1234
MOBILE (661) 555-9876
PATJOHNSON@EMAIL.COM

==
==

FINANCE/ACCOUNTING PROFESSIONAL
INTERNAL AUDITOR/FINANCIAL ANALYST/STAFF ACCOUNTANT
DETAIL ORIENTED, PROBLEM SOLVER WITH EXCELLENT ANALYTICAL STRENGTHS AND A TRACK
RECORD OF OPTIMIZING PRODUCTIVITY, REDUCING COSTS, AND INCREASING PROFIT CONTRIBUTIONS.
WELL-DEVELOPED TEAM BUILDING AND LEADERSHIP STRENGTHS WITH EXPERIENCE IN TRAINING AND
COACHING COWORKERS. WORKS WELL WITH PUBLIC, CLIENTS, VENDORS, AND COWORKERS AT ALL
LEVELS. HIGHLY MOTIVATED AND GOAL ORIENTATED AS DEMONSTRATED BY COMPLETING STUDIES
TOWARD B.S. IN FINANCE, GRADUATING WITH HONORS CONCURRENT WITH FULL-TIME, PROGRESSIVE
BUSINESS EXPERIENCE.

==

-CORE COMPETENCIES-
RESEARCH & ANALYSIS / ACCOUNTS RECEIVABLE / ACCOUNTS PAYABLE / JOURNAL ENTRIES /
BANK RECONCILIATIONS / PAYROLL / FINANCIAL STATEMENTS / AUDITING / GENERAL LEDGER /
ARTIST CONTRACTS / ROYALTIES / ESCALATION CLAUSES

==
==

PROFESSIONAL EXPERIENCE

MAJOR HOLLYWOOD STUDIO
HOLLYWOOD, CA
2000 TO PRESENT
ACHIEVED FAST-TRACK PROMOTION TO POSITIONS OF INCREASING CHALLENGE AND
RESPONSIBILITY
~~ROYALTY ANALYST-MUSIC GROUP, LOS ANGELES, CA
~~(2005-PRESENT)
PROCESS AVERAGE OF $8-9 MILLION IN PAYMENTS MONTHLY. REVIEW ARTIST CONTRACTS,
LICENSES, AND RATE SHEETS TO DETERMINE ROYALTIES DUE TO PRODUCERS AND SONGWRITERS FOR
LEADING RECORD LABEL. ENSURE ACCURACY OF STATEMENTS SENT TO PUBLISHERS IN TERMS OF
UNITS SOLD AND RATES APPLIED. RESEARCH, RESOLVE, AND RESPOND TO ALL INQUIRIES.

* RESOLVED LONGSTANDING PROBLEMS SUBSTANTIALLY REDUCING PUBLISHER INQUIRIES AND COMPLAINTS.
* PROMOTED TO "LEVEL 1" ANALYST WITHIN ONLY ONE YEAR AND AHEAD OF TWO STAFF MEMBERS WITH LONGER TENURE.
* PROVIDED SUPERIOR TRAINING TO TEMPORARY EMPLOYEE THAT RESULTED IN HER BEING HIRED FOR PERMANENT, LEVEL 1 POSITION AFTER ONLY THREE MONTHS.

~~ACCOUNTS PAYABLE ANALYST–MUSIC & VIDEO DISTRIBUTION
~~(2002–2005)

PROCESSED HIGH VOLUME OF UTILITY BILLS, OFFICE EQUIPMENT LEASES, SHIPPING INVOICES, AND OFFICE SUPPLIES FOR 12 REGIONAL BRANCHES. ASSISTED BRANCHES WITH PROPER INVOICE CODING AND RESOLVING PAYMENT DISPUTES WITH VENDORS.

* IDENTIFIED LONGSTANDING DUPLICATE PAYMENT THAT RESULTED IN VENDOR REFUND OF $12,000.
* CREATED CONTRACT–EMPLOYMENT EXPENSES SPREADSHEET; IDENTIFIED AND RESOLVED $24,000 IN DUPLICATE PAYMENTS.
* GAINED REPUTATION FOR THOROUGHNESS AND PROMPTNESS IN MEETING ALL PAYMENT DEADLINES.
* SET UP MACRO IN ACCOUNTS PAYABLE SYSTEM THAT STREAMLINED INVOICE PAYMENTS.
* CONSOLIDATED VENDOR ACCOUNTS, INCREASING PRODUCTIVITY AND REDUCING NUMBER OF CHECKS PROCESSED.

~~ACCOUNTS RECEIVABLE ANALYST–MUSIC & VIDEO DISTRIBUTION
~~(2000–2002)

PROCESSED INCOMING PAYMENTS; RECEIVED AND POSTED DAILY CHECK DEPOSITS, REVIEWED APPLICATIONS FOR VENDOR ACCOUNTS; DISTRIBUTED ACCOUNTING REPORTS AND ORDERED OFFICE SUPPLIES. HANDLED REBILLINGS OF INTERNATIONAL ACCOUNTS FOR SHIPMENTS BY VARIOUS LABELS.

* HIRED AS PERMANENT EMPLOYEE FROM TEMPORARY POSITION AFTER ONLY THREE MONTHS.

ADDITIONAL EXPERIENCE: BILLING CLERK/ACCOUNTING CLERK/BOOKKEEPER (DETAILS AVAILABLE UPON REQUEST)

===
===

EDUCATION

B.S. IN FINANCE; GRADUATED WITH HONORS
CALIFORNIA STATE UNIVERSITY
NORTHRIDGE, CA
2005
COMPLETED STUDIES CONCURRENT WITH FULL-TIME EMPLOYMENT
COMPUTER SKILLS: WINDOWS, MICROSOFT OFFICE (WORD, EXCEL, POWERPOINT), PEACHTREE,
J.D. EDWARDS, TRACS

Step three

Step three will create a resume that you will use to cut and paste directly into e-mails. While it appears to be the same as the previous version, this step will insert line breaks at the end of each line. Since the margins have already been set at 1" left and 2" right, the new file *with* line breaks will contain lines having no more than 65 characters. This is the standard width of e-mail windows, and will fit into a standard screen shot. If you cut and pasted the original e-resume into an e-mail without this step, the lines would scroll off the page and be hard to read.

1. Save again, using the "Save As" command, this time making sure that "Insert Line Breaks" *is* checked, as well as allowing character substitution. Use a save name such as NameE-MailResume.
2. This version will have line breaks and will fit a standard screen shot. Remember, this is the version to cut and paste directly *into* e-mail.

The resume will look like this:

PATRICIA JOHNSON
1234 Murietta Ave.
Palmdale, CA 93550
Residence (661) 555-1234
Mobile (661) 555-9876
PatJohnson@email.com
==
==
FINANCE/ACCOUNTING PROFESSIONAL
Internal Auditor/Financial Analyst/Staff Accountant

Detail oriented, problem solver with excellent analytical strengths and a track record of optimizing productivity, reducing costs, and increasing profit contributions. Well-developed team building and leadership strengths with experience in training and coaching coworkers. Works well with public, clients, vendors, and coworkers at all levels. Highly motivated and goal orientated as demonstrated by completing studies toward B.S. in Finance, graduating with honors concurrent with full-time, progressive business experience.

==
-Core Competencies-
Research & Analysis / Accounts Receivable / Accounts Payable / Journal Entries / Bank Reconciliations Payroll / Financial Statements / Auditing / General Ledger / Artist Contracts / Royalties / Escalation Clauses
==

==
PROFESSIONAL EXPERIENCE

MAJOR HOLLYWOOD STUDIO
Hollywood, CA
2000 to Present
Achieved fast-track promotion to positions of increasing challenge and responsibility
~~Royalty Analyst-Music Group, Los Angeles, CA
~~(2005-Present)
Process average of $8-9 million in payments monthly. Review artist contracts, licenses, and rate sheets to determine royalties due to producers and songwriters for leading record label. Ensure accuracy of statements sent to publishers in terms of units sold and rates applied. Research, resolve, and respond to all inquiries.

* Resolved longstanding problems substantially reducing publisher inquiries and complaints.
* Promoted to "Level 1" analyst within only one year and ahead of two staff members with longer tenure.
* Provided superior training to temporary employee that resulted in her being hired for permanent, Level 1 position after only three months.

~~Accounts Payable Analyst-Music & Video Distribution
~~(2002-2005)

Processed high volume of utility bills, office equipment leases, shipping invoices, and office supplies for 12 regional branches. Assisted branches with proper invoice coding and resolving payment disputes with vendors.

* Identified longstanding duplicate payment that resulted in vendor refund of $12,000.
* Created contract-employment expenses spreadsheet; identified and resolved $24,000 in duplicate payments.
* Gained reputation for thoroughness and promptness in meeting all payment deadlines.
* Set up macro in accounts payable system that streamlined invoice payments.
* Consolidated vendor accounts, increasing productivity and reducing number of checks processed.

~~Accounts Receivable Analyst-Music & Video Distribution
~~(2000-2002)
Processed incoming payments; received and posted daily check
deposits, reviewed applications for vendor accounts; distributed accounting reports, and ordered office supplies. Handled re-billings of international accounts for ship-ments by various labels.
* Hired as permanent employee from temporary position after only three months.

Additional Experience: Billing Clerk/Accounting Clerk/Bookkeeper (details available upon request)
==
==
EDUCATION

B.S. in Finance; Graduated with Honors
CALIFORNIA STATE UNIVERSITY
Northridge, CA
2005
Completed Studies Concurrent with Full-Time Employment
Computer Skills: Windows, Microsoft Office (Word, Excel, PowerPoint), Peachtree, J.D. Edwards, Tracs

HTML Multimedia Resume Considerations

An HTML or multimedia resume can be a sensible option if you work in a field where visu-als and sound and/or graphics represent critical skills. About 50 percent of resume banks and social networking sites accept HTML resumes, plus a simple HTML resume can be created by using the "Save as HTML" feature you can access when you save and name your documents.

You can add a hotlink within your standard resume, or add a hotlink in your cover letter / e-mail that takes the reader to your web-hosted resume rather than adding an attachment or pasting in an ASCII version. This has the advantage of allowing you to add audio, video, and graphics and the viewer can see your background positioned exactly as you wish it.

Some disadvantages include:

- Adding the graphics and visuals and video and audio is a time consuming process, and can be expensive if you hire someone to do it for you; most professionals don't need to present themselves in this way.
- If you want your HTML resume to be web based, you'll need to build a website or have one built. This website will then have to be hosted somewhere and you'll have registration fees and hosting fees and announcement fees (elementary optimization) to host it. Apart from paying to have such a site built, these costs are usually small, but they are ongoing and add up over time.
- If you build it yourself without any experience, there is a learning curve involved.
- Because the content is more complex, these documents take longer to open and work through, so the content needs to be compelling if you are going to hold anyone's attention.
- You will build a web-based resume because you hope to *send* people to see it. You can't expect recruiters to flock to it because anything to do with resumes is fiercely competitive in terms of achieving a reasonable search ranking. So unless you spend a small fortune on optimization, you can't realistically expect much traffic.

HTML and multimedia design considerations

- Don't be seduced by design capabilities for the sake of their flashiness; remember the end user and your communication goals. Instead use technology to make life easier for the visitor. For example, your e-mail address can be a hotlink, so that clicking on it immediately launches the user's e-mail to contact you.
- If the HTML resume ends up being a complex document with graphics, sound, and video, layout is going to be a major consideration. You don't want the mission-critical topics—performance profile, core and technical competencies, education, work samples, etc.—to get lost in the glitz.
- Provide a hotlink that allows the user to print out that beautifully formatted PDF version of your resume.
- Don't start from ground zero; find an example you like and copy it.

Is an interactive portfolio/web-based resume a waste of time?

Much depends on your situation and what you are trying to sell and to whom. For anyone it is a nice thing to have, but not mandatory unless:

- Your profession is web-based
- Your work involves visual and auditory components
- Your work is technology based with a communications component
- Demonstrating technological savvy is a plus for your branding

As an online portfolio is the most complex resume document you can create, you want the core content of the site to be finished before you start creating this version with all its bells and whistles. The most practical approach is to get your MS Word resume completed along with the necessary ASCII text versions. Once you've done your due diligence research as you developed the other versions, and have your job search up to speed, you can decide if you need to develop this third variation.

Proofread and Test E-mail All Versions of Your Resume

Before you send any version of your resume, proofread it carefully. Send your electronic cover letters and resume attachments to yourself and to a friend or family member. Ask them for printouts of your practice e-mail messages and resumes to ensure that what you intended to send is actually what was received and can be printed out. Often, this exercise will help you find mistakes, bloopers, or larger problems incurred during the conversion process. If you find typos at this late stage, reward yourself with a smack up the side of the head for being sloppy. The most common and annoying problem is that the contact information you carefully put at the top of the second page now appears half way down it, these are the important mistakes you can easily catch with this exercise.

CHAPTER 10
COVER LETTERS INCREASE YOUR BANG

A JOB SEARCH is all about getting into conversation as quickly and frequently as possible with people in a position to hire you. Because a letter introducing your resume enables you to differentiate your message and your brand, it dramatically increases your odds of an interview and helps position you appropriately for that interview.

When you build a great resume but don't learn how to use it properly, your job search will take longer, and the job you get may not be the best your skills deserve. So if all you are going to do is load your resume into resume databases (the two most common but ineffective job search approaches), a cover letter isn't going to do you a lot of good, because its main benefit is personalizing your message to a specific company and person.

When you develop a plan of attack for your job search that enables you to reach out directly to decision makers, (something that's covered in the latest edition of *Knock 'em Dead: The Ultimate Job Search Guide*) the right cover letter significantly increases your bang.

The quicker and more frequently you get into conversation with the people who have the authority to hire you, the faster you will land that new position. Whenever someone like this reviews your resume, your odds of getting an interview increase dramatically, because you have skipped right over needing to be pulled from the resume database. You have sidestepped the recruiter's evaluation process and you have the opportunity to make a personalized pitch.

When an e-mail or envelope is opened, your cover letter should be the first thing the reviewer sees. A cover letter personalizes your candidacy for a specific job in ways that are impossible for the impersonal nature of your resume. It sets the stage for the reader to accept your resume, and therefore you, as something and someone special. It can create common ground between you and the reader and demonstrate that you are well qualified and suitable for *this* job with *this* company.

Your target for direct communication is always someone who can hire you (typically one to three title levels above yours) although any management title offers opportunity for referral. Even HR contacts are valuable. Although these contacts can't make the hiring decision (although they can have a strong influence), the pivotal nature of the job makes them aware of all areas within a company that could use your skills. The point is, that any name is better than no name, and with the Internet at your fingertips there are almost countless ways to identify the names of people who carry the appropriate hiring titles for your needs.

Who to Target in Your Job Search

The hiring titles to target during your job search are:

- Those titles most likely to be in a position to hire you
- Those titles most likely to be involved in the selection process
- Those titles most likely to know people involved in the selection process

What Makes a Cover Letter Work

When you know how to find the names that go with your target hiring titles, you can approach these people directly, and then a cover letter really delivers for you. Direct research and approach is one of the best strategies to get hired fast. With Google, Bing, and other search engines, you can find something to show knowledge of the company and perhaps the name of the executive you intend to approach.

Try keyword searches for your target hiring titles (each search engine will get different results), execute general web searches and news searches; the news link is usually just above the regular search box.

For example, a professional in pharmaceutical sales trying to make direct contact with potential hiring authorities for a job at a specific company in the Pittsburgh area could try all the following keyword searches and gather new useable info from each search. Remember this person is most likely to be hired by someone with a management rank one, two, or three levels above his own.

Pharmaceutical sales (company name)
Pharmaceutical sales (company name) Pennsylvania
Pharmaceutical sales (company name) Pittsburgh
Pharmaceutical Mgr sales (company name) Pennsylvania
Pharmaceutical Mgr sales (company name) Pittsburgh
Pharmaceutical Director sales (company name) Pennsylvania
Pharmaceutical Director sales (company name) Pittsburgh
Pharmaceutical VP sales (company name) Pennsylvania

Try this approach on Google and Google News, both with and without the company name. Drill down five or ten pages, and you will come up with people holding titles at this and other target companies in your geographical area.

News items

When you do a Google News (right above the standard dialog box) search and find relevant intelligence you can use it as an opener for your letter or e-mail:

- Refer to the article and its relevance in your letter
- In an e-mail, paste the article and attach it.
- In a traditional letter, enclose a copy of the article.

Of course, not every company you approach will have been mentioned in *Newsweek*, but if there are no media hits or otherwise useful intelligence, the chances are still good that the company website can give you some insight that can be turned to similar bridge-building advantage.

Readability Is Critical

You can also grab attention with the appearance of your letter. From a branding perspective it should echo the fonts and font sizes of your resume.

The font must be legible for hiring managers: anyone who has been staring at computer screens for ten or more years, i.e., people who can hire you. I recommend using 11-point or 12-point fonts.

Your branding message stays strong and consistent by using the same font choices and paper for your letters as you use for your resume. Therefore, the font you used for contact information and headlines in your resume is the same font you will use for your letterhead. As well, the font you chose for your resume's body copy will be the same one you will use for the message in your letter.

You should obtain matching paper for resumes, cover letters, and envelopes. When the opportunity arises to send a resume by traditional mail you will want resume, letter paper, and envelope to match.

> Sending your resume and letter by traditional mail when the opportunity arises is a way to get your resume read because most people aren't thinking about using traditional mail right now.

Remember: Written communication is a critical skill in the workplace. Typos are *verboten*!

Your letters should always be laid out with short paragraphs and lots of white space so that reading is easy on the eye. Your letters have the same reader accessibility concerns as your resume. Say everything succinctly so that your copy never exceeds one page.

Your Professional Brand in Written Communication

The personal brand you've established for MeInc will always be transmitted through the materials you send out to reviewers. Remember that the object of your brand is to differentiate you from others.

- Getting your resume directly under the nose of a manager, who just wants to make a good hire and get back to work, makes you special.
- Introducing your resume with a covering letter that establishes connectivity between you and the reader makes you special.

- Getting your resume to a manager in a creative way makes you special, and showing that you know what you are doing is a big plus too. Your letter might say in part, "I sent my resume by e-mail but thought you might appreciate a screen break, so you'll find it attached to this letter . . . ."
- Ensuring that your paper is good quality and that fonts are legible and coordinated make you special.
- Writing a message that's clear and succinct makes you special.
- Differentiating your behavior and actions from others, will make you stand out as someone different. If the packaging that captures your written communications has high production values, looks good, carries a succinct, relevant message, and makes that message readily accessible, showing a professional with a clear sense of self, you are on your way to establishing a viable professional brand.
- Following up your meetings through the selection cycle with thoughtful letters that continue the messaging of a consummate professional, confirm your professional brand and make you special.

Good brands are those that live up to their promise or value proposition. Integrate this suggested behavior with the other strategies and tactics we have discussed and your candidacy is going to nudge that unique branded status.

Tone

When your "look" is determined, the content of your letter has to be succinct and to-the-point: reflecting a professional whose resume just might have something to say. Here are a few examples that grab attention and cut to the chase:

> *I have been researching the leading local companies in _____, and the name of _____ Products keeps coming up as a top company. This confirmed an opinion I've developed over my three years in the profession.*

> *Right after my mentor mentioned _____ as one of the top companies in our industry, I heard you speak at the association meeting last _____. I really resonated with your comments about productivity, and as I am looking to harness my _____ years logistics expertise to a major player, felt this was the right time to introduce myself.*

> *First things first, Carole Mraz over at C-Soft told me to say hello. You and I haven't spoken before but Carole thinks we might have an interesting conversation, especially if you anticipate the need for an industrious young marketing acolyte who comes equipped*

with a great education, two years and one mouth, and a great desire to start at the bottom learning from an acknowledged master in the field.

I understand you are a manager who likes to get things done, and who likes competent, focused, goal-oriented employees . . . .

I'm focused on finding the right boss to bring out the best in a consistently top-producing _____ who wants to make a contribution as part of a hard driving team.

I thought the best way to demonstrate my drive and creativity was to get you my resume in this priority mail envelope. I also sent it to you by e-mail and into your company resume bank, but sales is all about stacking the odds... and I knew you'd also appreciate a break from the computer screen.

I've been meaning to contact you ever since I attended / read / heard about _____. It encouraged me to do a little research, which has convinced me that you are the kind of company I want to be associated with, and that I have the kind of qualifications that can be successfully applied to your current projects.

I have been following the performance of your company in Mutual Funds Newsletter. With my experience working for one of your direct competitors, I know I could make significant contributions . . . .

Recently, I have been researching the local _____ industry. My search has been for companies that are respected in the field and . . . which prize a commitment to professional development. I am such an individual and you are clearly such a company.

Within the next few weeks, I will be moving from New York to _____. Having researched the companies in _____, I know that you are the company I want to talk to . . . .

The state of the art in_____ changes so rapidly that it is tough for most professionals to keep up. The attached resume will demonstrate that I am an exception, and eager to bring my experience to bear for your company.

If you haven't managed to include the reason for writing in your opening, as we see in some of the above examples, you should introduce it now and go on to identify something desirable about the professional you.

I am writing because . . .

My reason for contacting you . . .

. . . you may be interested to know . . .

If you are seeking a _____, you will be interested to know . . .

I would like to talk to you about your staffing needs for _____ and how I might be able to contribute to your department's goals.

If you have an opening for someone in this area, you will see that my resume demonstrates a person of unusual dedication, efficiency, and drive.

With a short paragraph or a couple of bullets, you might highlight one or two special contributions or achievements; these can include any qualifications, contributions, or attributes that brand you as someone with talent and energy to offer.

If an advertisement or a telephone conversation with a potential employer reveals an aspect of a particular job opening that is not addressed in your resume (and for some reason you don't have time to update it), you can use the cover letter to fill in the gaps.

Or you can use the cover letter to emphasize a key requirement, for example:

I noticed from your posting that training experience in a distance-learning environment would be a plus. You will see in my enclosed resume that I have five years experience writing and producing sales and management training materials in new media.

You want the reader to move from your letter to the resume with the feeling that you can do this job; the above reference to a job's key requirement does just that. Because you want the reader to move straight on to your resume, brevity is important—leave your reader wanting more. The letter doesn't sell you, that's the resume's job, but it does position you for serious consideration; whet the reader's appetite, no more.

Make it clear to the reader that you want to talk

Explain when, where, and how you can be contacted. You can also be proactive, by telling the reader that you intend to follow up at a certain point in time if contact has not been established by then. Just as you worked to create a strong opening, make sure your closing carries the same conviction. It is the reader's last personal impression of you, so make it strong, make it tight, and make it obvious that you are serious about entering into meaningful conversation.

Useful phrases include:

It would be a pleasure to give you more information about my qualifications and experience . . .

I look forward to discussing our mutual interests further . . .

While I prefer not to use my employer's time taking personal calls at work, with discretion I can be reached at _____.

I will be in your area around the 20th, and will call you prior to that date. I would like to arrange . . .

I hope to speak with you further, and will call the week of _____ to follow up.

The chance to meet with you would be a privilege and a pleasure, so to this end I shall call you on _____.

I look forward to speaking with you further, and will call in the next few days to see when our schedules will permit a face-to-face meeting.

May I suggest a personal meeting where you can have the opportunity to examine the person behind the resume?

My credentials and achievements are a matter of record that I hope you will examine in depth when we meet . . . you can reach me at _____.

I look forward to examining any of the ways you feel my background and skills would benefit [name of organization]. I look forward to hearing from you.

Resumes help you sort out the probables from the possibles, but they are no way to judge the caliber of an individual. I would like to meet you and demonstrate that I have the professional personality that makes for a successful _____.

I expect to be in your area on Tuesday and Wednesday of next week, and wonder which day would be best for you. I will call to determine. In the meantime, I would appreciate your treating my application as confidential, since I am currently employed.

With my training and hands-on experience, I know I can contribute to _____, and want to talk to you about it in person. When may we meet?

After reading my resume, you will know something about my background. Yet, you will still need to determine whether I am the one to help you with current problems and challenges. I would like an interview to discuss my ability to contribute to your company.

You can reach me at [home/alternate#] to arrange an interview. I know that your time investment in meeting with me will be repaid amply.

Thank you for your time and consideration; I hope to hear from you shortly.

I will call you for an interview in the next few days.

A brief phone call will establish whether or not we have mutual interest. Recognizing the demands of your schedule, I will make that call within the week.

Some people feel it is powerful in the closing to state a date—"I'll call you on Friday if we don't speak before"—or a date and time—"I'll call you on Friday morning at 10 A.M. if we don't speak before" when they will follow up with a phone call. The logic is that you demonstrate that your intent is serious, that you are organized, and that you plan your time effectively; all of which are desirable behavioral traits and support the brand of a goal-oriented and consummate professional.

A complete idiot in my business once said that an employer would be offended by being "forced" to sit and await this call. In over thirty years of involvement in the hiring process, as a headhunter, as a hiring manager, as an HR executive, and as a writer on these issues who speaks to executives all over the world, I have never met anyone who felt constrained to wait by the phone for such a call. What sometimes does get noticed, though, is the person who doesn't follow through on commitments as promised. Therefore, if you use this approach, keep your promise: its part of the value proposition in your professional brand.

More on Cover and Other Job Search Letters

Writing cover letters for resumes, or any of the other letters you can write to advance your candidacy during a job search (there are at least ten different kinds), is not a topic that we can cover properly in the few short pages we have available here. You can get complete comprehensive advice, with 150 plus examples, in the companion book to this one, *Knock 'em Dead Cover Letters*.

CHAPTER 10
THE RESUMES

I HAVE INCLUDED resumes from a wide range of jobs so you will probably find a resume telling a similar story to yours. However, *resume layouts are never designed for specific professions or job titles; they are designed to tell a person's professional story.* So when you see a resume layout that works for you, use it; don't be restrained because the example is of someone in another profession.

Trauma Treatment

Richard is transitioning out of the Navy, where he gained a great deal of experience in trauma treatment and crisis management.

RICHARD P. ISAACS, RN, BSN
529 SPRINGDALE ROAD
SPRINGWATER, NEW YORK 14560
585-555-6184
RICHI@CS.COM

DISASTER RESPONSE • ACUTE & CRITICAL PATIENT CARE • MEDICAL/SURGICAL CARE
Pediatrics / Geriatrics / Post-Surgical / Nuclear & Biological Hazards

Health care professional with over eight years' intensive experience in fast-paced military hospital environments. Demonstrated capacity to provide direct patient care and effectively supervise support staff in a variety of clinical settings. Specialized training in dealing with nuclear and biological exposure, as well as experience treating patients with infectious diseases including typhoid, meningitis, AIDS, and other contagions. Proven capacity to function well in crisis situations, plus excellent ability to relate to patients from diverse cultural backgrounds and various age groups.

PRIMARY CLINICAL EXPERIENCE:

LIEUTENANT, UNITED STATES NAVY (2003 – Present)
US Naval Hospital; Tokyo, Japan
Patients encompass infants through geriatrics, with conditions including a broad range of infectious diseases and physical injuries.

Staff Nurse / Charge Nurse – Adult & Pediatric Care   **May 2007 – Present**

- Provide bedside care to patients; administer medications and implement physician orders.
- Confer with physicians and other care team members on treatment plans for various patients.
- Address the needs of patients in isolation with typhoid, meningitis, and other contagious diseases.
- Train and provide leadership for staff of seven RNs and LPNs in Charge Nurse role.
- Participate in field exercises to maintain readiness for combat deployment in support of Marine units.

Key Accomplishment:
Restructured medical supplies inventory and wrote new Standard Operating Procedures (SOPs) to improve departmental efficiencies.

Staff Nurse / Division Officer – Post-Anesthesia Care Unit   **May 2006 – May 2007**

- Served needs of post-operative patients, addressing special concerns of post-anesthesia recovery.
- Otherwise supported surgical teams in treating patients with a broad range of medical conditions.

US Naval Hospital; Annapolis, Maryland
Patient base included military dependents and retirees, as well as active military personnel, including several "VIP" patients.

Staff Nurse – Medical / Telemetry Acute Care Unit   **Apr. 2003 – Apr. 2006**

- Addressed acute care needs of medical patients, including oncology and infectious disease patients.
- Cared for patients in isolation wards with tuberculosis, AIDS, and other contagious diseases.
- Monitored cardiac activity of patients using state-of-the-art telemetry technology.

Accomplishment:
Selected to serve as part of Humanitarian Relief Response Team.

Richard P. Isaacs, RN
Resume – Page Two

PRIMARY CLINICAL EXPERIENCE *(continued)*:

LONG ISLAND GENERAL HOSPITAL; Riverhead, New York
Suburban/rural facility (eastern Long Island, New York) providing full range of medical services.
Staff Nurse / Charge Nurse – Medical / Surgical Unit   2000 – 2003

- Provided direct patient care including telemetry monitoring.
- Served needs of incarcerated individuals in conjunction with Suffolk County (NY) Sheriff's Office.

ADDITIONAL CLINICAL EXPERIENCE:

EXPOSERVE MEDICAL SERVICES; Annapolis, Maryland
Per Diem Registered Nurse – Maryland Children's Center   2003 – 2006

- Served the needs of pediatric patients in a clinical outpatient setting.

HEARTLAND NURSING SERVICES; Riverhead, New York
Per Diem Registered Nurse   2002 – 2003

- Cared for burn victims, cardiac patients, post-surgical patients, ICU patients, and the terminally ill.

EDUCATION:

MICHIGAN STATE UNIVERSITY; East Lansing, Michigan
Master of Science, Community Service
Anticipated May, 2007

STATE UNIVERSITY OF NEW YORK AT ALBANY; Albany, New York
Bachelor of Science, Nursing   May 2001
Sigma Theta Tau Honorary / Gold Key Award / Silver Key Award

JOHNSON & WALES UNIVERSITY; Providence, Rhode Island
Associate of Science, Hotel & Restaurant Management   June 1986

CERTIFICATIONS / SPECIALIZED TRAINING:

Registered Nurse
Advanced Cardiac Life Support (ACLS); Basic Life Support (BLS)
Pediatric Advanced Life Support (PALS I)
Intravenous Conscious Sedation (IVCS)

Nuclear & Biological Hazard Medical Training
Mass Casualty Training; Field Hospital Training; Shipboard Hospital Training
Suturing; Chest Tube Insertion

References Provided On Request

145

Ophthalmic Doctor Assistant/Technician

Career transition: This former sales representative attained her ophthalmic certification and then obtained successful employment in her new field.

THERESA R. KEEBLER
404-555-6822 • 3248 Derry Lane, Decatur, GA 30035

OPHTHALMIC DOCTOR ASSISTANT / TECHNICIAN
Building organizational value by assisting with diagnostic and treatment-oriented procedures

Technical Skills:
Precise Refracting/Work Up
Scribing
Goniometry
Sterile Techniques

Procedures & Treatments:
Chalazion Surgery
Glaucoma Treatments
Conjunctivitis
Diabetes Monitoring
Retinopathy of Prematurity
Macular Degeneration
Strabismus
Cataracts
Palsy
NLD Obstruction
Blepharplasty

Equipment:
A Scans
Lasers
Tonometry
Slit Lamp
Lensonetry
Keratometer
Visual Fields
Topography

QUALIFICATIONS SUMMARY

Personable and capable professional experienced in conducting diagnostic tests; measuring and recording vision; testing eye muscle function; inserting, removing, and caring for contact lenses; and applying eye dressings. Competently assist physicians during surgery, maintain optical and surgical instruments, and administer eye medications. Extensive knowledge in ophthalmic medications dealing with glaucoma, cataract surgery, and a wide variety of other diagnoses.

PROFESSIONAL EXPERIENCE

AUGUSTA EYE ASSOCIATES, Decatur, Georgia — since 2005
Hired as a **Technician/Assistant** for a cornea specialist in a large ophthalmic practice. Performed histories, vision screenings, pupil exams, and precise manifest refractions. Assisted with a variety of surgical procedures. Quickly build trust and rapport and streamline processes to ensure physician efficiency.

GUGGINO FAMILY EYE CENTER, Atlanta, Georgia — 2004 to 2005
Taught customer service techniques and promoted twice within two months to an **Ophthalmic Doctor Assistant** for a pediatric neurology ophthalmologist performing scribing, taking histories, preparing patients for examination, and educating patients on treatment procedures.

DAVEL COMMUNICATIONS, Atlanta, Georgia — 2001 to 2003
Recruited as a **Regional Account Manager** and promoted within 3 months of hire to **National Account Manager**. Contributed to the company doubling in size within 10 months; maintained a 100% satisfied customer retention rate.

CHILI'S BAR & GRILL, Decatur, Georgia — 1995 to 2000
Hired as a **Hostess** and quickly promoted to **Server**.

EDUCATION

Bachelor of Science, Organizational Communication — 2001
University of Georgia, Athens, Georgia

CERTIFICATION

Certified Ophthalmic Assistant (COA) — expected July 2006

Medical Assistant

Jennifer's actual paid experience was minimal and dated; her skills needed to be brought to the forefront. This new resume was presented at a job fair where she was hired on the spot.

Jennifer Martin
(555) 555-5555
email@address.com
1234 West Street
Hometown, NY 01234

MEDICAL ASSISTANT

Triage	Injections	Patient Scheduling
Medical Terminology	Phlebotomy	Chart Updating
Patient Intake	Vital Signs	ICD and CPT Coding
Dosage Calculations	Infection Control	Insurance Claims
Sterilization Procedures	Urinalysis	Accounts Payable/Receivable
Blood Smears and Blood Tests	Hematocrit	Collections
Lab Equipment Operation	EKG	Data Entry

EXPERIENCE

Patient Care
- Cared for in-home patients with complex, multi-symptom illnesses for three years
- Eased patient discomfort by conducting accurate assessment and drawing techniques
- Fostered healthy environment for diabetic patient through meal preparation, medication dispensing, and glucose level monitoring

Administrative
- Improved cash flow by recovering uncollectible accounts in excess of $1,000,000
- Increased accuracy of patient files by designing and implementing new patient update sheet
- Exceeded daily quotas and minimized overhead expenses with effective scheduling and management of part-time employees

Computer Skills
- Microsoft Windows, Word, Excel, and Works
- Corel Word Perfect
- Medical software including Medical Manager and Great Plains

EDUCATION

College of Medical Careers, San Diego, CA
Medical Assistant Certificate, 1999
Valedictorian

High School, Anytown, PA
Diploma – Science Emphasis, 1997

RELATED EMPLOYMENT HISTORY

Billing Specialist, Bookkeeper, Medical Assistant (various – Indiana and Somerset, PA)	1999–2000
Medical Assistant (Internal Medical Office – San Diego, CA)	1999
Long-term/Acute Care Provider (self-employed – Anytown, PA)	1995–1998

147

Occupational Health Services Manager

Susan was successful in finding an Occupational Health Services management position in another industry after being a casualty of airline downsizing.

SUSAN BROWN, RN, COHN-S/CM

Manchester, NH
Mobile: 603-555-9944
Pager: 800-555-3642 PIN#1937761
E-mail: susanbrown81@hotmail.com

OCCUPATIONAL HEALTH SERVICES MANAGER

Certified Occupational Health Nurse Specialist / Certified Case Manager / Certified Occupational Hearing Conservationist / Case Management / OSHA & DOT Compliance / Ergonomics / Workers' Compensation / Corporate Safety / Training / Customer Service / Problem Solving / Quality Assurance / Sales & Marketing

- 10 years direct experience developing innovative occupational health programs and establishing clinics.
- 14 years experience in trauma centers and critical care units.
- Success in driving revenue stream and cost-saving initiatives through strong combination of business management and clinical skills.
- Licensed Registered Nurse: New Hampshire and Massachusetts
- Proficient in Sign Language, Microsoft Office, and Outlook.

PROFESSIONAL EXPERIENCE

Supervisor, Occupational Health Services, Southwest Air Lines, Manchester, NH   2001–Present

Recruited to implement and manage Southwest's first onsite employee health clinic in eight years. Accountable for care of work-related and non-occupational injuries and illnesses for 5000 airport employees (from baggage handlers to pilots). Coordinated care for another 1500 employees in New Hampshire and 1000 employees in Chicago. Hired and directly supervised 13 registered nurses. Managed $1,000,000 budget. Assisted with the launch of new Southwest clinics in four other airports. Standardized policies and procedures and created training programs.

Developed position to also encompass system-wide responsibilities, and established self as the resource for OSHA-related matters, insourcing opportunities, ergonomic issues, and post-job offer testing programs. Updated operational managers on daily events, occupational health program progression, new programs, ongoing testing, compliance achievement, drug testing program, etc.

Achievements

- Overcame resistance and established first-ever Manchester airport onsite clinic as an integral part of operations. Planned the department design, oversaw the architect and contractors, hired and trained staff, and developed an orientation manual from scratch.
- Conceived and implemented matrix to document value of occupational health services to Southwest. Demonstrated an average of 55% ROI each month.
- Generated annual revenue of $120,000 by spearheading a drive to insource business from other airport companies, promoting the utilization of the Southwest clinic instead of an offsite clinic.
- Initiated joint venture with Comair and opened a lucrative satellite clinic in Manchester for Comair employees.
- Innovated a post-job offer functional testing program to address the high percentage of injuries among new hires. Worked closely with Southwest Legal and Human Resources and researched vendors.
- Negotiated inpatient services volume discount with most utilized hospital system that will save $60,000+ per year.
- Developed an improved nurse orientation process and a charting quality assurance program.

- Coordinated availability of appropriate emergency care for passengers aboard flights that were diverted to Canada on 9/11. Arranged for medical providers to meet over 17 staggered flights and 1100 passengers that arrived over the course of the next 6 days following the event.

Trainer, Manchester, NH   1999–Present

Provided continuing education, with CEU's approved by New Hampshire Board of Nurses, on Workplace Violence Guidelines for Health Care Workers, Nuts and Bolts of Occupational Health Nursing, OSHA Compliance and the Occupational Health Nurse, and Workers' Compensation Fraud Prevention and Update.

Program Supervisor, Allied Health Corporation, Boston, MA   1998–2001

Accountable for providing a broad range of quality services in a convenient, efficient, and cost-effective manner for this 8,000-employee Hospital Based Occupational Health Services Program dedicated to "Business Health." Supervised staff of 50 at 35 different companies.

- Managed successful start-up of 8 freestanding occupational medicine walk-in clinics.
- Instrumental in winning $600,000 in new business through marketing the placement of clinics, doctors, and/or nurses at company sites.

Manager, Occupational Health Services, Cumberland Farms, Salem, NH   1995–1998

Managed department, workers' compensation benefits, OSHA compliance issues, and health and wellness initiative for this multi-million dollar division of Sara Lee Industries with 1,000 employees.

- Decreased compensation costs by 66% over three years.

Occupational Health Nurse, Granite Industrial Constructors, Boston, MA   1994
Provided occupational health and case management services to this large construction company.

Previous experience working at several medical centers and a trauma center providing direct emergency nurse care as a lead trauma nurse and charge nurse.

EDUCATION & TRAINING

Associate's Degree, Nursing, University of New Hampshire, Durham, NH   1983

Select Ongoing Professional Development (attended numerous occupational health and case management continuing education programs):

- 28 hours toward Bachelor of Science, Nursing, University of New Hampshire and Manchester Community College
- Certification Programs for Occupational Health Nurse Specialist, Certified Case Manager, and Occupational Hearing Conservationist
- 50 hours of OSHA Training

PROFESSIONAL MEMBERSHIPS

- Member, American Association of Occupation Health Nurses (AAOHN)—10 years
- International Airline Occupational Health Nurse Association
- American Board of Occupational Health Nurses (ABOHN)

COMMUNITY SERVICE

Manchester Association for the Hearing Impaired (1995–Present)

Pharmaceutical Sales and Service

Catherine was a bright sales and service specialist who was growing in her career responsibilities and accomplishments and wanted to move into more advanced management positions.

Catherine Atree
1441 Meadowbrook Road #A12 • Novi, Michigan 48375
248.555.6101 • catherineatree@yahoo.com

EXPERTISE:
PHARMACEUTICAL SALES & SERVICE

High energy sales professional with experience developing product awareness through building business relationships. A proven performer with a track record of outperforming sales goals, delivering high levels of customer service, and achieving successful sales results built on key strengths of:

- **Consultative Sales Skills** — experience and education involving custom pharmaceutical and consumer products
- **New Business Development / Territory Management** — prospecting and building a territory; identifying and capitalizing on opportunities, knowledge of sales cycles
- **Customer Retention / Relationship Building** — excellent communication (listening, speaking) and interpersonal skills
- **Goal Setting** — experience in setting and achieving both independent and team-driven targets

PROFESSIONAL EXPERIENCE

QUALIFIED HEALTHCARE INCORPORATED; Grand Rapids, Michigan
Largest domestic contractual sales and marketing partner providing solutions to pharmaceutical & healthcare industries
Pharmaceutical Sales Specialist, 2003–current
Manage team-driven pharmaceutical sales responsibilities in southeast Michigan territory. Interact with physicians, nurses, physician assistants, and medical professionals to represent a premier product line. Interact with other sales reps to do strategic planning, problem solving, and collaborative thinking. Manage 35–40 weekly calls on physicians to increase market share in territory.

- Coordinated product launch for new acid reflux drug (AstraZeneca).
- Petitioned physicians to contact their HMOs and recommend formulary status; received formulary standing in January 2005.
- Member of market-leading Prilosec sales team.
- Consistently over sales quota; won highest call activity contest. Regional sales leader for hypertensive drug.

OFFICE MAX [2000–2003]; Columbus, Ohio
Multibillion-dollar global retailer of office supplies, furniture, and technology
Business Development Specialist, 2001–2003
Promoted to develop new business while maintaining current business in competitive southeastern and central Michigan territories; focused on small to medium-size companies. Managed complete sales cycle from initial contact, through presentation and consultation, to close of sale. Acted as liaison between sales center rep team and corporate office in Boston.

- Consistently maintained above-expected goal percentage in regional and corporate sales.
- Trained new reps in all areas of product presentation, solution selling, and customer service.

Sales Representative, 2000–98
Managed sales and account maintenance with companies. Independently maintained relationships with company personnel to increase visibility and credibility. Developed leads through cold calls; met with customers to identify needs.

- Developed new customers; maintained high goal percentages; recruited to higher position.

EDUCATION & TRAINING

UNIVERSITY OF MICHIGAN; Ann Arbor, Michigan
Bachelor of Science degree in Interdisciplinary Studies/Social Science with a focus in Health & Humanities; Minor: Psychology, 1998
Seminars: Leadership Sales, Presentations Skills

References available on request

Medical Equipment Sales

Erik is seeking to transition from pharmaceutical sales to sales of medical equipment. The resume demonstrates a track record of accomplishments and outstanding sales and account development capabilities.

ERIK CLAYTON

erikclayton@email.com

5555 W. 55th St.
New York, NY 10024

Residence (212) 555-1234
Mobile (212) 555-4321

MEDICAL EQUIPMENT SALES

Top-producing sales professional with five years progressive experience, including three years in pharmaceutical sales. Natural communicator with expertise in forging solid working relationships with professionals at all levels. Proven ability to identify and capitalize on market opportunities to drive revenues and capture market share. Strong closer who consistently exceeds targets in a consultative sales environment.

—Core Competencies—

Sales & Marketing • Business Development • Account Development & Retention
Client Relations • Team Building & Leadership • Training & Educating
Prospecting & Closing Negotiations • Consensus Building
Problem Solving • Presentations • Public Speaking

PROFESSIONAL EXPERIENCE

Sales Representative • 2003 to Present
INDUSTRY-LEADING PHARMACEUTICAL CO., New York, NY
Represent leading pharmaceutical company in consultative sales of select medications to MDs, Pharmacists, Pharmacy Technicians and Pharmacy Managers throughout Metro New York area.

- Call on 250 accounts monthly; consistently exceed company targets.
- Increased product market share from 25%-46%.
- Educated clients on launch of product, achieving 35% market share within three months.
- Selected by District Manager, out of 12 representatives, to anchor and train new hires.
- Placed #2 in nation for sales of main product out of 2,500 reps.
- Achieved #1 in district two consecutive years, 2005, 2006.
- Nominated for *Representative of the Year* award (2005).
- Nominated for company's most prestigious award (2004).

Account Executive • 2001 to 2003
COMPUTER MASTER, New York, NY
Gained valuable sales and client relations experience with $5 million computer sales company.

- Serviced existing accounts and developed new business, including several major corporations.
- Increased territory gross sales by 20%.

EDUCATION

B.S. in Communications
NEW YORK UNIVERSITY, New York, NY; 2001

Professional Development
Company Sponsored Sales Training; 2005
Team Train the Trainer (Company home office, one week); 2005

Computer Skills: Windows, Microsoft Word, PowerPoint

Melanie Moore

459 Birch Avenue * Austin, IL 60000
(555) 555-2809 * mmoore@yahoo.com

WHAT I CAN OFFER **CROSLEY** AS YOUR **NEWEST PHARMACEUTICAL SALES REPRESENTATIVE**

Meeting demanding customers' needs * "Selling" ideas to doctors * Communicating to get results under tough conditions * Using creative ideas to solve problems on my own

RECENT WORK HISTORY WITH EXAMPLES OF PROBLEMS SOLVED

Investigator *promoted from six eligibles to* **Hospital Liaison;** *promoted to* Training Supervisor *and* Hiring Manager, Illinois Department of Protective and Regulatory Service, Austin, IL 00–Present

CAPABILITY: Well informed, senior, busy judges and **doctors usually approve my recommendations quickly because I've built their trust** without the benefit of formal training.

CAPABILITY: Regularly **win the day** with my ideas, even **after** penetrating **cross-examination** by some of the best attorneys in the business.

CAPABILITY: Persuaded senior decision makers to help us deliver better quality, reduce turnover, and make our employees more effective. Our **clients were served even better.**

CAPABILITY: My new training program lowers **costs, despite our diverse workforce. Team members** now **master training** that once intimidated them.

Child Specialist, State of Missouri, Division of Family Services, Kansas City, MO   99–00

CAPABILITY: Convinced a decision maker that **my plan would help his patient stay with a demanding treatment protocol.** Patient and her unborn child protected.

Account Manager, Dunhill Staffing, Austin, IL   98–99
Dunhill provided temporary clerical and light industrial workers to local employers.

CAPABILITY: Boosted our client's productivity and made us more productive at the same time. **Complaints fell to zero** and stayed there.

EDUCATION

B.S., University of Illinois, Austin,   97
Earned this degree while working up to 20 hours a week. GPA: 3.2.

COMPUTER SKILLS

Expert in Word and Excel; proficient in proprietary customer information software suite and Outlook; familiar with Internet search protocols

Biochemistry Researcher

Young professional making first job change with a powerful and well-focused resume.

SOPHIA L. MEYERS

15993 MAYFAIR COURT
WEST BLOOMFIELD, MI

(248) 555-8520
sophialmeyers@aol.com

Talented young professional with skills and training in:
NEUROBIOLOGY AND BIOCHEMISTRY RESEARCH

Highly-accomplished, quick learner with an impressive **hands-on knowledge base** encompassing the entire spectrum of **neurobiological research**, with special expertise in Organic, Inorganic, Analytical, Solutions, Instrumental Analysis, and Physical Chemistry. Regarded by peers and mentors as an overachiever who is **committed to excellence in this field**, as demonstrated by **outstanding academic achievement**. Demonstrate thorough and detailed research capabilities. *Experience and academic preparation include:*

- Molecular Theory
- Quantum Mechanical Modeling
- Mathematical Modeling
- Particle Location and Density
- DNA Analysis and Separation

- Reagent Preparations
- EDTA Titration Process
- Electron Neutron Diffraction
- Electrophoretic Techniques
- Thermodynamic Principles

- Ethology
- Blood Typing
- Diffusion Principles
- X-Ray Diffraction
- GCMS/MS

EDUCATION

Bachelor of Science in Biology and Biochemistry
Michigan State University, East Lansing, MI ~ Graduated with the Highest Honors ~ 2006

RELEVANT EXPERIENCE & EMPLOYMENT

Scheduling Coordinator ~ Oakland Radiology Consultants, Oak Park, MI ~ 5/2006 to present
Neuroscience Intern ~ Michigan State University, East Lansing, MI ~ 8/2005 to 5/2006
Medication Care Manager ~ Sunrise Assisted Living, East Lansing, MI ~ 2/2003 to 7/2005

Clinical Trials: Administered a significant drug trial and established a dosage response curve for the identification of invertebrate behavior using neuromodulators.

Medication Management: Completed state requirements training to confidently, legally, and safely administer patient medication and effectively document their immediate reaction. Managed a staff of 10, ordered and controlled the administration of all narcotics.

Ethology: Performed pet care behavioral science medical procedures, including the administration of both local and general anesthesia, catheters, IV, and injectables. Confidently handle x-rays and assess behavior modifications due to hormones, neuroreceptors, and neurotransmitters.

Quality Assurance and Statistical Analysis: Delivered 3+ years in-depth reagent preparation and reaction writing capstone project culminating in and solidifying expertise in testing chemicals to determine molarity of any solution.

Spectroscopy: Trained in Chemical Detection Methods including UV detection, chromotrography, and polarity, as well as finding unknown chemicals by running samples using search criteria.

Gamete Shedding/In Vitro Fertilization: Oversaw a developmental biology project devoted to the in vitro fertilization of insects, rats, and invertebrates, whereby deliberate injection led to gamete shedding, fertilization of eggs in petri, and ultimately the reintroduction of eggs into animals.

PRESENTATIONS & CONFERENCES

Presented Topic: "Octopomine vs. Serotonin as a Neuromodulator and Neurotransmitter" Society for Neuroscience National Conference - 2005 and West Virginia Academy of Science - 2006

MEMBERSHIPS, CERTIFICATIONS & AFFILIATIONS

Society of Neuroscience ~ American Chemical Society for Analytical Inorganic and Organic Chemistry
Sigma Phi Epsilon Fraternity ~ National Honor Society ~ MENSA ~*Who's Who* Listed

153

Registered Nurse

Clean layout, plenty of white space, easy on the eyes. The serif fonts don't detract here (they show a caring professional). The original had all the serif headings in blue and the employer endorsement near the top of the page. Eye-appealing and works well.

Laraine Brook Elliott, RN, BSN

nurse_elliott@yahoo.com

1234 Rexwood Drive ◆ Columbus, Ohio 43230 ◆ 614.555.0000

Registered Nurse

Compassionate nursing professional qualified by a **Bachelor of Science in Nursing**, RN Licensure and numerous certifications including ACLS, BLS and CNC. Provide high quality nursing care and unsurpassed patient service.

- Competent in **infectious disease containment** with proper universal precautions for tuberculosis; hepatitis A, B and C; VRE; MRSA; West Nile; meningitis, necrotizing infections and others
- **Procedure expertise**—intubation/extubation, ventrulostomies, chest tube placement, lumbar punctures, thorocentises, paracentesis, tracheostomy exchanges, central line insertions, swan guiding, arterial line insertions, peritoneal dialysis, continuing hemodialysis
- Excellent **critical thinking skills** utilized throughout career on a daily basis

" … functions effectively in an emergency situation, including Code Blue procedures … independent worker who needs little supervision … can be counted on to complete assignments … thoughtful and courteous … is an important contributor to the morale and success of the MICU team …" ~ Excerpts from performance evaluations

Education & Licensure

MT. CARMEL COLLEGE OF NURSING, Columbus, Ohio (May 2005)
Bachelor of Science in Nursing

Licensure & Certification
- RN License – State of Ohio, License #1234567
- Advanced Cardiac Life Support (ACLS)
- Continuous Renal Replacement Therapy (CRRT)
- Code Nurse Coordinator (CNC)
- Basic Life Certified (BLS)
- Disaster Relief Certificated with the American Red Cross

Related Professional Experience

BSN, Registered Nurse
THE OHIO STATE UNIVERSITY MEDICAL CENTER, Medical Intensive Care Unit, Columbus, Ohio (July 2005–present)
Provide superior care for patients with critical and/or life-threatening illnesses/injuries in a 25-bed intensive care unit.
- Serve as Code Nurse Coordinator (CNC) for hospital and assist with codes on my unit patients as well as others.
- Perform numerous procedures ranging from intubation/extubation to central and arterial line insertions while maintaining sterile environment and managing/maintaining lines.
- Issue medications, perform lab draws, specimen cultures, wound care and maintain wound vacs.
- Withdraw life support providing comforting care for patients and comfort and counsel for grieving families.
- Perform post-morgue care and transport bodies to morgue.

Nurse Resident
THE OHIO STATE UNIVERSITY MEDICAL CENTER, Nurse Residency Program, Columbus, Ohio (August 2005–August 2006)
Year resident involved in research of new graduates analyzing progression the first year out of nursing school with a guided program compared to new graduates without the program.
- Gave presentations on legal issues and numerous issues encountered during first year as an RN with strong focus on professionalism and dealing effectively with other members of medical team.

Laraine Brook Elliott, BSN, RN
Page 2

Related Experience (cont'd)

Nurse Intern
THE OHIO STATE UNIVERSITY MEDICAL CENTER, Nurse Internship, Columbus, Ohio (July–September 2005)
Rotated throughout surgical intensive care, medical intensive care and emergency room care units to gain insight and experience in all areas of operation and patient care

Patient Care Assistant (PCA)
MT. CARMEL MEDICAL CENTER, Columbus, Ohio (May 2004–May 2005)
Provided prescribed medical treatment and personal care services to ill, injured, convalescent and handicapped persons maintaining high standard of excellence throughout department
- Performed a variety of care including taking vitals, applying compresses and ice bags, administering medications and wound care.
- Cared for patients with chest tubes, central venous catheters, peripheral inserted central catheters, dialysis AV shunts and ventilators
- Observed patients and reported adverse reactions to medication or treatment to medical staff.
- Assembled and used equipment such as catheters, tracheotomy tubes, oxygen suppliers and SCDs with TED hose.
- Examined and passed food trays for prescribed diets.
- Inventoried and requisitioned supplies.

Dental Assistant
RACINE DENTAL CLINIC, Racine, Ohio (August 1998–August 2001)
Rotated throughout clinic providing assistance in various areas as needed.
- Performed central sterilization and processed dental impressions.
- Reviewed patient history and prepared patients for procedures.
- Scheduled appointments and assisted with clerical support functions.

Community Involvement / Activities

- Numerous hours of community service work with Mt. Carmel College of Nursing in various settings including Columbus Public Schools
- Mt. Carmel College of Nursing – Member of softball team (two years) and volleyball team (one year)
- Volunteer at Faith Mission – Prepared and served meals at homeless shelter
- American Red Cross Volunteer – Volunteer for disaster relief gathering supplies and updating medications
- Mission Trip to Mexico – Helped set up a clinic for the relief and medical care of people in Nuevo Progresso

Trauma Coordinator

Clean layout, easily readable subject headings, and well focused.

FIONA PATTERSON

Address	Phone
City, State Zip	Email Address

CAREER TARGET: TRAUMA COORDINATOR

Experience in Coordinating and Executing Outreach Programs to Meet Preventive Education Goals; Strong Background in Training, Mentoring, and Supporting Employees; Effective Communicator, Fluent in Spanish

Dedicated, resourceful health care professional with previous success in planning and implementing programs that emphasize preventive measures for injuries and illnesses. In-depth knowledge of principles, methods, and procedures of trauma and medical care. Strong advocate of health care organization's role as teacher within society. Knowledge and skill areas include:

Program Development & Implementation • Training Development & Delivery • Public Speaking & Presentations
Data Analysis & Evaluation • Community Outreach Initiatives • Trauma System Procedure Standardization
Emergency Medical Services Processes • Local, State, and Federal Regulations • Quality Assurance

Education & Credentials

Bachelor of Science in Nursing, In Progress: Lubbock Christian University, Lubbock, TX / Expected
Associates Degree in Science: Eastern New Mexico University, Roswell, NM

Certifications: ACLS, BLS, PALS, TNCC, ENPC
Affiliations: Member, Emergency Nurse Association
Attended National ENA Convention for the past 3 years
Currently serve as Injury Prevention Chairperson for local and state chapters

PROFESSIONAL EXPERIENCE

COVENANT MEDICAL CENTER – Lubbock, TX   2001 – Present

Staff Registered Nurse

In charge of implementing instructional outreach program. In addition to nursing responsibilities within 43-bed Emergency Room (over 40 nurses at any given time), perform Relief Charge Nurse duties at least once per week. Match patients with nurses at various levels and direct ambulances to different stations. As senior nurse within unit, serve as official mentor for organization, trainer for new graduates, and resolution specialist to address conflicts between staff members. Sat on Nurse Staff Council for the Emergency Department over the past 2 years, functioning as liaison between nurses and management.
Challenges: Implementing strategies for upholding high level of morale within under-staffed, stressful situations while maintaining optimal patient care.

KEY CONTRIBUTIONS & ACHIEVEMENTS:

❑ **Coordinated successful, well-received Injury Prevention Outreach Program. Landed Academy and Master** Locks as sponsors for events, oversaw Health Fairs to address various topics/issues, and worked with local fire departments (spanning from Ransom Canyon to Levelland) to disseminate information regarding fireworks safety measures.

❑ **Served as key member of Student Advocacy Subcommittee, ensuring proper training for high school, nursing, and** EMT students. Took on educator role with students circulating through ER, contributing to improved capabilities.

❑ **Assisted unit in ensuring fulfillment of standards for JCAHO, as well as improving Quality Assurance and Safety** objectives. Maintained and improved morale through continual communications and team building exercises.

❑ **Earned "Excellent" ratings on performance evaluations and received acknowledgment from multiple patients for** high level of care and personal attention. Leveraged bilingual background to serve Spanish-speaking population.

** Prior position as Staff Registered Nurse with the Eastern New Mexico Medical Center, Roswell, NM, 1997–2001. Performed various nursing duties, including those revolving around Emergency Room. Participated in extreme trauma cases.

Hospital Management Professional

Clean layout, generic target job title followed by three key strengths relevant to job and a core competency section

Dianne Martino

555 Gayle Avenue • Los Angeles, California 90049
Residence (310) 555-1234 • Mobile (310) 555-5678 • DianneMartino@email.com

HOSPITALITY / HOTEL MANAGEMENT
Strengths in Operations / Sales / Marketing

Top-flight hospitality management professional with 10+ years progressive experience and a track record of delivering measurable revenue and profit contributions. Team building and leadership strengths with proven ability to hire, train, and motivate top performing teams. "Big-picture" thinker, highly organized, with the ability to multitask in a fast-paced environment and respond quickly and effectively to problems. Learns quickly and thrives on challenges.

—Core Competencies—
Customer Service / Client Relations / Team Building / Hiring, Training, & Motivating
Operations Management / Marketing / Advertising / Time & Task Management / Policy & Procedures
Revenue Optimization / Cost Containment / Productivity Enhancement / Problem Solving

PROFESSIONAL EXPERIENCE

STAR CITY RESTAURANT, Los Angeles, CA
Achieved fast-track promotion to positions of increasing responsibility at world-renowned establishment.

Assistant General Manager—Hollywood (2004–Present)
Oversee day-to-day food and beverage operations of $5+ million fine-dining establishment that averages 250 covers daily. Train, manage, and mentor cross-functional team of 60+, ensuring highest standard of customer service and brand integrity. Supervise food & beverage inventories, manage costs and maximize profitability, monitor safe handling best practices & procedures; prepare sales and labor forecasts. P&L accountability. Payroll responsibility. Accounting & POS support.

- Orchestrated scheduling initiative that minimized overtime, captured 10% increase in productivity, and reduced payroll by over 10%.
- Hired, trained, and supervised cross-functional front- and back-of-the-house staff of 60 with minimum turnover; achieved impact ratio over 100%.
- Generated mystery shopper score of 90+% annually.
- Slashed food cost by over $150,000 annually.
- Created marketing strategies that increased top line sales.
- Consistently ensured excellent service within critical time frame for 300+ pre-theater patrons as required.
- Organized liquor perpetual inventory and streamlined daily procedures, capturing cost reduction of 2%.

157

Administrative Manager—Hollywood (2002–2004)
Promoted after nine months to initiate and manage administrative affairs for new location including daily cash and credit reconciliations, employee file maintenance, accounts payable, office administration, benefits administration, new hire processing, etc.
- Achieved 95% or better on all audits
- Appointed as corporate administrative trainer; trained six managers during tenure.
- Authored Positouch Procedural Guide for use at all locations.
- Designed employee file initiative that was adopted for use companywide.
- Implemented side work, floor plan, and scheduling charts to organize restaurant opening.
- Assumed responsibility for OSHA and Workers' Comp that resulted in perfect scores on corporate audits.

Bartender—Santa Monica (2000–2001)
Hostess—Santa Monica (2000)

PROFESSIONAL EXPERIENCE, continued
CARLA'S DINNER HOUSE, Los Angeles, CA • 1996–2000
Shift Supervisor / Bartender / Server
Advanced to shift supervisor with responsibility for opening/closing, scheduling staff, maintaining inventory, purchasing, reconciling cash drawer, etc., for busy Upper East Side restaurant.
- Gained valuable experience in all aspects of restaurant operations.
- Developed "spotter" system to eliminate theft that has been implemented by other establishments throughout the area.
- Increased sales through "door to door" advertising program.

Additional Experience—*Worked Part-time as Server/Hostess at various establishments concurrent with University studies*

EDUCATION
UNIVERSITY OF CALIFORNIA, Los Angeles, CA
BA in Humanities
Professional Development / Certifications
Stellar Service Training (Phoenix, 2004)
Servsafe, FMP (Food Management Professionals) Certified Trainer

ADDITIONAL INFORMATION

Professional Affiliations—Member, NAWBO (National Association of Women's Business Owners)

Computer Skills—(PC and Macintosh), Word, Excel, Databases, POS Systems (Positouch, Squirrel, Micros), Restaurant Magic

Foreign Language Skills—Conversational Spanish in the Workplace

Teacher

Normally I'm against warm and fuzzy fonts like this, but for this teacher, they work. Note how clean and professional the rest of the layout is.

1234 Dove Lake Road
Athens, Ohio 45701
740.555.3996
sjkramer@hotmail.com

Shannon J. Kramer
Elementary School Teacher

Excerpts from Letters of Recommendation

"...her enthusiasm for teaching, love for children, and ability to plan creative and effective lessons will be definite assets ..."

~ Dr. Diane J. DePeal
Ohio University Professor and
Mentor, Chauncey Partnership

"...extremely organized ...very helpful with room set-up ...eager to learn as much as possible ... seeks resources to help her accomplish her goal ... great knowledge on the computer–uses it as a tool to support classroom management ... excellent rapport with students, their families ... communicates well with other teachers ... aware of what it takes to be the best teacher she can be!"

~ Amy Martin
Cooperating Teacher
Barrington Elementary School

Summary of Qualifications

- Self-directed, resourceful and enthusiastic teaching professional with a genuine interest in fostering students' cognitive and social growth

- Skilled in the design of developmentally-appropriate, enriching, innovative and hands-on activities and lessons to meet social and emotional needs of students as well as state standards

- Combine strong passion for literacy, motivation and inspiration to create a fun and challenging learning environment with strong connections to community

- Active team member effectively communicating and collaborating with all levels of staff to ensure optimum learning environment for students

Education & Certification

OHIO UNIVERSITY, Athens, Ohio (November 1999)
Bachelor of Science in Elementary Education • Reading Endorsement

Certification
State of Ohio Five-Year Professional License (1-8) with K-12 Reading Endorsement (Effective June 2007)

Related Teaching Experience

First and Second Grade Multi-Age Teacher
HIGHLAND PARK ELEMENTARY SCHOOL, Grove City, Ohio (August 2000–June 2002)
- Integrated first and second grade curriculum while establishing an independent, self-directed multi-age classroom. Conducted Developmental Reading Assessments (DRAs) as well as other routine assessments setting individual student performance goals based on results. Successfully implemented new science curriculum. Developed home/school relationships with communication through weekly newsletters and grading period conferences. Utilized a variety of teaching methods including Guided Imagery, Process Drama and hands-on sensory activities to facilitate learning process.

Long Term Substitute/First Grade Classroom
BARRINGTON ELEMENTARY SCHOOL, Upper Arlington, Ohio (February–June 2000)
- Developed and implemented weekly lesson plans and units in absence of regular classroom teacher. Created and fostered a child-centered, literacy rich environment. Established individual student goals across curriculum. Scheduled daily parent involvement and held parent/teacher conferences.

159

1234 Dove Lake Road
Athens, Ohio 45701
740.555.3996
sjkramer@hotmail.com

Shannon J. Kramer
Elementary School Teacher

Page 2

Related Teaching Experience (cont'd)

Student Teacher
BARRINGTON ELEMENTARY SCHOOL, Upper Arlington, Ohio (Fall 1999)

- Assumed full teaching responsibility in first grade classroom developing, planning and implementing weekly lesson plans and units. Assisted cooperating teacher with assessments. Completed DRA and Everyday Math training; integrated Everyday Mathematics into lesson plans. Attended staff meetings, parent information night and parent/teacher conferences.

Ohio University Literacy Partnership (400 hours)
CHAUNCEY ELEMENTARY SCHOOL, Chauncey, Ohio (September 1998–June 1999)

- Collaborated with both 2nd and 6th grade teachers and students in challenging school demographic of 30% IEP and 25% identified students. Taught individual small group and whole class assignments. Created and taught lessons using rich text aligned with thematic units. Used various reading assessments to set reading goals, develop lessons with appropriate reading strategies to support students' literacy growth and track progress throughout the year.

Technology Skills

Competent in both Microsoft Windows and Macintosh OS X operating systems and the following software packages:

- Microsoft Word and Powerpoint
- WordPerfect
- AutoCAD
- Scholastic Reading Inventory
- Power Media Plus
- Chalkwaves
- Internet and e-mail packages
- Working knowledge of Quicken

Current Professional Experience

Designer/Sales Associate
KITCHEN CREATIONS & RENOVATIONS, Athens, Ohio (January 2007–present)

- Coordinate sales and manage large- and small-scale projects from initial design through final install. Projects range from kitchen remodels to custom cabinetry layouts.

Computer Support Technician

Joshua is a recent graduate of a computer help desk/computer support technician program, and his resume demonstrates commitment to excellence, team spirit, and customer focus—all qualities needed in his new line of work.

Joshua Michael Peterson

4 Borderland Court • Montclair, NJ 12345 • tel: 555-555-5555 • petersonjm22@aol.com

OBJECTIVE: HELP DESK / COMPUTER SUPPORT TECHNICIAN

PROFILE
✓ **Recent computer center graduate with proven technical abilities.**
✓ Demonstrated track record of achieving goals in a team environment.
✓ Highly motivated and dependable. Proven skills in problem solving, customer relationship management, and organization.

EDUCATION

The Computer Learning Center, **Skillman, NJ**   **2005 – 2006**

Computer Coursework completed in:

✓ **Networking Essentials**	✓ Beginning Windows NT
✓ A+ Certification	✓ Administering Windows NT
✓ Intermediate Word 2003	✓ Windows NT Core Technologies
✓ Beginning Word 2003	✓ Windows NT Support by Enterprise
✓ Beginning Access 2003	✓ Beginning Business on the Internet
✓ TCP/IP Protocol	✓ Beginning FrontPage 2003

Montclair University, **Montclair, NJ**   **2003 – 2004**

General first-year courses in Bachelor's Degree program (24 credits).

EMPLOYMENT

A Cut Above, **Montclair, NJ**   **2002 – 2006**

Receptionist / Cashier
- Successfully handled front desk and three incoming telephone lines for busy, upscale hair salon. Greeted and logged in steady stream of customers, coordinating appointments with hairdresser availability.
- Developed cooperative, team-oriented working relationships with owners and co-workers in this 12-station salon.
- Managed customer problems and complaints with tact and attention to prompt customer service. Received team and customer service awards.
- Experience gained in opening and closing procedures, cash register receipts, counter sales, light bookkeeping, and telephone follow-up.

Pro Soccer Camp, **Princeton, NJ**   **Summers 1999 – 2002**

Trainer / Coach
- Assisted Women's Soccer Coach in 200-participant soccer camp. Asked to return as trainer for 3 seasons. Worked with individuals, as well as teams, to improve their attitude and resulting soccer performance.

ACTIVITIES

Jersey Waves **Soccer Semi-Pro Team**   **1999 – 2003**

✓ **Team consistently ranked in top 10 semi-pro teams in the nation.**

Washington Crossing High School Soccer Team   **1998 – 2001**

✓ Captain of team that won State Soccer Title in 2000
✓ Recognized as one of the top two mid-fielders in the state in 2001

Jackson A. Lewis

1532 W. 35th Terrace, Dallas, Texas 75032 Phone: 276-555-7225 Email: jacklew@sbc.global.net

SOFTWARE DEVELOPMENT / PROJECT MANAGEMENT

Expertise

Software Development Life Cycle, Process Automation, Vendor Management, Software Interfacing
Systems and Hardware Analysis, Maintenance, Upgrade, Customization, & Modification
Client & Vendor Presentations / Employee Recruiting / Employee Mentor and Trainer, Improved Efficiency

Operating Systems

UNIX, Solaris, IBM AIX, HP-UX, DOS, Windows 95/98/NT/2003/XP

Languages

Java (JSP, Servlets, Applets, EJB, J2EE), JavaScript,
Visual Basic, HTML, XML, C/C++, COBOL, PL/SQL

Databases

Oracle, SQL, JDBC, ODBC, Microsoft Access

Software/Programs

Weblogic Application Server, Websphere Studio Application Developer, Eclipse, Forte for Java
(Sun One), NetBeans, Visual Age for Java, MQ Series, TOPLink, CVS, RCS, Visual Source Safe,
Dreamweaver, Microsoft Project, Word, Excel, Outlook, PowerPoint, FrontPage

SUMMARY OF EXPERIENCE

SBC Corporation, Dallas, Texas
Software Engineer IV, April 2003 – Current
Software Engineer III, October 2001 – April 2003
Software Engineer II, July 2000 – October 2001

*Integrated communications provider serving 85 million customers,
and employing a workforce of 90,000 worldwide.*

- **Lead Analyst** for **multiple projects** and **subprojects** (with Regional, National, and International clients and vendors), performing supervisory functions, including task assignment, quality assessment, scheduling, and employee evaluation.
- Vendor development and management, including **Cingular Wireless, Telcordia,** and **RLG Systems.**
- Designed and developed Web-based production job scheduling system with multi-threaded server component, **automating scheduling process.**
- Managed Customer Records Database project, interfacing with vendor software, affecting **1 Million+** SBC customers and **700** internal personnel.
- **Improved** operational **efficiency** of Sierra Online Scheduling, **reducing personnel by 50%.**
- **2004 SBC Award of Distinction.**
- **Multiple Monthly SBC Awards of Distinction,** including May 2006, December 2005, March 2005, April 2004, August 2003, November 2002, July 2001, and September 2000.
- Developed **configuration management process** allowing multiple team members to access system without interference to other users.
- Created and presented seminar for EDP (Enterprise Development Project) process to client and software team. Implemented **customization or updating processes** to meet team needs.
- **Trained** over **40 employees** in use of systems and processes.
- **Mentored 20 employees** in technical and professional business aptitude, including associates in Sales and Marketing Systems, Operational Systems Support, and Resolution Support Services departments.

- Experienced in managing hardware-related projects.
- Maintain existing systems, upgrade existing hardware and operating systems, establish new hardware, and provide on-call support.

BPC, Ft. Worth, Texas
Programmer/Analyst, May 1998 – July 2000

*Medical-based applications company marketing software to
healthcare industry, including hospitals, laboratories, pharmacies, and doctors.*

- 24/7 on-call crisis management for all clients accessing Patient Management Systems.
- Enhanced Patient Management software with additional functionalities, utilizing COBOL, and Discern Explorer.
- Modified Patient Management software to correct flaws/errors.
- Planned and executed all phases of project management, including design, coding, testing, and implementation.
- Analyzed and resolved client software issues.
- Educated clients during troubleshooting process in resolution of software issues, while preparing them to independently repair similar issues in the future.
- Assisted management team in selection of new associates, including interview process.
- Lead Developer for Patient Management Team, guiding other developers and software specialists.

CIVIC CONTRIBUTIONS

Habitat for Humanity, May 2006

Grande Point Homeowners Association, Vice President 2004, Member 2002 – Present

EDUCATION & PROFESSIONAL DEVELOPMENT

Baylor University, Waco, Texas

B.S. Business Administration – Computer and Office Information Systems, May 1998

SBC Corporation, Dallas, Texas

"Advanced Project Management" April 2004
"Project Management Principles and Practices" May 2003
"Negotiations" August 2002
"Process Analysis and Maturity" January 2002
"Advanced C++" December 2001
"C++" November 2001
"Conflict Prevention and Resolution" October 2001
"Presentation Skills" March 2001
"Managing Basic Projects (Project Management)" February 2001
"Seven Habits of Highly Effective People" January 2001
"Java Workshop" December 2000
"Visual Basic" December 2000
"UNIX: Advanced Shell Programming" November 2000
"UNIX: Shell Programming" November 2000
"Oracle for Application Developers" September 2000

Network Administrator

David wants to transition his impressive and broad experience from technical consulting with the military to commercial endeavors in the corporate sector.

DAVID J. WAGNER, MCP

217 MAGNOLIA COURT, OAKLAND, NJ 07436
(201) 405-5555 HOME • (201) 405-8888 MOBILE • DJWAGNER@CSN.COM

Networks / Systems
Hardware Configuration:
Windows, UNIX, Cisco
Software Configuration
Systems Integration
Systems Configuration
Router Configuration
Intrusion Detection Systems
Frame Relay Networking
Network Planning
Network Firewalls
Peer-to-peer Networks
Ethernet Networks
Telephony & Fiber Optics
Internet Information Server
Switches & Hubs
ISDN/T1 Lines

Media & Peripherals
Voice & Data
TCP/IP

Project Management
Technology Consulting
Technology Management
Networking Infrastructures
Systems Implementation
Virtual Team Leadership
Relationship Management
Advanced Communications
Telecommunications
Security Analysis
Security Development
Applications Development
Evaluation & Testing
Troubleshooting
Resource Utilization
Inventory Management
Technology Training
End-User Training
Knowledge Transfer
Executive Presentations
Strategic Planning
Project Team Development
Team Building
Client Relations
Quality Assurance
Problem Solving

TEAM LEADER • PROJECT MANAGER • DEPARTMENT MANAGER
Network Administration • Systems Security Technology

✓ **Microsoft Certified Professional. A+ Certification.**
Accomplished technology consultant and project manager adept in desktop and network security / systems architecture planning, design, installation, configuration, maintenance, and smooth project delivery.

✓ Accustomed to supporting multi-user networks, as well as leading high-performance technology and telecommunications solutions. Successfully employ technology to improve operations efficiency, reduce costs, and meet reliability and security goals and deadlines.

✓ Proven track record in team leadership and training, supplying a balanced mix of analytical, management, coaching, and technical skills.

PROFESSIONAL EXPERIENCE

Senior Computer Scientist   2003 – present
S5 Systems Group (US Army technology consulting firm), Stockton, NJ

Technical Lead – Army Computer Systems Office (2004 – present)
Focus: Rollout of Army Partnership Tool Suite (APTS) system, implementing new functionality into live networks and systems.

- Lead Consultant and liaison (chosen by government project manager) in 7-member cross-functional team deploying integrated networks, systems, and technologies. Introduced real-time, peer-to-peer collaboration via new application, bringing far-flung team together and eliminating disconnects.
- Key player in development, testing, and implementation process, including custom tool suite development, to fit client needs. Integrate configuration, and supply installation support for pioneering technology collaboration.

Lead Network Engineer
Information Systems Engineering Office (2003 – 2004)
Focus: $24 million Communications Update & Planning System (CUPS). Evaluated, selected, and integrated advanced communications and networking products for the Communications Collaboration Team.

- Key role (network engineer/administrator/technician) leading 6-member team. Honed end-to-end project management and presentation skills.
- Pioneered first-ever use of security hardware/software, including intrusion detection systems (IDS), Cisco routers, and network management apps.
- Designed robust, mobile communications (and upgrades) to facilitate efficient network convergence and bandwidth utilization. Developed network management tools for real-time monitoring and troubleshooting.
- Field-tested flying local area network (FLAN), utilizing wireless Ethernet technology, which interconnected en route aircraft to ground-based units.
- Proposed equipment purchasing savings of $2.5 – $6 million through services analysis, reducing duplication of physical space and equipment.
- Introduced new traffic routing method (tech) utilizing a defense satellite channel for communications, enabling netmetting in worldwide locations.

continued

DAVID J. WAGNER, MCP
(201) 405-5555 Home • djwagner@csn.com

Page 2

HARDWARE:
Sun Microsystems
IBM PCs & compatibles
SCSI & IDE Hard Drives
Cisco Routers & Switches
3COM Switches & Hubs
Ascend Pipeline Series
Netgear Hubs
RAID Arrays (Sun)
Ethernet NICs
Printers, Scanners
CD-ROMs, Modems
CD-R & CD-RW Drives
Sound Cards, TV Cards
Tape Drives

Software (UNIX):
Solaris, Linux
HP UNIX, SCO UNIX
Cisco Works Essentials
BIND 4 & 9 (DNS)
X-Windows, Open Windows
SSH, Lynx, Pine, ELM
sh, csh, bash
ftp servers & clients
Eagle Raptor Firewall
Apache, Sendmail, IRC

Software (PC):
Windows, DOS
Novell Netware
MS Office, MS Outlook
WordPerfect, FrontPage
IRC, IE, Netscape
FTP Servers & Clients
Norton, Cisco
HyperTerminal, Kermit
HP Openview
Cisco Works Essentials
Carbon Copy
Seagate Backup Exec.
SCO Xvision

Software (Cisco IOS):
Internetworking OS
Network Address Trans.
Access Lists
Context Based Access
Intrusion Detection
Remote Syslog Logging
Routing Protocols

Signal Officer   1994 – present
113th Signal Battalion, NJ Army NG, Stockton, NJ

- Platoon Leader – Mobile Subscriber Equipment Company. Lead, develop, and motivate 40 soldiers. Oversee inventory management of $4.8 million in vehicles, weaponry, security, and communications equipment.
- Mission – establish mobile subscriber equipment network (mobile phone network for combat soldiers in the field).

Computer Scientist   2001 – 2003
Computer Development Services, Inc., Oakland, NJ

- Lead technical consultant – Computer Services Security Branch (U.S. Army) for setup, testing, and evaluation of networks/systems security technologies. Established configuration, installation procedures, and network topologies for all support tasks. Tech reports used as management measurement tool.
- Designed secure test bed network/domain on UNIX, Windows, and Cisco IOS providing e-mail, DNS, firewalls, routing, file serving, and accounting.
- Selected to serve as test bed manager for dry run and official testing, personally resolving testing challenges and intrusion issues.

Systems Administrator   2000 – 2001
Technical Solutions & Services Corporation, Oakland, NJ

- Installation, configuration, and troubleshooting software (UNIX, Linux, Windows, Solaris) on HP workstations, Toshiba laptops, and servers (Compaq, Diversified, HP, Sun). Prepared backups on multiple platforms and provided 24/7 technical support to data warehousing center.
- Oversaw corporate telecomm system, LAN physical extension, and technical purchasing (POs, quoting, authorizations, and receiving).

Technology Consultant   1999 – 2000
Campbell & Cohen (legal firm), Trenton, NJ

- Systems and network troubleshooting (Windows & Novell Netware) at multiple locations. Peer-to-peer training. Proposed LAN and equipment recommendations to stay ahead of the curve, which were implemented.

Systems Instructor / Client Support   1998 – 1999
Healthcare Information Group, Oakland, NJ

EDUCATION & CERTIFICATIONS

MS, Telecommunications Management, Rutgers University – in progress
BS, Accounting, The College of New Jersey, Ewing, NJ – 1998

Microsoft Certified Professional – Windows NT, Network Essentials
A+ Certification – Computer and Network Repair
Cisco Switching 2.0 & Routing 2.0 – towards CCNP in progress
Building Scalable Cisco Networks (BSCN) course – in-house training

PROFESSIONAL ASSOCIATION

Institute of Electrical & Electronics Engineers (IEEE)

Computer and IT

165

Software Designer

Regina updated her resume after being off from work for quite some time due to surgeries after an accident. She wanted an updated resume just in case (after being away from work for over a year) the company decided to downsize her.

Regina Pierce

1974 Paramount Way
Toledo, OH 43623
Phone: 419.555.5555
Email: reginapierce@msn.com

* SOFTWARE DESIGN ENGINEER *
DELIVERING SOFTWARE TO REDUCE COSTS AND INCREASE EFFICIENCIES

Detail-oriented, highly motivated SYSTEMS SOFTWARE CONSULTANT with 8+ years of successful experience in design-ing, developing, and implementing software solutions to support strategic business objectives. Keen **problem-solving skills** evidenced by the implementation of innovative technologies across dissimilar architectures and multiple platforms to provide quality product functionality. An **effective communicator** who can easily interface with end-users, technical teams, and professionals on all levels.

Technology Expertise Includes:

- Astute strategic understanding of mainframe, client/server, and Internet environments.
- Experience in Object-Oriented design and development.
- Empirical knowledge of all system development life cycle phases and a structured approach to project management. Accurately develop end-user documentation.
- Proven ability to acquire knowledge rapidly and to apply new technologies for process improvement.
- Functional knowledge of the finance, billing, and operations areas of **Customer Information Systems.**

KEY PROJECT MANAGEMENT & LEADERSHIP

ERNST & YOUNG – * LEAD TECHNICAL ANALYST *
Customer Information System for Southeastern Utility Company

Challenge: To identify and resolve critical errors of newly developed software in the Primary Test region before migrating online and batch programs to Regression Testing region.

Action: Extensively used problem-solving skills while interacting with eight-member team, Software Engineers, Data Con-version, project manager, and end-users to understand client requirements. Executed and analyzed test suites resulting in quality assessments that verified product require-ments and high quality code.

Result: Delivered high quality software that exceeded client expectations and was specifically requested to stay on as Technical Analyst of the Regression Test Team, supporting both test teams through first- site implementation.

ERNST & YOUNG – * CUSTOM DEVELOPMENT LEAD / SUPERVISOR*
Customization of Client / Server Customer Information System

Challenge: To resolve technical issues of the Open Client architecture that were slowing progress on the development of a $1.8M CIS system at a Canadian utility company. To develop a detailed design of Powerbuilder software modifica-tions in the Operations area.

Action: (1) Supervised two developers in identifying the cause of the Open Client issues and in the completion of software modifications to resolve those issues.
(2) Developed detailed design of Powerbuilder software modifications to increase functionality and efficiency.

Result: My team successfully identified and resolved the Open Client issues ahead of schedule, streamlining the rest of the project back to schedule.

COMPUTER TECHNOLOGIES

Languages: SQL, SQL*Plus, PL/SQL, Transact SQL, C, Java, HTML, COBOL, Pascal, Scheme ■ **Databases:** Oracle 8.x, DB2, Sybase, MS Access ■ **Environments:** Microsoft Windows 95/98/NT/2003, DOS, UNIX, VMS, CICS ■ **CASE Tools:** ADW 1.6, ADW 2.7 ■ **Development Tools:** JDeveloper v.2.0, Oracle Designer v.6.0, Oracle Developer 2003 v.2.0, Oracle Forms v.5.0, Oracle Reports v.2.5, Dreamweaver 3.0
■ **Methodologies:** Oracle's Applications Implementation Methodology (AIM) & Custom Development Methodology (CDM); Ernst & Young's Application Implementation Methodology (SMM).

PROFESSIONAL EXPERIENCE

Corporate Affiliations: Oracle, Healthnet, Bell South, Eaton Corporation, Kellogg Company, Kelly Services Corporation, Price Waterhouse, Niagara Mohawk Power Co., Alabama Gas Co., Atmos Energy, Consumers Gas, Consolidated Natural Gas

ORACLE CORPORATION, **Senior Consultant / Technical Analyst**   2000 – 2006
Installed and configured Oracle Financial Applications at five large North American companies to enhance the accuracy, availability, and timeliness of financial data for strategic planning and reporting. Identified, designed, developed, and documented customizations and interfaces to Oracle applications. Delivered excellent results to each client. Consistently commended for ability to work independently or as a team member to complete assignments on time and under budget.

- Designed and developed online Help for a customized installation of Oracle's iBill – iPay system, a $1.2M Oracle initiative. Extensive use of Dreamweaver 3.0 to develop 16 HTML Web pages.
- Developed work plans for a $2.5 million implementation of the Oracle CPG/Oracle Financials solution using Project Workbench and Microsoft Project '98.
- Developed Configuration Management Standards for a $1.5 million global implementation of Oracle Applications at a large international temporary services agency. Developed initial template of the project's global work plan.

ERNST & YOUNG LLP, **Consultant / Programmer Analyst**   1996 – 2000
Demonstrated outstanding technical skills in design, development, and implementation of a large Customer Information System package at five North American companies.

- Conducted analysis of Finance System on the CIS project of a large utility holding company. Prepared and presented Joint Application Design sessions, creating modification control reports, and proposing and estimating solutions for complex system enhancements in the following areas of Finance: Credit and Collections, Accounts Receivable, and Payment Processing.
- Programmer/Analyst. Modified existing batch and online (CICS) programs and constructed new programs to support general ledger journaling and credit collection processes in the implementation of a COBOL/DB2 Customer Information System at a northeastern electric and gas company.

EDUCATION & TRAINING

BOWLING GREEN STATE UNIVERSITY, Bowling Green, OH
Bachelor of Science in Computer Information Systems

ORACLE PRODUCT TRAINING:

Oracle CRM eCommerce 3i (iStore)
Java Programming with JDeveloper v.2.0
Developer/2003 Release 2: Build Forms I and Report Builder v.3.0
Oracle Receivables Release II
Oracle Financials 10.7 SC Bootcamp: General Ledger, Purchasing, Payables, Receivables, & Application Implementation Methodology (AIM) 2.0
Ernst & Young MCS Information Technology Individual Study (MITIS 1) & Study 2 (MITIS 2)

Technical Support Specialist

Gloria needed to present her technical, project management, and technical training/supervisory qualifications for an upcoming promotion possibility within her department.

Gloria Bartlett

6463 Apple Valley Road, Stevens Point, WI 54481
(715) 555-5555 Home ■ (715) 555-8888 Mobile ■ gloriabar@boi.com

Application Support Administrator / Technical Support Specialist / Desktop Support

Technologically sophisticated, bilingual (Spanish / English) IT Support & Training Specialist with hands-on experience in project life-cycle management for technical and intranet applications, Web site development and maintenance, and workgroup support. Proven desktop and network troubleshooting skills. Expertise in:

- ✓ Help Desk & Hardware Support
- ✓ System Upgrades / Conversions
- ✓ Peer-to-Peer User Groups
- ✓ First-Level PC Support
- ✓ LAN / WAN Architecture
- ✓ Web Content Upgrades
- ✓ Project Management
- ✓ Escalation Resolution
- ✓ Customer Service

TECHNOLOGY SUMMARY

Networking – LAN / WAN, Windows 2000 / NT 4.0 Server, TCP/IP, SQL Server

Operating Systems – Windows 95 / 98 / 2000 / XP, Windows 2003 / NT 4.0 Server, DOS 6.0

Applications – MS Office Suite 97/2000/2002 (Word, Access, Excel, PowerPoint), MS FrontPage 2003, Macromedia Dreamweaver 3.0, Adobe Acrobat 5 and PDF, Flash 4.0, Novell GroupWise 5.5, Adobe Pagemill 3, Lotus Suite 96, Corel Suite 96, Corel 9, Adobe PhotoShop, Kodak digital software, Symantec pcAnywhere 32, Internet Explorer, Netscape Communicator, and WinZip

Programming – HTML code, CGI, Java, JavaScript, C Programming, RPG 400, SQL, Visual Basic 5.0, Visual InterDev 6.0, AS/400, ASP code

PROFESSIONAL EXPERIENCE

WISCONSIN STATE TREASURY DEPT., DIV. OF TAXATION, Madison, WI   1998 – present
Senior Technician, MIS – Technical Support Activity (2004 – present)
Promoted to provide help desk support for 2003+ end-users (including remote users) in 9 locations throughout Wisconsin, as well as project management team leadership for special technical assignments. First-point-of-contact (Tier 1 Help Desk Technician) for support incidents, as well as end-user training.

- **Help Desk.** Ensure effective "one-stop" technical support for mainframe, WAN, LAN, and remote system. Install and update software, and set up, configure, and troubleshoot Reach Center equipment. Track and de-escalate technology and workflow problems, and assist Desktop Support Group and other IT groups.
- **Web Site Development.** Project-managed Division of Taxation's Web site redesign to text-only version, enabling fast and easy access for all users, including vision-impaired. Supervised staff of 8.
- **Intranet Development.** Key player in creation, launch, and maintenance of Division of Taxation intranet site, providing management with easily retrievable, up-to-date information for operations decisions. Initiated, created, and maintain Access users group intranet to facilitate information sharing and learning.
- **Project Management.** Led WIX CD-ROM project for 2 years, delivering interactive CD-ROMs with 1000+ tax-law-verified documents for simplified tax preparation (tax years 2004 & 2005) on schedule.
- **ASP Development.** Played pivotal role in beta-test programming and development of causal sales application (upgraded Alpha 4 database into back-end of Access 2000 and SQL Server, front-end into Internet Explorer via ASP programming).
- **End-User Training.** Expanded Reach Center offerings by designing, developing, and delivering advanced programs and manuals for MS Office, GroupWise, Novell Network, and Internet, making information easily understood and usable. Manage all Access courses, training and supervising 5 adjunct team instructors.

WISCONSIN STATE TREASURY DEPT.– continued
Technical Assistant, MIS – Technical Support Activity   (2002 – 2004)
First-level technical support for software installation, as well as setup and configuration of new equipment used in Division of Taxation (PCs, laptops, printers, scanners, projectors, digital & video).

- **IT Software Training.** Designed curriculum and materials, and delivered technical training, for introductory programs in Microsoft Office Suite (Word, Excel, Access), as well as Windows 95, keeping staff motivated and focused while improving job satisfaction and productivity.
- **Web site Support.** Functioned as Web Editor for Division of Taxation's Internet/intranet Web site, proofing and updating Web site information on a daily basis.
- **Database Maintenance.** Upgraded and maintained link-shared employee Access database with Chief of Staff's office, ensuring data integrity for training. Created database reports for management evaluation.
- **Technical Development Project.** Pioneered development and implementation of storage, archive, and retrieval system for electronic presentations used throughout Division of Taxation.

Principal Clerk – Technical Education   (2000 – 2002)
Promoted to provide installation, configuration, and troubleshooting support for new equipment and software in REACH Center, as well as evaluation and modification of skills assessment.

- **Training Center Database.** Initiated and implemented data gathering system in Access to compile, store, and retrieve statistics on computer training classes. Researched and wrote monthly reports used to evaluate training trends and staff training needs.
- **WI Saver Rebate Program.** Key team participant in initial, large-scale data compilation for WI Saver Rebate Program, including retrieval, distribution, quality control, and storage of data.

Senior Clerk Typist, Clerk Typist – Corporation Business Tax   (1998 – 2000)
Assisted auditors by researching taxpayer information on mainframe, ordered work files for Supervising Auditor using HLLAPI information system, and prepared report statistics using Excel spreadsheets.

WISCONSIN STATE DEPT. OF BANKING, Madison, WI (temp contract)   (1997 – 1998)
Data Entry Specialist / Legal Secretary
Front office support for attorneys and accountants: records management, legal document preparation, purchasing, and equipment maintenance. Used IS software for research and to process taxpayer complaints.

FIRST AMERICAN BANK, Stevens Point, WI   (1993 – 1996)
Customer Service Representative / Supervisor Teller
Instructed employees in use of computerized banking systems and procedures. Verified and audited financial reports and balance sheets. Cash management responsibility exceeded $100,000.

EDUCATION

Instructor Certification, **HRDI, Blue Bell, PA – 2003**
Courses: Curriculum Design, Performance Consulting, Training Presentations, Design Surveys and Questions, Determining Training Needs, and Active Techniques for Teaching.

Certificate in Computer Programming, The Computer Institute, Madison, WI – 2002
Courses: HTML, CGI, Java Programming, JavaScript Programming, RPG 400, C Programming, SQL, Visual Basic 5.0, AS/400 Subfiles & Common Language Queries, MS Office, Windows NT 4.0

Ongoing Professional and Technical Development in-house and at vendor locations (1998 – present)

Technology Strategist

Technology strategist following basic resume principles and adapting them to showcase some impressive and wide-ranging achievements

BRENDA R. HINESVILE

Droid: (214) 721-5687   4658 Lovers Lane   http://brendahinesville.com
iPhone: (214) 723 7856   Dallas, TX 75240   brenda@brendahinesville.com

Technology Strategist / Senior Software Architect
Solid Leadership – Software Architecture – Mobile Application Development – Internet Marketing

Proven Leadership — Rare blend of theoretical and practical understanding of open source applications and server environments. Leadership and hands-on experience in regulated financial services and mobile software industries.

Senior-Level Software Professional — Strong leader. 12+ years of experience developing and managing open source software. Successful in building solid technology platforms and leading technology organizations. Career includes senior-level positions, contributing to corporate, board and division-level strategic planning, policy formation, and decision-making.

CORE COMPETENCIES

Software Development	Management Leadership	System Administration
• Advanced Objective-C on iPhone OS • Advanced C/C++ on OS X, BSD, Linux • UNIX Systems Programming • Application Architecture & Design • Network & Security Protocols • Mobile Hardware/Software Limitations	• Personnel Recruiting/Management • Regulatory Accountability/Compliance • Translation/Communication of Technology Needs & Issues • Process & Policy Creation & Implementation • P&L Accountability	• Server & Network Administration • Extensive Work in UNIX Shells • Expert in Terminal Environments • Thorough Knowledge of OS Internals • FFIEC Technology Regulations • Web and Server Security • Network Protocol Analysis

PERFORMANCE PROFILE

Developed iPhone App for commercial transportation industry • Ranked #2 on App Store top free business apps, June 2010. • Featured on App Store - New and Noteworthy, June 2010. • Featured in numerous freight publications and Dallas Morning News. • Online Gallery, HD Screencasts, technical overview available on Project URL.	2009 to 2010
Contributed Documentation to Plone – Open Source CMS • How to configure a Plone 3 production server with Squid and Apache 2 + SSL on a FreeBSD 7 server with PF, the packet filter. Comprehensive instructions for secure installation.	2009 to 2010
Developed Open Source Enterprise Software for Federal Savings Bank •Deployed loan pricing and eligibility software across nation-wide network on hardened Linux servers. •Designed extensive schema in PostgreSQL, C++ DFA for parsers, and TCL for dynamic content. • Achieved near 100% system uptime and significantly increased bank profit margins. •500+ mortgage programs, 50K+ underwriting/pricing rules, $1M daily changing mortgage interest rates.	2003 to 2008
Migrated Bank Infrastructure to Open Source Platforms • Deployed, managed Open Source mail / web servers on hardened Linux at SAS 70 Type II data center. • Drastically reduced costs, near 100% uptime, and significantly mitigated security/regulatory risks. • Developed CRM on Open Source CMS and deployed across nation-wide branch network. • Deployed Open Source mail / web clients on corporate workstations - trained IT department on Linux server administration and workstation software management.	2003 to 2005
Led startup of IT department for Federal Savings Bank •Established bank's online presence and branded "Cofedbank". •Integrated custom CRM with Google Adwords to track lead conversion quality and ratios. •Provided technical, financial and managerial oversight of bank's technology infrastructure. •Ensured compliance with FFIEC Regulations.	2003 to 2005

Brenda Hinesville   Droid: (214) 721-5687   iPhone: (214) 723 7856   brenda@brendahinesville..com

PROFESSIONAL EXPERIENCE

LEAD SOFTWARE ARCHITECT / DEVELOPER APPLICANDY, LLC - MOBILE APPLICATION DEVELOPMENT, DALLAS, TX	2009 to Present

Designed and developed iPhone application, iLogMiles, for commercial transportation industry. Led project, including all development, and provided training on software standards, Apple guidelines and Internet marketing. Closely followed agile design principles. Designed and managed web site and web application framework.

• App released for the iTruckers on the road" - Today's Trucking Magazine, April 2010.
• "New iPhone App Provides Daily Log Book" - Heavy Duty Trucking Magazine, April 2010.
• "Amid industry discussion…, smartphone logging apps proliferate" - Overdrive Magazine, April 2010.
• "Two Dallas iPhone/iPad app developers hit milestones with iLogMiles…" - Dallas Morning News, April 2010.
• "Software developers keep churning out the apps" - Dallas Morning News, March 2010.

PRESIDENT / SOFTWARE CONSULTANT HINESVILLE MORTGAGE & INVESTMENT CO., DALLAS, TX	2008 to 2009

Consulting services for regulated banks and financial institutions – Enterprise software architecture, capital markets consulting - Mark to Market, Fall-Out analysis, and Hedged Pipeline analysis reports. Deployed Plone on hardened FreeBSD server at SAS 70 Type II data center.

VP — INFORMATION TECHNOLOGY / MANAGING DIRECTOR COLORADO FEDERAL SAVINGS BANK (COFEDBANK), DALLAS, TX	2003 to 2008

Led and managed technology department and created tech strategy for bank. Architected and managed technology infrastructure, including migration strategies for accounting and loan origination systems. Trained personnel on network protocols, system admin, server security and data modeling. Performed technology assessments of prospective acquisitions. Managed project life-cycles for several software interfaces. Performed database migrations, server installations, server upgrades, performance tuning & security assessments. Managed vendor contracts.

SOFTWARE DEVELOPER MORTGAGE PORTFOLIO SERVICES, DALLAS, TX	2001 to 2002

Designed, developed & deployed mortgage lock platform using CGI and C++.

C++ and UNIX TUTOR COLLIN COUNTY COMMUNITY COLLEGE, PLANO, TX	2000 to 2001

Tutored 200+ students in C++ and UNIX courses.

OPEN SOURCE DEVELOPER, DALLAS, TX	1996 to 2002

UNIX systems programming on Solaris, Open/FreeBSD, RH/Slackware Linux.
Developed thread-safe, streams library in C++. The library is an extension of the C++ iostreams hierarchy. Customized streams provide support for sockets, shared memory, pipes and text files.   Project URL – http://mls.sourceforge.net

EDUCATION

BS — Computer Science, University of Texas at Dallas, Dallas, TX • Graduate-level coursework in Computer Science • Emphasis on operating system architecture and database design Member of iEEE Computer Society	2002

Notable Conferences: Apple World Wide Developer Conference; Apple iPhone Tech Talk – San Jose, 2009.
Administering Linux in Production Environments - USENIX; Online Analytics – Omniture Inc.; Search Engine Strategies – Chicago, 2006.

Systems Engineer

Technical Skills section (Core Competencies) is right up front on this engineer's resume. It tells the story quickly, and the body copy fills in the details.

PARAG GUPTA

104 W. Real Drive • Beaverton, OR 97006 • (503) 555-4286 • parag.gupta@technical.com

SYSTEM ENGINEER

Motivated and driven IT professional offering 9+ years of hands–on experience in designing, implementing, and enhancing systems to automate business operations. Demonstrated ability to develop high-performance systems, applications, databases, and interfaces.

➤ Part of TL9000 CND audit interviews which helped Technical get TL9000 certified which is significant in Telecom industry. Skilled trainer and proven ability to lead many successful projects, like TSS, EMX, and TOL.

➤ Strategically manage time and expediently resolve problems for optimal productivity, improvement and profitability; able to direct multiple tasks effectively.

➤ Strong technical background with a solid history of delivering outstanding customer service.

➤ Highly effective liaison and communication skills proven by effective interaction with management, users, team members, and vendors.

TECHNICAL SKILLS

Operating Systems:	Unix, Windows (2000, XP), DOS
Languages:	C, C++, Java, Pascal, Assembly Languages (Z8000, 808x, DSP)
Methodologies:	TL9000, Digital Six Sigma
Software:	MS Office, Adobe Framemaker, Matlab
RDBMS:	DOORS, Oracle 7.x
Protocols:	TCP/IP, SS7 ISUP, A1, ANSI, TL1, SNMP
Tools:	Teamplay, Clearcase, Clearquest, M-Gatekeeper, Exceed, Visio, DocExpress, Compass
Other:	CDMA Telecom Standards – 3GPP2 (Including TIA/EIA-2001, TIA/EIA-41, TIA/EIA-664), ITU-T, AMPS

PROFESSIONAL EXPERIENCE

Technical, Main Network Division, Hillsboro, OR   Jan. 1999 – Present

Principal Staff Engineer • Products Systems Engineering • Nov. 2004 – Present

✓ Known as "go-to" person for CDMA call processing and billing functional areas.

✓ Create customer requirements documents for Technical SoftSwitch (TSS) and SMS Gateway products. All deliverables done on/ahead schedule with high quality.

✓ Solely accountable for authoring and allocation, customer reviews, supporting fellow system engineers, development, and test and customer documentation teams.

✓ Support Product Management in RFPs, customer feature prioritization, impact statements, and budgetary estimates.

✓ Mentored junior engineers and 1 innovation disclosure (patent) submitted in 2007.

✓ Resolve deployed customer/internal requirements issues and contribute to Virtual Zero Defect quality goal.

✓ TOL process champion and part of CND focus group that contributed to reducing CRUD backlog (NPR) by 25% and cycle time (FRT) by 40%.

✓ Recognized as the TL9000 expert. Triage representative for switching and messaging products.

✓ Achieved 'CND Quality Award' for contribution to quality improvement in May 2007.

Senior Staff Engineer • MSS Systems Engineering • May 2002 – Oct. 2004

✓ Led a team of 12 engineers for 3 major software releases of TSS product included around 80 features/enhancements to create T-Gate SE deliverables.

✓ Mentored newer engineers to get up to speed on TSS product.

✓ Created requirements for TSS product, 30 features/enhancements contributing to 5 major software releases. *Recognized as overall product expert with specific focus on call processing and billing.*

✓ Played integral role in successfully implementing proprietary commercial TSS billing system.

✓ Supported PdM organization by creating ROMs, technical support for RFPs (Vivo, Sprint, TELUS, TM, Tata, Inquam, Alaska, Reliance, Pakistan, PBTL, Mauritius, Telefonica, Brasicel and Angola).

✓ Proactively identified functional areas of improvement for requirements coverage, contributed to resolving several faults, improved customer documentation, and provided reference for future releases as well as other customers.

✓ *Received 'Above and Beyond Performance Award' – Oct. 2003.*

Senior Software Engineer • EMX Development • Aug. 2000 – Apr. 2002

✓ Successfully led and coordinated the cross-functional development teams, 30 engineers, to meet the scheduled design, code, and test completion dates ensuring Feature T-Gates are met.

✓ Feature Technical Lead for Concurrent Voice/Data Services feature, the largest revenue-generating feature for KDDI customer.

✓ Feature Lead for Paging Channel SMS feature. Created requirements and design; led implementation phase of five engineers' team; supported product, network, and release testing; and created customer reference documentation.

✓ Performed the role of functional area lead for Trunk Manager and A1 interface functional areas. Provided 2-day Technical Workshops for internal/customer knowledge sharing and functional area transition from Caltel.

✓ Provided customer site testing and FOA (First Office Application) support for major EMX releases and off-hours CNRC (Customer Networks Resolution Center) support.

✓ *Received 'Bravo Award' – May 2001, Sep. 2001, Jan. 2002*

Software Engineer • EMX Development • Jan. 1999 – Jul. 2000

✓ Developed design and code for SMS feature as a Trunk Manager functional area lead for the largest FA impacted by the feature. Supported product, network, and release testing.

✓ Contributed to customer release documentation. Supported feature-level SMS testing at various internal labs and customer sites resulting in successful deployment at customer sites.

✓ Designed and coded phases for wiretap and virtual circuits feature development, initial assessment of internal and customer EMX PRs (problem reports) to route/classify issues and providing problem assessments for many of these PRs.

✓ Created an implementation process to serve as reference for new hires.

✓ Provided CNRC support during the Y2K transition.

✓ *Received 'Above and Beyond Performance Award' – Jan. 2000, Dec. 2000 and 'Certificate of Outstanding Achievement' – Jun. 1999*

EDUCATION

Master of Science in Computer Engineering • University of Portland, Portland, OR • 1998

Bachelors of Engineering in Electronics • Technology and Science Institute, India • 1996

Significant Trainings Include

- Open Source Software
- WSG Requirements Process
- WiMAX
- Product Security
- Agile Management for Software Engineering
- Fagan Inspection and Moderation

173

Information Technology Manager

A good technical resume that worked for the owner. Notice the technical skills at the end of the resume. While this doesn't matter in the resume database, it would have been more helpful to human eyes had it come after the Core Competencies section on the first page.

Dan Newcomb, PMP

82 Nowhere Ave. • Nowhere, NJ 08820

Cell: 732.555.1212 • aresumesolution.com

INFORMATION TECHNOLOGY MANAGEMENT

Hands-on technology manager with multifaceted experience in mainframe and client server environments with multiple relational databases; Informix, Oracle Sybase, and SQL server. Exceptional team building and management capabilities. Strong background in relational database management, performance tuning, and high availability techniques. Skilled project manager with ability to obtain project requirements and implement solutions that drive bottom line. Talented in providing technology risk management. Leverages wide-ranging talents in computer technology, staff leadership, and SDLC to effectively manage organizational change, mitigate risk, infuse new ideas, and deliver large-company capabilities.

➤ Excellent ability to analyze business needs and implement cost-effective solutions meeting business objectives.
➤ Solid record of achievement building and aligning organizations with strategic IT business objectives to achieve dramatic bottom-line results.
➤ Expertise providing project management, technology expertise, and staff leadership.
➤ Demonstrated talents in database architecture, design, and maintenance.

KEY COMPETENCIES

– $MM Project Management	– Staff Leadership
– Process Management	– Release & Change Management
– Software Development Lifecycle	– Disaster Recovery Management
– Telecom Systems	– Vendor Management
– Client Relationship Management	– Database Administration

PROFESSIONAL EXPERIENCE

XYZ FINANCE COMPANY, Parsippany, NJ 2003 – Present
Consumer division of Cleveland based 92 billion key bank providing lending/leasing of auto and home mortgages to customers all across America.

Application System Team Manager

Provides team leadership and project management for IT projects with price ranging in value from $50K to $1.5M, ensuring timely completion. Directs and mentors four Application/Database Designers, providing prototype, design, development, and implementation of database architecture and strategies and 24/7 support of databases and applications. Oversees organizational change management functions, providing support and approval of over 100 change requests in one release cycle. Designs and implements ETL solutions for XML-based interface of Origination data. Assists audit organizations, providing engineering and architecture changes to necessary applications, databases, and servers for SOX compliance. SME for origination data and ensures persistence of data across downstream systems. Provides 24/7 support for back applications.

Accomplishments:
• Increased client leads by 20% through development and implementation of lead registration system.
• Directed team in development and implementation of Disaster Recovery Planning efforts, providing quick restoration of critical applications.
• Spearheaded major 18 month application and database design project for implementation of application and database security ensuring SOX compliance for entire organization with budget of $1.5M.

NEW MORTGAGE, Parsippany, NJ   2001
– 2003
Leader in sub-prime lending in Tri-state area with presence in 22 states subsequently acquired by key bank.

<u>*Database Consultant*</u>

Designed and implemented the Enterprise wide Data Warehouse and reporting framework for the mortgage line of business with departmental data mart. Performed Dimensional data modeling to implement the data warehouse. Managed the Application and Physical DBA role for Enterprise wide Oracle and Informix databases ranging from 50 GB to 250 GB size. Established database backup and recovery strategies using RMAN and ONBAR utilities.

Performed expert object management technique like object partitioning. Performed capacity planning based on transaction volume and expected growth. Developed and implemented shell scripts, stored procedures, functions, and triggers. Ensured all databases were functioning appropriately and resolved any issues on a timely basis.

Accomplishments:
- 10% reduction of time between receipts of inquiry to funding with the help of availability of daily Sales, appraisal effectiveness reports.

TELCORDIA TECHNOLOGIES, Piscataway, NJ
Leading provider of technology solutions for Telecom Industries around the globe.   2000
– 2001

<u>*Senior Database Consultant*</u>

Developed and maintained telecom clearinghouse software for telecom services providers to manage 1 million customer requests per day. Directed team of developers in support and maintenance for Exchange Link project running on an Oracle 8-I database with capacity of over 200 GB. Performed application and database tuning with object and index redesign resulting in 66% improvement in application performance. 24/7 support of application in an ASP model. Handled configuration management, change management, business analysis, and project management.

Accomplishments:
- Increased customer satisfaction through improved application support, increasing revenue from $1M to $10M.

ABC TECHNOLOGIES, Somerset, NJ   1998
– 2000
Leading provider of software for telecom service providers.

<u>*SAP Production Support Database Administrator*</u>

Served as Oracle database administrator for large 600GB database, providing 24/7 support of numerous SAP R/3 systems. Learned and quickly adapted to new technology. Analyzed and resolved complex issues with over 1000 batch jobs in SAP R/3 environment. Developed and implemented shell scripts, providing escalations based on procedure and severity. Provided support for end users on complex issues. Configured and maintained various files. Ensured application security and provided user administration.

Accomplishments:
- Key member of team that turned six-month pilot SAP project to company-wide implementation, providing coordination between vendors, clients, and implementation team.

EDUCATION
Bachelor of Science, Engineering

Regional Engineering College, St. Louis, MO

Training:

- Certified training in COBOL, DMSII, UNIX, C, and Oracle
- Certified training in "Structured Systems Analysis and Design"

TECHNICAL SKILLS

Databases: SQL Server2000, DMSII, Sybase, Oracle 7, 8, 9I, 10G
                          Informix 7.3/9.X, SQL Server 7.0

Systems: HP9000 (HP-UX 11, 10.20), SUN SPARC-Enterprise 2000(Solaris 2.5),
                          SUN SPARC 6500 (Sun OS 5.6), Sun Fire 880, AIX, Linux, UNISYS A
                          series, Windows NT

Languages: C, COBOL74, SQL, Oracle Pro*C, PRO*COBOL, PL/SQL, VB, ASP

UNIX Programming: Shell scripting, AWK/SED Scripting

DB Tools: Oracle (Enterprise Manager), SQL*DBA, Import, Export, SQL Loader,
                          SQL (Report Writer), Microsoft SQL Server Data Transformation Ser-
                          vice, Oracle RMAN

CASE Tools: ERWIN/ERX (both IE and IDEF1X)

Methodologies: UML, Rational Unified process, SCRUM, Agile

Graphic Designer/Illustrator

Today every resume needs to be data-dense and appealing to the eye, and never more so than with a graphic designer, a beautiful example of form following function.

NORA PATTERSON

Address	Phone
City, State Zip	Email Address

ILLUSTRATOR ✍ GRAPHIC DESIGNER ✍ VISUAL ARTIST

CORE SKILL AREAS:

Textbook Illustration

❖ ❖ ❖

Scientific Drawings

❖ ❖ ❖

Museum Exhibits Illustration

❖ ❖ ❖

Storybook Illustration

❖ ❖ ❖

Cartoon Image Design

❖ ❖ ❖

Greeting Card Design/ Illustration

❖ ❖ ❖

Artifact Replications

❖ ❖ ❖

Surface Coloration Restoration

❖ ❖ ❖

Original & Production Artwork

❖ ❖ ❖

Visual Aid Preparation

❖ ❖ ❖

Photo-Realistic Illustration

❖ ❖ ❖

Logo Design

❖ ❖ ❖

Full-Figure Drawing

❖ ❖ ❖

CAREER PROFILE

Creative, diverse illustrator and artist with extensive experience in designing and developing broad range of visual pieces to meet business and program objectives of both employers and their clients. Particularly adept in creating original, vibrant artwork that captures attention from serious and casual viewers. Additional skills:

- *Developing Products* — Able to translate concepts into well-designed products by integrating various elements, including illustration, formatting, photography, and typography. Combine innovative thinking with logical design elements.
- *Conveying Messages* — Create illustrations that articulate key ideas and earn recognition for aesthetic quality. Excel in reinforcing positive messages.
- *Meeting Expectations* — Maintain consistent track record of fulfilling organizational goals. Highly adaptable to changing needs and requirements.

SELECTED WORKS *(a full portfolio is available for immediate review)*

Marketing Material & Product Design

- International Colloquium for Biology of Soricidae — **Logo, image, and product development** for line of merchandise used in international conference.
- Carnegie Museum of Natural History — **Sweatshirt** *The American Mastodon* for the museum's gift shop. Designed and produced original artwork for full line of products sold in association with the Walton Hall of Ancient Egypt. Created full-sized, full-color paintings for children's area the Discovery Room.
- H. J. Heinz Pittsburgh Historical Center — **Photo-mural retouching** activities to enhance key display areas.
- Tucson Children's Museum — Initial design and development of **cartoon images** for outside banner/T-shirt image and other museum merchandise.

Book & Magazine Illustrations

- *The Carnegie Magazine, Pittsburgh Magazine* — Miscellaneous illustrations and graphics.
- *The New York Times, Time, Johns Hopkins Magazine, others* — Widely published illustrations through the United Press International.
- Dr. L.E. McCullough — Instructional drawings for *The Making and Playing of Uilleann Pipes*, including musical notation.
- Dr. Sandra Olson — Reconstruction illustration of Paleolithic horse fetish for *Horses Through Time.*

Scientific Illustrations

- *National Geographic* — 11"x14" acrylic reconstruction of *Eosimias sinesis.*
- Cultural & Environmental Systems — Artifacts for Technical Series #56.
- Walton Hall of Ancient Egypt — Scientifically accurate recreation of 18th dynasty tomb walls and entire hall as graphics artwork. Built complete scale models, coordinated all illustration production with various collaborators, and earned commendation from Egyptologists for accuracy of reconstruction.

TESTIMONIALS

"Nora is a dedicated and highly talented artist....[her] ability to work in close collaboration with others, together with her innate artistic talents, were the key elements that allowed her to produce such stunning works of art..."
K. Christopher Beard, PhD Associate Dean of Science, Carnegie Museum of Natural History

"Nora's passion for a subject comes across in her artwork...[she] is a talented illustrator able to work in a variety of media...more importantly, she is a team player used to dealing with multiple aspects of a project to effect a successful outcome..."
- James R. Senior Chairman, Division of Exhibits, Carnegie Museum

"In addition to her skills, Nora has proven to be extremely dedicated and a very amiable coworker and colleague. I am quite happy to recommend her as an excellent candidate for a wide range of positions in which precision, talent, patience, and attention to detail are important assets.
- Sandra Olsen Curator of Anthropology, Carnegie Museum

"I strongly recommend Nora at the highest level...has very well-developed critical thinking skills...novel ideas for designs...a true artist with great creative ability."
- Sankar Chatterjee Professor of Geology, Curator of Paleontology, Museum of Texas Tech

SELECTED PROFESSIONAL EXPERIENCE *(in order of professional importance)*

Illustrator/ Exhibits Preparator, The Carnegie Museum of Natural History
Built distinguished record of achievement and extensive portfolio of work for one of the 4 museums comprising the Carnegie Museums of Pittsburgh family. Employed with museum for 20+ years until 1998.

- *Work Summary* – Served as exhibits/scientific illustrator and designer for installation of traveling and temporary exhibits. Collected, researched, and accurately reproduced artifacts (both for 3-dimensional and 2-dimensional venues) and vegetation for permanent installations.
- *National/Global Recognition* – Collaborated with Dr. K. Christopher Beard on production of life restoration for 40 million-year old fossil primate *Eosimias* centennicus, featured in *Science* magazine (1996) and receiving global coverage in the following:

National Geographic, Science et Vie (Paris), Earth, U.S.A Today, Pittsburgh Post-Gazette, Dallas Morning-News.

- Leadership Role – Supervised gallery technicians, staff, and volunteers in general and specific activities, providing expertise and support to facilitate project completion.

Freelance Artist, Various Clients
Contracted to design and develop illustrations and artwork for broad range of companies, organizations, and individual buyers. Period spanned from 1985 to 1999.

- Satisfying Requirements – Aligned client/employer needs with artwork to ensure satisfaction, leading to frequent repeat and referral business.
- Meeting Deadlines – Worked often under tight timelines; consistently exceeded expectations in delivering work on time with zero effect on quality.
- Earning National Recognition – Received placement in national, well-respected publications and garnered recognition for breadth/quality of creations.

Preparator, The Texas Tech Museum
Oversee preparation and surface treatment of dinosaur cast exhibit specimens for university museum in Lubbock, TX. Arrange artwork for display in large and small exhibits, prepare works on paper for exhibitions, and perform accurate replications of surface coloration for cast specimens. Work jointly with internal team members and external partners to ensure success of exhibitions. Hired in 2003; currently held position.

Held additional positions with J.C. Penneys, S-K Designs, Cultural & Environmental Systems, and Holland Gardens, among others. A full employment history will be provided on request.

EDUCATION & CREDENTIALS

Bachelor of Fine Arts ❖ Major in Drawing, Minor in Painting
TEXAS TECH UNIVERSITY, Lubbock, TX

Former Affiliations
- Member, Guild of Natural Science Illustrators
- Member, Society for the Preservation of Natural History Collectors
- Member, National Association of Museum Exhibitors

Computer Summary
- Appleworks 6, Photoshop 7 (rudimentary level), Internet research

Guidance Counselor

Sharon wanted to get into another district closer to her home, as she had a daily commute of over one hour.

SHARON WISE

500 Nottingham Street ~ Plymouth, MI 48170
444.555.1111 ~ sharon _wise@hotmail.com

SCHOOL GUIDANCE COUNSELOR

Dedicated elementary, middle, and high school guidance counselor, skilled at providing positive direction for students' academic, social, and emotional well-being. Work effectively with children with ADHD and with multicultural and diverse populations. Counseling Skills include:

Guidance Curriculum:	Classroom Guidance Lessons; Career Awareness; Conflict Resolution/ Social Skills; Developmental Awareness
Individual Planning:	Student Assessments; Student Placement & Scheduling; New Student Transition; Academic & Career Advisement
Responsive Services:	Mental Health; Family & Teacher Consulting; Crisis Intervention & Grief Management; Psycho-Educational Support Groups
Systems Support:	Program Evaluation; Program Development & Coordination; Needs Assessment; Committee Participation

EDUCATION / CERTIFICATION

MA, *School Counseling,* UNIVERSITY OF DETROIT-MERCY, Detroit, MI.
MA, *Teaching,* MARYGROVE COLLEGE, Detroit, MI
BA, *Teaching – Social Studies/French,* MICHIGAN STATE UNIVERSITY, East Lansing, MI

Certified – *Counseling* – K–12 – State of Michigan
Certified – *Social Studies & French* – grades 7–12 – State of Michigan
Certified – *LLPC* – expected completion 7/03

PROFESSIONAL EXPERIENCE

HARTLAND COMMUNITY SCHOOLS, Hartland, MI   2005 – 2006
SCHOOL COUNSELOR

Provide individual and small-group counseling sessions and large-group counseling presentations within classroom and guidance office environments for a school with 800 students. Participate in parent/teacher meetings to discuss and develop emotional and behavioral strategies for students with physical, mental, and emotional challenges.

- Developed 45-minute Bully-Proofing classes and presented them to each of 30 classes in the building.
- Wrote a monthly article for the school newsletter on a topic of relevance.
- Facilitated students participating in the Midwest talent search for the Gifted & Talented program.
- Held orientation for new students and their parents, providing them with a schedule of classes and showing them around the building.
- Created 30-minute Career Awareness/Exploration sessions so students would become exposed to various career options. Organized a Career Day, arranging for 40 speakers in various fields to talk with the students about their profession.
- Facilitated support groups dealing with social and coping skills, and conducted needs assessment and program evaluation with staff and students.
- Designed a survey for students and teachers to evaluate the guidance program.
- Hung a display of bully-proofing pledges in the shape of the American flag, with children earning hearts instead of stars for "acts of kindness."

- Participated as a team member for the School Improvement Team (SCIT).
- Performed Title I coordinator duties, planning and organizing initial structure mailings, assigning students to teachers, adhering to budgets, and scheduling classes.

NOVI COMMUNITY SCHOOLS, Novi, MI   2003 – 2005
GUEST TEACHER

Substituted in the middle school and high school, teaching most subjects, including special ed. Immediately tried to develop a rapport with students and engage in discussion of relevant topics. Facilitated the discussion to steer towards daily lesson plan. Discussion and debate kept students centered, entertained, and open to learning.

- Given long-term teaching assignment for students with disabilities. Taught math, science, and social studies in grades 6–8 for a full semester. There were 5 – 10 students in each of four classes, ages 11–13; many students had ADHD. Wrote lesson plans, graded assignments, and consulted with parents.

DETROIT PUBLIC SCHOOLS, Detroit, MI   1996 – 2003
FRENCH & SOCIAL STUDIES TEACHER

Taught five classes each day, with each class having between 30 – 35 students, engaging their curiosity and research abilities in structured classroom activities. Provided lectures, notes, study guides and projects for courses in American History, Government, Economics, World Geography, Global Issues, and French.

- Devised an effective structure for parent communication.
- Gathered resources as supplemental materials to be used in conjunction with assigned texts to give students a richer experience.
- Assigned different subjects each year, showed flexibility in providing first-rate learning experience for each subject.
- Developed a system to track work and assignments while moving to different rooms for each class period.
- Provided students with practical experience, such as making menus and calendars in French.
- Member of School Improvement team and on the committee to improve student self-esteem.

PROFESSIONAL MEMBERSHIPS

- American Counseling Association
- American School Counselor Association
- Michigan Counseling Association
- Michigan School Counselor Association

RECENT CONFERENCE PARTICIPATION

Launching Career Awareness – Oakland Education Service Agency
Legal Issues for School Counselors – Washtenaw County Counselors Association
Counseling Groups in Crisis – Michigan Association of Specialists in Group Work
A.D.H.D in the New Millennium – Oakland Schools
Bully-Proofing Your School – Oakland Schools
The Human Spirit & Technology – Michigan Counseling Association
Understanding Attachment Disorders – Medical Educational Service
Grief Counseling Skills – Cross Country University

Law Enforcement Officer

Because James is a recent graduate, his education section needed to come first; however, he also wanted to emphasize his experience as a trainer and team leader.

JAMES BURLINGTON

9803 Clinton Avenue
Lubbock, TX 79424

(806) 555-9900
jamesb@door.net

Career Profile

GRADUATING STUDENT
Career Targets: Law Enforcement ▪ Criminal Justice
Dependable, service-focused professional with strong background knowledge in Human Services and Criminal Justice, complemented by work experience reflecting promotion, excellent service delivery, and meticulous attention to detail. Able to manage multiple tasks and responsibilities in fast-paced, demanding environments; exercise calm approach in pressure situations.

Areas of Ability

- Customer Service
- Team Leadership
- Business Ethics
- Quality Standards

- Law & Rules Enforcement
- Public Service Delivery
- Public Speaking
- Team Collaboration

- Problem Solving/Resolution
- Workplace Organization
- Multi-Task Management
- Classroom Presentations

Education

Texas Tech University, Lubbock, TX
BSOE in Human Services, Emphasis in Criminal Justice
Completed August, 2006

Selected Upper-Level Coursework:

- Police Administration
- Minority Relations
- Criminal Investigations

- Vice & Narcotics
- Theories of Personality
- Introduction to Social Work

- Organized Crime
- Police-Community Relations
- Forensic Psychology

Work Experience

Certified Trainer / Bartender / Team Leader (2002 – Present)
Orlando's, Lubbock, TX
Promoted from original busser position to train staff of eight bussers in all duties; hand-selected by management to work bartending shifts in addition to training schedule. Provide hands-on instruction to new and established bussers; team with management to ensure fulfillment of all service and quality goals. As Bartender, interact directly with guests and team members, including servers, kitchen personnel, hosts, and managers; handle large amounts of cash on each shift.

Key Contributions/Accomplishments:

- Contribute comprehensive, quality training for diverse group of bussers; demonstrate patience with new employees and provide assistance during busy periods.
- Place uncompromising focus on guest service delivery; commended by management team for positive attitude and attention to guests' needs.

Garden Shop Associate (2001 – 2002)
Sutherland's, Lubbock, TX
Held responsibility for organizing garden shop, with emphasis on outside garden area; worked with team of five in arranging tables, displays, product placement, and inventory storage areas. Maintained area cleanliness and assisted customers as needed.

Key Contributions/Accomplishments:

- Earned consistently favorable performance evaluations and recommendation for promotion to Lead Associate position based on training and mentoring abilities.
- Maintained well-organized, attractive outside garden area to secure attention of customers and influence buyer decisions for key product offerings.

Volunteer – University Medical Center, Lubbock, TX. Worked in outpatient pharmacy for 18-month period; assisted with verifying inventory and filling prescriptions.

181

Transportation Security Specialist

This is a resume for a federal job, so it includes information you won't normally find in commercial sector jobs. It's also six pages long; here are the first two pages.

Edward William Hastings

7896 White Pine Lane

Kingston, New York 12401

Day Phone: (518) 444-3456

Secondary Phone: (518) 555-6789

Social Security Number:	xxx-xx-xxxx
Citizenship:	U.S. Citizen
Veteran's Status:	N/A
Federal Civilian Status:	N/A
OBJECTIVE:	Transportation Security Specialist (ASI), SV-4357-A
	Vacancy Announcement Number TSA-R-0274D
	Albany International Airport, Albany, New York
	Department of Homeland Security
	Transportation Security Administration

PROFILE:

Experienced Police and Security Specialist with 20 years of expertise, excellence and outstanding service as a Patrolman, Investigator and Sergeant in the Albany City Police Department, and 4 years of specialized experience as a Security Officer and Supervisor at the Albany International Airport.

EXPERTISE:

- 24 years experience as a city police officer with high level of expertise as a criminal investigator and firearms trainer. Six years experience as a Police Sergeant responsible for up to 35 officers in the line of duty.
- Expertise as security/police supervisor at the Albany Airport in daily security of airport buildings, facilities, and personnel through use of Federal, state, local, and FAA regulations.
- Expert knowledge in use and deployment of physical security systems to safeguard airport buildings, facilities, staff, and travelers.

AWARDS & RECOGNITION:

- Received many commendations for Recognition of Service in situations including making burglary arrests, gun arrests, and homicide arrests. Awarded two medals for heroism.
- Ranked second in the city in arrest/conviction rate in the first year on the job.
- Recipient of Mayor's Achievement Award for saving several people from a burning building.

PROFESSIONAL HISTORY:

Albany Police / Albany International Airport
North Albany, New York 14708 11/01 – Present

SERGEANT/SUPERVISOR, PATROL OFFICER (Airport)

Part time: 20 hours/week Col.
Salary: $XXXXX/year

Conduct Albany Police Department law enforcement and security operations at the Albany Airport, ensuring the daily safety and security of hundreds of passengers and employees of the Albany Airport.

Sergeant/Supervisor:

- Oversee a staff of four security officers during the day shift, ensuring officers are at their assigned posts, and coordinating breaks to assure that all posts are continually manned.
- Responding to all potential arrest situations to assure that all state and federal procedures are followed. In the event of a major incident I am responsible for notifying and deploying the proper personnel to various locations as needed.
- Make crucial decisions when situations call for immediate attention.

Patrol Officer:

In addition to being a supervisor I have worked at four different posts at the airport, involving:

- Assisting the Transportation Security Administration (TSA) employees with weapons and contraband discovered during their screening process, and taking custody of any weapons or contraband to determine if that person possessed it legally or if they were in violation of federal or state law.
- Monitoring all vehicle traffic as it entered in front of the terminal. Conducted over five hundred vehicle inspections ensuring nothing hazardous was brought into the terminal area by means of a motor vehicle.
- Monitoring all vehicle traffic entering airport service entrances, including jet fuel trucks, construction vehicles, airport personnel vehicles, sanitation trucks, and United Parcel Service vehicles. Verifying the drivers' identification, and, where applicable, visibly checking the contents of the vehicle to ensure it matched the manifest presented to me. Checking all deliveries entering the restricted Airport grounds that were eventually brought into the Airport terminal and on the airplanes. Checking the validity of the drivers' identification and then visibly checking the contents of the delivery truck, and contacting the appropriate Airport divisions to respond and escort delivery vehicle into restricted areas.
- Checking and verifying identifications from all truck drivers entering restrictive areas during the construction phase of the Airport runways and pads, inspecting over 60 vehicles a day.

Law Enforcement Manager

Strong resume for a seasoned professional in the public eye for thirty years and looking for a promotion.

EDWARD ROYCE

1400 Everett Street
San Jose, CA 95111

e.royce@mindspring.com

408-555-2222 (cell)
408-555-1212 (home)

LAW ENFORCEMENT MANAGEMENT

Moving organizations forward by putting people before paper and projects

More than 29 years of law enforcement experience, with a track record of consistently delivering improved results in each new assignment. Successful performance as acting Captain in 3 divisions during the absence of division commanders. Commitment to achieving high standards, both personally and for subordinates, to ensure providing outstanding public service. MA in Leadership and BA in Management.

Core Strengths & Expertise

- Large-scale event planning & management
- Community outreach
- Emergency & incident management
- Risk assessment
- Community & media relationship management
- Group training & public presentations
- Peer-to-peer & inter-organization collaboration
- Personnel counseling & investigations

PROFESSIONAL EXPERIENCE

San Jose Police Department, San Jose, CA   1979–Present
Lieutenant, Investigations (current)

As Investigations Lieutenant, oversee and manage 6 sergeants, 6 officers, 1 community service officer, and 2 office specialists. Coordinate daily operations of the Investigations Division, which includes managing major investigations, performing case assignments, conducting personnel counseling and background investigations, controlling narcotics "flash funds," and informally supervising an undercover unit. Previous assignments as Lieutenant: Media Relations; Administrative Services / Community Services; Field Operations; Honor Guard.

SPECIAL ACCOMPLISHMENTS:

Managed the planning and completion of a new custody facility within 9 months versus expected 18-month time-frame.

Orchestrated successful planning and completion of July 4th festivities attended by about 100,000 people. Coordinated development and implementation of a plan involving 4 police departments, 1 fire department, 65 personnel, and 10,000 residents and business owners.

Developed an effective Public Information Officer unit with 24-hour availability. Major actions and benefits included the following:

Achieved broader community outreach through diverse composition of the unit, including male, female, gay, white, and bilingual Hispanic, Vietnamese, and Korean members.

Established and fostered beneficial relationships with 135 media agencies.

Created a media resource book for future reference.

Formed and motivated a volunteer team that achieved the most successful Special Olympics fundraising campaign in the agency's history. Inspired commitment in team members and others to achieve challenging goals and negotiated support from corporate sponsors. Garnered positive media coverage, both print and television. Spearheaded a project to provide detectives with an electronic investigation facility that incorporated all required elements. Identified remedial actions, instituted training, and established accountability for outside vendors and department personnel. Achieved a working, digitally recorded interview system that included 4 interview rooms and extensive equipment.

Sergeant: Field Operations; Administrative; Detective; Department Training; Traffic / Motors; Patrol; Services Division; Honor Guard; TAC Squad; Field Training

Major actions and results as Sergeant included the following:

Selected as first person to hold Administrative Sergeant position, which required defining its responsibilities. Coordinated construction, creation, and implementation of the department's first temporary holding facility, from policy-manual writing through equipment acquisition.

Created and facilitated curriculum for the 3 most successful Advanced Officer Trainings in the department's history. Established strong new relationships with vendors, private industry, and city staff. Through successful budgetary control, helped increase training budget by 50% and returned 66% of training dollars spent through a variety of reimbursement processes.

EDUCATION & PROFESSIONAL DEVELOPMENT

Master of Arts in Leadership & Bachelor of Arts in Management, University of Santa Clara, Santa Clara, CA: graduated with Honors; achieved Distinction for Top Research Project
Level 1 Management Certificate, West Valley College, Saratoga, CA
POST Management Certificates including **Supervisory, Advanced, & Reserve,** POST Supervisory Leadership Institute, Class 46, Sacramento, CA; selected as Auditor for Class 56
POST Executive Development Course, San Mateo, CA
21st Century Leadership Course, City of San Jose, San Jose, CA
Crisis Communication #1, #2 & PIO Certificates, California Specialized Training Institute, Shell Beach, CA
FEMA ICS Training, San Jose, CA / Online
7 Habits of Highly Successful People, Covey Leadership Center, San Jose, CA

AWARDS & RECOGNITION

Distinguished Service Award, San Jose Police Department
"Top Cop" Award, Santa Clara County Criminal Justice Training Center
Silver & Gold Medals, Northern California Special Olympics Fundraising / Coordination

PROFESSIONAL AFFILIATIONS & CONTRIBUTIONS

Vice-President, Santa Clara County Training Managers Association
Co-Chair, South Bay Regional Criminal Justice Training Center Academy Advisory Committee
Associate Member, International Association of Chiefs of Police
Board Member, San Jose Police Officers Association
Speakers' Bureau Member, representing San Jose Police Department at diverse functions
Member, International Police Officers Association & Santa Clara County Peace Officers Association

COMMUNITY INVOLVEMENT

San Jose Kiwanis: current member; past member of Board of Directors
Special Olympics: past Chairman, Santa Clara County Law Enforcement Torch Run
San Jose High School Grad Night Committee Member, 2004

Security Guard

For a moment, imagine that you're a Hollywood star in need of a bodyguard and driver. Now read the first third of the page.

JOHN HARRISON

12345 Gilbert Street, #140 • North Hollywood, California 91442
Residence (818) 555-1111 • Mobile (818) 555-8998 • josehern1@email.com

SECURITY GUARD / DRIVER
—Bilingual English / Spanish—

- Over 20 years experience in all aspects of security including transport of goods and protection of residential and commercial properties.
- Possesses a strong work ethic with a verifiable record of perfect attendance and punctuality.
- Professional in appearance and work habits.
- Experienced in training and supervision.

CERTIFICATIONS

Security Guard License
Mace & Baton Certification
Gun Permit (.38. 98 mm 42 mm)
Health/Drug Certificate

Class B Driver's License
Forklift Certificate
Licensed Auto Mechanic
CPR / First Aid Certified

EXPERIENCE

Security Guard • 1999 to Present
FARGO, INCORPORATED, Van Nuys, CA
- Promoted to Messenger with full responsibility for security of armored truck, crew performance, and custody of goods.
- Coordinate daily activity of crew and truck; ensure safekeeping and security of shipments; control safe.
- Supervise crew members in safe and efficient performance of duties; assist in training new hires.

Recognition / Awards:
- 10 Year Anniversary Award for Contributions to the Success of Company, 2005
- Recipient of Safe Worker Awards 1995, 1998, 2000, 2005
- Inside Sales Manager/Office Manager

Armed Security Guard • 1997 to 1999
ESTELLA NIGHT CLUB, Sylmar, CA
- Maintained security of patrons and premises (including parking lots) at popular night club.
- Checked IDs; searched male patrons for weapons; assisted law enforcement agencies as required.

Security Guard • 1995 to 1997
NORTH VALLEY HOSPITAL, Granada Hills, CA

International Sales/Marketing Manager

Meghan had worked her way through a fast-track entry-level program and was ready to strike out on her own with another company.

MEGHAN M. ENGLAND

327 Bristol Circle • New Fort, NY 12345 • (888) 555-2200 • email@email.com

INTERNATIONAL SALES/MARKETING MANAGER
Strategic Planning/Staff Supervision & Training/Business Development

Highly accomplished and innovative marketing professional with key domestic and international experience in penetrating new markets, expanding existing accounts, and boosting profits. Fluent in English and Spanish. Results-oriented and visionary leader with proven success in new market identification, regional advertising, branding, and competitor analysis. Skilled in staff supervision and training, client relations, and strategic planning. Polished communication, presentation, negotiation, and problem-solving skills. Thrive in an intensely competitive, dynamic environment.

Core competencies include:

- Strategic Business Planning
- Budget Management
- Business Development/Planning
- Staff Training & Development
- Marketing Program Design

- Market Identification
- Team Building & Leadership
- Account Relationship Management
- International Client Relations
- Key Networking Skills

PROFESSIONAL EXPERIENCE

SAP AMERICA/SAP CHILE/LATIN AMERICA
Fast-track progression through the following key international marketing management positions:

Latin American Marketing Manager, **TAPP LATIN AMERICA – Newton Square, NY (2003 to Present)**
Direct and manage 360 degree company marketing programs throughout Argentina, Bolivia, Brazil, Chile, Colombia, Mexico, Paraguay, Peru, Puerto Rico, Venezuela, Uruguay, and the Caribbean Islands for the third largest software company worldwide. Oversee all aspects of Latin American regional marketing operations with broad responsibility for strategic planning and the indirect supervision of a staff of four marketing managers and various partner PR/advertising agencies.

Initiate, develop, and nurture new leads to generate additional sales revenues; collaborate with sales representatives to turn over leads and establish key relationships. Accomplish marketing goals by launching comprehensive marketing, advertising, and branding plans. Manage PR marketing functions through press releases, C-level executive interviews, press conferences, professional networking, and by creating an educational focus to allow greater company exposure. Ensure top-level customer satisfaction; collaborate with various outside agencies to administer and analyze customer surveys.

Develop and manage a $3 million marketing budget encompassing strategic industries such as banks, the public sector, and utility companies, as well as strategic solutions involving customer relationship management, enterprise resource planning, supply chain management, and small to mid-sized businesses. Design and implement regional advertising/branding strategies, and analyze progress through brand-tracking studies and competitive reports. Pioneer and manage key relationships with high-profile industry analyst firms. Interact with an outside global advertising agency to effectively leverage internationally syndicated relationship marketing campaigns. Serve as a company representative, liaison, and central point-of-contact for providing vital information, managing market research, and resolving issues at all levels.

Key Accomplishments:

- Spearheaded and manage a highly effective electronic quarterly newsletter, resulting in increased communications among Latin American employees.

- Directed an extensive 8-month regional team project in successfully training and educating all Latin American marketing personnel on the newly implemented CRM system in the areas of budgeting/planning, campaign planning, preparation, execution/analysis, lead management, and reporting.
- Developed and initiated the first regional budget with the global marketing team.
- Pioneered the centralization of advertising, resulting in greater discounts and significant savings.
- Accomplished greater recognition for the company including the first, and many additional publications of the company president in regional magazine articles.

Marketing Manager, **TAPP CHILE – Santiago de Chile (2001 to 2003)**

Spearheaded, built, and launched the first marketing department for the company's Chilean subsidiary, with full responsibility for hiring, training, scheduling, supervising, mentoring, and evaluating marketing coordinator and marketing analyst staff members. Managed an $800,000 Enterprise Resource Planning marketing budget. Interacted directly with the sales team to implement marketing strategies and meet goals. Managed extensive market research and analysis functions by collaborating with a local agency to conduct focus group interviews in evaluating both company and competitor solutions. Involved in all aspects of production, public relations, sales, relationship building, and customer service.

Key Accomplishments:

- Created and implemented a lead-generation program, resulting in an increased amount of qualified leads for Account Executives and improved revenues due to shorter sales cycle.
- Built solid PR operations by developing and managing high-impact press strategies; concurrently continued to initiate key media relationships, conduct press conferences and executive interviews.

Latin American Coordinator, **TAPP LATIN AMERICA – Wayne, NY (1998 to 2001)**

Managed the international roll-out and training for the company's Sales and Marketing Information System. Traveled extensively to various international locations to oversee all implementation and training functions. Concentrated on providing a full range of support to Finance and Marketing Directors.

Spanish Teacher, **CHASE CHEMICAL CORPORATION – Exton, NY (1998)**
Taught Spanish to top-level corporate executives.

Education & Credentials

BS in International Studies
EDUCATIONAL UNIVERSITY – Ross, NY (1997)

Language Studies
Seville/Segovia, Spain (1997)

Comprehensive Spanish Language Studies
Adelaide, Australia (1996)

Additional Professional Training in Business and Communications

Private Pilot License with instrument and commercial ratings

– Excellent Professional References Available on Request –

Database Administration

Jackie enjoys most the database administration portion of her current job and will be targeting employers that will give transition from database marketing to database administration.

Jacqueline Alois

188-17 Greenway, Salt Lake City, UT 00000
000-000-0000
jacqueline@alois.net

Database Management ◆ Marketing Communications ◆ E-mail Template Design

Profile

Sales and Marketing Support Professional with more than 14 years of experience in time-sensitive, fast-paced environments. Highly developed skills in oral and written communications, multitasking, attention to detail, and perseverance to completion. Keen insight into clients' perspectives, goals, and target audiences. Proficient with various software programs including Word, Excel, Access, and Goldmine.

Key strengths include:

- Database administration
- Market research
- Sales lead qualification
- Proactive problem solving
- Promotional copywriting

- Internal/external customer service
- Computer and procedural training
- Project coordination
- Relationship building
- New account development

Professional Employment History

GRAYROCK COMMUNICATIONS INC., BEAR CREEK, UT   2002–PRESENT

Database Marketing Coordinator for trade-show design firm

- Assist the President, Creative Director, and sales force of 7 in developing targeted messages to promote company's services (trade-show display design and client training seminars). Contribute ideas in brainstorming sessions and translate concepts into persuasive written materials (brochures, Web pages, and e-mail templates).
- Generate leads through extensive phone contact, which has facilitated the closing of numerous sales by determining clients' interests and addressing their specific needs or concerns.
- Enter and update all pertinent information for up to 500 clients and prospects on Goldmine system; create profiles and periodically send electronically distributed promotional pieces to keep company in the forefront for future business.
- Initially train new sales consultants on data mining to their best advantage as well as empower them for success in prospecting and cold calling. Organize sales assignments to avoid duplication of efforts.
- Coordinate all pre- and post-sale details with various departments.
- Demonstrated versatility and talent in several areas; was retained on staff despite 2 company downsizings.

QUIGLEY & VANCE, CARRINGTON, UT   2000–2002

Inside Sales Representative for graphic arts supply company

- Performed duties of sales liaison, assistant purchasing agent, and customer service representative.
- Streamlined department by automating the quote process and systematizing sales literature.

Education

Westview County College, Randolph, UT – A.A.S., Marketing Communications, 2000
Shelton Institute, Shelton, UT – Applied Writing and Database Administration courses, 2001

Sales Executive

Mary Ann was a recent college grad looking for a job while she continued training as a performer in New York.

MARY ANN BURROWS

123 Randolph Street
Wilmington, Delaware 19801
(555) 555-5555

Outside Sales/Account Manager/Customer Service

Energetic and goal-focused sales professional with solid qualifications in large account management and customer relationship building/maintenance. Proven ability to develop new business and increase sales within established accounts and mature territories. Self-confident and poised in interactions across all business hierarchies; a persuasive communicator and assertive negotiator with strong deal-closing abilities. Excellent time-management skills; computer-literate. Areas of demonstrated value include:

- Sales Growth / Account Development
- Commercial Account Management
- Prospecting & Business Development
- Customer Liaison & Service
- Consultative Sales / Needs Assessment
- Territory Management & Growth

PROFESSIONAL EXPERIENCE

Morris Mtr. Co., Wilmington, DE   1998 – Present
SALES EXECUTIVE (2000 – Present)
Promoted and challenged to revitalize a large metropolitan territory plagued by poor performance. Manage, service, and build existing accounts; develop new business, establishing both regional and national accounts. Serve as key liaison for all customers and work as the only outside sales representative in the company. Produce monthly reports for major national accounts.

Selected Results
- Reversed a history of stagnant sales; delivered consistent growth and built territory sales 22%, to $4.75 million annually, in less than 2 years.
- Surpassed quota by a minimum of 20% for 14 consecutive months.
- Personally deliver 95% of all sales generated for the company's main site.
- Prospected aggressively and presented products to key decision-makers during cold calls; opened more than 60 new commercial accounts.
- Improved account service and applied consultative sales techniques; grew sales in every established account a minimum of 15%.

MANAGER, Harrisburg Store (1998 – 2000)

MANAGER TRAINEE, Wilmington Store (1998)
Initially recruited as a management trainee and rapidly advanced to management of a retail location generating $1 million annually. Supervised and scheduled 12 employees. Budgeted and produced advertising, oversaw bookkeeping, and set/managed sales projections and growth objectives.

EDUCATION AND CREDENTIALS

B.S., BUSINESS MANAGEMENT, 1998
Wilmington College, New Castle, DE

Additional Training

> Building Sales Relationships, 2001
> Problem Solving Skills, 2001

Professional & Community Associations

> Member, Chamber of Commerce, 1999 – Present
> Member, Country Club and Women's Golf Association, 1999 – Present
> Youth Soccer Coach and FIFA Certified Referee, 2002 – Present

Sales Manager

Although the costs of book publishing won't allow color printing in *Resumes That Knock 'em Dead*, this resume jumped out at me because every relevant keyword has been highlighted in yellow. Try this when customizing a resume to a specific set of requirements.

MAX STERN
22225 Mayfair Way • Reston, VA 20190 • cell: (703) 555-2406 • *maxstern234@aol.com*

NATIONAL SALES MANAGER / PARTNER ACCOUNT MANAGER
Internet....High-Tech....Software Industries

Award-winning and dedicated sales manager with over a decade of success generating revenue and securing high-profile clients for industry leading companies, such as AOL Time Warner and Monster, with excellent levels of retention. Recipient of numerous prestigious sales awards for consistently exceeding sales goals and forecasts, and creating win-win client solutions. Utilize a consultative approach to assess client needs and provide solutions that meet the client's strategic goals. Expertise in:

❖ New Business Development	❖ High-Expectation Client Relations	❖ Relationship Management
❖ Key Account Management	❖ Consultation and Solution Sales	❖ Contract Negotiations
❖ Strategic Alliance/Partners	❖ Sales Training & Team Leadership	❖ Vertical Channel Sales

Proficient in all sales cycle phases from lead generation and presentation to negotiation, closing, and follow-up. Excel in training and mentoring teams to outperform the competition. Possess a high level of discipline, professional integrity, a passion for achieving organizational success, and a desire to always play on a "winning team."

PROFESSIONAL EXPERIENCE

TELCORDIA TECHNOLOGIES - Sterling, VA   10/2005 – Present
Telcordia Technologies provides trusted, neutral, and essential addressing, interoperability, infrastructure, and other clearinghouse services for communication service providers and enterprises worldwide.

National Sales Manager   3/2006 – Present
Promoted from Account Executive to National Sales Manager in eight months due to the consistent attainment of breakthrough sales results. Oversee national sales programs and supervise 15 sales representatives. Recruit, interview, hire, and train staff and evaluate performance for regional placements. Conduct quarterly sales meetings, develop goals, and coordinate all local, regional, and national training efforts.

- **Sales Performance**. Achieved **100% of sales quota despite a 60% reduction in staff.**
- **Awards & Recognition. Received 2005 Polaris Award, Neustar's most prestigious distinction,** which rewards superior performance and strong commitment to operational excellence. Nominees undergo a rigorous nomination and selection process, and awards are granted to the **"top-talent" (less than 5%)** of the company.
- **People Leadership.** Empowered staff and built a focused and loyal national sales team that consistently generated higher-than-budget sales.
- **New Business Development.** Key player in cultivating relationships with national clients including Nutrisystem, Expedia, and Mediacharge. Personally conducted assessment interviews with prospective clients to identify needs and formulate appropriate solutions.

Account Executive   10/2005 – 3/2006
- **Vertical Sales Campaign Management.** Through rigorous cold-calling and prospecting, launched company into the online advertising vertical, setting the stage for colleagues to follow. As a result, an impressive 65% of all online advertising currently comes through Neustar, and recurring monthly revenue exceeds $150,000.

HOTJOBS.COM – Annandale, VA
Yahoo! HotJobs has revolutionized the way people manage their careers and the way companies hire talent, and puts job seekers in control of their careers, making it easier for employers and staffing firms to find qualified candidates.

Southeast Account Executive   6/2004 – 9/2005
Aggressively sold Monster business solutions including database, web job hosting, and job posting packages within the Mid-Atlantic and Southeast Regions. Applied a solutions selling methodology to the sales cycle, promptly completing proposals and sales activities, closing sales opportunities quickly and efficiently, and completing necessary paperwork steps to successfully set projects in motion.

- Revenue Generation. Consistently exceeded monthly revenue target of $15,000. Cold-called and closed new business with major retail clients including Safeway and Wal-Mart.

TNS SOLUTIONS – Herndon, VA

TNS is the trusted source for the complete Oracle suite of data-centric solutions, including database, Oracle Fusion Middleware, and packaged applications.

Account Executive   1/2004 – 6/2004

Managed Sales for Oracle's 9iAS and Collaboration Suite, and developed new territory in district, including several key accounts such as RSA and Comstore. Managed a staff of 25 sales representatives.

- **Marketing.** Generated $1 million in new business development by creating local and state-wide marketing programs to generate buzz around Symantec products and DLT's Commonwealth of Virginia contract.
- **Campaign Management.** Prospected for new business through various marketing campaigns, including telemarketing, direct mail, targeted seminars, and partnerships with leading software firms.
- **New Business Development.** First to sell the hosted Collaboration Suite product to the Armed Forces Retirement Home, and secured the RSA relationship at DLT.
- **Trade Show Participation.** Networked extensively throughout the business community at industry trade shows, obtaining over 7,000 leads on average per event.
- **Awards and Recognition.** Generated the highest volume of accounts company-wide and was recognized with the DTL's prestigious "Sales Leader Award."
- **Partner Development.** Liaised with DLT staff and Oracle team to successfully manage the Symantec relationship.

AOL TIME WARNER – New York, NY

AOL Time Warner is a leading media and entertainment company, whose businesses include interactive services, cable systems, filmed entertainment, television networks, and publishing.

National Account Sales Manager   3/1998 – 10/2003

Sold print and online advertising across all AOL Time Warner properties (159 websites and publications) including People, Time Inc, Fortune, Netscape, and Compuserve. Interfaced directly with C-Suite executives, negotiated high-dollar contracts, and coordinated implementation. Managed accounts in three major verticals (retail, travel and tourism, and online gaming) and orchestrated post-sale professional services and resources. Recognized market needs and provided clients with new solutions, ultimately expanding their customer base.

- **Revenue Generation.** Booked $2.3 million in new revenue from a previously dormant category, exceeding $1.8 million revenue quota within eight months.
- **New Business Development.** Created $1.5 million in new business opportunities through presentations, cold calling, and successful final negotiations.
- **Training Course Development.** Designed and implemented a live prospecting training class focused on topics such as utilizing unique online tools (ad relevance and niche online sites, etc.) and capturing contact information from prospects and leads.
- **Customer Relations and Retention.** Forged strong partnerships with both clients and ad agencies, and increased advertisers' retention rates by encouraging collaboration between both groups.
- **Sales Presentations.** Completed intensive national sales and presentation training, and ranked #1 (out of 30) and #7 in the country in both 2000 and 2001, based on number of deals closed.

EDUCATION & TRAINING

Advanced Leadership Program

Telcordia Technologies • Sterling, VA • 2008
Bachelor of Arts in Business Administration
George Mason University • Fairfax, VA

Salesperson

The first page tells a strong, focused story. Notice the MBA after the name. Some object to this as not traditional. My view? Hard-earned and well-respected, it makes a powerful statement about the candidate. If you've got it, flaunt it!

SARA FERNANDEZ, MBA

22451 Blue Onyx Way • Fairfax, VA 22033 • cell: (703) 555-8791 • *sara123@comcast.net*

EXPERIENCED MULTIMEDIA SALES PROFESSIONAL
Advertising, Communications, and Media Industries
Strategic Sales & Marketing / New Product Launch / Advertising Strategy / Team Building

Ambitious, high-performing sales professional with a twenty-year track record of success generating revenue and securing high-profile clients for "best in class" companies. Recipient of **numerous prestigious sales awards** for consistently **exceeding sales goals and forecasts,** and creating win-win client solutions. Utilizes a consultative approach to assess client needs and provide "turnkey" solutions and programs that meet the client's strategic goals. Possesses deep expertise in branding, managing and positioning product lines, and implementing innovative solutions that drive revenue and bring unique products to the community. Expertise in:

❖ Business Development	❖ High-Expectation Client Relations	❖ Overcoming Objections
❖ Relationship Management	❖ Employee Communication Strategy	❖ Contract Negotiations
❖ Strategic Alliance/Partners	❖ Staff Motivating and Mentoring	❖ Channel Sales Strategies

Gifted sales strategist and tactician who excels in driving revenue through innovative channel development programs. Candidate differentiators include: the ability to produce ROI with passion, tenacity, and an ethical, compliance-based stance that nurtures respect and supports growth. Excels in training and mentoring teams to outperform the competition. Possesses a high level of personal and professional integrity, a passion for achieving organizational success, and a desire to **always play on a "winning team."**

VALUE LINE, INC. - Alexandria, VA • 3/2007 - Present
Sr. Sales Account Executive

Promoted and sold online advertising packages for leading investment and personal finance website. Identified and targeted key accounts and built relationships with senior level, often C-suite, clients and advertising agencies, building for them a "soup to nuts" online campaign and suite of services that generated results. Charged with delivering $1-3 million in advertising revenue, by analyzing existing sales channel relationships and developing a new strategy focused on market leaders.

THE LOUDOUN EASTERNER – Ashburn, VA • 7/1998 - 3/2007
Account Manager (3/2006 - 5/2007) • **National Ad Agency Channel Sales Representative** (2/2005 - 5/2006)
National Recruitment Sales Representative (7/1998 - 2/2005)

Aggressively recruited to develop, revitalize, and nurture productive relationships with *Fortune* 1000 companies and government agencies such as Inova Healthcare, BAE Systems, Lockheed Martin, and the FBI and CIA. Packaged and sold targeted multimedia integrated talent solutions and services to maximize effectiveness and reach to key clients.

Key Accomplishments:

➤ **Multimedia Campaign Development.** Offered existing clients an opportunity to "fish in a different pond" by developing and recommending new and alternative multimedia account strategies targeted at niche and passive candidate markets. Packaged and sold nontraditional campaigns from non-print sources targeted at key audiences.
➤ **Product Development.** Credited for designing and spearheading the execution of a cutting edge hotjobs.com product offering whereby keyword searches served up product-related ads along the margins of the website, generating more than $50K in incremental revenue per year.
➤ **Increased Advertiser Revenue.** Through a combination of face-to-face visits to 13-15 domestic markets, the creation of various telephone sales programs, and multiple e-mail marketing campaigns, grew Easterner JOBS Advertising Unit by $10 million, an increase of 25%, representing one-third of all sales for the unit.
➤ **Sales Performance.** Consistently met and exceeded quarterly and annual sales revenue goals, up to 131% above quota.

➤ **Awards & Recognition.** Recipient of Presidents Club Year End Award for demonstrating a commitment to customers that is reflected in business performance, a high-level of sales achievement, and customer satisfaction. Recipient of several prestigious awards including two Vice Presidents Club Awards, three Sales Achievement Awards, two Sales Excellence Awards, and a Publishers Award for Sales Excellence.

HOTJOBS.COM - Annandale, VA • 1991 - 1998
Vice President/General Manager - (1997 - 1998) • **Director of Client Services** - (1996 - 1997)
Account Executive - (1991 - 1996)

Progressed rapidly through and promoted into positions with increasing responsibility during tenure with Hot-Jobs.com. Directed all aspects of sales, marketing, and operations functions, and managed full P & L ($10 million in revenue) for Washington, D.C., office. Generated significant new client business and produced employer-branded recruitment and retention advertising campaign and execution strategies.

Key Accomplishments:

➤ **Cost Containment.** Spearheaded key cost-containment initiatives, saving thousands of dollars, resulting in a Top 10 (out of 35) "managerial profitability" ranking for the Washington, D.C., office.

➤ **New Business Development.** Partnered with the HotJobs sales channel in the design and implementation of a "business case building" sales contest, increasing HotJobs revenue by $2 million.

➤ **Sales Productivity.** Noted for driving $1 million in new business development in one year.

➤ **Process Improvement.** Spearheaded from conception to implementation an employee retention initiative. Launched monthly new hire performance appraisals (30/30's), which fostered a welcoming new hire experience, and drastically improved retention. Hired, trained, and supervised a staff of 12 account managers, and provided ongoing staff mentoring and support enabling them to grow company's client base.

➤ **High Expectation Client Relations.** Painstakingly researched and subsequently instituted the recommended solutions outlined in the business book classic *The Nordstrom Way: The Inside Story of America's #1 Customer Service Company* to maximize HotJob's customer satisfaction.

➤ **Employer Branding.** Partnered with senior level Human Resources clients in the design and development of uniquely branded corporate recruitment advertising strategies. Recommended tactical approaches for campaign execution.

➤ **Marketing Solutions.** Presented competitively positioned employee communication solutions and executed delivery of solutions such as collateral development, diversity strategies, university/college relations, and creative ad design to maximize employee communication programs.

Education

Masters of Business Administration
The Kogod School of Business – American University
Fully financed way through Business School

Bachelor of Science in Marketing
Michigan State University – East Lansing, MI

Member - National Society of Hispanic MBAs

Sales Account Manager

All I need to see before calling this candidate is the target job titles, the first two subheads, and three demonstrative graphics (graph bars in blue in the original). A picture is worth a thousand words in this instance.

TODD GUNDERSON

945 Main St. ♣ Lubbock, TX 79400 ♣ 806-555-9900 ♣ *todd_gunderson34@yahoo.com*
♣ Relocating to Las Vegas region

SALES DEVELOPMENT ♣ ACCOUNT MANAGEMENT ♣ CUSTOMER SERVICE

Career Overview:

Determined, customer-driven sales professional with extensive experience and track record of success in B2B sales and account management within the vending product industry, demonstrating ability to gain customer trust and secure win-win results. Build strong "partnerships" with individuals ranging from small business owners to decision-makers within high-profile customers (e.g. Wal-Mart, McLane) and business partners (Coca-Cola, Pepsi). Recognized for over-achieving goals and delivering exceptional service. Quick, on-the-spot learner.

Knowledge & Skill Areas:

❖ Consumer Product Sales	❖ Prospecting & Lead Generation	❖ Account Management/Retention
❖ Customer Relationships	❖ Order Writing & Fulfillment	❖ Backroom Inventory Management
❖ Product Merchandising	❖ Point-of-Sale Advertising	❖ Customer Needs Fulfillment

PROFESSIONAL EXPERIENCE

VENDING, INC., Lubbock/Amarillo, TX

Specializing in sales, installation, and maintenance of vending machines throughout Texas.

Sales Representative / Account Executive (1989 – Present)

Gained increase in responsibilities as business grew from wholesale liquor distributor to include sales and service of vending machines. Conduct extensive field research to determine optimal locations for machines; develop and deliver presentations to prospective customers detailing how merchandise will add to their bottom line. Negotiate contract terms and handle all closing and follow-up service activities. Additionally serve as Acting Manager in overseeing performance of 12 team members. *Key Contributions & Accomplishments:*

- *Revenue Growth* – Maintained consistent, year-over-year pattern of increasing revenues through robust and downturn economies, from $50,000 to $1.2 million as illustrated below:

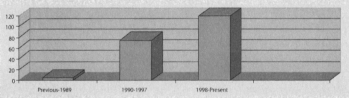

- *Product Placement & Market Share* – Grew number of machines from **1** to **450** from 1989 to 1998 prior to Lubbock opening; expanded inventory from **89** machines in 1998 to **780** by 2004, buying out some of the largest vendors in the area. Earned position as one of top vendors market-wide.
- *Key Account Management* – Built strong, sustainable relationships with broad range of accounts, including: **X-Fab of Texas • Industrial Molding • McLane • Owens-Corning • Wal-Mart**
- *Customer Service* – Provided excellent service for customer companies throughout tenure, characterized by immediate, thorough resolution of problems with equipment and friendly service.

* Prior roles as Sales Associate and Service Worker with Quality Vending. Played key role in expanding company's market presence and driving sales growth from **zero** to **$50,000** in annual revenues.

PROFESSIONAL DEVELOPMENT

Sales Training: Attended seminars and workshops featuring highly recognized speakers, including:

Zig Ziglar • Paul Tracy • Anthony Robbins

Technical Skills: Able to operate forklift, pallet jack, and other equipment. Skilled in MS Office and Internet tools.

Sales Account Manager

The entire first third of the page consists of highly relevant keywords relating to the job's deliverables. The sales chart breaks up the text, draws the eye, and packs a serious punch.

Thomas Vargas

3799 Millenia Blvd. Miami, FL **** | Phone: ***-***-*****
revenuedriver@aol.com

Account Management | **Product Marketing** | **Program Management**—IT Industry
Skillfully combining sales cycle management and technical expertise to drive revenue growth

LEADERSHIP PROFILE

Profit-driver and technology-expert professional with more than eight years' experience exceeding sales quotas, generating increased revenue, managing highly technical projects, and developing executive relationships. Well-rounded knowledge of the telecommunications industry with strong academic preparation: Master of Business Administration with Marketing and Management Information Systems majors; Cisco technical certifications.

Areas of Strength

Sales Goals | Territory Sales | Marketing | Executive Presentations | Emerging Technologies | Prospecting
Consultative Sales | Negotiations | Public Speaking | New Client Acquisition | Market Assessment
Competitive Market Intelligence | Corporate Communications | Account Management | Long-term Planning
Customer Service | Networking | Product Solutions | Vendor Relations | Strategic Initiatives

~ Solid career history of sales goal deliveries ~

Projection	Sales	Percentage
$240,000	$425,000	177%
$90,000	$106,200	118%
$102,000	$114,000	112%
$114,000	$123,120	108%
$185,000	$192,816	104%
$120,000	$121,000	102%

Top performing professional with a unique ability to implement technology knowledge into sales presentations. Technical expertise: install, configure, operate, and troubleshoot medium-size routed and switched networks, including implementation and verification of connections to remote sites in a WAN.

PROFESSIONAL EXPERIENCE & ACHIEVEMENTS

Corporate Account Manager III, WorldCom, Orlando, FL   2002–Present

Sales, Marketing, and Revenue Generation:
Prospect, qualify leads, and gain new business with persuasive presentations. Lead high-powered negotiations with corporate executives; develop proposals and create enticing sales presentations that include in-depth product education and executive briefings. Combine efforts with marketing specialists to study market trends, create customized and effective marketing strategies.
- Influenced prospective clients of *Fortune* 1000 companies; convinced them to close on multi-million-dollar, long-term contracts by demonstrating value over the competition.
- Managed total revenue of $5M and more than $250K per month customer revenue base.
- Grew revenue by 10% within one year by building and strengthened relationships with existing customers.

Technology Projects:
Design and lead complex network-implementation projects. Demonstrate expertise in Wide Area Networking including IPVPN, Private IP (MPLS), Frame Relay, ATM, and Private Line; local voice and private branch exchange service including class 5 and class 3 switching technologies. Introduce emerging technologies such as VoIP, VoFR, PoE, FCoIP, hosted IP Centrex, and Managed IP PBX.
- Increased profits by selling entire suite of telecommunication products and services, leveraging partner vendors like Cisco, Nortel, Avaya, and Checkpoint.

Network Solutions Consultant, Business Solutions, Houston, TX   2001–2002

Devised sales plans to cater to new and existing customer base and yielded higher revenue. Provided consultation on sales strategies, emerging technologies, existing line of products, and small networks to large client servers. Combined effort to work on projects that included WAN technologies, both data bandwidth and telephony solutions multiple platform networks.

- Developed new marketing techniques that increased sales opportunities and propelled sales from $110,000 in 2000 to $425,000 in 2001.

Network Design Consultant, Network Media, Austin, TX   2000–2001

Designed, installed, and maintained structured voice and data cabling projects, both Inside Plant and OSP. Prepared bids and estimations for structured cabling projects per RFP and RFQ.
- Collaborated and played an instrumental role in the winning bid for a $1.5M structured cabling job with the State of Texas Corrections Department.

EDUCATION

UNIVERSITY OF TEXAS AT DALLAS, Richardson, TX
MBA, dual concentration in Management Information Systems and Marketing, 2002
Activities and Societies: National Scholars Honor Society, UTD MBA Society, AITP

TEXAS A&M UNIVERSITY, College Station, TX
Bachelor of Business Administration in Information and Operations Management, 2000

CERTIFICATIONS

Cisco Certified Network Associate | Cisco Sales Expert

Sales and Marketing

All the right component parts. Of interest is the Selected Achievements section, which acts as a focusing tool for the reader who reads "achiever."

BOB M. SMITH

resumes@aresumesolution.com

#2 Nowhere St. • New York, NY
Home: 973.555.1212 • Mobile: 973.555.1313

Sr. Account Executive
❖ ❖ ❖

Highly qualified professional with strong background in sales, sales management, new business development, and account management in collaborative environments. Skilled in Enterprise Software Sales, Enterprise Content Management (ECM), Business Process Management (BPM), and Business Process Outsourcing (BPO). Increased sales by developing strong relationships with clients, staff, partners, and management from initial contact through implementation. Demonstrated talents in building name brand awareness through various marketing techniques.

- Exceptional ability to research, analyze, and translate information to diverse audiences.
- Skilled in developing and implementing marketing techniques that drive revenue and increase sales.
- Excellent communicator with a consultative sales style, strong negotiation skills, and a keen client needs assessment aptitude.
- Strong background in selling to C-level executives of large organizations.

Key Proficiencies Include:

➢ Business Process Analysis ➢ Contract Negotiations ➢ Order Management

➢ Sales & Marketing ➢ Relationship Development ➢ Strategic Accounts

➢ Document Management ➢ Technical Sales ➢ Business Development

SELECTED ACHIEVEMENTS

✓ Created a niche market at Pyramid Solutions, providing a repeatable business process management (BPM) solution for national financial services and mortgage industries, utilizing FileNet technologies. Project resulted in significant increase in deal profit margin by 35%.
✓ Awarded FileNet's "Innovative Solution of the Year" at Pyramid Solutions for development of a repeatable Business Process Management Solution in financial services industry. (2002)
✓ Met and exceeded quota by 103% and added (4) new named accounts in 2006 at Thunderhead Limited.
✓ Recognized as "Top Partner - Kofax Midwest Region" at Pyramid solutions. (2001 – 2004)
✓ FileNet Presidents Club Achiever 125% > of Quota. (1991–1996)

PROFESSIONAL EXPERIENCE

THUNDERHEAD, LTD. – London, England

Senior Sales Executive / Business Development Director   **2005 – Present**

Performs direct software sales for organization which specializes in 100% Open Standards-based Enterprise Document Generation. Focuses on financial services and government programs, including lending and unemployment insurance. Negotiates contracts with new vendors and partners. Cultivates relationships from initial contact through implementation with partners, clients, staff, and management.

- Hired as first direct sales staff member in for start-up operations in North America, gaining four new named accounts in first year
- Organized "Lunch & Learn" program for FileNet System Consultants and integration partners to provide product education.
- Established strategic partnerships with UNISYS, BearingPoint, and IBM Global Services, as well as several other system integrators.

TECHNICAL SOLUTIONS, INC. – New York, NY

DIRECTOR OF SALES & MARKETING   2001 – 2005

Charged with providing sales and marketing for systems integration and professional services organization. Increased brand awareness through development of comprehensive marketing materials. Analyzed business needs and implemented solutions that drove business growth. Created new pricing model and product structure. Provided sales and deployment of ECM and BPM solutions nationwide. Managed relationships with FileNet, Captiva, and Kofax. Implemented Business Process Analysis methodology that analyzed and documented customer's current processes, and how the technology could streamline these processes. Customers included: Flagstar Bank, Sun Trust, PMI, Comerica, Washtenaw County, Muskegon County, Oakland County.

- Awarded FileNet's "Innovative Solution of the Year" for development of Business Process Management Solution in financial services industry. (2002)
- Exceeded quota by over 100% two out of four years.
- Earned membership in FileNet's ValueNet Partner Million Dollar Club. (2002 – 2004)
- Developed and implemented new change management marketing program, assisting companies with installation of complex technology.

NEW SYSTEMS, INC. – New York, NY

REGIONAL SALES DIRECTOR   1997 – 2001

Directed and managed sales staff throughout the United States. Oversaw and managed budget of $6.2M. Created and implemented new value-based sales process for rapid prototyping technology. Developed and installed Rapid Manufacturing Application within the Aerospace industry. Provided global sales support for Ford Motor Company, DaimlerChrysler, and GM. Trained sales and engineering staff members. Oversaw all regional operations, including deals and resources on a national basis. Established and managed relationships with Business Process Outsourcers (BPO).

- Reduced operating costs for field operations by combining facilities.
- Facilitated professional sales training boot camps.
- Discovered highly complex application, resulting in creation of InVisiLine braces.
- Transformed 3D Solutions sales force from product focus to solutions-oriented focus, through process analysis, training, and ROI models.
- Grew annual sales 15% by focusing sales teams on solution sales.

ABC CORPORATION – New York, NY

DISTRICT MANAGER / SENIOR ACCOUNT EXECUTIVE   1990 – 1997

Promoted from Senior Account Executive in 1995. Provided direction and management to 14 staff members, charged with providing large enterprise document management and BPM solutions. Gained new channel partners with application providers and consulting vendors. Charged with selling $MM solutions to C-level executives at large organizations, including GE Aircraft Engines, Medical Mutual of Ohio, Goodyear Tire and Rubber, Steelcase, Dow, Ford Motor Credit, U of M Health Systems, Comerica, Huntington Banks, and Key Banks.

- Increased indirect sales channels by 100%.
- Awarded "Presidents Club" for exceeding quota by 125%, 1991 – 1996.
- Earned "Rookie of the Year," 1990.
- Received "Eastern Region Top Producer," 1993.

EDUCATION
Bachelor of Science, Business Administration • The Ohio State University – Columbus, OH

Sales and Marketing

Brand/Product Manager

I like this resume targeted to a specific job and taking part of the job posting as the content for what otherwise might be an objective/summary/profile. It works well for human eyes and will come out tops in the employer's database searches.

Jackie Byrd

Address City, State Zip

Home Phone Cell Phone E-mail Address

Career Target

BRAND/PRODUCT MANAGEMENT, GAMING INDUSTRY

Brand/Product Manager, WizKids.com

Looking for experienced Brand Manager to direct product lines, develop strategic marketing promotions, product research & positioning, and cross-departmental interfacing. Minimum 3 years management/marketing experience. A+ with game marketing experience.

Qualifications

Over 15 years of overall experience in sales and marketing leadership positions. Demonstrate strong commitment to maintaining highest level of product quality while driving revenue growth through multiple marketing and promotional strategies. Able to identify and convey Unique Selling Proposition (USP) to customers/business partners. Skilled in all core marketing and business development disciplines, with particular strength in product evangelism. Hold deep passion and interest in gaining market share for gaming company. <u>Certified HeroClicks Facilitator.</u>

- As key point of distinction, recognized as lifelong participant in the field of gaming, with experience in the '80s working for gaming pioneer Chaosium under the tutelage of renowned game designers Sandy Petersen and Greg Stafford. Completed all editing, mapping, layouts, and writing for SuperWorld Companion of SuperWorld; worked on supplemental modules for Cthulhu. In addition, managed gaming store during similar time period; eventually sold business that remains profitable two decades later. *

Knowledge & Skill Areas

Strategic Marketing & Promotional Campaigns — Branding & Competitive Positioning — Game Marketing
Product Research & Analysis — Customer Relationship Building — Team Building & Leadership
Product Line Management — Point-of-Sale Displays — Collateral Material Development
Sales Prospecting & Lead Generation — Presentations, Negotiations & Closing

Professional Experience

Marketing Manager   (2000 – Present)

ANVIL BUSINESS DEVELOPMENT, Seattle, WA

In charge of developing company marketing plan, managing vendor relationships, hiring/training sales staff, evaluating team performance, and completing sales in hands-on account executive role. Contract with companies to develop market presence for telecommunications products and services, working with broad range of clients that includes retailers, software development firms, and real estate developers.

- Redeveloped Web site and all marketing materials for key client Pacific Rich Homes. Tracked results of advertising placements, created sales/marketing plan, and secured exposure in *Everett Business Journal.*
- *Results: Increased sales and established pre-selling pattern affecting every community.*
- Improved management of product line (profile assessments) by writing brochure for customization to **5 industries,** including health care and non-profit organizations.

Account Executive   (2000 – 2001)
ESCHELON / ICM COMMUNICATIONS

Oversaw all aspects of sales in both employment positions, with focus on medium-sized companies. Scope of responsibility included making cold calls, conducting fact-finding research, delivering presentations, securing new accounts, and creating referral partner network.

- Introduced sales and marketing strategies that contributed to product improvement and revenue growth in downturn, heavily competitive market.

Account Executive   (1996 – 2000)
NORTHWEST WIRELESS, Seattle, WA

Directed sales and marketing initiatives for business clients. Managed all phases of sales cycle, transitioning to consultative selling approach as company increased lines to accommodate customers.

- Played key role in driving company from start-up to Nextel New Dealer of the Year recognition in 1998. Assisted in migrating company from one to multiple carriers.

Broker   (1994 – 1996)
AFLAC, Seattle, WA

Represented supplemental insurance programs to companies and their employees.

- Created "package" approach to sell multiple insurance lines simultaneously, resulting in **228%** revenue increase and average sales growth from **$360** to **$820** annual premium.
- Earned formal recognition as Number One Producer for largest supplemental insurance company worldwide; received commendations for opening most new groups in WA/OR regions in 1995.

Senior Partner   (1985 – 1993)
RESOURCE MANAGEMENT CENTER, Seattle, WA

Initially hired as Sales Manager and earned subsequent promotions to GM and Senior Partner, respectively. Delivered consulting and training seminars in all areas of business management, including finance and accounting, business growth, personnel law and management, taxes and reporting, and personal development.

- Spearheaded company's expansion into computer market to offer high-end accounting systems, wide area networks, centralized processing solutions, and ISDN to customers.

Professional Experience

Professional Training Courses:

Dale Carnegie Sales Training — Brian Tracy-Strategic Sales Training — Tom Hopkins Sales Training — Nextel Basic, Advanced, and Consultative Selling Training — Certified PSI Disk Cashing Controllers — Certified PC Multi-User Operating System — Certified Novell Netware — License in Insurance for Health, Life and Disability / Certified & Certified Trainer in Cafeteria Plans/Section 125 — Telecommunications Training Courses: PBX Trunks, Digital Switched Service, Digital Data Service, ISDN, Frame Relay Service, Self-Healing Network Service, DS1 (includes SHARP/SHARP+), DS3, Analog Private Line

Computer Skills: Skilled in Excel, Word, PowerPoint; experienced with sales programs Onyx, Gold Mine, & ACT
Community Involvement: Community Advocate, Role Playing Game Association (RPGA). Work with at-risk youths in running games on late Friday and Saturday nights, providing fun, appealing alternative to prohibited activities.

* Certified HeroClicks Facilitator; run demos of CreepyFreaks (under company's authorization) and promote Pirates of the Spanish Main, both products by the WizKid Corporation *

Sales Professional

Strong one-page sales resume with a layout that packs in lots of data and keywords. The chart speaks loudly of a young, motivated professional who can close the deal.

MARK BIENLICH
SALES REPRESENTATIVE

Clinical Sales • Territory Sales • Customer-focused Selling Strategies

SUMMARY OF QUALIFICATIONS

Performance-focused sales professional, recognized for consistently increasing sales in challenging territories. Track record exceeding sales goals and generating more than $4M in combined revenue throughout career.

More than ten years' experience in all aspect of sales cycle management: lead generation, customer needs assessment, multimedia presentation, negotiation, closing, follow-through, relationship management, and development of customer loyalty. Experienced in pharmaceutical sales and preparing engaging clinical presentations, which include visual and audio appeal. Computer literate: MS Access and PowerPoint.

Areas of Strength:

- ➢ Sales Presentations
- ➢ Sales Closing
- ➢ Direct Sales
- ➢ Revenue Growth
- ➢ Consultative Sales
- ➢ Customer Retention
- ➢ Product Demonstration
- ➢ Staff and Customer Training
- ➢ Account Development

PROFESSIONAL EXPERIENCE & ACCOMPLISHMENTS

Account Manager, O'BRIEN PAINT CORPORATION, Minneapolis, MN   2005–Present
Manage 130 accounts in 12 Midwestern states and three Canadian provinces. Gain new accounts, prepare proposals, and negotiate aggressively. Report to the district manager of one of the top manufacturers in America with an annual revenue over $1B.

- Reached sales goals, consistently increased sales by 12% each year:

	2005	2006	2007
Sales Revenue Growth	$1M	$1.12M	$1.25M

- Gained 11% market share by renegotiating and convincing clients to extend contracts on existing accounts from six months to three years.
- Improved customer service by 32% for 2006 by following up after the sale, leveraging position with customers, and reassuring their decisions.
- Generated 65 new accounts and $50K additional revenue on existing accounts by leading-high-powered negotiations.

Sales Representative, CIM CLARK-SHEEHAN, Chicago, IL   2002–2005
Sold multiple pharmaceuticals for a multimillion-dollar corporation. Generated leads, cold called, made clinical presentations, nurtured customer relationships, and managed accounts.

- Produced $450K sales increase and surpassed company's record quota by 9%.
- Earned salesman of the year for three consecutive years by driving revenue growth via enticing, client-focused product presentations.
- Converted new hires into strong sales closers that became top-territory producers.

EDUCATION

Bachelor of Science Degree, SOUTHERN ILLINOIS UNIVERSITY, Carbondale, IL, 2001

PROFESSIONAL DEVELOPMENT

Seminars: Situational Leadership | Successful Selling | Sales and Motivation Skills
2122 S. Main St., Jacksonville, IL 62650 • Home: 217-555-0098 • Cell: 827-555-7629 • Email: *mark2@aol.com*

Bank Branch Management

SCOTT E. BOWMAN

19 Harrington Lane • Manalapan, NJ 07726 • 555.770.8956 • boman4765@hotmail.com

FINANCE ~ BANKING
Branch Management/Customer Service

Well-qualified and results-oriented **Finance and Banking** professional with experience and demonstrated accomplishments developing corporate growth, stability, and financial performance. Skilled analyst with strong organizational and communication abilities, and proven leadership qualities. Broad-based understanding of financial needs at all levels of business including evaluating, analyzing, and communicating financial data. Demonstrated broad-based strengths and accomplishments in:

Finance & Banking	Project Management	Teller Operations
Marketing Financial Services	Customer Service Relations	Loan/Account Origination
Team Management	Sales Management	Problem Solving
eBusiness Management	Communications	Continuing Education
Supervision/Leadership	Branch Management	Strategic Management

Recipient – Commerce Capital Markets Referral Award – July/August 2004

PROFESSIONAL EXPERIENCE

COMMERCE BANK, New Brunswick, NJ ~ 2004 to Present
CUSTOMER SERVICE REPRESENTATIVE (CSR)
Counsel clients in the selection of financial products in order to meet their financial planning and banking needs. Create and process client accounts providing excellent customer service. Sell and refer bank products based on specific sales focus (Commerce Capital Markets, Commerce National Insurance and Residential Mortgage). Identify prospective clients and develop and implement presentations for clients. Originate and process consumer and mortgage loan applications. Extensive knowledge of bank lending policies, practices, compliance, and underwriting criteria. Familiar with processing collateral loans, unsecured personal loans, asset-based loans, and mortgage-based loans. Process a myriad of loan documentation performing research activities when necessary.

Accomplishments:

- Consistently met and exceeded sales quotas and standards by cross-selling and up-selling bank products and services.
- Increased branch loan production volume.
- Sold a variety of loans by pulling CBA, creating loan worksheets, and making recommendations to lenders upon request.
- Ensured that loan policies and procedures were followed in accordance with audit guidelines.

STAR FIRE AUTOGRAPHS, Manalapan, NJ ~ 1999 to Present
BUSINESS MANAGER/PRINCIPAL
Established and currently manage Internet and mail order entertainment media business. Implemented strategic marketing programs successfully retaining clients and achieving market position. Instituted pricing structure after conducting extensive marketing research utilizing industry resources. Explored marketing and advertising opportunities adding value to new initiatives. Tracked data and improved business operations accordingly.

Accomplishments:

- Grew annual revenues to $30K.
- Authored inventory item descriptions and managed customer service relations.

EDUCATION/TRAINING

FAIRLEIGH DICKINSON UNIVERSITY, Madison, NJ
BA – History, Minor – Politics

COMMERCE UNIVERSITY BANK COURSES
Finance, Supervision, Business Management, Consumer Lending, Customer Service, Loan Products, Privacy Compliance, Loan Underwriting, BSA/AML, Foreign Assets Control, Bank Secrecy, etc.

COMPUTER SKILLS
Microsoft Office, Lotus Notes, dBase, Basic, HTML

Finance, Banking, and Insurance

203

Credit and Collections

James is a bank executive who wanted to relocate to the Dallas/Fort Worth area. This particular format showcased his credentials in a straightforward, results-driven manner.

JAMES HOFFMAN

2212 Gate Drive _ Phoenix, AZ 85001 _ 928.444.0888

PROFESSIONAL OBJECTIVE

Opportunity with a Dallas-based financial services organization where expertise in commercial collections, credit administration, and financial analysis/structuring contributes to increased profits.

PROFILE

- Extensive general business experience in the financial services industry, with credentials in both line and staff positions. Areas of expertise:

  - credit/portfolio administration
  - asset structuring/restructuring
  - commercial collections
  - loan documentation
  - regulatory compliance

  - financial analysis
  - risk assessment/underwriting
  - problem asset resolution/loan work-outs
  - operations/information integration
  - lender liability issues

- Background in diverse environments ranging from major regional financial holding companies to large and small community banks.
- Driving force in the establishment of a newly chartered commercial bank in the Phoenix area.
- Customer-focused professional whose philosophy is to "do it right the first time."
- Viewed by clients as an individual who is worthy of their trust, and who holds their best interests paramount.
- Effective at building sound internal/external relationships to support client and organizational goals.
- Actively involved in leadership roles focused on community development.

EDUCATION

M.B.A. **Financial Administration**
Northwestern University, Evanston, Illinois, 1982

B.A. **Business-Economics**
Vanderbilt University, Nashville, Tennessee, 1980

Executive Professional Development Programs:

- Northwestern University – Management School for Corporate Bankers
- University of Texas – National Commercial Lending Schools
- Certified Commercial Lender – American Bankers Association
- Computer School for Executives – Bank Institute of America
- Leadership and Lending – National Credit Executives Association

EXPERIENCE

RIVCOM STATE BANK, Phoenix, Arizona   1998 – Present
- Founder/Charter Director/Executive Vice President and Senior Lending/Compliance Officer.
- Member of three-person team that founded and organized a new state-chartered FDIC insured commercial bank. Established nine-member Board of Directors.

Key Accomplishments:
- Led efforts in generating $17.2 million in start-up capital.
- Grew bank into a profitable organization with $120 million in assets, while maintaining strong loan quality.
- Personally managed 70% of the bank's borrowing client base and 60% of $72 million in total loans outstanding.

U.S. LEASING COMPANY, Fort Worth, Texas   1995 – 1998
- Senior Vice President, Leasing – Managed lease origination process for a national leasing company. Offerings included private label programs for five Fortune 500 companies. Trained, supervised, and developed new team members.

Key Accomplishment:
- Introduced commercial bank quality underwriting procedures to correct prior portfolio deficiencies for leases averaging $75,000 per transaction.

STATE BANK AND TRUST, Springfield, Illinois   1989 – 1995
- Vice President and Senior Lending Officer – Responsible for bank's credit administration and management of commercial, consumer, and residential lending. Chaired loan and Community Reinvestment Act (CRA) committees.

Key Accomplishment:
- Developed and implemented new credit culture, achieving an all-time bank record of 1.12% ROA, from a negative .67%.

COMMERCIAL BANK, Chicago, Illinois   1983 – 1985
- Commercial Lending Officer – Special Loan Division – Established and managed new loan work-out activity to support the bank's domestic commercial lending group.

Key Accomplishment:
- Directed reduction of internally classified credits and nonperforming assets by 70% each.

CIVIC AND PROFESSIONAL ACTIVITIES

- Board of Directors and Past President, Local Chamber of Commerce
- International Association of Bank Executives, Charter Member and Board of Directors
- Senior Board Member, National Banking Institute of Arizona

Intern

This is an internship resume that will fast-track the start of any career.

Dan Tranner

San Jose, CA · 444.444.4444 · *dantranner@anyserver.com*

QUALIFICATIONS FOR BANK OF AMERICA INTERNSHIP

- Committed to a career combining formal education in economics with practical work. Experienced with analysis for project management, including budgets, labor resources, and timelines. Prepared and delivered numerous presentations on project status to city and PG&E officials. Researched and presented options to property owners and investors for construction materials.
- History of taking on responsibility and successfully managing personnel for multimillion-dollar project. Excellent communication with individuals, businesses, municipalities, and professional firms. Conversational Spanish.

EDUCATION

SAN JOSE STATE UNIVERSITY, San Jose

Masters, Economics

Expected completion December 2008

UNIVERSITY OF CALIFORNIA, Davis

Bachelor of Arts, Economics, 2005

PROFESSIONAL BACKGROUND

CONFIDENTIAL, San Jose, CA · 2006 – 2008

Installer of wet and dry underground utilities for new developers and municipalities

Project Manager

- Managed $3.6M project to install new underground dry utilities and new street lights on Main Street in Santa Cruz. Worked with city, PG&E, telephone and cable companies. Project took approximately 1-1/2 years for planning, execution, and completion. Averaged approximately 15 full-time crew, including both union and non-union.

INDEPENDENT CONTRACTOR · 2005, 2006

DAVÉ CONSTRUCTION · 2005

Residential and investment property new construction and renovation

Construction Manager / Project Manager

- Functioned as general contractor for construction of new $2M, 4,700 sq. foot residential property. Hired and managed approximately 300 subcontractors and vendors over the course of the project.
- Obtained building permits, and worked with general contractors and clients on architectural plans. Oversaw daily construction, and handled accounting, including paying all subcontractors.
- Worked with owner to convert 1,000 sq. foot home to 3,200 sq. feet. Same duties noted as above. Sale of home resulted in net profit of almost $400K for property owner.

RISK MANAGEMENT SOLUTIONS (RMS), Newark, CA

Global provider of expertise to manage catastrophic risk

Software Upgrade Aide · Summer 2001

Accounts Receivable Clerk · Summer 2000

LEADERSHIP EXPERIENCE

PHI DELTA THETA, Davis, CA · 2000 – 2005, Consecutively

President / Vice President / House Manager / Treasurer

Financial Manager

You read this resume and immediately know that the career direction is no accident. I fully expect to see this focused young professional submitting a resume for a VP position within twelve years.

Norman Stanley

5555 Ficus Lane #555   (310) 555-5555
Los Angeles, California 90049   nstanley@email.com

Target Positions—FINANCIAL SALES / PORTFOLIO MANAGEMENT
Strengths in Research / Analysis / Client Relations / Financial Planning

RECENT GRADUATE with demonstrated leadership strengths and proven ability to manage multiple responsibilities in a fast-paced environment with critical deadlines... Worked throughout college to partially self-finance education... Well organized with attention to detail... Works well independently as well as collaboratively in a team setting... Proven ability to "think outside the box" in identifying problems and implementing innovative solutions.

——Areas of Strength——

Sales & Market Research & Analysis • Competitive Intelligence • Strategic Planning • Project Management
Budget Management • Team Building & Leadership • E-commerce • Website Maintenance

EDUCATION

UNIVERSITY OF SOUTHERN CALIFORNIA, Los Angeles, CA; 12/ 2007
Bachelor of Science in Business Economics; Minor in Accounting
GPA: 3.8

Activities: Treasurer—Alpha Beta Gamma Fraternity... President—Student Accounting Society...
Vice President—Business-Economics Society

PROFESSIONAL EXPERIENCE

PORTER WARNER, INC., Century City, CA • Jan. 2006 to Nov 2007—*Concurrent with Studies*

Portfolio Manager / Finance Assistant to Senior Portfolio Managers
Set up and managed client accounts to ensure compliance with established policies and procedures. Collaborated with other financial institutions to facilitate money and account transfers. Conducted in-depth research utilizing Internet, Bloomberg, and direct corporate contact, etc.

- Implemented and maintained detailed database to accurately track clients and prospects.
- Streamlined client communication process.
- Collaborated with support staff to maintain account compliance and reduce missing documents.

INTERNAL REVENUE SERVICE, Los Angeles, CA • 2005, 2006, 2007 *(Tax Seasons)*

Volunteer Income Tax Assistance (V.I.T.A.)
Prepared income tax returns for low-income families and students; provided step-by-step instruction to guide taxpayers in filling out future returns.

ZEMAN & YOUNG, C.P.A.'s, INC., Los Angeles, CA • Oct. 2004 to Jan. 2006 *(Concurrent with Studies)*

Jr. Accountant
Prepared individual and corporate income tax returns; audited company records to identify fraud; investigated, compiled, and summarized data to support records for IRS audit.
- Maintained client books through financial statement preparation.
- Prepared investment proposal for start-up company.

Previous Experience: Camp Counselor *(Summers 2001 to 2003)*

Computer Skills—Microsoft Word, Excel, PowerPoint, Access, Outlook, Peachtree, QuickBooks, Turbo Tax
Foreign Languages—Proficient in Oral and Written Spanish, including business terminology
Community Activities—Little League Coach, Big Brothers

General Ledger Accountant

Powerful punch on the first page. The resume's organization gives fast access to the credentials of someone who clearly lives up to the target job title.

CURTIS SMITH

Confidential, CA   curtis.smith@comcast.net   C: 999.999.9999

EXPERIENCED GENERAL LEDGER ACCOUNTANT

Strong general ledger experience supported by accounts payable background. Takes leadership role in systems conversions, process improvement, and establishing better vendor relations. Communicates well with team members, purchasing department, and operations employees.

Selected Career Accomplishments – Confidential Corporation

- Team Lead in successful 1-1/2 year conversion to global SAP Purchase to Pay module.
- Reconciled $3.2M vendor discrepancy that was over one year old by working closely with another confidential location in the Netherlands. Researched and reviewed every individual invoice and payment, and corrected each transaction that had not been properly recorded.
- Eliminated significant backlog of past-due invoices, including establishing improved procedures to prevent future problems. Rebuilt vendor relations.

CORE COMPETENCIES

General Accounting

Accounts Receivable	Internal Controls
Billing	Intercompany Accounts
Bank Deposits	Inventory Control
Bank Statement Reconciliations	Journal Entries / Accruals
Budget Analysis – Cost Centers	Master Data: Vendors, Materials, Sources
Cash Applications	Month End Close
Cashier – Cash Controls	Payroll Processing
Fixed Assets	Staff Training

Accounts Payable

Account Reconciliations	Procurement Procedures
Credit Cards / Employee Expenses	Sales / Use Tax Returns
Full-Cycle Accounts Payable	Systems Conversion (SAP)
Invoice Discrepancy Resolution	Vendor Relations
Payment Monitoring / Verification	Wire Transfers

PROFESSIONAL BACKGROUND

CONFIDENTIAL CORPORATION, Anywhere, CA   **2001 – 2007**
Global supplier of confidential products and services
General Ledger Accounting Specialist, 2004 – 2007

Balance Sheet: Reconciled all accounts and subsidiary ledgers, including accounts payable, accounts receivable, and fixed assets.

Intercompany: Invoiced and reconciled for both domestic and international company locations.

Month End Close: Prepared reconciling and recurring journal entries. Compared cost center budgets to actual.

Fixed Assets: Tracked construction-in-progress and capitalized assets in accordance with GAAP.

Accounts Receivable: Assisted all functions, including cash applications and reconciling customer accounts.

SPECIAL PROJECT, SAP IMPLEMENTATION, 2005 – 2007

Team Lead – **Purchase to Pay:** Managed two other staff for successful implementation of Purchase to Pay process for SAP conversion.

Master Data: Set up and implemented Master Data accounts, including vendor, material, Product Information Record (PIR), and source listings.

Process Implementation and Documentation: Incorporated and revised existing purchasing and subcontracting processes into new system. Trained other team members.

Key User – General Accounting and Controlling: Resource for reviewing master data for general ledger setup. Assisted with GL account mapping for reporting and financial statement consolidation. Assisted users with cost center accounting. Assisted in transfer of accounts receivable and accounts payable to shared services department.

ACCOUNTS PAYABLE SPECIALIST, 2001 – 2004

Full-Cycle Payables: Handled all aspects of accounts payable, including general ledger coding. Processed 100 checks per week, $2.5M per month.

Vendor Relations: Eliminated significant backlog for processing vendor and freight invoices that happened with job predecessor. Improved vendor relations by bringing payables up-to-date.

Process Improvement: Streamlined process for accounts payable invoices. Implemented effective Excel report to keep track of discrepant invoices.

ISYS MANUFACTURING, INC., Concord, CA   **1998 – 2001**

$50M manufacturer of electronic components for semiconductor industry

ACCOUNTING CLERK

Payroll: Processed full-cycle payroll for 130 salaried and hourly employees.

Accounts Payable: Performed lead role for full-cycle accounts payable with approximately 100 weekly checks.

Accounts Receivable: Handled full-cycle accounts receivable including billing, cash applications, labor applications, and general ledger entries.

Inventory Control: Tracked parts and finished goods inventory worth approximately $5M. Implemented improved procedures for shipping and receiving.

ORCHARD SUPPLY HARDWARE, Concord, CA   **1996 – 1998**

CASHIER INSTRUCTOR / BACKUP CUSTOMER SERVICE

Managed front-end store operations. Trained and scheduled all cashiers.

TECHNICAL EXPERIENCE

Microsoft: Word, Excel, PowerPoint

Applications: *SAP:* Vendor, Purchasing

        PRMS: Accounts Payable, Accounts Receivable, Vendors, Customer Masters, Journal Entries

        Payroll: ADP

        Other: MAS90, FAS Fixed Asset Software, T Rowe Price 401k system, Lotus Notes

Non-Profit Fundraising Consultant

Senior re-entry resume of a retired executive targeting the non-profit sector and showing he's done his homework.

NORMAN BEACON

555 Valley Glen Ridge • Valley Glen, California 91405

Home (818) 555-1234 • Mobile (818) 555-9876 • NormanBeacon@email.com

PUBLIC RELATIONS / COMMUNITY / FUNDRAISING CONSULTANT— NONPROFIT SECTOR

- Retired Corporate Executive, committed to providing expertise in communications to promote the public good.
- Combines distinguished career building and leading successful company growth with extensive background contributing efforts to charitable causes.
- Proven strengths in the fine art of communications and negotiations with the ability to establish confidence and trust, resolve conflicts, build consensus, and motivate parties with divergent opinions toward common goals.
- Excellent listening skills with focus on a "win/win" philosophy.
- Extensive network of contacts.

Verifiable Record of Raising Significant Amounts of Money for Charitable and Public Causes

PROFESSIONAL BACKGROUND

Personal Sabbatical—Travel, Community Involvement • 2006 to Present

WEST COAST SPECIALTY CONFECTIONS, Los Angeles, CA

Managing Partner / Chief Operating Officer • 1982 to 2006

Launched and directed activities of confectionary manufacturing company from start-up through 20 years of successful operations.

- Built business from initial capital investment of $10,000 to annual revenues in excess of $40 million.
- Established and nurtured key contacts with retail and wholesale operations on local, regional, and national level including major chain stores.
- Sourced vendors and contractors and directed manufacturing operations in U.S. and abroad.
- Negotiated with union and non-union personnel, consistently achieving a win/win outcome.
- Generated widespread goodwill for company though extensive, ongoing involvement with numerous community charitable organizations. Recognized by city for contributions.
- Named "Local Business of the Year" by *Valley Glen Business Journal*.

EDUCATION

B.A. in Humanities, UNIVERSITY OF CALIFORNIA, Los Angeles

COMMUNITY ACTIVITIES —Partial List

Fundraising Chair—Friends of Valley Glen Hospital
Platinum Donor, Chair of Steering Committee—Valley Glen Youth Association
Member, Past-Officer—Valley Glen Chamber of Commerce
Member, Board of Directors—Neighborhood Youth Industries, Inc.
President—Valley Arms Homeowners Association

ADDITIONAL INFORMATION

Foreign Languages—Fluent in Spanish
Computer Skills—PC and Mac Proficient on Microsoft Office Suite
Military—United States Army, Honorable Discharge
Activities & Hobbies—Los Angeles Marathon (annually since 1995), Golf, TennisEvent Planner

Event Planner

George wanted a job closer to home. Some of his past job titles did not fit with his career aspirations, and he wanted to focus on the specific skills needed for an Events Manager, so he used a functional style format.

George S. Easton
12 Lee Street, Middleburg, VA 20118
540-555-5470

PROFILE SUMMARY
Meeting Planning ▪ Conferences ▪ International Events ▪ Fundraising ▪ Golf Tournaments

Creative professional with expertise in all aspects of successful event/program planning, development, and management. Excel in managing multiple projects concurrently with strong detail, problem-solving, and follow-through capabilities. Demonstrated ability to manage, motivate, and build cohesive teams that achieve results. Sourced vendors, negotiated contracts, and managed budgets. Superb written communications, interpersonal and organizational skills. First-class client relation and teaming skills. Proficient in Access, Excel, PowerPoint, Outlook, MS Project, Publisher, MeetingTrak, and Corel WordPerfect.

PROFESSIONAL EXPERIENCE
Meeting Planning Management

Planned and coordinated government, association, and private conferences, meetings, events, and fundraisers. Coordinated all conference activities, workshops, meetings, tours, and special events. Trained, directed, and supervised teams to accomplish goals. **Saved $72,000 on most recent meeting.**

- As Team Leader, coordinated 10-26 annual workshops for Centers for Disease Control and Prevention.
- Coordinated 2004 National Conference on Smoking and Health. (2,000 participants)
- Organized 6,000-participant national annual conferences.
- Coordinated Global Scholarship Pre-Conference Training for 200 third-world participants.
- Developed and supervised education sessions at CSI's 2001 National Convention.
- Directed CSI's National Seminar Series.

Meeting Coordination

As Team Leader, coordinated production, distribution, and grading of exam materials. Supervised registration and tracking of continuing education units. Negotiated hotel and vendor contracts. Prepared and administered budgets. Arranged all on-site logistics, including transportation, accommodations, meals, guest speakers, and audiovisual support. **Consistently come under budget for each meeting planned.**

- Developed and maintained 5,000-person database.
- Developed, promoted, and implemented CSI's National Certification Program.
- Managed logistics for a Regional Pacific Training in Guam.

Fundraising

Team player in the development, promotion, and implementation of membership and retention programs for BUILD-PAC. Coordinated PAC fundraising events. Supervised high-donor club fulfillment benefits. Provided updated donor reports.

- Coordinated 2 PAC fundraising golf tournaments.

EVENTS MANAGEMENT EXPERIENCE

Conferences / Meetings / Program Coordinator   1997–Present

- Centers for Disease Control and Prevention/Office on Smoking & Health
- Tobacco Control Training & Technical Assistance Project
- Health & Human Services Department's Administration on Children, Youth and Families Grant Review Contract
- Food and Drug Administration
- Centers for Disease Control and Prevention/National Center for Health Statistics
- National Library of Medicine
- Housing & Urban Development Grant Review Contract
- CSI National Seminar Series
- CSI 1998 & 1999 National Conventions and Exhibits

PROFESSIONAL EMPLOYMENT

CORPORATE SCIENCES ■ Rockville, Maryland   2003–Present
Senior Conference Specialist

ROCKVILLE CONSULTING GROUP ■ Arlington, Virginia   2000–2003
Logistics Manager
Senior Conference Coordinator

CONSTRUCTION SPECIALISTS ASSOCIATION ■ Arlington, Virginia   1997–1999
Assistant Coordinator of Education Programs

NATIONAL ASSOCIATION OF PIPE WELDERS ■ Washington, D.C.   1997
Assistant Director, Fundraising

EDUCATION & CERTIFICATIONS

VIRGINIA POLYTECHNIC INSTITUTE & STATE UNIVERSITY ■ Blacksburg, VA
B.S. Exercise Physiology ■ 1996
Minor Psychology

Go Members Inc. MeetingTrak Certification ■ 2004

Certified Meeting Professional (CMP) – Pending Jan. 2005

PROFESSIONAL AFFILIATIONS

- Meeting Professionals International – Annandale Chapter (AMPI)
- Logistical Committee
- Educational Retreat Committee
- Member Services Committee
- Community Outreach Committee
- Connected International Meeting Professionals Association (CIMPA)
- DC Special Olympics – Volunteer
- Hands On DC – Volunteer
- SPCA of Northern Virginia – Volunteer

Senior Accountant / Networking

Here we have one full resume for a well-credentialed accountant, followed by a one-page resume for networking.

CHARLENE DEDARBY

2084 Van Ness St #118 • San Francisco, CA 94105 • (415) 806-5478 • cdedarby@comcast.net

SENIOR ACCOUNTANT / ACCOUNTING MANAGER / FINANCIAL ANALYST

Results-focused Senior Accountant and Financial Analyst with 12 years progressive experience—through numerous mergers and acquisitions—including 5 years as Accounting Manager for leading global company. Proven ability to combine "big-picture" strategic picture with day-to-day policies and processes to deliver consistent on-time, accurate results in support of organization goals. Diligent in executing critical month-end closing process. Highly adaptable to change. Tech savvy; learns and implements new programs quickly. Works well with cross-functional/ cross-departmental teams, as well as public and co-workers at all levels.

—Key Areas of Expertise & Leadership—

Project Management ~ Financial Analysis ~ Research ~ Accounting Processes ~ GAAP ~ Compliance ~ SOX
Expense Review & Control ~ Productivity & Process Optimization ~ Complex Account Analysis & Reconciliation
Fixed Assets Management ~ Trend Analysis ~ Variance Analysis & Resolution ~ Training & Supervision
Internal / External Client Relations ~ Change Management ~ Teambuilding & Leadership

PROFESSIONAL EXPERIENCE

A GLOBAL FINANCIAL SERVICES COMPANY • 1998 to Present
$2T plus in assets and 200,000 employees

Accounting Manager II— Global Financial Services Company, San Francisco, CA (2008–Present)
Received promotion prior to acquisition by *************** in late September 2008. Overall responsibilities remained similar to Accounting Manager I position.
Selected Accomplishments

- Selected as primary accounting contact for project to determine disposition of outstanding customer rebate checks. Resolution reduced number of outstanding items > 90 days old from 130,000+ items to less than 60,000 and reduced reconciliation time 20%.
- Partnered with various areas to transition group's functions to Chase Card Services following acquisition by JP Morgan Chase, to reduce redundancies.

Accounting Manager— Global Financial Services Company San Francisco (2004–2007)

Promoted to newly created position, reporting to Senior Accounting Manager, and managing three staff accountants. Reviewed corporate expense analytics and variance analyses; oversaw balance sheet reconciliation process including cash accounts, fixed assets, various PPD accounts, and accrued expenses. Supervised processing of monthly accruals and reclassifications. Ensured on-time, accurate completion of key accruals including bonuses, workers compensation, etc.
Selected Accomplishments

- Oversaw variance analysis process for $1.5B credit card division—from initial identification and research—through collaborating with various business units on resolution.
- Participated in preparation and maintenance of SOX documentation and quarterly departmental testing.
- Researched tax code and identified division under-accrual that had resulted in $5M+ overpayment of taxes over 9-months; executed process that recaptured $1.2M+ per month.
- Created process ensuring timely and accurate completion of all business owner accruals and reclassifications.
- Worked with various departments within WaMu on transfer of assets following acquisition of Providian (2005)

Sr. Accountant— Global Financial Services Company, San Francisco (2000–2004)
Relocated to San Francisco and joined Providian prior to acquisition by WaMu. Prepared expense analytics for $40M in income statement accounts. Reconciled various balance sheet accounts; compiled cost allocations.
Selected Accomplishments

- Participated in creating and performing expense analytics process for Marketing Group; identified millions of dollars in past over- and under-accruals.
- Converted poorly formatted Accrued Expense account to well-organized, easy-to-identify and understand format that resulted in identifying and resolving $40M in excess accruals out of $100M total, dating back up to five years.

213

• Assisted management in determining correct accounting of third party partnership expenses.
• Reduced time required to prepare cost allocation database from five business days to half a day while increasing accuracy of data and reducing management review time from one day to less than two hours.
• Key person in standardizing, updating and cleaning up fixed asset system comprised of 35,000+ items. Worked with managers and key personnel across multiple departments in identifying owned vs. leased assets.

Accountant II— Global Financial Services Company, Northridge, CA (1998–2000)

Hired by WaMu to perform general accounting functions. Took over responsibility for reconciling, researching and clearing major GL account with average activity of $100M+ daily and up to $4B per month, three months after joining company. Reconciled GL accounts for company owned loans.
Selected Accomplishments
• Reduced unreconciled items in key GL account from 12,000+ items to less than 4,000 within four months and fewer than 1,400 within one year; concurrently eliminated all items aged > 60 days.
• Reversed prior steady increase in number of un-reconciled items.
• Gained support from another company group that led to improvement in fraud identification and paved the way for receiving payments of millions of dollars in loans.
• Recommended, and assisted in creating process for communicating with branches and loan centers on outstanding un-booked loans; became trusted point of contact for branches and loan centers for resolving un-booked loans.

COUNTRYWIDE HOME LOANS, Simi Valley, CA • 1997 to 1998
Mortgage company with $200B in managed loans during this period
Investor Accounting Analyst
Joined company with responsibility for mid-month and special loans for end-of-month investors. Completed period close within one day and reconciliations within two weeks of closing.
Selected Accomplishments
• Reconciled 160+ bank accounts and prepared $350M in wire transfers monthly.
• Researched and cleared variances in <1 day for significant investor on monthly basi

PAYPHONE SERVICES INC., Ventura, CA • 1996 to 1997
Regional business with 150 employees
Junior Accountant
Hired following college graduation to code accounts payable, rapidly assumed additional responsibilities. Prepared, processed and posted journal entries to GL; prepared financial statements for two small companies including general partnership. Worked with outside auditors during due diligence process following company sale.
Selected Accomplishments
• Participated in determining best accounting method inventory valuation in computing sales and use tax.
• Assumed A/P functions for 5 out of 18 companies with minimal training.

EDUCATION

DEVRY UNIVERSITY, Pomona, CA
BS in Accounting

Computer Skills
Microsoft Office (Excel, Word, Access, PowerPoint, Outlook)
Visio, Macola, Peoplesoft for Government, Extensity (GEAC) SmartStream

—Available for Travel and/or Relocation—

Finance, Banking, and Insurance

Trainer

Casandra lost her job and needed to move into a higher-level position for increased compensation. She did not have a college degree, so highlighting her skills helped employers get a quick overview of her many talents . . . and it worked!

CASANDRA B. JEELES

555 Riverside Drive • Houston, Texas 77027
713-555-1234 • casbjeeles@bxy.net

PROFESSIONAL OBJECTIVE

Training/Performance Development

PROFESSIONAL PROFILE

- Proven leadership and supervisory experience with ability to lead multiple projects/teams simultaneously.
- Outstanding project planning and project management skills, meeting tight time constraints/deadlines.
- Solutions-driven manager, mentor, and coach who relates well with all types of people at all levels.
- Strong organizational and analytical abilities applied to achieve desired goals, objectives, and results.
- Unwavering commitment to excellence in building teams who are best of the best in serving others.
- Personal traits: professional; common sense; adaptability; focused; skilled trainer and team builder.

CORE COMPETENCIES

Passion for Customer Care Excellence:
- Instill a philosophy of immediate response to customer inquiries – no such thing as "do it tomorrow."
- Value each individual customer, exceeding expectations and paying diligent attention to small details.
- Act and serve with integrity and trust, essential ingredients for successful, long-lasting customer relations.
- Create an environment where customers are ecstatic with service, creating action-oriented advocates.

Motivating and Training:
- Analyze company culture and structure to pinpoint obstacles and create new pathways or adopt existing model to build an environment of solutions and forward movement.
- Recognize hidden solutions, already existing or external, through research, active listening, observation.
- Help personalize company vision and goals by implementing strategies to create ownership/advocates.
- Analyze and monitor sales figures and statistics to establish firm foundation for future growth.
- Identify the extraordinary among the team, systems, and practices and build upon strengths.

Team Building:
- *"My job is to make the team successful"* – accomplished by coaching, nurturing, and stretching to reach beyond an individual's comfort zone to maximize personal/professional excellence.
- Discover talents/gifts of individual team members and build upon those to maximize results.
- Create an environment to link team members' strengths as the beginning of all endeavors.
- Capitalize on company structure, budgets, and timelines to build a *"let's do it"* framework.

Managing and Supervising:
- Orchestrate a team, discover core values of individual members, and build consensus of goals.
- Analyze budgets and expenditures to align with company vision, mission, and direction.
- Automate and systematize rote and mundane functions to improve operating efficiencies.

Solutions Oriented – Analysis to Action:
- Thrive on converting obstacles into opportunities by recognizing root cause and developing solutions.
- Structure work environment where fear, failure, and blame are not responses and/or defenses.
- Incorporate active listening to unravel challenges and rebuild – be it systems, technology, or people.

EXPERIENCE / EDUCATION

- Inside Sales/Assistant to Director – Strigle, Inc., Houston, Texas, 2002–2006
- Senior Executive Club/Top Sales – Halley Distribution, Inc., Midland, Texas, 1994–2002
- Various administrative roles, Houston, Texas, 1989–1994
- Numerous leadership, management, and customer relations courses – company sponsored, 1986–2006

Operations/Human Resources Manager

Ray needed to transition from seasonal work with national fairs into a more traditional management career.

RAY CHARLENE DEDARBY
2084 Van Ness St #118 • San Francisco, CA 94105 • (415) 806-5478 • cdedarby@comcast.net

SENIOR ACCOUNTANT / ACCOUNTING MANAGER / FINANCIAL ANALYST

Results-focused Senior Accountant and Financial Analyst with 12 years progressive experience—through numerous mergers and acquisitions—including 5 years as Accounting Manager for leading global company. Highly adaptable to change. Tech savvy; learns and implements new programs quickly. Works well with cross-functional/ cross-departmental teams, as well as public and co-workers at all levels.

Key Areas of Expertise & Leadership

Project Management ~ Financial Analysis ~ Research ~ Accounting Processes ~ GAAP ~ Compliance ~ SOX
Expense Review & Control ~ Productivity & Process Optimization ~ Complex Account Analysis & Reconciliation
Fixed Assets Management ~ Trend Analysis ~ Variance Analysis & Resolution ~ Training & Supervision
Internal / External Client Relations ~ Change Management ~ Teambuilding & Leadership

---

PROFESSIONAL EXPERIENCE

A GLOBAL FINANCIAL SERVICES COMPANY • 1998 to Present
Accounting Manager II— Global Financial Services Company, San Francisco, CA (2008–Present)
Accounting Manager— Global Financial Services Company, San Francisco (2004–2007)
Reviewed corporate expense analytics and variance analyses; oversaw balance sheet reconciliation process including cash accounts, fixed assets, various PPD accounts, and accrued expenses. Supervised team of three in processing monthly accruals and reclassifications.

- Partnered in transitioning group's functions to Chase Card Services following acquisition by JP Morgan Chase, to reduce redundancies.
- Oversaw variance analysis process for $1.5B credit card division—from initial identification and research—through collaborating with various business units on resolution.
- Participated in preparation and maintenance of SOX documentation and quarterly departmental testing.
- Collaborated on transfer of assets following acquisition of Providian (2005)

Sr. Accountant— Global Financial Services Company, San Francisco (2000–2004)
Prepared expense analytics for $40M in income statement accounts. Reconciled accounts; compiled cost allocations.

- Identified millions of dollars in past over- and under-accruals.
- Resolved $40M in excess accruals out of $100M total, dating back up to five years.
- Assisted management in determining correct accounting of third party partnership expenses.
- Reduced time required to prepare cost allocation database from five business days to half a day while increasing accuracy of data and reducing management review time from one day to less than two hours.
- Streamlined fixed asset system comprised of 35,000+ items.

Accountant II— Global Financial Services Company, Northridge, CA (1998–2000)
Performed general accounting functions. Reconciled, researched and cleared major GL account with average activity of $100M+ daily and up to $4B per month.

Early Experience

Investor Accounting Analyst—COUNTRYWIDE HOME LOANS, Simi Valley, CA; (1997 to 1998)
Junior Accountant—PAYPHONE SERVICES INC., Ventura, CA • 1996 to 1997

BS in Accounting; DEVRY UNIVERSITY, Pomona, CA

Computer Skills—Microsoft Office (Excel, Word, Access, PowerPoint, Outlook); Visio, Macola, Peoplesoft for Government, Extensity (GEAC) SmartStream
Available for Travel and/or Relocation

Purchasing Director

Peter's resume was shortened from a four-page resume which listed 30+ bullets outlining responsibilities for each job, and no impact/achievements/value-add.

PETER M. RABBIT
333 Court Hill ▪ Underhill, NY 11111
(H) 111.111.1111 ▪ (C) 111.111.1111
ptrrbt@aol.com

PURCHASING DIRECTOR
SENIOR PROJECT MANAGER
SENIOR OPERATIONS MANAGER

Professional Summary

Driven operations leader offers extensive hands-on experience and a consistent track record in **exceeding goals** for large-scale domestic and international capital projects, **fostering growth** and **delivering strong and sustainable gains**. A self-starter with a proven ability to conceptualize and implement **innovative solutions**. **Technologically competent,** past achievements demonstrate a clear ability to utilize new, **cutting-edge technologies** as a means of updating processes/systems. **Highly effective leadership and motivating skills** support the development of cohesive teams (union and non-union) in the collaborative achievement of strategic goals. **Extensive experience** partnering with influential business leaders within successful organizations.

▪ CORE COMPETENCIES ▪

Business Planning	Financial Analysis	Quality Assurance
Business Process Re-engineering	Influencing Skills	ERP/MRP
Contracts Administration	Negotiation Skills	Supplier/Vendor Management
Cost Containment	Logistics Management	Systems Implementation
Efficiency Improvement	Project Management	Warehouse Management

Selected Achievements

- Initiated the development of a **first-ever computerized purchasing/inventory system** for the Newspaper Company resulting in substantial reductions on labor and materials costs; these improvements resulted in a request for support in the implementation of the system from the USA-based Newspaper. Subsequently consulted on the second successful implementation.
- **Reduced operating costs by $500,000 per year** by outsourcing an "in-house" printing department.
- Provided comprehensive capital procurement services for the **$300 million construction and start-up of two large daily newspaper printing press facilities.**
- **Significantly increased waste recycling revenues by $545,000 per year** through successful negotiations with individual recycling firms.
- Directed an **operating budget of over $180 million** during construction and operations of the **Famous World Exhibition.**
- Initiated the development and implementation of a **first-ever budget tracking and reporting system in support of a $90 million capital project**; this system accelerated the project's successful completion—**90 days ahead of schedule and $1 million under budget.**
- Shortly after assuming responsibility for Security operations, **reduced in-house theft, drug and alcohol abuse by 99%, while reducing costs $100,000 per year.**

Relevant Experience

Independent Consulting   **2005 to Present**
- Sourced and introduced a comprehensive, cutting-edge finance management software solution, which enabled a $5 million business to more effectively manage sales, inventory, and distribution.
- Established warehouse management procedures, facilitating highly effective inventory planning and control practices; trained and coached warehouse crew.
- Established the foundation for a fully integrated logistics management function consolidating inventory, warehousing, and distribution.

NEWSPAPER COMPANY, Manager, Procurement & Security   **1991 to 2005**
*Hired as Assistant Manager of Purchasing. Quickly demonstrated **aggressive turnaround management capability,** resulting in **significant increases in responsibility**—Fleet, Security, Facilities, and $40 million in newsprint inventories.*
- Established clear processes and procedures, and centralized purchasing and inventory management via first-ever electronic system in the southern newspaper system, reducing costs by $500,000/year.

- Introduced new technologies resulting in **increased efficiencies and cost-savings**; technologies included fax services and color scanning, which increased turnaround in ad presentation and makeup and **saved $125,000/year**.
- **Reduced annual operating costs by $500,000/year through offshore purchasing and vendor partnerships.**
- Successfully **sourced national and international vendors, negotiated and administered contracts** and executed **procurement strategies** on several large-scale capital projects: Development of a new $60 million facility; $97 million development project for implementation of new printing processes.
- **Directed international sourcing and managed logistics,** which included customs documentation and inspections.
- Served as **Project Manager in the design of a waste management system,** providing detailed specifications and managing project activities; **generated a significant increase in revenue.**
- **Overhauled the Security function**—outsourcing, modernizing equipment, establishing and training contract staff on new procedures and roles; significantly reduced costs, and nearly eliminated all incidences of theft.
- **Initiated and implemented the "pay in advance" system**—now used internationally among all newspapers—which contributed to a significant increase in revenue.
- **Revamped First Aid and Safety program,** and **implemented Assassination Protection Program.**
- Managed sale of assets from old facilities, building deconstruction, and **seamless relocation of 900 employees.**

WORLD EXHIBITION, Manager, Site Operations Procurement   1987 to 1991
World Exhibition's 6-month World Fair exhibition is orchestrated and attended by over 70 countries, each with its own on-site pavilion. Managed comprehensive procurement services for construction and start-up of operations. Held signatory responsibility for all purchases, and spearheaded profitable vendor partnerships.

- **Hired and established a procurement team and introduced new technology,** which facilitated shared communications and increased procurement and materials handling efficiencies; Successfully managed procurement activities throughout liquidation and site deconstruction.
- **Orchestrated first-ever buyback contracts** for heavy equipment and machinery utilized by the Exhibition, regaining a full 50% of the initial purchase price; negotiated and received free maintenance, providing additional cost savings; **negotiated service contracts** for site equipment and operations.
- **Demonstrated creative problem-solving skills,** which enhanced operations ability to provide ongoing entertainment, while significantly reducing operating costs.

PAPER COMPANY, Project Budget Controller/Buyer   1984 to 1987
Provided project support for a $90 million operations implementation.

- **Led the development of an innovative financial tracking and control system.**
- **Controlled spending and ensured consistent use of the system, enabling a perfectly balanced budget.**
- Identified an opportunity to apply for a tax break, **saving an additional $600,000** at project's end.

Previous Experience

BIGWIG COMPANY, Project Expeditor, 1982–1984
CHEMICAL COMPANY A, Project Buyer, 1981–1982
CHEMICAL COMPANY B, Project Buyer/Expeditor, 1979–1981
BIG DOG COMPANY, Materials Supervisor, 1978–1979

Technologies

Accpac, Crystal Report Builder, Dun & Bradstreet, EDI, Microsoft Office, Purchase Soft, RAL, Visio

Professional Development

North American Newspaper Purchasing Association
American Society for Industrial Security
School Institute: Business/Marketing Management Diploma

Peter M. Rabbit, page 2.

Logistics Manager

A powerful combination resume that demonstrates a virtuoso grasp of the supply chain function. Any employer with needs in this area and at this level would want to talk to a person with these skills.

John William Wisher, MBA

☏ 630.555.2653 ☎ 630.555.9117

Expert leadership in cost-effective supply chain, vendor, and project management within *Fortune* organizations.

2541 Bainbridge Blvd.
West Chicago, IL 60185
jwisher@ameritech.net

EXECUTIVE PROFILE

A visionary, forward-thinking SUPPLY CHAIN AND LOGISTICS LEADER offering 20+ years of progressive growth and outstanding success streamlining operations across a wide range of industries. Excellent negotiation and relationship management skills with ability to inspire teams to outperform expectations. Proven record of delivering a synchronized supply chain approach through strategic models closely mirroring business plan to dramatically optimize ROI and manage risk.

Trust-Based Leadership *Vendor/Client Negotiations* *Cross-Functional Collaboration* *Supply Chain Mapping* *Financial Logistics Analysis*	**Supply Chain Strategy:** Successfully led over 500 supply chain management initiatives across a wide spectrum of businesses, negotiating agreements from $5K to $27M. Implemented technology solutions and streamlined processes to reduce redundancies and staffing hours, improving both efficiency and productivity. Industries include; automotive and industrial manufacturing, consumer goods, government and defense, healthcare, high-tech, and retail. **Industry Knowledge:** Extensive knowledge base developed from hands-on industry experience. Began career in dock operations with experience in Hub and Package Operations, multi-site retail operations management, to custom supply chain strategy development over 21-year career with UPS.
Contingency Planning *Risk Management* *Competitive Analysis* *Haz Mat Compliance*	**Supply Chain Process Costing:** Built several information packets on total cost of ownership (TCO) and facilitated several C-level negotiations to identify and confirm opportunities. Worked to increase awareness among stakeholders of efficiencies and cost-saving measures' ROI. Delivered $3.75M total cost savings to client base over three-year period. **Operations Re-organization:** Designed and implemented new sales force alignment and reporting structure; increased daily sales calls by 20%, reduced travel mileage 23%, and head count by nine; total annual cost savings of $920K.
Inventory Planning, Control, & Distribution *Recruiting/Training/ Development* *Project Management*	**Logistics:** Experienced across all modes of transportation; ocean, air freight, LTL, TL, mail services, and small package. Performs complex analysis to develop strategy based on cost and delivery requirements. **Project Management:** Implemented complete $1.2M redesign of 11 new UPS Customer Centers. Managed vendor and lease negotiations, developed budgets, training, and sales structure. All 11 centers up and operational on time and on budget.

Organizational Change Management	**Cost & Process Improvements:**
Distributive Computing	▸ Implemented complete warehouse redesign for a large optical distributor. Optimized warehouse operations through engineering a new warehouse design, integrating and automating technology, and synchronization of goods movement through ocean, air, ground, and mail services. Reduced transportation expense by 15%, increased production levels by 25%, reduced inventory by 15% and staffing by 20%.
Budget Management	
Labor Relations	▸ Built custom supply chain for a nationally recognized golf club manufacturer. Improved service levels by 30%, reduced damage by 45%, and integrated technology to support shipping process automation, reducing billing function staffing hours 50%.

PROFESSIONAL BACKGROUND

United Parcel Service (UPS), Addison, IL   **1986 – Present**
World's largest package delivery company and global leader in supply chain services, offering an extensive range of options for synchronizing the movement of goods, information, and funds. Serves more than 200 countries and territories worldwide and operates the largest franchise shipping chain, The UPS Store.

DIRECTOR / AREA MANAGER – SUPPLY CHAIN SALES, 2005–Present
Promoted to lead and develop a cross-functional sales force of 18 in consultative supply chain management services to Chicago-area businesses. Directs development of integrated supply chain management solutions across all modes of transportation, closely mirroring client business plans. Mentors team in Demand Responsive Model, a proven methodology to quickly align internal and external resources with changing market demands, situational requirements, and mission-critical conditions. Manages $100M P&L.

Accomplishments:
- Implements over 100 multimillion-dollar supply chain integrations per year with 14% annual growth on 8% plan.
- Develops future organizational leaders; four staff members promoted through effective mentoring and development.
- Choreographed a supply chain movement from the Pacific Rim for a global fast food chain to deliver 300k cartons to 15k locations all on the same day. Utilized modes of ocean, TL, air, and ground services, allowing for a national release synchronized to all locations on the same release date.
- Designed and implemented an automated reverse logistics program for a nationally recognized health food / supplement distributor. Automated returns process to reduce touches and costly staffing hours. Eliminated front end phone contact using technology and web automation.

MARKETING MANAGER, 2004–2005
Fast-tracked to streamline sales processes increasing performance. Performed analysis of sales territory, historical data, operations alignment, reporting structure, and sales trends to devise solutions. Managed and coached area managers in business plan development and execution of sales strategies. Delivered staff development in cost-reduction strategies and compliance requirements. Accountable for $500M P&L.

Accomplishments:
- Drove $500M+ in local market sales. Grew revenues 2004/2005 revenues 12% and 7% respectively.

RETAIL CHANNEL / OPERATIONS MANAGER, 2002–2004
Charged with turning around this underperforming business unit. Managed development and implementation of new retail strategy across northern Illinois. Re-branded UPS Customer Centers and The UPS Store. Performed vendor negotiations and collaborated with nine regions to support additional implementations.

Accomplishments:

- Developed key revenue-generating initiatives across multiple channels. Attained 65% growth in discretionary sales. Several strategies adopted across the national organization.
- Re-engineered inventory for over 1,000 drop-off locations, reduced lease expenses by 45% and inventory levels by 40% through weekly measurement, inventory level development by SKU, order process automation, and order consolidation.
- Implemented new retail sales associate structure in 1,100 locations; scored highest national service levels by mystery shoppers.
- Selected as Corporate team member on Mail Boxes Etc. acquisition integration.

PROJECT MANAGER, 2001–2002

Selected to support several underperforming business areas. Managed key segments of district business initiatives and compliance measures for 1,000 drop-off locations. Reported on status to corporate management. Supervised office staff of 16. Negotiated vendor and lease agreements.

Accomplishments:

- Rolled out and managed ongoing Haz Mat compliance program for all locations.
- Generated $6M in sales through cross-functional lead program and increased participation from 20% to 100%.
- Attained Union workforce sponsorship of support growth program through careful negotiations and persuasion.

Additional UPS Positions Include:

SENIOR ACCOUNT MANAGER, 1999–2001
Delivered $2.8M in growth on $1.1M plan, rated 3rd of 53 managers in revenue generation.

ACCOUNT MANAGER, 1997–1998
Top producer out of 53; $1.3M sales on $500K plan.

SERVICE PROVIDER, 1994–1996
Managed final service delivery to consumers; operated 378 hours under plan first year with zero accidents or injuries.

SUPERVISOR OF PACKAGE OPERATIONS, 1994
Managed 65 full-time service providers. Performed post-routine analysis, operating strategy development, compliance, payroll, service failure recovery, and new technology implementation. Met 100% DOT and Haz Mat compliance. Reduced post-delivery staffing time by 50% and missed pickups by 65%.

SUPERVISOR OF HUB OPERATIONS, 1988–1994
Managed up to 100 union employees and staff processing 75K pieces per day involving 40+ outbound bays. Performed complex staff scheduling and maintained low turnover rates. Designed new management reporting format reducing administrative time by 20% and improved load quality by 30%.

OPERATIONS DOCK WORKER AND TRAINING LEAD, 1986–1987

EDUCATION

MBA
National Louis University, Wheaton, IL, *4.0 GPA*

BA, Business, Supply Chain Management
Elmhurst College, Elmhurst, IL, *3.84 GPA, Magna cum laude*

Additional Specialized Courses:

- Supply Chain Mapping, 20 Hours
- Financial Logistics Analysis (FLOGAT), 10 Hours
- Hazardous Materials, 20 Hours
- Labor Relations, 30 Hours
- Managers Leadership School, 100 Hours
- Supervisors Leadership School, 100 Hours
- Managing from the Heart, 30 Hours

International Trade Manager

Nothing fancy, just the relevant information clearly laid out. The last four subheads at the end of the second page make this a powerful resume from start to finish.

DAVID M. GOLDEN

943 Hartford Pike
Baltimore, MD 13257

(803) 555-1212 (Home)
dmgolden@yahoo.com

———— INTERNATIONAL TRADE COMPLIANCE PROFESSIONAL ————

TACTICAL MANUFACTURING OPERATIONS • INTERNATIONAL LOGISTICS • AUDITING • GLOBAL TRADE • TRANSPORTATION MANAGEMENT

Task-oriented, resourceful professional offering diversified management and leadership background highlighted by significant accomplishments governing global trade compliance. Innate ability to motivate and empower cross-functional groups to accomplish objectives and resolve complex import and export issues. Visionary and creative problem solver who controls cost and minimizes risks while simultaneously driving desired results for bottom-line profitability. Talent for analyzing business data and identifying opportunities to improve operational efficiencies and reduce ongoing expenses within domestic and international marketplaces.

———— CORE COMPETENCIES ————

- Strategic Business Planning
- Contract Negotiations
- Business Reengineering
- Regulatory, Compliance & Auditing
- Import and Export Operations
- Research and Data Management
- Transportation & Logistics
- Project Management
- Reporting & Administration

EDUCATION

Master of Business Administration—University of Southern Florida (3.7 GPA)

Bachelor of Science, Finance—The Pennsylvania State University

PROFESSIONAL EXPERIENCE

INTERNATIONAL TRADE INC., Baltimore, MD   2000 to Present
Senior Consultant, Policy & Compliance
Focal point leader and advisor for Trade Compliance Program within and across 120+ countries. Maintain knowledge of current import / export regulations, evaluate proposed regulatory changes, and write business impact and recommendation reports. Create manuals, guidelines, standard operating policies, internal control programs, and other tools needed for import / export compliance. Develop and conduct customs / export training programs for employees, customers, and third-party logistics providers.

Key Achievements:

- Discovered $1.5 billion in errors and other significant compliance deficiencies during international audit.

- Recognized as subject matter expert for development of numerous software applications. Automated and streamlined operations by at least 50% while simultaneously increasing global trade regulatory compliance.

- Conceived, developed, and implemented countless ideas for increasing Global Trade Compliance among numerous business units around the world, including immediate funding and IT resources. Successful in improving productivity and increasing due diligence for regulatory requirements.

AMERICAN FREIGHT CORPORATION, Lancaster, PA   1995 to 2000
Senior Transportation Analyst
Produced Request for Quotations for domestic and international transportation, freight forwarders, and other logistics services. Analyzed bid packages and participated in negotiations with carriers and logistics service contracts. Identified corrective actions for domestic and international shipments. Supervised and trained three staff members in export compliance, packaging, freight damage claims, and freight payment with full accountability for budget of over $4 million.

Petroleum Operations Supervisor

Military to civilian transition. The first third of the page shows he is qualified and "gets" the target job.

MICHAEL W. MILLER

675 Bishy St. • Watertown, NY 13601 • millermichaelw@aol.com • 315.555.2345 Home
• 315.555.2347 Cell

FUEL DISTRIBUTION SYSTEMS SUPERVISOR, FOREMAN, OR SYSTEMS OPERATOR
Convoy Operations • Staff Training & Leadership • Refueling Point Inventory Management & Control

Top-performing, respected, and loyal petroleum operations supervisor possessing vast knowledge of petroleum operations. Expertise in supervision of pipeline and pump station operations, petroleum supply storage facilities, water supply and distribution systems, supply point and terminal operations, pipeline systems, water supply operations, and laboratory tests. Track record of excellence in leading, training, and developing staff; supervising maintenance activities; and property accountability. Recognized for outstanding performance and service and exceptional technical skill and discipline. Prepared to contribute in a dangerous environment. *Core competencies include:*

- Strategic Planning & Implementation
- Fuel Systems; Inspections
- Safety & Compliance
- Preventive Maintenance
- Employee Relations
- Recordkeeping & Administrative Functions
- Team Building & Leadership
- Organization & Time Management

PROFESSIONAL EXPERIENCE

U.S. ARMY, 1984–3/2008
Built impressive record of achievement and advancement through a series of progressively responsible positions leading petroleum operations functions and staff.

PETROLEUM OPERATIONS PLATOON SERGEANT, 2006–8/2008
Afghanistan

Supervised, trained, advised, inspected, and maintained responsibility for the health, morale, discipline, and welfare of 10 non-commissioned officers, and 41 enlisted soldiers, in petroleum operations at four separate locations in Afghanistan. Coordinated daily training requirements to meet unit refueling goals. *Group issued over 2.9 million gallons of aviation grade fuel with no safety issues and no damage to equipment or environment.*

Selected accomplishments:

- Converted four mismanaged areas into highly effective centers. Maintained an operational readiness rate above 97% on all ground vehicles. Managed responsibility for more than $8M of property.
- Assisted Platoon Leader in daily platoon functions, overseeing all training including convoy operations and providing battle-focused training and counseling.
- Directed construction of new living quarters for personnel.
- Served as the go-to person, continually sought out by leaders, subordinates, and peers throughout the organization for technical and tactical advise and expertise.
- Experienced zero accidents for entire period, due to stressing of the importance of safety.
- Developed a Soldier Study Board to encourage and assist staff in attending and passing boards.
- Awarded the Bronze Star Medal for meritorious service.

- From Aug. 2006 evaluation:
"Concerned, caring leader of the highest caliber … instilled confidence in his soldiers"
"Among the best … a unique NCO whose technical knowledge and experience are above his peers"
"Demonstrated unlimited potential … continue to assign to tough positions of increased responsibility"

PETROLEUM DISTRIBUTION TRAINER, 2001–2005
National Training Center, Ft. Irwin, California

Trained, coached, and observed platoon leaders, NCOs, and enlisted soldiers in the doctrinal employment of Forward Arming and Refueling Point (FARP) assets. Conducted after action reviews and debriefings for up to 10 units per year. Monitored and incorporated changes in operational policy and procedure. Scheduled and coordinated painting and maintenance overhaul of all team vehicles.

Selected accomplishments:

- Rapidly assessed operational and organizational strengths and weaknesses and provided complete programs for improvement.
- Coached and mentored new distribution platoon leaders. Provided quality after action reviews in one-on-one leadership format, as well as 3/5 platoon, small group format.
- Recognized for high degree of self-motivation and initiative, for providing exceptional leadership and training guidance, and for continual willingness to go the extra mile.
- Awarded the Meritorious Service Medal, Army Commendation Medal, and Army Achievement Medal. Received Certificate of Training Excellence, three Certificates of Achievement, Certificate of Appreciation, the Order of the Condor Award, and the Order of St. Michael medal for contributions to Army aviation.

PETROLEUM PLATOON SERGEANT, 2000–2001
Ft. Irwin, California

Shouldered responsibility for maintaining equipment valued in excess of $3M, including nine fuel tankers, nine tractors, two HEMTT's with trailer, a tanker aviation refueling system, two cargo trucks with tank, and pump unit. Accounted for supplies received, stored, and issued. Supervised, trained, and developed 16 soldiers and junior non-commissioned officers.

Selected accomplishments:

- Managed and directed a driver's training program which continuously qualified 100% of assigned personnel regardless of rank or MOS.
- Maintained accurate accounting of all bulk fuel issued.
- Ensured platoon received highest ratings during Aviation Fuel Inspections.
- Received an excellent performance rating as acting First Sergeant leading up to the Division Capstone Exercise.

** ** **

Additional experience as a Sergeant of a Support Platoon assigned to an attack helicopter cavalry squadron in the Republic of Korea, as Section Sergeant in a FORSCOM Petroleum Supply Company, as Supervisor in a refueling platoon, and as Section Sergeant and Fitness Trainer.

──────────── EDUCATION & CREDENTIALS ────────────

Graduate, Petroleum and Water Specialist ANCOC – Quartermaster School, Fort Lee, VA 1999
Graduate, Petroleum Supply Specialist Course BNCOC – Quartermaster School, Fort Lee, VA 1993
Graduate, Petroleum Supply Specialist Course – Quartermaster School, Fort Lee, VA 1987

Professional Development:

Specimen Collection Class – Fort Riley, KS 1996 **Hazardous Materials Training** (45 hrs.) – Fort Riley, KS 1995
Environmental Officer Course (40 hrs.) – Health Consultants, Inc. 1993 **Bus Training School** – Fort Story, VA 1989
Physical Inventory Management – Logistics Management College 1990 **Train The Trainer** – Fort Story, VA 1989
Primary Leadership Development – Armour School, Fort Knox, KY 1989 **Division Artillery Leadership Course** – Schofield Barracks, HI 1986

Purchasing Manager

You get a great feel for the caliber of this candidate from the first third of the page. Get my attention that fast, and I'll read on.

HERMAN KEYNES

5488 Sherman Drive
(818) 555-9880

Toluca Lake, CA 91455
Hkeynes818@email.com

PURCHASING

Buyer/Planner Skilled in Sourcing, Negotiations, and Inventory Management

➤ Expertise in purchasing, inventory planning/control, warehouse operations, and customer service.
➤ Skilled in sourcing and selecting suppliers, with a track record of consistently negotiating highest quality merchandise at favorable prices and terms.
➤ Accurate in monitoring inventory levels to minimize lead times, ensure accuracy, and contribute to efficient, cost-effective operations.
➤ Analytical, with excellent decision making strengths, team building and leadership qualities.
➤ Highly computer literate with experience on mainframes and PCs. Systems/applications include AS-400, CAPRMS, BPCS, COPS, UPS Online, Simbill, Microsoft Word, Excel, and Outlook; Internet, e-mail.

EXPERTISE

MRP ◆ JIT ◆ TQM ◆ ISO 9001 ◆ KanBan Inventory ◆ Vendor Sourcing, Selection, & Negotiations
Raw Material & Inventory Planning/Control ◆ Spreadsheets & Report Design/Preparation

PROFESSIONAL EXPERIENCE

MAJOR HEALTH PRODUCTS, Thousand Oaks, CA * 1998 to Present
$54 million international manufacturer and distributor of medical devices. Division of *Fortune* 100 company with 350 employees.

Buyer/Planner *(2000–Present)*
Oversaw material planning, inventory management, vendor sourcing/selection, and negotiation of pricing and delivery terms for components required for custom surgical kits, injection molded products, foam positioning products, and surgical kits. Worked closely with cross-functional teams including marketing, R&D, and product development. Processed material rejections and replacements; resolved quality and vendor problems; maintained intercompany transfers. Authorization for purchase orders up to $50,000.

- Served as key member of team in charge of transferring product line to Mexican manufacturing facility, implementing closure of Tennessee facility, transfer of inventory to Thousand Oaks facility, and transfer of new product line into facility — all within 10-month period.
- Reduced costs by $500,000 annually through new vendor sourcing and purchase negotiations.
- Identified and selected local vendors, reducing lead time by 50%.
- Implemented Kan Ban inventory management system.

Shipping Lead Man — Moebius Controls / Stilton Industries (1998–2000)
Supervised staff of 20 including warehousemen, fork-lift drivers, order pullers, and office staff. Responsibilities were diverse and encompassed overseeing order processing and shipment at 66,000 sq. ft. warehouse.
Maintained inventory transaction accuracy of 99%.

➤ Established procedures for online receipts of inventory to create live inventory transactions.
➤ Assisted management in closing and opening out-of-state distribution facilities.

EDUCATION / WORKSHOPS / SEMINARS

TQM (including problem solving, team skills, and conflict resolutions)
ISO 9001, GMP Overviews & Practices, Kaizen Blitz Training

Operations Manager

An executive's networking resume. Not for job applications but a condensed version of deep skills for passing out to networking colleagues and contacts.

HOWARD MORRIS

249 Alpine St. #57 ◆ Morgan, CA 91677 ◆ (555) 555-9605 ◆ howard.morris@myemail.com

Operations Management

Information Technology • Process Improvement • Financial Services

"[The company President] wanted [to hire] someone who understood not only computers but also business and people – a management-level leader who could sell the changes to the staff, handle outside consultants, and make sure the company's choices positioned it for growth."
– Article titled "Hail to the Chiefs," *Inc. Technology Magazine*, Fall 1998

Profile of Qualifications

Highly accomplished visionary Executive with a solid background in operations, business development, information technology, staff training / development, change management, project management, and turnaround situations with large and small organizations in multiple industries. Results-oriented, decisive leader, with proven success in streamlining operations, reducing costs, and boosting profits. Thrive in a fast-paced, growth-oriented, highly competitive environment.

Core Competencies

- Visionary Leadership
- Operations Management
- Process Restructuring
- Project Management
- Technology Integration
- Business Development
- Market Identification
- Strategic Business Planning
- Turnarounds
- Strategic Alliances
- Staff Development
- Communication

Professional Experience

Project Manager / Process Improvement Manager
AT&T – Ferris, CA / KAVESH AND TAU – Morgan, CA (1999 to Present)

CIO / Vice President of Operations & Technology
ACT CONSULTANTS, INC. – Jordan, CA (1996 to 1999)

Vice President / Client Administrative Services
RESOURCE MANAGEMENT GROUP, INC. – Temple, CA (1995 to 1996)

Business Manager / Agent
NORTHWESTERN LIFE – Jarod, CA (1993 to 1995)

Project Manager / Systems Engineer
APPLE COMPUTER / MARKETING & SERVICES DIVISION – Long Beach, CA (1982 to 1993)

Education & Training

UNIVERSITY OF SOUTHERN CALIFORNIA – Los Angeles, CA
MBA in Finance & Marketing ◆ BS in Mechanical Engineering

Business ◆ Project Management ◆ Leadership ◆ Finance ◆ Management ◆ Sales
Customer Service ◆ Technical ◆ Product Information & Education

Professional Certifications: American Society of Pension Actuaries ERISA Consulting
Exams (Completed four exams; *first person in company history to pass all exams on first try*)
Registered Representative, Series 6 & 63, Life & Disability License
Certified Financial Planner Classes, UCLA (Completed two classes)

Community Leadership

Alumni Mentor, UNIVERSITY OF SOUTHERN CALIFORNIA – Los Angeles, CA (1995 to Present)

Executive Chef

Well-structured, easy to read, and—because it is focused—clearly represents a professional of some account.

JACKLYN LaFLAMME

Address City, State Zip
Home Phone Cell Phone Email Address

EXECUTIVE CHEF

Seeking to Leverage 15 Years of Management/Culinary Experience in Food Service Operations and Passion for Food Preparation and Exemplary Guest Service in Executive Chef Position

Quality-driven, guest-focused, and award-winning chef with a track record of building and maintaining optimal guest satisfaction and excellent productivity/profit performance. Place uncompromising focus on guest needs fulfillment while striving to meet and surpass corporate sales and production goals. Effective communicator, listener, and troubleshooter. Able to manage multimillion-dollar operations, prioritize multiple tasks in high-volume environments and relate to employees/guests with a wide range of backgrounds and personality types. Proficient in Execuchef, Cheftec, and MS Office suite applications; thorough knowledge of kitchen equipment.

Core competencies and knowledge base include:

- ✓ Front-of-House Management
- ✓ Banquet Operations
- ✓ Team Building/Leadership
- ✓ New Operations Launch
- ✓ Guest Satisfaction/Retention
- ✓ Food Preparation & Preservation
- ✓ Staff Training & Evaluation
- ✓ Menu Planning & Pricing
- ✓ Service Improvements
- ✓ Purchasing & Receiving
- ✓ Quality Assurance Standards
- ✓ Time/Resource Management

Professional Experience

COMPANY CONFIDENTIAL – Washington, D.C. 1998 – Present
Food operations included 2 restaurants, patio/café, 12,000 sq.ft. banquet and catering space, in-room dining for 314 rooms, and 100-person employee cafeteria.

EXECUTIVE CHEF

Senior Food Service Executive with full accountability and decision-making authority for all food/kitchen operational functions, directing staff of 3 managers, 3 sous chefs, and 7 dish staff. Hold additional roles as Director of Purchasing/Receiving for all food and non-alcoholic beverages and Executive Steward; signified as 1st Executive Chef in American division of company. Established and implemented all systems guiding kitchen operations, instituted sanitation policies and HAACP guidelines, and developed all menus for restaurants and banquet/catering functions.

- ✓ **New Systems Implementation** – Introduced software to manage inventory, labor/costing schedules, and recipe/plate costing, leading to 3.5% decrease in overall food cost, 4% reduction in kitchen labor cost, and overall increase in consistency.
- ✓ **Food Cost & Labor Reduction** – Generated over $84,000 in food cost savings since restaurant's opening (01/99) through price modifications, improvements in portion control, and negotiations with vendors to secure better purchasing deals, Reduced kitchen labor to annual rate of 9.84.

✓**Operations Launch & Renovation** – Currently consulting with management on new hotel kitchen opening in 2004. Rewrote menus, designed recipes, trained cooking staff, and set up other aspects of Courtyard by Marriott franchise. Directed 2 kitchen renovations to meet increased business.

✓**Critic Reviews** – Led operations to receive outstanding reviews from leading local critics, including:

- *Washington Blade*, rated "Very Good"
- *Washington Times*, rated "Excellent"
- *Capitol Cuisine*, featured 2000, 2001, 2002
- *Sidewalk.Com*, rated "Best Pub in D.C."
- *City Paper*, rated "Very Good to Excellent"
- *AAA*, rated "3 Diamond Hotel"
- *Mobil*, rated "3 Star Property"
- *Where Magazine*, featured May, 2000

Professional Experience Continued

COMPANY CONFIDENTIAL – New Brunswick, NJ   1998/1993–1994
New Jersey's premier New Orleans-style restaurant with food sales exceeding $3 million annually.

EXECUTIVE CHEF (1998) **/ SOUS CHEF** (1993 – 1994)

Recruited for return after previously successful tenure as Sous Chef to lead all kitchen operations while assisting General Manager and Proprietor in developing strategies for profit and quality improvements. Supervised team of 170, created daily specials, and standardized written recipes and operational procedures.

✓**Menu Planning & Design** – Developed new bar, late night, and café menus that provided additional revenue centers and led to $200,000 revenue increase; continued development on new menu of Creole and Acadian cuisine with modern influences.

✓**Process Automation** – Introduced new inventory and recipe software that resulted in 3.2% decrease in overall food cost.

✓**Formal Recognition** – Selected to Princeton University Garden State Great Chef Culinary Series; chosen as one of 5 "Great Chefs of New Brunswick" for City Market dining promotion/festival.

✓**Restaurant Reviews** – Achieved excellent reviews from local critics and publications:

- *New Jersey Star Ledger*, "3 stars"
- *New Jersey Home News*, "4 stars"
- *NJ Home News Tribune*, "4 stars" "Best of Central New Jersey" 1998
- People Choice, "Best in the State"
- *New York Magazine*, "Best Beer Bar/Restaurant"

Education & Credentials

Professional Development Courses:

- ♦ ServSafe Train the Trainer Sanitation Course - National Restaurant Association - Washington, D.C. – 2002
- ♦ ServSafe Foodservice Sanitation Certification - National Restaurant Association - Washington, D.C. – 2001
- ♦ Diversity Awareness Skills Training Seminar - Jurys Washington Hotel - Washington, D.C. – 2001
- ♦ Big Tastes, Small Plates; Appetizers Class – The Culinary Institute Of America - August, 2003

Affiliations:
- National Restaurant Association (NRA) – 1997 – Present
- New Jersey Restaurant Association (NJRA) – Former member
- International Association of Culinary Professionals (IACP) – 2002 – Present
- Nation's Capital Chefs Association (NCCA) – 2002 – Present

Recognitions:
- Selected as an Honored Member in the American Registry of Outstanding Professionals 2002, 2003
- Won Second Place-People's Choice Award Chef's Gumbo Cook-Off 2003 - Sponsored by the Chesa-peake Chefs Association - Sanctioned & certified by the American Culinary Federation
- Awarded 3rd Place Entrée Magazine's "Cooking with Beer" Dessert Contest - Sponsored by the New Jersey Restaurant Association - Judged by the Culinary Institute of America, 1994
- Selected as the Garden State Series guest Chef for Princeton University Culinary Great Chef Series, 1998

Presentations & Community Work:
- Hosting James Beard Foundation Fundraiser Dinner, 2003 – "Once In 100 Years" chef's dinner
- Featured on "The Best Of" on the TV Food Network – Washington, D.C.
- "Great Chef of New Brunswick" – New Brunswick Food & Music Festival
- Zoofari / Star Chefs, March of Dimes / Best Chef Fundraiser – Washington, D.C.
- Special Olympics Chef's Degustation Dinner – Washington, D.C.
- Mentor for the Marriott Charter Hospitality High School – Washington, D.C.
- Volunteer cook for Salvation Army at the Pentagon following September 11, 2001, terrorist attack

Operations Manager

Entry-level resume targeting a specific job and successfully leveraging internship experience.

NATHAN W. BETHEL

4563 Woodstock Manor Road • East Otselic, NY 34216

(315) 555-2203 Cell • (315) 555-9897 Home • nwb4536@yahoo.com

BUSINESS MANAGEMENT PROFILE

• EXPERTISE IN WATER PARKS •

Operations/ Project Management • Staff Training & Management • Safety Initiatives

Dynamic, top-performing water park operations management professional with a broad range of business, organizational, and interpersonal skills. Natural leader, able to develop strong, easy working relationships with management, staff, and the general public to ensure positive, high-quality guest experiences. Expertise in company revenues through engendering customer loyalty. *Seeking part-time work while still a full-time student.*

Areas of Expertise

- Outstanding track record of strategic contributions in visioning, planning, strategizing, and accomplishment of a range of business-related initiatives, with significant success in developing emerging concepts into full-fledged, high-performance realities.

- Offer a valuable blend of leadership, creative, and analytical abilities that combine efficiency with imagination to produce bottom-line results. Proven success in planning, directing, and coordinating staff activities to maximize cost options and produce optimal outcomes.

- Calm under pressure; diplomatic and tactful with professionals and non-professionals at all levels. Recognized for ability to negotiate, manage, and deliver positive results and to readily transcend cultural and language differences.

- Technically proficient in use of Microsoft Office Word, Excel, PowerPoint, Outlook, on Windows and Macintosh platforms.

Relevant Professional Experience

WALT DISNEY WORLD – LIVERPOOL, NY   2006–2007

Professional Internship, Blizzard Beach
Recruited, following a productive four-month lifeguard internship, to contribute to the ongoing success of this popular Disney water park attraction.
Performed a variety of management-level functions and team-building training for staff, and developed key organizational systems to standardize strategic functions.

Key Contributions:
- Spearheaded, developed, created, and implemented the Blizzard Beach and Typhoon Lagoon Evacuation Operations Report, coordinating all strategic safety and evacuation information. Document included map of park, procedures, phone lists of all lifeguard stands, and inventory supply lists.

- Promoted the Disney anniversary theme of "A Year of a Million Dreams" by participating in the "Magical Moments" program to create special, unique, memorable guest experiences.

- Developed a signage system for the Lazy River to assist river patrons in finding their way through the park.

- Conducted monthly in-service staff trainings. Developed and delivered training materials on a variety of topics including CPR, team building, and water rescues.

230

- Selected to serve as a "Safety in Motion" (SIM) instructor, training staff in becoming aware of workplace safety issues and how to safely perform all required responsibilities.
- Achieved 100% completion of Blizzard Beach staff United Way Fundraising Drive.
- Assisted in planning and executing various events, including a get-to-know-you party for interns.

Lifeguard Internship

Served as one of 80 lifeguards at Disney's famous Blizzard Beach water park.

Received special training in the 10/20 Waterpark Rule of Lifeguarding (Ellis Lifeguard Training), and rotated throughout the water park with fellow staffers to provide assistance and protection to participants. Patrolled or monitored recreational areas on foot or from lifeguard stands. Rescued distressed people using rescue techniques and equipment. Contacted emergency medical personnel in case of serious injuries. Examined injured persons and administered first aid or cardiopulmonary resuscitation as required, utilizing training and medical supplies and equipment. Instructed guests in proper use of waterslides and other features and provided safety precaution information. Reported to the Lifeguard/Recreation Manager.

Key Contributions:

- Saved several lives in backboard and other types of rescues and resuscitations.
- Received many commendations for performance above and beyond the call of duty.

Manager, Miniature Golf

Completed internship in the Miniature Golf park to further develop management knowledge.

Oversaw a wide variety of staffing and administrative functions, supporting Disney initiatives and instructing others in company policies and procedures.

Education

Associate of Arts in Business Administration Candidate

PEACH COUNTY COMMUNITY COLLEGE, OTSELIC, NY

Anticipated Graduation, May 2008

Completed Organizational Leadership practicum at Walt Disney World, Orlando, Florida.

Serve as campus representative for the Walt Disney World Internship Program.

Ellis & Associates Lifeguard Training

WALT DISNEY WORLD, ORLANDO, FL

Operations Management and Human Resources

Human Resources Manager

Focused, comprehensive, and well laid out—an overall easy, engaging read.

SAM MILLER
#2 Nowhere Court • New York, NY

(H) 973-555-1212 • (C) 973-555-1313 • resumes@aresumesolution.com

HUMAN RESOURCES MANAGER

~ Over 25 years of experience in Human Resources, Management, and Labor Relations ~

◆ ◆ ◆

Seasoned and accomplished Human Resources Management professional with strong background in leading, and managing HR initiatives. Proven senior-level experience in decision-making policy, direction business planning, government relations, and research. Talented in development and enforcement of policies and procedures. Skilled in analyzing staffing needs and creating effective solutions that result in maximized efficiency and reduced overhead. Exceptional interpersonal capabilities, able to cultivate relationships with clients, staff executives, and union leaders.

KEY PROFICIENCIES

Labor Relations	Arbitration Management	Union Negotiations
Policies and Procedures	Human Resource Functions	Budget Development
Staff Hiring	Management	Grievances

PROFESSIONAL EXPERIENCE

HUMAN RESOURCE SERVICES – New York, NY

STAFF MANAGER – LABOR RELATIONS   2001 – PRESENT

Direct all aspects of Labor Relations team through implementation of third step grievance, arbitration, NLRB, and labor relations training process. Research past bargaining minutes, history, and arbitration decisions to develop contract interpretations and clarify intent of collective bargaining agreements. Review grievance reports for identification of trends. Handle third step grievances, arbitrations, and bargaining preparation though research of background information for field labor managers and legal staff. Collaborate with union officials, Labor Relations Managers, and attorneys.

• Key member of team that served on National Bargaining Table with CWA and IBEW Unions in 2002.

XYZ CORPORATION– New York, NY

HR PARTNER – LABOR RELATIONS   1998 – 2001

Designed and implemented organizational budget. Oversaw monthly reports for operating budget results. Served as Labor Relations liaison for HR on performance development, benchmarking, merit review, and employee survey results. Facilitated the Employee Survey Results team, which analyzed the results of the survey, and prepared recommendations for action for the leadership team and LR organization based on the results. Directed performance management and merit review process for organization, while ensuring Labor Relations compliancy on budget and timeline. Managed communications to the union on numerous issues. Member of the LR leadership team. Managed the development and maintenance of LR's 1999 operating budget, which was under ran by 19%, which allowed LR to contribute $1.5M to the overall HR budget reduction.

XYZ CORPORATION– New York, NY

BUNDLES PORTFOLIO ANALYST – AT&T ACCOUNTS RECEIVABLE MANAGEMENT   1997 – 1998

Analyzed accounts receivable portfolio results for long distance accounts, local bundled accounts, and wireless bundled accounts. Served as primary financial advisor for direct billing. Analyzed delinquent accounts. Calculated financial ratios for identification of trends, risk assessment, and performance evaluation. Prepared monthly presentations, through evaluation of AT&T's business performance against estimates. Examined uncollectible rates versus targeted objectives.

• Reconciled MultiQuest account adjustments in 2 Business Units, which yielded an annual $1.1 million improvement to uncollectible expense in one of the units.

XYZ CORPORATION– New York, NY

ASSISTANT MANAGER – HUMAN RESOURCES   1996 – 1997

Served as Human Resources Generalist for Law and Government Affairs organization. Oversaw staffing process from advertisement of open position though hiring and placement of candidate, which included telephone interview screenings. Advised clients on labor relations issues, benefits, leave of absence, performance management, employee misconduct, and terminations.

• Developed business/process assumptions and applied them to the existing Public Relations organization to create a plan for a new occupational design that maximized resources within the client group.

EDUCATION

Bachelor of Science – Business Administration   Nowhere University – New York, NY
Associate of Science – Business Administration   College of New Horizon – New York, NY
Certification – Secretarial   Katharine University – New York, NY
Contracts Administration Certification – Labor Relations   School of Industrial and Labor Relations, Cornell University – New York, NY

SOFTWARE KNOWLEDGE
MS Word • MS Excel • MS PowerPoint

Director of Recruiting

So *this* is what I might have been, had I kept my day job. Clearly the writer really knows the recruitment business.

Anneke Smith　　　2423 Fairfax Court　　　Home: 248.555.2323
　　　　　　　　　　　West Bloomfield, MI 48322　　e-mail: annekes@aol.com

---

Director of Recruiting
Process Re-engineering / Project Implementation / Organizational Growth and Turnaround

Talented and forward-thinking senior recruitment leader with proven track record of success turning around company performance by distilling and managing processes, enhancing organizational structure, and developing skilled self-managed teams. Known as the "go-to" person for diverse organizational and process-related challenges. Confident and passionate individual with a mission to create "best in class" recruiting departments through comprehensive utilization of marketing tools and cutting edge sales practices.

✓ Project Implementation	✓ Strategic Planning	✓ On-boarding/Referral Programs
✓ Process Reengineering	✓ Sales and Marketing	✓ Role Competency Design
✓ Training and Development	✓ Recruitment Metrics	✓ Workforce Planning

Proven success collaborating with internal and external stakeholders to execute business-growth strategies that generate revenue and exceed client expectations. Demonstrate expert communication skills, analytical thinking, financial analysis, strategic planning, and business management capabilities.

PROFESSIONAL EXPERIENCE

A & E CORPORATION, *Bloomfield, MI*
A & E Corporation has been an innovative leader in Recruitment Process Outsourcing (RPO) for over a decade. A & E offers innovative recruiting, consulting, and staffing solutions.

Recruitment Process Outsourcing Manager　　　　　　　　　　　6/2006 to present
- Design the recruitment and sourcing strategies to support the strategic, operational, and business plan for the company. Influence senior business executives on strategy, resources, hiring forecasts, and capacity planning.
- Establish and oversee maintenance of effective candidate sourcing channels and both internal and external resume tracking systems to speed the process of identifying qualified candidates and tracking effectiveness and efficiency metrics.
- Assist with proposal generation, implementation, training, and daily oversight of key account service delivery teams, overall delivery of key account results, and the management and nurturing of client relationships to deliver the highest caliber client results.
- Provide timely feedback to management and clients regarding workload and accomplishments, ensuring accuracy of data and timely, thorough completion of assignments.

SMITH & WILLIAMS CONSTRUCTION, INC., *San Francisco, CA*
Established as a general contractor in 1961, and consistently ranked among the largest local Contractors by the San Francisco Business Journal, *the Top 400 Contractors and the Top 100 Design/Builders in the nation by* Engineering News Record.

Vice President, Recruiting　　　　　　　　　　　　　　　1/2005 to 6/2006
Designed, implemented, and oversaw 230-person corporate recruiting function. Reported directly to the CEO and provided strategic direction and tactical follow-up on all levels of hiring. Established executive construction talent pipeline through direct networking, cold-calling, online niche boards, and an employee referral program.
- Managed the internship program and volunteered to represent student construction organizations establishing a future flow of qualified construction management majors.
- Improved the "candidate experience" by instituting full life cycle recruiting to the company.
- Spearheaded company-wide skills matrix to aid in succession planning and resource management.
- Partnered with IT to create and launch career site to meet OFCCP and EEOC compliance requirements.
- Orchestrated a comprehensive multi-prong employee retention process overhaul.
- Established a 30-60-90 new employee review process, introduced buddy system and re-engineered new hire on boarding procedures, reducing communication breakdowns and ensuring employees' complete preparedness for first day of employment.

START UP AIR, *Dulles, VA*
A low-cost airline based in Fairfax County, Virginia (near Washington, D.C.) that operated from 1989 until 2002.
Recruiting Manager   12/2003 to 12/2004
Hired to develop and implement a large-scale recruiting function for a pre-launch start-up airline to support 2000 hires. Assisted with the creation and management of a $1M advertising budget. Presented detailed and comprehensive reports and analysis on staffing metrics including attrition, program results, time-to-fill, and recruiter performance. Assisted with creation and follow-through of function's new Sarbanes-Oxley narrative.

- Exceeded 2004-headcount targets by 20%, employing 2000 external and 500 internal employees.
- Conducted months of research, built a business case, and gained C-level buy in for the implementation of an applicant microsite, which significantly increased the ease and effectiveness of the baggage handler screening process. Developed tool questions based on role competencies, and rolled out "plug-and-play" microsite to *www.startupair.com*.
- Dismantled and rebuilt all hiring processes and procedures to accommodate AAP, EEOC, and OFCCP guidelines with an eye towards the U.S. government's newest definition of an applicant and conducted quarterly internal audits to ensure compliance.
- Created a robust Employee Referral Program (ERP) that propelled referrals to 13% of total hires resulting in lower cost-per-hire for hourly airport employees.
- Implemented legally defensible behavioral interviewing with recurrent training for hiring managers, resulting in a significant reduction in EEOC claims.
- Designed and implemented a measurement tool to assist with monitoring the "candidate experience," ensuring a positive experience and takeaway after interviewing with Independence Air and increasing candidate satisfaction levels 20%.
- Designed and implemented a Service Level Agreement (SLA) greatly impacting the time-to-offer metric by eliminating communication disconnects. Time-to-offer on corporate hires went from 65 days to 30 days.
- Influenced two major internal departments to utilize in-house recruiting function rather than headhunting services, resulting in a savings of approximately $300K in 2004.

TNET COMMUNICATIONS, *Dulles, VA*
TNET Communications provides leading voice, data, converged, and managed services for businesses, enterprises and carriers who need a proven, responsive and cost-effective alternative to traditional service providers.
Staffing Manager (promoted to full-time in July 2001)   8/2000 to 12/2003
Promoted to take nationwide 37-market telecommunications corporate, technical and sales recruiting efforts for 1200-member organization to the next level. Reported to multiple VPs/Directors and charged with maintaining order through chaos of company's bankruptcy filing.

- Orchestrated and launched organizational measurements and metrics against specific and desired corporate outcomes.
- Engaged external agencies and internal recruiters in a massive hiring effort for top performers in sales arena meeting the business objective of 300 hires in a time frame of 3 months, dramatically impacting sales for the last quarter.
- Introduced SLA to firmly establish the recruitment strategy, reducing time-to-offer by 5 days. Significantly reduced time-to-offer to 27.01 and time-to-start to 40.01 after the initiative implementation completion.
- Successfully established solid customer service best practices and hired 700 sales employees.
- Reduced offer turnaround to a 5-day administrative cycle from a 2–3 week cycle.
- Implemented technical pre-screen process to eliminate unqualified candidates to meet OFCCP and EEOC guidelines.

PRIOR ENGAGEMENTS

CONCERT/FOLIO FN/BRITISH STANDARDS INSTITUTE/MANPOWER

Recruiter   3/1996 to 8/2000
Utilized both traditional and non-traditional search resources and techniques to identify and target top talent professionals including cold-calling, advertising, networking, and professional associations.

- Sourced, reviewed, and screened resumes for a variety of technical and corporate positions.
- Conducted preliminary IT candidate interviews and arranged for subsequent interviews with hiring managers and clients.
- Expanded growth of business by initiating direct placement contracts and placements service.

Louis Edwards

1234 Ocean Road • Wilmington, NC 97979 • (999) 999-9999 • louis@email.com

Emerging Technologies Globalization Executive
Deal Maker / Market & Product Strategist / Business Developer / Negotiator

Results-driven and innovative Telecommunications Industry Executive with a 20+ year successful track record driving revenue growth and winning market share primarily in turnaround, start-up, and high growth situations. Consistently deliver strong and sustainable revenue gains through combined expertise in Strategic Business Planning, Product Management, Market Strategy, Contract Negotiations, and Customer Relationship Management. Recognized for exceptional ability to assess business unit capabilities, identify and implement appropriate business and product re-engineering measures thus assuring bottom line growth. Rare ability to establish the organization's vision, develop "C" level relationships and negotiate the deals that guarantee success.

Key Accomplishments

- "C" level relationship builder with a track record personally negotiating contracts with companies such as Xerox, Lockheed Martin, Bank of America, Morgan Stanley, EDS, Visa, Oracle, Microsoft, Nortel, Boeing, Nordstrom, and The Gap.
- Consistent track record developing contracts and terms that utilized company capabilities and met customer needs, including the first prepaid international contract. This allowed the company to accelerate into the international market achieving $1+ billion in revenue. This approach became the industry standard.
- Turned around an underperforming business unit lacking leadership by redesigning and motivating the sales and services teams, successfully recovering 60% of the lost accounts and adding new business to increase revenues to $5+ million annually in the first 12 months.
- Conceived and coordinated the global account management process; identified customer needs and product capabilities, spearheaded product and service level agreement changes to win the first global contract. Not only did this grow market share from 7% to 100% and revenue from $330,000 to $6 million per month, it set new industry standards in global business practices.
- Revitalized a product offering by identifying and implementing an International Reseller Channel, re-engineering the existing product through the addition of a conversion process adding packaging enhancements and aligning a service/support structure extending the product life by 2 years and capturing a potential revenue of $10 million annually.
- Within 45 days, conceived and implemented a National Accounts Program, establishing pricing model, sales organization structure, and customer service delivery format, successfully increasing revenue from $12 million to $27 million per month. This program became the standard for the entire company.
- Led the company's new technologies market development (VPN, Web Hosting, co-locating Internet) securing sales in excess of $15 million within 6 months.

Employment Summary

Software Company, Inc.   **2004 – Present**
Vice President, Business Development and Alliances, Philadelphia, PA
Recruited to drive the product development process and expand market reach through the implementation of an international reseller channel and strategic business alliances.

- Negotiated contracts with Fuji Xerox, Xerox, Accenture, and Lockheed Martin, capturing $10 million in potential revenue.
- Managed the renegotiation of two existing alliances that will net the company at least $2 million over the next 12 months.
- Established a new technology relationship with Open Text extending the company's reach in the Life Sciences market.

235

International Telecom, Inc.   1997 – 2004
Regional Vice President National Accounts, Nashville, TN
Recruited to develop a major account program and subsequently developed a national account program. Responsibilities included full P&L, $20 million operational budget, and more than 250 personnel.
- During a 15-company acquisition period, including the ITI acquisition (the largest in Telecom history), consistently exceeded all business objectives.
- Managed the best corporate A/R and bad debt levels, achieved outstanding customer retention level of 94% and managed corporation's lowest employee turnover rate of 10%.
- Developed and implemented a National Account Program expanding revenues within the first year from $180 million to $260 million and achieved Top Regional Vice President award for outstanding revenue increase.
- Averaged a 21% annual internal revenue growth and was selected to the President's Club from 1998 through 2003 by continually identifying new business opportunities and establishing the right teams, resources, and support to grow the organization and meet the customer's expectations.

ABC Telecom, Inc.   1995 – 1997
Executive Director – Global Accounts, California
Promoted to manage the Western U.S. team of 139 sales and support staff, 5 direct reports and to oversee 35 national accounts.
- Managed and negotiated $750 million in contracts with "C" level players including BOA, Visa, Microsoft, The Gap, Sun, Apple, Oracle, AMD and Nordstrom. Grew market share from less than 15% to 48% in two years.
- Averaged 122% of revenue target every year.

ABC Telecom, Inc.   1992 – 1995
Branch Manager, California
Recruited to grow and manage the Bank of America account, successfully leading a team of 39 cross-functional members.
- Grew annual sales and revenue from $3.6 million to $80 million within two years, attaining 100% market share.
- Spearheaded largest commercial sale in ABC history, valued at $400 million, successfully converting the entire Bank of America network to ABC in less than 6 months while maintaining 100% customer satisfaction.

BS&S   1986 – 1992
Field District Manager, San Francisco, CA
- Consistently exceeded quota, averaging 112% and made President's Club every year while in sales/sales management positions.
- As staff member for the President of BS&S Information Systems, was responsible for revenue and issues for all national accounts west of the Mississippi, approximately 200 accounts, achieving 109% of the revenue quota.

BS&S   1983 – 1986
National Account Management, BS&S Headquarters, New York, NY
- Negotiated and implemented the largest state government equipment contract, valued at $20 million.
- Named to Management Development Program (top 2% of all management personnel), recognized for superior executive and leadership potential.

Education
Bachelor of Arts, New York University
Career Development: Intensive 18-week BS&S account management and product training seminar

JANE B. URATA

3131 Carmel Road • San Diego, California 92109
Home: (858) 555-0234 • Cellular: (858) 555-0235 • E-Mail: ju_arborist@plantnet.com

New Business Development • Strategic Partnerships • Product Marketing

Accomplished Senior Executive with a strong affinity for technology and a keen business sense for the application of emerging products to add value and expand markets. Proven talent for identifying core business needs and translating into technical deliverables. Launched and managed cutting-edge Internet programs and services to win new customers, generate revenue gains, and increase brand value.

Unique combination of technical and business/sales experience. Articulate and persuasive in explaining the benefits of e-commerce technologies and how they add value, differentiate offerings, and increase customer retention. Highly self-motivated, enthusiastic, and profit-oriented.

Expertise in Internet services, emerging payment products, secure electronic commerce, smart card technology, and Java.

AREAS OF QUALIFICATION

Business

- Sales & Marketing • Business Development • Strategic Initiatives
- Business Planning • Project Management • Strategic Partnerships
- Business & Technical Requirements • Revenue Generation
- Contract Negotiations • Relationship Management

Technical

- Electronic Commerce • Encryption Technology • Key Management
- Public Key Infrastructure • Firewalls • Smart Cards • Stored Value
- Digital Certificates • Internet & Network Security • Complex Financial Systems
- Authorization, Clearing, Settlement • Dual and Single Message

PROFESSIONAL EXPERIENCE

ABC Credit Card Corp., San Diego, CA   *2002 to Present*
E-COMMERCE AND SMART CARD CONSULTANT

- Developed strategic e-commerce marketing plans for large and small merchants involving Web purchases and retail transactions using a multifunctional, microcontroller smart card for both secure Internet online commerce and point-of-sale offline commerce.
- Combined multiple software products for Internet and non-Internet applications: home banking, stored value, digital certificates, key management, rewards & loyalty program, PCS/GSM cell phone, and contactless microcontroller with RF communications without direct POS contact.
- Consulted on business and technical requirements to define new e-commerce products and essential deliverables for ABC Credit Card, valued at $2.5 M, supporting and enhancing Internet transactions.
- Analyzed systems relating to the point of sale environment in the physical world and at the merchant server via the Internet for real-time authorization, clearing, and settlement.
- Managed projects including the requirements management system for electronic commerce products affecting core systems: authorization, clearing, and settlement. Provided expertise about business and technical issues regarding SET and the Credit Card Payment Gateway Service.

Management

237

Communications Technology Corporation, Miami, FL   *1997 to 2002*
MANAGER OF WESTERN REGION CHANNEL PARTNER PROGRAM
- Developed and maintained business relationships with large Fortune 500 customers and partners that use or resell client-server software for applications and contracts involving e-commerce and smart card technology for a variety of Internet/intranet products: home banking, EDI, stored value, digital certificates, key management, perimeter defense with proxy firewalls, secure remote access.
- Negotiated an exclusive contract with one of the largest government and commercial contractors in the industry, projected to generate $2–4 million over a 24–36 month period. Contract includes secure remote access, telecommuting, secure health care applications.

Avanta Corp., Miami, FL   *1993 to 1997*
SENIOR SOFTWARE ENGINEER / SOFTWARE INSTRUCTOR
- Designed new programs and trained software engineers in object-oriented analysis and design using UML. Solutions were implemented in C++ in a UNIX environment.
- Managed a software engineering group of 53 individuals. Developed in-house program that saved over $150,000 in training costs for state-of-the-art communications system software development.
- Received Peer Award for outstanding performance; earned a performance evaluation rating of 4.2/5.0.
- Developed and maintained C and C++ communication software in a UNIX environment.
- Created curriculum and course materials that reduced overall training costs by more than $150,000. Coordinated and presented software training programs.

EDUCATION AND CREDENTIALS

- B.S., Electrical Engineering, University of Miami: Emphasis, software engineering; Minor: Psychology. President of the Sigma Sigma Fraternity
- Top Secret Security Clearance with Polygraph

Management

238

BRENDA FRANKS

95 Lane Road   Los Angeles, CA 900071   (888) 888-9888   Bfran@yahoo.com

SENIOR TECHNOLOGY EXECUTIVE

Project Management ◆ *Multimedia Communications & Production* ◆ *MIS Management*

Exceptionally creative management executive uniquely qualified for a digital media technical production position by a distinctive blend of hands-on technical, project management, and advertising/communications experience. Offers a background that spans broadcast, radio, and print media; fully fluent and proficient in interactive and Internet technologies and tools.

Proven leader with a strength for identifying talent, building and motivating creative teams that work cooperatively to achieve goals. Highly articulate with excellent interpersonal skills and a sincere passion for blending communications with technology. Capabilities include:

- Project Planning & Management
- Account Management & Client Relations
- Multimedia Communications & Production
- Information Systems & Networking
- Conceptual & Creative Design
- Work Plans, Budgets, & Resource Planning
- Department Management
- Interactive / Internet Technologies
- Technology Needs Assessment & Solutions
- Team Building & Leadership

PROFESSIONAL EXPERIENCE

LaRoche Investments, Inc., Los Angeles, CA   *1989 – Present*
VICE PRESIDENT OF MIS (2000 – Present)
ASSISTANT VICE PRESIDENT OF IT/CORPORATE COMMUNICATIONS   (1995 – 2000)
CORPORATE COMMUNICATIONS OFFICER   (1991 – 1995)
ASSOCIATE   (1989 – 1991)

Advanced rapidly through a series of increasingly responsible positions with this U.S. based, European investment group. Initially hired to manage market research projects, advanced to plan and execute corporate communications projects, and in 1995, assumed responsibility for spearheading the introduction of emerging technologies to automate the entire company.

Current scope of responsibility is expansive and focuses on strategic planning, implementation, and administration of all information systems and technology. Lead technical staff members, manage budgets, select and oversee vendors, define business requirements, and produce deliverables through formal project plans. Manage systems configuration and maintenance, troubleshoot problems, plan and direct upgrades, and test operations to ensure optimum systems functionality and availability.

Technical Contributions
- Pioneered the company's computerization from the ground floor; led the installation and integration of a state-of the-art and highly secure network involving 50+ workstations running on 6 LANs interconnected by V-LAN switching technology.
- Defined requirements; planned and accelerated the implementation of advanced technology solutions, deployed on a calculated time frame, to meet the short- and long-term needs of the organization.
- Orchestrated the introduction of sophisticated applications and multimedia technology to streamline workflow processes, expand presentation capabilities, and keep pace with the competition.
- Administered the life cycle of multiple projects from initial systems/network planning and technology acquisition through installation, training, and operation. Saved hundreds of thousands in consulting fees by managing IS and telecommunication issues in-house.

Management

239

Business Contributions
- Created and produced high-impact multimedia presentations to communicate the value and benefits of individual investment projects to top-level company executives. Tailored presentations to appeal to highly sophisticated, multicultural audiences.
- Assembled and directed exceptionally well-qualified project teams from diverse creative disciplines; collaborated with and guided photographers, videographers, copywriters, script writers, graphic designers, and artists to produce innovative presentations and special events.
- Performed market research and analyses to determine risks and feasibility of multiple investment projects valued at up to $150 million. Developed and recommended tactical plans to transform vision into achievement.

Broadcast, Print, and Radio Advertising & Production   *1974 – 1988*
DIRECTOR OF ADVERTISING, Schwarzer Advertising Associates, New York, NY (1986 – 1988)
ADVERTISING ACCOUNT EXECUTIVE, Schoppe, New York, NY (1987) / Rainbow Advertising, Brooklyn, NY (1984 – 1986) / Marcus Advertising, Phoenix, AZ (1983 – 1984) / WCHN, WTYR, AND WSCZ, Boston, MA (1982 – 1983) / WFDX-TV, WFDX-FM, WKLU, WERS, WQRT, Lehigh Valley, PA (1974 – 1981)
WRITER/PRODUCER, RADIO PROGRAMMING, WPTR, Detroit, MI (1974)

Early career involved a series of progressive creative and account management positions spanning all advertising mediums: multimedia, television, radio, and print. Worked directly with clients to assess complex and often obscure needs; conceptualized and developed advertising campaigns to communicate the desired message in an influential manner.

Achievement Highlights
- Designed, wrote, produced, and launched advertising campaigns that consistently positioned clients with a competitive distinction. Developed a reputation for ability to accurately intuit and interpret clients' desires and produce deliverables that achieved results.
- Hand-selected and led creative teams consisting of graphic designers, artists, musicians, talent, cartoonists, animators, videographers, photographers, and other freelancers and third-party creative services to develop and produce multimillion-dollar advertising campaigns.
- Won accolades for the creation, production, and launch of a 4-color fractional-page advertisement that generated the greatest response in the history of the publication. Honored with a featured personal profile recognizing achievements.
- Developed and applied a unique style and advertising philosophy that accounted for the nuances of human psychology and utilized innovative, brainy, and sometimes startling techniques to capture attention and influence the target market.

EDUCATION & TRAINING
A.A.S. Broadcast Production, Russ Junior College, Boston, MA, 1974
Continuing education in Marketing Research and Broadcast Production, 1984 – 1986
The School of Visual Arts, New York, NY

TECHNICAL QUALIFICATIONS
Innate technical abilities and interest in emerging technologies and digital communications. Trained and fully versed in all aspects of network design, implementation, installation, and maintenance. Advanced skill in the installation, configuration, customization, and troubleshooting of software suites and applications, hardware, and peripherals within the Windows environment (3.x, 95, 98, NT 3.5, NT 3.51, NT 4). Proficient with most Web development, multimedia, word processing, spreadsheet, graphic/presentation, and database tools and applications.

Management

Manager

The creative layout is appealing and breaks up the dense data in the first half page. It's all there: Target Job, Performance Profit, Core Competencies, and even an endorsement.

KEN DAVENPORT

864 Bentley Road ◆ Campbell, CA 95008 ◆ 408-555-0606 ◆ kendaven@sbcglobal.net

Electronic Manufacturing Management Performance Profile
Delivering value to the "bottom line" by recognizing and maximizing opportunities.

Customer-driven manager with more than 15 years of electronic manufacturing services experience involving operations, finance, project management, materials management, and supply chain management, including 6 years managing cross-functional teams and customer relationships. Skilled at evaluating complex issues, identifying key elements, creating an effective action plan and guiding its execution. MBA in Finance and General Management. APICS-certified: CPIM and CSCP.	**Core Strengths & Expertise:** • **Revenue & Profit Increases** • **Cost Reduction & Cost Avoidance** • **Process & Efficiency Improvement** • **Customer Relationship Management** • **Contract Development & Negotiation** • **Team Building & Leadership** • **Materials & Supply Chain Management** • **P&L Management** • **Metrics Management & Analysis**

Consistently promoted to positions with increasing responsibility. Recognized by management as a key contributor, with comments such as the following: *"Ken is a strategic thinker. He is respected as a role model of integrity—he sets a good example for others to follow. He knows how to get things done through channels. Ken's good judgment has helped him identify several opportunities for the company; he not only recognizes opportunities but takes decisive action to make the most of them."*

PROFESSIONAL EXPERIENCE

High-Tech Circuits, Inc., San Mateo, CA   1998–Present; 1989–1997

Business Analyst, Business Unit Financial Analyst *(2006–Present)*
Perform extensive analysis and reporting for a business unit group of 300+ employees. Key actions and accomplishments include the following:
- Revitalized the Time Clock project, which was behind schedule. Established close interaction with offsite project manager and completed assembly, installation, and testing ahead of schedule. Recognized for contribution to efficiency improvement and more effective plant operation.
- Compiled and updated quarterly customer QBR reports using Excel pivot tables and Access database information. In addition, generated and reported quarterly bonuses for employees.

Business Unit Manager *(2003–2006)*
Managed a challenging $25 million/year account and approximately $18 million of materials to maintain profitability. Major areas included forecasting, contract negotiations, supplier performance, financial management, and HR issues. Developed and coordinated activities of cross-functional teams. Key actions and accomplishments included the following:
- Spearheaded revision and execution of full manufacturing contract within 4 months versus expected 6-12 months.
- Grew revenue 330% in fiscal year 2006.

Business Unit Coordinator *(2001–2003)*
Managed accounts valued at $12 million per year. Interacted with customers to ensure high satisfaction. Contributed to cost-reduction and efficiency improvements that included developing Excel macros to use purchasing and inventory data more efficiently and an Access database to track ECN changes and impact.

Master Planning Supervisor *(1998–2001; 1996–1997)*

Established rules, procedures, tools, and techniques to move plant from prototype to volume production. Managed master scheduling for multiple programs, as well as work cell material management and metrics. Key actions and accomplishments included the following:

- Achieved smooth transfer of $30+ million program to another facility through detailed material transactions and planning.
- Reduced excess inventory by $400,000 and increased inventory turns 20%.
- Originally earned promotion from Master Planner position within less than a year.

Previous positions: Master Planner; Accounting Manager

Peterson Laminate Systems, Phoenix, AZ   1997–1998

Production/Scheduling/Inventory Manager

Served as a member of Plant Leadership Team and as High Performance Work Team coach for Shipping department. Additional actions and accomplishments included the following:

- Participated in Kaizen event that promoted continuous improvement and elimination of waste by initiating changes that included reducing product travel from 5,000 to 2,000 feet.
- Contributed to $500,000 inventory reduction and 98% on-time shipping record.

EDUCATION & CERTIFICATION

Master of Business Administration-Finance & General Management
Boston University, Boston, MA

Bachelor of Science-Accounting
Northeastern University, Boston, MA

Certified in Production & Inventory Management (CPIM): earned in less than one year
Certified Supply Chain Professional (CSCP): earned in less than 6 months
APICS, Alexandria, VA

PROFESSIONAL AFFILIATION

Member, American Production & Inventory Control Society

COMPUTER COMPETENCIES

MS Office: Word, Excel (including pivot tables and macros), PowerPoint, Access; Visio; SAP ERP

Marketing Director

Good one-page networking resume for an executive that captures the big points; wouldn't be used to make a serious pitch but for getting the word out, useful.

Terri Williams

Los Angeles, CA 90066 □ (310) 390-7943 □ isom@verizon.net

Strategic Marketing Director

Identifies and establishes footholds in new markets

Innovative business development leader offers 12 years of international expertise identifying market opportunities, defining market strategies, developing reseller channels, and establishing profitable distribution networks. Collaborative by nature; works within teams to build strong relationships and strategic business partnerships. Experienced across a range of industries; create competitive advantage by taking the lessons learned from one industry and applying to others.

Areas of Expertise

Business Development ~ Relationship Building / Strategic Partnerships ~ Marketing ~ Channel Management
Strategic Market Planning ~ Reseller Channels ~ Distribution Networks ~ Market Penetration ~ Market Growth
Program Development & Management ~ Marketing Communications ~ Brand Awareness ~ Market Research

PROFESSIONAL SUMMARY

Ontario Market Development Group, San Francisco, CA (1996–Present)

International Business Development Manager

Helped more than 300 Quebec-based companies penetrate the US market

Assist various Ontario-based industries (technology, food, environmental, and others) in penetrating and developing distribution networks within the US market. Define and identify market opportunities, analyze and create market entry strategies, establish and manage market development plans, develop key contacts, recruit agents and distributors, make formal introductions, train companies in promoting their businesses, craft and manage promotional programs and events, perform market research, and generate valuable business intelligence. Initiate and implement licensing, OEM, and other partner relationships. Teach companies how to identify, negotiate, and establish reseller networks.

- Identified, qualified, and selected appropriate markets and distribution channels for 800+ companies; developed strategic business and marketing plans for 150 clients.
- Planned, coordinated, and managed promotional events that have generated tens of millions of dollars in new revenues for Ontario-based businesses; 1999 Hollywood animation promotion generated $34M (Canadian) in contracts.
- Developed network of high-level, strategic contacts in numerous industries; taught companies to profit through channel distribution.

California Computer, Los Angeles, CA (1992–1995)

Sales Support Administrator

Coordinated reseller channel strategy implementing channel marketing programs for printers, plotters, and other peripheral products. Supported 15 outside sales representatives and 1 international subsidiary, helped resellers understand and leverage marketing programs, managed accounts, resolved conflicts between sales channels and internal departments, and provided world-class customer service.

- Improved marketing program tracking and reporting time 30% through automation.

EDUCATION

Master of Business Administration—International Management & Marketing
University of California—Los Angeles

Bachelor of Arts—Economics
University of Florida, Gainesville

Marketing Director

Strong combination-style resume. Target job followed by relevant credentials and section detailing mission-critical core competencies.

TINA JOHNSON, MBA

22761 River Bank Drive Reston, Virginia 20165
703-555-7667 (h) • 703-555-6840 (m) • tinajohnson14@comcast.net

Online and Brand Marketing Strategist/Director

Over 20 years experience in every facet of marketing in positions such as marketing director, consultant, and/or owner with a solid successful background in traditional and entrepreneurial venues. Use a real-world approach to problem solving and a deep well of experience to meet the challenges of this fast-paced function.

◆ Demonstrate project planning and management skills in supremely high-stress scenarios where failure is not an option and the wrong decision could deliver substantial client loss.

◆ Utilize a consultative approach to assess client needs and provide "turnkey" solutions and programs that meet the client's strategic goals.

◆ Possess strategic business sense, an uncompromising work ethic, and a natural sincerity to help create consistent, "magic" marketing solutions and win loyal support from clients, partners, managers, and business owners.

◆ Possess deep expertise in branding, managing and positioning product lines, and implementing innovative marketing messages that drive revenue and bring unique product "stories" to the community.

MBA - Marketing - Rutgers University, New Jersey • **BS in Business Administration** -
College of New Jersey, New Jersey

Results-Oriented Catalyst:

◆ Built a packaged employee communication strategic roll-out plan for Montgomery General Hospital, partnered with senior internal HR leaders and directed launch time frame for new employee subscription benefit (PepPods, an online emergency preparedness and personal home record system).

◆ Met with potential investors on behalf of Zigzag.net, marketed online learning management system to military and law enforcement professionals, and identified a $1 million investor who was ultimately secured.

◆ Developed from inception to implementation an interactive kiosk concept whereby banking clients received instant product and service information during busy bank periods, receiving praise from customers nationwide during testing and rollout.

Marketing and Events Planner:

◆ Created and launched the AT&T "No More Excuses" multimedia cell phone campaign, the most successful January campaign to date in company history.

◆ Assisted in locating creative team to design Mascot Percy's character costume. Lined up stimulating children's entertainment musicians and artisans, and food and health screening vendors, and launched direct mail campaign to the Mercy Health Plan members, resulting in an impressive 900-person turnout.

◆ Organized and launched a hugely successful White Glove Car Wash charity grand opening event, and donated a portion of the proceeds to the Make-a-Wish Foundation.

Multi media Marketing Strategist:

◆ Created the Magistar public corporate identity, including the marketing language on the corporate website, trade show participation strategy, and public relations presentations.

◆ Established strong rapport with TMC Labs editor who agreed to conduct an extensive product evaluation and testing, resulting in a rave product review for Magistar in the January 2001 issue of *Internet Telephony Review* entitled "VoIP 'Click-to-Talk Shootout'"

Gifted Leader:

Developed a turnkey fundraising program for immediate online client use complete with a fundraising microsite, fundraising, sales and pricing procedures, and training and sales support materials such as scripts and FAQs. Improved the volume and quality of traffic to ActiveMedia client websites from search engines via "natural" search results, raising their resulting online rank, and improving their click-through numbers.

THE RIVER BANK GROUP • Marketing Consultant – Reston, VA • 2001–present
MAGISTAR • Director, Brand Marketing (VOIP) - Reston, VA • 1999–2001
NATIONS BANK/BARNETT BANK, INC. – Advertising Project Manager - Jacksonville, FL • 1997–1998
URBAN DESIGN, INC. – Director of Marketing - Philadelphia, PA • 1994–1995

Online Faculty at UNIVERSITY OF PHOENIX • 2002–2003

Facilitated asynchronous online undergraduate courses in Marketing, Integrated Marketing Communications, Management, and Organizational Behavior. Developed marketing rich content and designed final group project, whereby students created a viable business and marketing plan and delivered presentation to final class.

Senior Finance Manager

Here the target job title, giving instant focus to the reader, is immediately followed by bolded credentials highlighting relevant skills.

BOB JOHNSON

5401 68th Street ◆ Lubbock, TX 79424

Home: 203-000-0000 ◆ Cell: 913-000-0000 ◆ Email: bobjohnson@hotmail.com

SENIOR FINANCE MANAGEMENT EXECUTIVE / CFO

17+ Years of Progressive Experience, Including Position as CFO for Global Division of Wal-Mart

MBA in Finance; Graduate of Wal-Mart Financial Management Program; Green Belt Certified

Executive Board Member for Several Asian Financial Services Companies

Senior-level finance executive/CFO with track record of directing and re-engineering large-scale corporate finance functions. Strategic analyst, forecaster, and planner with proven risk assessment and sound decision-making background.

Core Financial & Executive Knowledge/Skill Areas Include:

Corporate Finance Management	Acquisitions & Divestitures	Financial Forecasting & Modeling
Corporate Reorganization Affairs	Financial Analysis & Reporting	International Financial Affairs
Cost Reduction & Avoidance	Risk Assessment Management	Banking & Investor Relationships
Senior Executive Collaboration	Team Building & Leadership	Multi-Location Operations Leadership

PROFESSIONAL EXPERIENCE	WAL-MART, 1989 – Present *Progressed through increasingly responsible positions and challenging assignments over 17-year period, demonstrating ability to generate quantifiable results on national and international scale.* **Global Financial Planning & Analysis Leader** – Wal-Mart Insurance (2004–Present) Currently lead financial reporting and forecasting functions for $10 billion Revenue Insurance division with $40 billion in assets. Supervise local and international (India) team. Work hand-in-hand with CFO and CEO on mission-critical objectives and serve as primary point of contact to Corporate Finance organization. Create reports for BOD Audit Committee and CEO reviews. Assist top-level senior management in key strategic communication and presentation activities. **Challenges: Bring heightened visibility to key business information within complex, restructured organization. Improve financial reporting methods (previously lacking insightful analysis) to provide better view for senior management and Board into financial health of large operations.**
FINANCIAL FORECASTING & REPORTING	Built Center of Excellence team that took charge of financial reporting for $100 million in expenses, leading to significant improvements in cost control and immediate benefits to business operations. Led successful forecasting improvements through design and development of new modeling tools; instituted new SG&A reporting infrastructure for ~$800 million cost base.
MERGERS & ACQUISITIONS	Played key role in supporting largest re-insurance transaction in history (Wal-Mart Insurance sale to Swiss RE), performing due diligence functions to facilitate process.
EXECUTIVE MANAGEMENT SUPPORT	Provided value-driven recommendations and support to Chief Financial Officer and Chief Executive Officer, including preparation of strategic communication and presentation materials for delivery at Board of Directors and other key meetings.

	Chief Executive Officer – Wal-Mart Hong Kong (2002–2004) Hand-selected for return to top leadership position following previously successful management tenure with Wal-Mart Capital Hong Kong, overseeing team of 150–160. Held full P&L responsibility for Consumer Financial Services Operations ($600 million in assets, $200 million in revenues) consisting of Mortgage, Personal Loans, and Automobile Financing divisions. Functioned as Capital's Lead Representative to Hong Kong Monetary Authority and Finance House Association of Hong Kong. **Challenges: Engineer turnaround for underperforming business affected by heavily saturated financial services market in Hong Kong and SARS epidemic, with continual downsizing initiatives.**
NEW BUSINESS DEVELOPMENT	Transformed Hong Kong's mortgage strategy by strengthening operations and launching new product introductions, generating 30% growth in asset base as a result.
COST REDUCTION & AVOIDANCE	Achieved $1.5 million cost savings through several productivity improvement solutions, including outsourcing and rationalization initiatives, leading to fulfillment of turnaround goals.
	Chief Executive Officer – Wal-Mart Finance Indonesia/Malaysia (2000–2002) Promoted to hold full P&L accountability for Finance Indonesia, directing multi-branch platform with 800+ team members. Directed Credit Card, Personal Loans, and Automobile Financing divisions. Served as Board member for several Asian leading financial services businesses. Challenges: Reverse 5-year history of declining profits as operations emerged from Asian economic crisis of late 1990s. Restructure debt necessitated by difficulties of commercial financing customers. Drive improvements for low employee morale.
OPERATIONS TURNAROUND	Met turnaround objectives by leading Indonesian business to first profitable year in 5 years by growing credit card/personal loan revenues and customer base over 150%.
BUSINESS DEVELOPMENT	Launched Visa co-brand credit card with largest bank in Indonesia that became #1 Visa-issued card in Indonesia during 2001.
QUALITY ASSURANCE	Utilized Six Sigma processes to improve operations through collection autodialers, application scanning, and system migration to Vision+
EDUCATION & CREDENTIALS	Masters of Business Administration in Finance UNIVERSITY – New York, NY (1997) Bachelor of Science in Information Technology
Professional Development	Financial Management Program (FMP)
	Information Management Leadership Program (IMLP)
	Six Sigma Green Belt Training & Certification
	Financial Analysis for Business Development

Receptionist

With this resume, Keisha had no trouble finding another job after her last employer moved out of state.

Keisha A. Jackson

1305 Lakeshore Drive ◆ Apartment 10-B ◆ Chicago, IL 00000 ◆ (555) 555-5555 ◆ kaj200@netmail.com

PROFILE

Responsible and dedicated office professional with 15 years of experience in heavy-volume, fast-paced environments. Cooperative team player who enjoys working with people and utilizing direct telephone contact. Detail-oriented, thorough, and accurate in taking and relaying information. Well-organized to handle a variety of assignments and follow through from start to finish. Strong work ethic, with eagerness to learn and willingness to contribute toward meeting a company's goals.

- Visitor reception and routing
- Multi-line phone system operations
- Data entry and retrieval (Word and Excel)
- Customer relations
- Sales department support

- Account maintenance/reconciliation
- Order processing and billing
- Research and resolution of problems
- Regular and express mail distribution
- Office supplies and forms inventory

WORK HISTORY

CONCORD GROUP, INC., CHICAGO, IL   1998–2007
Personal and commercial insurance company
Receptionist
- Represented the prestigious image of this company in a high-profile position requiring public contact with important clients in the sports and entertainment field as well as various other industries.
- Entrusted with opening the office daily and handling confidential material.
- Operated 24-line Premiere 6000 phone system, routing calls/faxes appropriately, and relaying messages accurately. Saved managers' time by screening unwanted calls.
- Reorganized shipping room to run more efficiently and operated automated labeling/tracking system (Powership), processing 5 to 50 outgoing packages daily.
- Ensured prompt delivery of express packages.
- Took initiative to update insurance certificates on computer.
- Participated in hiring a new assistant and trained her in company procedures.

PAPERCRAFT USA, CHICAGO   1994–1997
Nation's largest distributor of specialty paper
Telephone Account Coordinator (Customer Service Representative)
- As one of 80 employees in a busy call center averaging 200 incoming calls per hour, handled the ordering process, billing, and issuing credits or rebills to ensure accurate account records.
- Consistently achieved excellent scores in the mid-90s on monitored activities.
- Provided support to sales representatives all over the country.
- For four months in 1996, assisted the product director, creative director, and vice president of sales, providing them with daily sales activity reports and analyses, pricing updates, and sales strategy presentations for company's two divisions.
- Processed invoices and deliveries for international shipments.

HJR VENDING COMPANY, CHICAGO, IL   1992–1994
Distributor of confectionery items sold in vending machines
Customer Service Representative
- Worked in a team of six, processing telephone orders from individuals and retailers, including four house accounts. Resolved billing discrepancies.
- Offered information on promotions and discounts, which encouraged larger orders.

THE PLAYHOUSE, CHICAGO, IL   1987–1997
Director of Day Care Center
- While raising a family, owned and operated a full-service day care center for preschool children.
- Administered all aspects of the business (billing, accounts payable, accounts receivable, and maintaining client files).

Office Support Professional

Janet is a long-time (15 years) worker within the veterinarian field who successfully moved into an administrative assistant's job in a medical office. She sent out one resume and got the job.

JANET COOPER

813-555-9988 • JCOOPER@EMAIL.COM

2833 Newsome Road, Valrico, FL 33594

OFFICE SUPPORT PROFESSIONAL

Receptionist ... Clerk ... Administrative Assistant

EXPERTISE

Records Management

Customer Liaison

Front Office Operations

Workflow Planning / Scheduling

Troubleshooting / Problem Solving

Inventory Control

COMPUTER SKILLS

- Microsoft Word
- Cornerstone Proprietary Contact Management Software

TRAINING

Eastern States Conference in Orlando – Annual training for receptionists and managers

Top-performing office assistant with a reputation for professionalism, integrity, creativity, resourcefulness, and competence. Superior communication and listening skills. Strong client focus, with attention to detail and excellent follow-through.

SELECTED CONTRIBUTIONS

- Redesigned administrative processes to streamline functions, eliminate redundancy, and expedite workflow. Initiated the conversion from manual processes to a fully computerized office. Implemented the automated Gevity HR Payroll Program.
- Improved customer service by developing a new client survey, soliciting feedback to quickly resolve client complaints and ensure top-quality service and satisfaction.
- Launched an employee-of-the-month incentive program to build unity and promote outstanding customer service.

PROFESSIONAL EXPERIENCE

Practice Manager – 1993 to 2006
Receptionist – 1992 to 1993
COMPLETE ANIMAL HOSPITAL, Tampa, Florida
(Veterinary clinic comprised of 6 doctors, 10 technicians, and 7 receptionists with annual revenues of $1.4 million)
Oversaw scheduling, managed inventory, and trained receptionists. Accountable for financial reports including daily deposits, monthly billings, and collections.

Receptionist – 1990 to 1992
WILLIAM SMITH, DVM, Fayetteville, North Carolina
(One-doctor veterinary clinic, 2 technicians, 2 receptionists)
Professional and cheerful first point of contact. Broad-based experience in answering multiple telephone lines, scheduling appointments, and filling prescriptions.

RELATED EXPERIENCE

Administrative Assistant
CENTEL BUSINESS SYSTEMS, Fayetteville, North Carolina

Clerking Assistant
OSTEOPATHIC SCHOOL OF MEDICINE
Ohio University, Athens, Ohio

Management

248

Office Assistant (Initial Resume)

After interviewing Barbara, it became clear that she did more than her resume reflected. Aside from her initial resume being poorly formatted, it lacked focus, an interesting summary, and a content-rich presentation of her experience.

BARBARA WINSTON

190-12 Arthur Avenue, Brentwood, NY 11717

• • • 631-555-5555 • • •

OBJECTIVE

TO OBTAIN AN OFFICE ASSISTANT POSITION, ENABLING ME TO UTILIZE MY SKILLS AND DEVELOP CAREER PROGRESSION.

SKILLS

WORD PERFECT 5.0 AND 6.0
LOTUS 123
MICROSOFT WINDOWS 98
KEYBOARDING
DICTAPHONE, OFFICE PROCEDURES
KNOWLEDGE OF BUSINESS AND ORAL COMMUNICATIONS
MEDICAL FORMATS
WORK HISTORY

12/01 to Present

SIX AREAS UNIVERSITY, BRENTWOOD, NY
LIBRARY CLERK

ORGANIZING CIRCULATION DESK. ATTENTION TO DETAIL, EDITING, DATA ENTRY, XEROXING, FAXING, FILING, ASSISTING STUDENTS WITH RESEARCH, ADMINISTERING TESTS.

3/99 to 6/00

BRENTWOOD SCHOOL DISTRICT, BRENTWOOD, NY
TEACHER'S AIDE / CLERICAL

ASSISTED TEACHERS WITH SPECIAL EDUCATION STUDENTS, COMPUTER LAB, LUNCH ROOM MONITOR, PERFORMED DUTIES IN PUBLICATIONS DEPARTMENT, CLERICAL DUTIES SUCH AS COLLATING, HAND-INSERTING, AND PROOFREADING.

EDUCATION

10/97

SECRETARIAL SCHOOL OF AMERICA
MORRISTOWN, NY
Certificate In Information Processing
CUMULATIVE GPA – 3.6

1/85

JOHN WILSON TRAINING SCHOOL
BRENTWOOD, NY
Certificate In Medical Assisting

EXCELLENT REFERENCES AVAILABLE UPON REQUEST

Office Assistant (Revised Resume)

The result of this before-and-after resume is dramatic in many ways. It has gone from a confusing document to a personal marketing tool that clearly expresses Barbara's objective. Most importantly, the experience section has become very detailed and interesting to read.

BARBARA WINSTON
190-12 Arthur Avenue, Brentwood, NY 11717 ◆ 631-555-5555 ◆ BWinston@aol.com

Seeking a position in the capacity of **OFFICE SUPPORT ASSISTANT** within a general business or medical office environment, bringing the following experience, skills, and attributes:

Extensive experience working in general public, educational, and medical office settings.
Interface well with others at all levels including patrons, patients, professionals, children, and students.
Caring and hardworking with excellent interpersonal communication, customer service, and office support skills.
Windows 98/DOS, MS Word, Dictaphone, CRT data entry, basic Internet skills, and medical terminology.

Work Experience

Circulation Desk Associate, Six Areas University, Brentwood, NY   12/00 – Present
Provided diversified information services and research assistance to the general public and student populations

◆ Assisted patrons in obtaining a broad selection of books, periodicals, audio-visuals, and other materials.

◆ Catalogued library materials, prepared bibliographies, indexes, guides, and search aids.

◆ Performed multifaceted general office support, and administered academic placement tests.

Teacher's Aide / Office Assistant, Brentwood School District, Brentwood, NY   3/96 – 6/00
Assigned to the Publications Department, Computer Lab, Special Education Resource Room, and Lunch Hall

◆ Assisted grade-level teachers with diversified clerical support in areas of document proofreading, duplication, collating and distribution, classroom management, student monitoring, and miscellaneous assignments.

◆ Easily established rapport with students, and interfaced well with parents and school-wide faculty members.

Nursing Assistant, Our Lady of Consolation, West Islip, NY   6/90 – 1/96
Physical Therapy Aide, Mother Cabrini Nursing Home, Dobbs Ferry, NY   3/85 – 6/90

Held the following combined responsibilities at Our Lady of Consolation and Mother Cabrini Nursing Home:

◆ Obtained vital signs and followed up with timely and accurate medical records-keeping procedures.

◆ Interfaced extensively with patients, staff personnel, orthopedic surgeons, and neurologists.

◆ Observed and reported changes in patients' conditions and other matters of concern.

◆ Performed ambulatory therapeutic treatments such as range of motion, gait training, and whirlpool baths.

◆ Transported patients to and from the hospital for emergency care and scheduled tests.

◆ Ensured the proper use of equipment and medical devices such as wheelchairs, braces, and splinters.

◆ Assisted patients with personal hygiene, grooming, meals, and other needs requiring immediate attention.

◆ Maintained sanitary, neatness, and safety conditions of rooms in compliance with mandatory regulations.

Education

Certificate, Information Processing, 1997
SECRETARIAL SCHOOL OF AMERICA, Morristown, NY

Certificate, Medical Assisting, 1985
JOHN WILSON TRAINING SCHOOL, Brentwood, NY

BRENDA FORMAN
45 Duquesne Street
Parlin, New Jersey 08859   Residence: 732-555-4681

CUSTOMER SERVICE PROFESSIONAL

SENIOR CUSTOMER SPECIALIST • BILLING • CREDIT

Shipping and Dispatching • Inventory Control

Top-performing customer service specialist with more than 20 years experience in diverse environments. Outstanding reputation for keeping and maintaining excellent customer service standards. Experienced in working with high volume calls and answering intricate inquiries.

Train and observe other customer service staff. Take pride in order processing accuracy and efficiency; receive excellent customer feedback. Punctual in meeting deadlines. Interact with the President of my present company on a daily basis. Known to go the "extra mile" for customers and colleagues. Dedicated, efficient, task-oriented employee.

Perform the functions of Order Processing Specialist, Diversified Account Specialist, and Crediting/Billing Specialist. Skilled planner with the ability to analyze client needs and achieve objectives. *Professional strengths include:*

- Customer Service
- Shipping Receiving
- Manufacturing Processes
- Troubleshooting Accounts
- Leadership/Supervision
- Sales Force Support
- Accounts Receivable
- Inventory Control Functions

- Pricing/Quoting Customers
- Processing Orders
- Expediting Deliveries
- Tracking
- Special Attention Order Entry
- Customer Service Observations
- Billing
- Written Reports

BUSINESS EXPERIENCE

EDWARD SMITH, Cranbury, NJ   2000 – Present

Senior Customer Service Representative and Trainer
Team Leader

- Currently serve as a Team Leader for this fine art and supplies manufacturer. Responsible for training and observation of other customer service employees. Lead customer service meetings and prepare written reports of findings.
- Replace supervisor in her absence.
- Ensure that discounts are applied correctly, and credits are entered in a timely fashion.
- Work with orders from start to completion. Interact daily with Daler-Rowney sales force and district manager.
- Handle customer requests. Take orders via fax, place on our system, send to purchasing; then send to warehouse, edit order, bill, print, and send to customers.
- Process all orders from Wal-Mart, our largest customer, through an EDI system.
- Work with Internet order processing systems including Microsoft Orbit program, Navision Financial Program, Trading Partners, Retail Link, Microsoft Word, and Excel.

251

BRENDA FORMAN PAGE TWO

- Attend trade shows and handle special orders in the field. Work with export customers.
- Print back order reports on a weekly basis. Work with potential new clients and their sales representatives regarding administrative work.
- Process numerous order per day including 500–1,000 keyed lines. Write reports in Microsoft Excel and Word.
- Responsible for the issuance of all return authorization numbers and UPS call tags. Research credits and input information into our system.

ROLL INDUSTRIES, Cranbury, NJ   **1991–2000**

Shipping/Receiving Coordinator
Customer Service Representative

- Responsible for a wide range of shipping/receiving and customer service functions for this *Fortune* 500 carpet manufacturer. Handled an extremely high call volume. Processed orders, answered customer inquires, tracked inbound/outbound shipments, expedited deliveries, and set up delivery schedules. Prepared UPS shipments and participated in cycle counting and quarterly inventories.
- Attended trade shows and expedited special attention orders.
- Coordinated with and supported sales representatives in the field. Performed cash receipt reconciliations and resolved customer complaints, disputes, or discrepancies.
- Received Employee of the Month Award out of 300 people.

CONTINENTAL LIFE INSURANCE, Plainfield, NJ   **1989–1991**

Customer Service Representative

- Responsible for pricing/quoting customers, answering phone inquiries, processing orders, and expediting deliveries along with troubleshooting accounts.

CHILDCRAFT, Plainfield, NJ   **1988–1989**

Customer Service Representative

- Duties similar to above. Position required ability to work in a high-pressure/fast-paced environment.

ACTION TUNGSTROM, East Brunswick, NJ   **1985–1988**

Shipping/Receiving Coordinator/Accounts Receivable Clerk

~ LETTERS OF RECOMMENDATION AND REFERENCES UPON REQUEST ~

Retail Manager

Scott needed a resume that would highlight his strong retail and store management experience.

SCOTT KELLY

761 Stoneham Avenue
Woburn, MA 01801

(781) 555-6093
ScottKelly3@hotmail.com

RETAIL ~ SALES & MANAGEMENT

Successful retail manager with over 14 years of experience in Sales, Purchasing/Buying, Customer Service, Inventory Management, Merchandising, Staff Recruitment, and Supervision. Proven ability to increase sales revenue and improve profitability through effective sales consultation, merchandising, purchasing, and inventory management. Demonstrate a high level of motivation and enthusiasm in all aspects of work.

- **Record of improving sales, successfully introducing new products, and growing customer base.** Expanded business for large volume – wine specialty – liquor establishment.
- **Excellent leadership skills**—can communicate effectively with employees and motivate them to perform at their best. Can set direction for the team. Hands-on approach to training.
- **Established record of dependability and company loyalty.**
- **Experience in both general merchandising and specialty retail sales.** Extensive knowledge of the wine industry including suppliers, distributors, and consumers; extensive product knowledge.

PROFESSIONAL EXPERIENCE

Manager (General Operations), *O'Leary's Discount Market,* Woburn, MA   **1996–present**

Direct the daily operation of a high-volume liquor/wine specialty store, servicing over 1,000 customers per week. Manage staff of 15 in the areas of sales and customer service, cash management, budgeting, sales forecasting, employee relations, merchandising, promotions, and security.

- Steadily increased revenues through strong focus on customer service, excellent merchandising, and teamwork.
- Attracted new clientele to store through the development of a full-service wine department. Expanded product line, increased sales and special-order purchasing by implementing specialized sales methods, such as promotional wine-tasting events.
- Established strong reputation in the area as leader for extensive wine inventories at competitive pricing, including regularly stocked hard-to-find selections.
- Trained staff in selling through increased product knowledge and food and wine pairing.
- Participated regularly in trade tastings, shows, and vintner dinners, including Westport Rivers Vineyard, Nashoba Valley Vineyard, Prudential Center and World Trade Center events.

Manager (Stock and Display), *Ames Department Stores,* Boston, MA   **1994–1995**

Managed a staff of 12 in a large, national general merchandise store. Marketed and sold products; developed merchandise and promotional displays; maintained stock levels.

- Increased profits through effective displays and merchandising.
- Improved operations through effectively supervising daily staff assignments.

Stock/Inventory Manager, *Beantown Gift,* Boston, MA   **1992–1994**

Managed purchasing and supervised sales staff for a high-traffic specialty gifts store.

- Expanded customer base by offering a wide range of attractive product displays and creating a welcoming atmosphere that increased the comfort level of patrons.
- Supervised staff of three, ensuring quality of store display and product inventory levels.

Additional experience includes entry-level inventory/shipping-receiving position at Boston University (1990-1982).

253

Merchandise Buyer

The use of a title and keywords list allows the reader to see exactly what Mary's objective is and the scope of her skills in relation to the position of interest. Notice the keywords are very specific rather than general attributes.

Mary J. Sanders

111 East End Avenue • Elmhurst, New York 55555 • (555) 888-0000 • shop2drop@retailworld.net

Assistant Buyer

Skilled in areas of:

- Wholesale / Retail Buying
- Product Merchandising
- Inventory Replenishment
- Product Distribution and Tracking
- Sales Analysis & Reporting
- Regional Marketing Campaigns
- Information Systems
- Vendor Relations
- Order Management

Professional Experience

Merchandise Buying / Coordination

- Report directly to London-American's Director of Sales, providing support in areas of commodities buying and merchandising activities that reach annual sales volumes of $3 million for the division.
- Collaborate with multiple buyers to facilitate the marketing efforts of new products, and development of promotional calendars, product launches, and employee incentive programs.
- Maintain open lines of communication between manufacturers, sales teams, vendors, and warehousing personnel to expedite product orders, distribution, and problem resolutions.
- Reported directly to the Senior Buyer of Steinway Bedding in charge of day-to-day retail merchandise buying and merchandising activities impacting bedding sales across 37 Northeast locations.
- Successfully trained 45+ Steinway employees on a complex LAN database management system.

Sales Tracking, Analysis, & Reporting

- Perform LAC's weekly sales analysis activities on regional/local transactions, achieving a recovery of $1,800,000 from 2001 to 2007 resulting from identification and resolution of accounting discrepancies.
- Develop sales books reflecting product lines, monthly promotions, discontinued items, order forms, and transparencies utilized by sales teams and personnel throughout 26 store locations.
- Formulate price breakdowns and track sales levels to determine product volume adjustments, replenishments, and allocations with a demonstrated proficiency in internal networking systems.
- Researched, compiled, and recorded Steinway's historical data to develop innovative sales strategies through close examination of inventory and product availability, pricing, and store promotions.

Work History

Assistant Buyer / Sales Analyst   7/00 – Present
LONDON-AMERICAN COMMODITIES, LTD. (LAC), Valley Stream, New York

Assistant Buyer / Merchandise Coordinator   4/96 – 7/00
STEINWAY BEDDING, Woodbury, New York

Education

Associates in Science, Business Management, 1996
STATE UNIVERSITY of NEW YORK at COBLESKILL

Sommelier

Angelica's resume was tricked out to look like a menu.

Angelica Merceau

242 W. 103rd Street, Olathe, Kansas 66206
Phone: 913-555-2323 Email: wineangel@yahoo.com

Sommelier Extraordinaire

Piedmonts by the Bay, San Francisco, CA

Master Sommelier, September 2001 – Present

➤ Expertise in all aspects of wine, including regions of the world and their products, grape varietals, fortified wines, methods of distillation, international wine law, cigar production, and proper storage and handling.
➤ Manage wine inventory averaging over 12,000 bottles, worth $2,550,000.
➤ Supervise and personally train staff of 25 sommeliers and wine stewards in pairing wines with cuisine, presentation of wine, brandies, liqueurs, and cigars, and selection, preparation, and placement of glassware.
➤ Coordinate all wine-tasting events, and varietal seminars.
➤ Handle all client inquiries and complaints.

Bordeaux Steak House, New York, NY

Sommelier, May 1999 – January 2001
Lead Wine Steward, December 1997 – May 1999

➤ Supervise and train staff of wine stewards in all aspects of wine presentation, pairing with cuisine, and glassware selection and placement.
➤ Choose appropriate cuisine and wine pairings, assist clients in selection of wines, brandies, liqueurs, cigars, properly present and decant wines, and select and place stemware.

Education, Certifications and Professional Development:

➤ Columbia University, New York, NY
B.A. Food History, May 1997

➤ Court of Master Sommeliers, Napa, CA
Master Sommelier, 2001

➤ International Sommelier Guild, Grand Island, NY
*Sommelier Diploma Program, 1999
*Wine Fundamentals Certificate, Level II, 1999
*Wine Fundamentals Certificate, Level I, 1998

➤ Sommelier Society of America, New York, NY

Varietal Courses:
*Cabernet Sauvignon, 1999   *Sauvignon Blanc, 1999   *Chardonnay, 1999
*Merlot, 1999   *Sangiovese, 1999   *Syrah, 1998
*Pinot Noir, 1998   *Riesling, 1998

Professional Memberships

➤ *Association de la Sommellerie Internationale (ASI)*
Member, 2001 – Present
➤ *The Sommelier Society of America*
Member, 1999 – Present

Restaurant Server

Valerie uses an "Outstanding Achievements & Recommendations" section to bring attention to her strengths, and she has done a nice job identifying the type of restaurants in which she has gained experience.

Valerie W. Butler

333 S.E. Riveredge Drive • Vancouver, Washington 33333
222-222-2222 cell • home 555-555-5555

≈Server≈

Professional Profile

Energetic and highly motivated **Food Server** with extensive experience in the food service industry. Expertise lies in working with the fine dining restaurant, providing top-quality service, and maintaining a professional demeanor. Solid knowledge of the restaurant business with strengths in excellent customer service, food and wine recommendations.

Get along well with management, coworkers, and customers. Well-developed communication skills, known as a caring and intuitive "people person," with an upbeat and positive attitude. Highly flexible, honest, and punctual, with the ability to stay calm and focused in stressful situations. Committed to a job well done and a long-term career.

Outstanding Achievements & Recommendations

- Served notable VIP clientele including clients associated with Murdock Charitable Trust.
- History of repeat and new customers requesting my service as their waitress.
- Known for creating an atmosphere of enjoyment and pleasure for the customer.

"...Valerie was warm, friendly, kind and very efficient.
We didn't feel rushed – she handled our requests and
we appreciated her genuine 'May I please you' attitude...."

Related Work History

Waitress • Banquets • Heathman Lodge • Vancouver, Washington • *2005–present*
Northwest seasonal cuisine.

Banquets • Dolce Skamania Lodge • Stevenson, Washington • *2004–2005*
Casual to fine dining restaurant.

Waitress • Hidden House • Vancouver, Washington • *1996–2004*
Exclusive fine dining restaurant.

Waitress • Multnomah Falls Lodge Restaurant • Corbett, Oregon • *1995–1996*
Historic Columbia Gorge Falls restaurant serving authentic Northwestern cuisine.

Waitress • The Ahwahnee at Yosemite National Park • California • *1 year*
World renowned award-winning fine dining restaurant – sister lodge to Timberline Lodge.

Customer Service Representative

Well laid out. Everything important is up front and center.

JUANITA FLORES

1523 Wisteria Avenue • Sherman Oaks, California 91423

Residence (818) 555-5555 • Mobile (818) 555-1234 • jflores555@email.com

Customer Service Representative / Administrative Support Specialist

—Bilingual English / Spanish—

Highly reliable professional who consistently demonstrates integrity and sound judgment.

Verifiable record of low absenteeism and punctuality; performs tasks with enthusiasm and efficiency.

Well organized with good time management habits; completes assignments in a timely and accurate manner.

Works well independently as well as collaboratively in a team environment.

Reputation for exceptional customer relations; easily establishes trust and rapport with public, demonstrating good listening skills and compassion.

Strong problem solving abilities; can be counted on to follow through to resolution.

Computer Skills: Windows, Microsoft Office (Word, Excel, PowerPoint)

PROFESSIONAL EXPERIENCE

Administrative Assistant, Trust Division • 2005 to Present

CITIBANK, Los Angeles, CA

Provide outstanding customer service handling and directing incoming telephone calls, assisting clients with inquiries and requests, and processing trust account transactions.

Directly support two vice presidents and team of trust specialists with administrative and clerical tasks.

Administrative Assistant • 2001 to 2005

LA OPINION NEWSPAPER, Los Angeles, CA

Provided sales and administrative support to advertising account executives. Assisted customers with inquiries and marketing information in Spanish and English.

Performed translation services.

Handled English and Spanish language correspondence.

Apartment Building Manager • 2001 to 2004 (*concurrent with above*)

SHERMAN PARTNERS PROPERTIES, Sherman Oaks, CA

Collect rents, ensure grounds and units are well maintained, prepare vacancies for rental, screen applicants, and write up rental agreements.

EDUCATION

LOS ANGELES VALLEY COLLEGE, Valley Glen, CA

Major: Business Administration—currently attending

UNIVERSIDAD MICHOACANA DE SAN NICOLAS DE HIDALGO, Mexico

Completed two years of studies in International Business

Steamfitter

Fred had experience in highly specialized jobs. His expertise and training were attractively empha-sized with graphic lines.

Fred G. Jamisen
9999 Abernethy Road • Oregon City, Oregon 99999
555-555-5555

Steamfitter

Professional Profile

Highly skilled, conscientious, and precise **Steamfitter** with over 6 years experience and 10,000+ hours of training in all aspects of Steamfitting. Familiar with all required codes, appropriate use of equipment, steamfitting techniques, safety standards, and proper procedures to prevent injuries. Proficient in reviewing plans, blueprints, and specifica-tions for steamfitting projects with proven ability to provide expert recommendations. Well-developed troubleshoot-ing skills with accurate and precise repairs. Experienced EMT willing to volunteer EMT services on the job. Excellent communication skills, personable, trustworthy, adaptable, and committed to a long-term career.

Expertise and Training Includes:

- Air Conditioning and Refrigeration Systems and Equipment
- Boilers
- Commercial and Industrial
- Conduit Flex, Duct, and Controls
- Electrical and Electronic Contracting
- HVAC, Air Conditioning, and Refrigeration
- Instrumentation
- Outdoor Installations
- Overhead and Underground
- Process Systems and Equipment
- Steam and Heating Systems and Equipment
- Troubleshooting and Maintenance
- Welding Processes including Orbital Welder Arc 207
- Wire Pulling, Wiring Devices, Removal, and Finish

Licenses

Pressure Vessel and Boiler License Class V • *State of Oregon*
United Association of Steamfitters • *Local 290*

Employment History

Steamfitter • United Association of Steamfitters • Portland, Oregon • *6 years*
Assignment to various companies and projects as needed.

Paper Machine Operator • Crown Zellerbach Corp. • West Linn, Oregon • *11 years*
previously owned by James River and Simpson Paper Company
EMT *(Emergency Medical Technician)* • Served as volunteer EMT for the paper mill.

Sales Representative • Pepsi Bottling Company • Portland, Oregon • *8 years*
Beverage sales.

Military

U.S. Army • **Specialist E-4 – Nuclear Missile Technician** • *Honorable Discharge* • *1979*

Education

Associates of Applied Arts • **Humanities**
Carroll College • Helena, Montana *and* Clackamas Community College • Oregon City, Oregon

TOM PARSONS

52 Dune Drive
Matawan, NJ 07747

732.555.3896
E-mail: dtjnpar@aol.com

AUTOMOTIVE SERVICE MANAGER

Twenty-three years successful customer service management experience within the automotive industry; proven track record meeting challenges and creatively solving a variety of problems. Extensive knowledge of automotive warranty policies and procedures. Decisive hands-on manager with an interactive management style able to lead several service teams and administrative staff. Ability to motivate employees' performance levels and develop rapport with diverse audiences; excellent employee relations. Developed excellent product and service knowledge throughout career. Computer-literate with experience of Microsoft Office. Broad-based responsibilities and knowledge include:

- Customer Service
- Problem Solving
- Leadership, Supervision, & Training
- Service Repair Analysis
- Safety & Quality Control
- Warranty Expertise
- Product Knowledge
- Conflict Resolution
- Team Building
- Service Accounting (Expenses/Revenues)
- Technical Knowledge/Efficiency
- Operational Policies & Procedures

PROFESSIONAL EXPERIENCE

KEASBY NISSAN & SUBARU, Keasby, NJ ~ 1992 to Present
Service Manager

- Direct reports include 35 staff (Service Advisors, Service Teams, Cashiers, Receptionists, Lot Attendants, & Detailers)
- Manage Nissan and Subaru Service Departments while supervising service advisors and administrating client issues; ensure customer satisfaction.
- Solve product issues for both departments while working with company representatives and senior management.
- Improve department productivity and solve warranty issues when necessary.
- Monitor departmental budget, taking correct actions when required.
- Oversee the development and implementation of new Subaru franchise, and obtain required certification for service department.
- Achieve 2.2 hours per service order ratio for each customer.
- Eliminate expense and waste while reducing employee time-schedule loss.
- Perform repair order analysis, and monitor team efficiency improving shop utilization and work in process ratios.
- Analyze monthly owner first reports for Nissan, and communicate findings with staff.

ESSEX COUNTY NISSAN, Stanhope, NJ ~ 1987 to 1992
Service Manager

- Direct reports included 13 staff (Service Advisors, Service Teams, Cashiers, Lot Attendants, & Detailers)
- Oversaw entire Service Department ensuring complete customer satisfaction.
- Communicated with Nissan Service Representatives regarding product issues and warranty concerns.
- Improved departmental productivity, implementing several new programs.
- Conducted repair order and service department analysis.
- Substantially increased service revenues and volume by 60% during first fiscal year.
- Maintained warranty expenses within manufacturers' guidelines.
- Transferred to another location to manage larger department.

HAYNES NISSAN, Bloomfield, NJ ~ 1982 to 1987
Service Consultant

- Handled and wrote over 20+ customer service orders per day.
- Sold service and maintenance plans to clients.
- Coordinated service orders with technical staff ensuring quality control through entire service process.
- Prepared final accounting of orders.
- Implemented first statewide service team model for dealerships.
- Transitioned to new organization after company purchase.

259

Heavy Equipment Driver

Treavor was interested in driving heavy equipment in the Middle East.

TREAVOR BLACK
9999 CR7555 + Rolling Hills, Texas 79000
(999) 999-9999 + (806) 777-7777 (C)

+ DRIVER / HEAVY EQUIPMENT +

PROFILE

- Skilled driver with Class A Commercial Driver's License (CDL), Expires 1/29/08
- Over two million miles driving commercial vehicles loaded with general or refrigerated freight.
- Superior driving / safety / inspection record and on-time delivery.
- Excellent health and physical condition.
- Mechanically inclined and maintenance-minded.
- Customer-service oriented; personable with instructional communication skills.

VEHICLE EXPERTISE

- Several tractor / trailer rigs including refrigerated vans   32 years
- National 2003 Flatbed Trailer   3 years
- 2006 2T Ford F550 with Jerr-Dan Bed, Hydraulic Winch, Diesel   1 years
- 2004 35T Pete Wrecker with Nomar Bed, Hydraulic Winch, Diesel   3 years
- Racetrack road graders and water trucks   13 years

TRUCKING EXPERIENCE

Truck Driver, ROLLING HILLS WRECKER, Rolling Hills, Texas   2003 – present
Clean up heavy equipment wreck sites and transport vehicle remains to Rolling Hills Wrecker storage facility. In addition to using wrecker with hydraulic winch, utilize refrigerated vans, cow trailers, flatbed trailers, and Jaws of Life, as situation requires. Interface with customers and insurance providers. Maintain daily log and State / Federal paperwork. Worked dispatch and accepted management responsibilities as needed.

- Receive consistent raises due to outstanding performance.
- Underwent police background check to secure driver's position.

Truck Driver, GORGE TRANSPORT, Rolling Hills, Texas   2000 – 2001
Leased refrigerated truck to haul produce and meat products throughout California, Washington, Oregon, and Texas. Worked 12–14 hour days; maintained daily logs and trip sheets; and hired own loaders (lumpers) at docks.

Owner / Driver, BLACK TRUCKING, Rolling Hills, Texas   1993 – 2000
Leased out transport truck during summers to clients that included Blackcrest Transportation, WWW Trucking, and Gorge Transport. Drove during winters.

OTHER EMPLOYMENT

Promoter, SUN CITY SPEEDWAY, Sun City, Texas (summers)   2002 – 2003
Manager / Promoter, PLAINS SPEEDWAY, Rolling Hills, Texas (summers)   1990 – 2002
Auctioneer, Panhandle Texas Area   1996 – 2002

EDUCATION

High Plains College, Rolling Hills, Texas, Real Estate License   1998
Buddy Lee Auctioneer School, Freeze, Montana, Auctioneer   1996

Material Handler

Glenda used her "Outstanding Accomplishments and Achievements" section to bring strong focus to her capabilities.

Glenda Pension

356 N.E. Musical #303 • Portland, Oregon 88888
Email: pen333333@attbi.com • 555-555-5555

Material Handler

Professional Profile

Energetic, highly motivated, and organized Material Handler with extensive experience in purchasing, inventory control, and shipping / receiving. Strong liaison and negotiator for improving product delivery and lowering expenses. Well developed tracking and research abilities. Outstanding communication skills. Personable, independent, and committed to producing top-quality work. Positive and upbeat attitude; get along well with coworkers and management. Thoroughly enjoy a challenge and committed to a long-term career.

Experience Includes

• Accuracy Assurance	• Import	• Order Pulling	• Quality
• Customer Service	• Inventory Control	• Ordering	• Receiving
• Dedication	• Liaison	• Organization	• Shipping
• Export	• Negotiator	• Purchasing	• Tracking

Outstanding Accomplishments and Achievements

- Advocated to get certification through Quality Control to achieve FAA approval on specific products.
- Secured credit, due to my personal reputation, for a company in Chapter 11 bankruptcy.
- Negotiated effective contracts to obtain product shipment with little or no shipping charges.
- Recaptured thousands of dollars in warranty monies for company.
- Developed and implemented inventory tracking system.
- Reorganized and set up efficient stock room.

Professional Experience

Enlargement Printer • Qualex, Inc. • Portland, Oregon • *2003–2007*
Temporary Associate • Manpower • Portland, Oregon • *2002–2003*
Inbound Auditor / Quality Control • Columbia Sportswear • Portland, Oregon • *2001–2002*
Warehouse Tech / Quality Control • Dr. Martins Airwair • Portland, Oregon • *1999–2001*
Records Clerk • America West Airlines • Phoenix, Arizona • *1998*
Purchasing Agent • MarkAir Express, Inc. • Anchorage, Alaska • *1996–1998*
Japan Airlines Liaison for Inventory Management by Alaska Airlines
   Alaska Airlines • Anchorage, Alaska • *1994–1996*
Purchasing Manager / Warranty Administrator / Inventory Control
   Stateswest Airlines – USAIR Express • Phoenix, Arizona • *1991–1994*

Education and Training

Beechcraft Warranty Training • Indianapolis, Indiana • *2001*
Various classes offered by OSHA and Japan Airlines
Hazardous Materials Training • San Francisco, California • *1995*
Business *emphasis* • University of Alaska – Anchorage • Anchorage, Alaska • *1995*

Apartment Management (Joint Resume)

Pamela and Katherine needed a combined resume for use in applying as Team Managers. This format was highly effective.

Pamela Heshe & Katherine Heshe

1234 S.E. 23rd Avenue	Rhododendron, Oregon	555-555-5555

Apartment Managers

PROFESSIONAL PROFILE

- Highly motivated, dynamic, and energetic with over 30 combined years experience successfully working with diverse personalities.
- Experienced management and maintenance of various houses and plexes.
- Possess strong organizational skills and effective paper processing techniques.
- Expert bookkeeping abilities.
- Skills include: Minor repairs, simple plumbing, light electrical, painting, pool maintenance, landscaping, strong maintenance and clean-up experience.
- Effective in pre-qualifying new lease applicants and collecting rents in a timely fashion.
- Personable, loyal, honest, committed, creative, able to maintain property impeccably, and get along well with tenants and management.
- Able to be bonded, if necessary.
- Computer literate.

Pamela Heshe

EMPLOYMENT HISTORY

Medical Assistant • Portland, Oregon • *1993–2007*
- OHSU Sellwood/Moreland Clinic • *2002–2007*
- Medical Temporaries • *1993, 1994, 1998, 2000, 2002*
- Mount Tabor Medical Group • *1999–2000*
- Dr. Samuel Miller • *1994–1998*

EDUCATION

Medical *Emphasis* • *1988*
- Clackamas Community College
Oregon City, Oregon

Graduate
- Portland Community College
Portland, Oregon

Graduate
- Oregon X-Ray Institute
Portland, Oregon

Katherine Heshe

EMPLOYMENT HISTORY

Accounting Manager / Administrative Assistant
- National Metal Distributors, Inc. • *2003–2004*
Vancouver, Washington

Bookkeeper • *2001–2003*
- Aerospace & Corrosion International
Vancouver, Washington

Letter Carrier • *1979–2000*
- United States Postal Service
Portland, Oregon

MILITARY

United States Air Force • *1974–1978*
- Disbursement Accountant

EDUCATION

Elliott Bookkeeping School • *2001*
Accounting • *1979*
- Portland Community College
Portland, Oregon

Fitness Trainer

Anna has a great start in her career as a fitness trainer with super client results that are detailed in the resume for an action-packed, results-oriented document.

Anna Mead 5235 N. Halsey Drive, Richmond, Texas 77853 • 256-555-7772 • fitness77@sbcglobal.net

Physical Fitness Specialist

BACHELOR of SCIENCE KINESIOLOGY
December 2004
Texas A&M University   *College Station, Texas*

PROGRAMS DEVELOPED

- Volleyball League
for health club members

- Women's Self Defense

- "Silver Hearts"
group exercise class for mature members over sixty years of age

- "HealthPlex Holiday Challenge"

- "Suit Up for Summer"

- Personalized exercise programs for clients

- "Tiny Mites"
gymnastics for preschool

- "Gymnastic All-Stars Cheerleading Program"

GROUP EXERCISE CLASSES

- Yoga for Fitness

- Muscle Pump

- Rock Bottoms

- Aquafit

Proficient in the use of PC and Macintosh computers.

Motivated and driven

FITNESS SPECIALIST

brings eighteen months of ENERGETIC professional training experience to health and wellness programs yielding enthusiasm, commitment, and results.

SELECTED ACHIEVEMENTS

- Develop strong and strategic weightlifting program for male clients.

- Implement customized fitness programs for group and individual clients.

- Manage personal training programs, results, and profiles for 13 clients.

PROFESSIONAL CERTIFICATIONS

- IDEA Personal Trainer • YogaFit Certified Instructor
- CPR & First Aid • NSCA & ASCM Professional Member

PROFESSIONAL PHYSICAL FITNESS EXPERIENCE

EXERCISE PHYSIOLOGIST

- **Develop, produce and implement** internal and external marketing plans.
- **Instruct and create** programs for Cardiac Rehabilitation Phase III members.
- **Organize** Fitness Team and Health Assessment Testing schedules
- **Exceed expectations** and **deliver excellent customer service**.

PERSONAL TRAINER

- **Develop** personalized exercise programs for each client.
- **Monitor** the transition and progressions of each client into new, more effective exercises.
- **Prepare** exercise prescriptions.

FITNESS INSTRUCTOR

- **Instruct** various Group Fitness and Yoga classes.
- **Conduct research** on the latest trends and newest exercises.

GYMNASTICS COACH

Head Level Five Compulsory Coach

CLIENT PROFILES

Profile: Female, age 33 – Stay-at-home mom
Goal: Lose weight and get in shape after birth of baby.
Results: Within 4 months, weight: 147 to 128 lbs; body fat: 30.8% to 18.9%

Profile: Senior male, age 57 – Retired
Goal: Exercise to maintain and get the benefits for his heart.
Results: Developed regulated fitness program to reach target heart rate.

Profile: Female, age 40 – Professional
Goal: Lose weight (100 lbs.) and get in shape.
Results: Lost 12 lbs. and 14 inches in a six-week period.

PROFESSIONAL EXPERIENCE

ABM HEALTHPLEX – Richmond, Texas   **January 2005 – Present**
UNITED GYMNASTICS – Richmond, Texas   **2001 – 2004**
SPELLING GYMNASTICS – Richmond, Texas   **1999 – 2001**

Aesthetician

Anita is an aesthetician moving up in her chosen profession.

ANITA KELLER

9001 E. Aspen Drive, Fountain Hills, AZ 85233
480/555-0000 • akeller@123.net

PROFILE

An experienced state-licensed **Aesthetician** seeking a rewarding career opportunity in a service-driven, team-centered spa / resort setting.
Consistently exceed client expectations; recognized for a gentle, soothing touch with a pleasant attitude, while demonstrating capability in areas of:

- skin care / facials • body treatments / wraps • waxing • lymphatic drainage • chemical peels • masks
- aromatherapy • multivitamin treatments • makeup • acupressure and Oriental massage treatments

Familiar with a wide product range including:

- Dermalogica • Murad • Obagi • Trucco • Jan Marini • Epicuren • Bio Elements
- Biomedics • Skinceuticals • MD Forte • Neo Clean • Magica

Licensure:

- State of Arizona Aesthetician License
- State of California Aesthetician License

AESTHETICIAN EXPERIENCE

HUDSON WILLIAMS DAY SPA, 3/03 – 7/06   Palm Springs, California
NITA FOSHEE, 4/03 – 7/06   Costa Mesa, California
Aesthetician
Working by appointment, provided comprehensive aesthetology services, from oxygen facials and anti-aging skin treatments, to waxing, body wraps, and aromatherapy for these upscale spas.

- Noted for customer service excellence to build a loyal customer base.

OTHER

PARSONS AGENCY, 7/06 – Present   Fountain Hills, Arizona
Personal Assistant
Provide production support for advertising agency, monitoring media placement, preparing and analyzing invoices and coordinating / scheduling talent for ads.

- Additionally serve as **makeup artist / stylist** on location / photo shoots to maximize visual impact.

EDUCATION

International Dermal Institute   Los Angeles, California
Continuing Education in Aesthetology 2005
Classroom and hands-on training in:

- European Skin Care Techniques • Vitamin Therapy for Skin Health • Aromatherapy • Body Therapy
- Wellness Therapies for Body, Mind, and Spirit • Results-oriented Tips for Maximum Prescriptive Retailing

Walters International School of Beauty   Costa Mesa, California
Aesthetology Certificate Program (600 hours) 2003
Course work encompassed:

- Microdermabrasion • Salt Glow Body Scrub
- Advanced Skin Care • Makeup Techniques
- Color Theory • Contouring and Corrections
- European Skin Care Techniques • Vitamin Therapy for Skin Health
- Aromatherapy • Body Therapy
- Wellness Therapies for Body, Mind, and Spirit
- Results-oriented Tips for Maximum Prescriptive Retailing

265

The New Executive Resume

Traditional thinking has it that resumes only get a cursory first-time reading (about 45 seconds, and 90 percent of that time spent on the first page) and rarely get thoroughly examined, and so consequently all resumes must be as brief as possible. The standard chant for professionals who think constantly about these matters says this: "One page for every ten years experience and never more than two pages." This still holds true for the majority of professionals, but not for all.

In certain quarters I may be regarded as a resume heretic, because I believe that for some professionals in some situations such as senior technologists, scientists, and certain medical professionals—as well as many Director level, most VPs, and just about all C-suite executives—this rule no longer holds true; in fact, adhering to it can be a detriment to a successful job search.

The practical issues creating the need for this change are really quite simple: The increasingly complex requirements for more senior jobs creates the need for adequate reflection of these multifaceted competencies in a written document.

Such competency must be shown through ever-deepening experience supported by steadily increasing responsibility and illustrated by achievement. Management expertise and its achievements separate from professional and market sector skills also need clear illustration; additionally there are the necessities of professional visibility through publishing, speaking, and other leadership roles that are relevant in many senior level jobs. For example, I recently advised a big Pharma COO with a half-page history of board appointments, all of which had utmost relevance given his target job. Science is one of the "publish or perish" professions, and you'll see a resume example in the next few pages that contains almost a full page addressing publications, presentations, and professional affiliations; in such instances, mass adds weight.

Let's take a moment to recall the roles your resume plays in a successful job search: It gives you an achievable focus (without which you cannot be successful); opens doors; it acts as a road map for interviewers; and it is your spokesperson long after the last interview is over. The thinking that goes into the focus and execution of your resume has a significant impact on every facet of your successful job search. Not surprisingly for professionals in the higher ranks of some professions, an adequate story sometimes cannot be told in two pages, and cramming it in with 9- and 10-point fonts is certainly not the answer—the people in a position to hire such candidates are simply not going to struggle with the fine print. At the same time the Internet has changed the face of recruitment advertising in at least two dramatic ways:

1. Space is no longer an issue, so recruitment advertising has changed from a few terse lines to hundreds and sometimes thousands of words.
2. The descriptors used in the recruitment advertising and job descriptions increase need for a data-dense resume—one that is going to be retrieved from the resume databases because it uses the right keywords in adequate frequency to catch the attention of database spiders.

Putting these considerations together: The complexity of some professional and most executive work, along with the need to communicate effectively by using the traditional device of the resume in the new electronic media, has birthed knowledge-era executive resumes of considerable length and density.

My thinking has changed to such a degree on this issue that in my private coaching practice, where I work with senior professionals on the national and international stage, I am suggesting, encouraging, supporting, and approving data-dense resumes in the three-to-eight-page range, because these resumes are clearly necessary to hit home runs for players in the major leagues.

Executive resumes still get a cursory first-time review, whether they come directly to human eyes or are from a database. This means that, just as much as ever, a resume needs to be clearly focused on a job with that first page screaming understanding, capability, and achievement in the target area of expertise.

When the first resume page communicates clearly and contains a compelling message, the subsequent pages will get read with serious attention. The established standards of clarity and brevity (wherever possible) still hold; it's just the complexity of work at the higher levels that has increased and requires explanation. So resume length for today's executive becomes a clear-cut issue of form following function. The examples you'll see in the next few pages are courtesy of my colleagues at the Phoenix Career Group *(www.phoenixcareergroup.com)*, where we work with executives like this every day. If you are in need of powerful executive documents, Phoenix or MartinYate.com is the place to go.

DONALD T. THOMAS

2009 Churchill Drive
Aliso Viejo, CA 92656
donaldthomas@gmail.com

Home: 949-555-9396

Mobile: 949-555-2709

SENIOR-LEVEL EXECUTIVE
FINANCE, CORPORATE STRATEGY, & DEVELOPMENT

Expert in Leading & Partnering Corporate Finance with Enterprise Strategies, Initiatives, Transactions, & Goals

PROFILE & VALUE	QUALIFICATIONS & EXPERTISE

PROFILE & VALUE

Strategic Finance Expert—Dynamic CFO with extensive experience and exceptional success in conceiving, planning, developing, and executing strategic and tactical finance initiatives that drive top-line performance and bottom-line results. Technically proficient in all aspects of the finance and accounting functions, and expert in partnering corporate finance with enterprise strategies, initiatives, and objectives.

Corporate Strategy & Development Specialist—Characterized as a rare visionary, strategist, and tactician. Consistent originator of bold, innovative business strategies that have extraordinary results on growth, revenue, operational performance, profitability, and shareholder value. Heavy transactions background including startup financing, industry rollup, merger of equals, acquisition, and sale.

Consummate Management Executive—Top-performer and valuable contributor to corporate executive teams. Extremely versatile with high-caliber cross-functional management qualifications, experience-backed judgment, and excellent timing. Outstanding role model. Talented team builder, mentor, and leader.

Diverse Industry & Situational Experience—public and private; small and *Fortune* 500; startup, rapid growth, turnaround, post-IPO, post-acquisition integration, bankruptcy—consulting services, real estate, hospitality, resort/vacation property, travel companies doing business in highly regulated industries in U.S., European, and global arenas.

Extraordinary Personal Characteristics—Articulate, intelligent, ambitious, self-driven, and creative. Outstanding corporate ambassador to customers, industry groups, regulatory bodies, private investors, Wall Street analysts, board members, and other internal and external stakeholders. Speak conversational French and German.

QUALIFICATIONS & EXPERTISE

Vision, Strategy, Execution, & Leadership

Strategic Corporate Finance

P/L & Performance Improvement

Financial Forecasting, Analysis, & Reporting

Cost Analysis, Reduction, & Control

Treasury, Tax, Internal Audit

GAAP, SEC, & Statutory Reporting

Corporate Development & Strategic Alternatives

Due Diligence, Deal Structuring, & Negotiation

Financial & Legal Transactions

Growth Management & Business Development

Organizational Design & Transformation

Turnaround & Restructure

Crisis & Change Management

Internet Strategies & IT Projects

Team Building & Leadership

Investor, Analyst, & Board Relations

Executive Advisory & Decision Support

PROFESSIONAL EXPERIENCE

DTT Management Consulting, San Diego, CA   2000 to Present
Successful Management Consulting Firm—Significant Repeat Business and Value-Added Partner to Leading Consulting Firms (e.g.,
Alix Partners, PKF Consulting)—Retained by Start-up, Small-Cap, and Fortune 500 in US, UK, and ASIA

PRINCIPAL

Operate an independent firm specializing in the delivery of a full-range of consulting services—strategic business planning; strategic finance; corporate strategy, development and financing; organizational design; operational and financial turnaround; marketing; and market research and strategy. Identify and acquire new business, and manage all aspects of the project lifecycle—from scope of work through provision of deliverables, follow-up, and relationship management—for large-scale, long-term projects. Engaged by corporate clients representing a broad-range of industry sectors—travel and tourism; hospitality; real estate development; marketing services; and technology and Internet.

Management Successes
• Leveraged professional reputation contacts worldwide to build and grow a successful management consulting firm.
• Acquired significant repeat business and positioned the firm as a value-added partner to high-profile management consulting firms in the U.S. and U.K. (e.g., ABC Partners, DEF Consulting).

Key Engagements

- **Turnaround & Change Management**—Retained (by principal consultancy group) to evaluate a key strategic business unit of a $500 million resort/vacation sales company in Chapter 11. Performed in-depth analyses of operations, identified deficiencies and risks, and presented recommendations for restructure and turnaround of call center operations, program management, inventory control, and member services functions. Engagement contract was extended to serve as Chief Business Architect during execution and post-C11 transition/recovery phases.
- **Operational Start-up & Financing**—Retained by U.K.-based client of a $10 million marketing services business to advise and participate in creating a business plan, raising capital, and executing a startup in the global event management and incentives sector.
- **Corporate Strategy & Finance**—Retained by independent U.S. resort developer to determine the viability and ROI of expanding into international markets. Analyzed business, financial, marketing, competitive intelligence, and geopolitical issues impacting the world tourism and hospitality sectors. Pinpointed key target markets, and authored business strategy and financial plan for launch of a luxury boutique hospitality brand.
- **Corporate Strategy**—Engaged in joint consultancy project with ABC Consulting in developing a full-scale corporate strategy plan for $500 million public hospitality company. Researched and analyzed internal and external organizations, market opportunities, competitive differentiators, business models, and challenges.

CDE Group, Ltd., London, England — 1999 to 2000

Venture Capital–Backed Dot-Com Start-up Operating in a Niche Sector—Fine Arts and Antiques Online Sales/Auction

MANAGING DIRECTOR

Held full P&L accountability—recruited by and reported to the investor group and Chairman of the Board—for an early-stage Internet company. Developed and executed strategy, managed finance and operations, directed sales and marketing, steered technology development, and managed relationships with internal and external stakeholders. Led a core team of three executives—Director of Sales, Director of Operations, Manager of Finance & Administration—and provided indirect oversight to team of 18 in sales, operations, IT, finance, and administrative roles.

Strategy & Leadership Successes

- Revised corporate strategy to leverage core competencies—a well-established network of dealerships and virtually unlimited source of product—and position the firm as inventory and distribution solution to another company.
- Conceived and executed viable exit strategy—vs. minimum requirement of additional 2+ years' investment to achieve break-even—by identifying a buyer and negotiating sale of the company to a U.S.-based business. Provided investors with ROI on their original investment/commitment of 660%+.

STUV Corporation, Inc., Orlando, FL — 1997 to 1999

$500 Million Company—One of Largest Resort and Vacation Development/Sales Companies in U.S.—in Rapid Growth Through International Expansion, Strategic M&A, Industry Rollup, and IPO

VICE PRESIDENT—BUSINESS DEVELOPMENT

Key member of the executive committee—retained in company's buyout of U.K.-based LSI Group—in charge of the strategic and tactical business development activities during period of dynamic growth and change. Crossed-over functional lines to address product development, marketing, branding, sales, corporate communications, legal, and regulatory matters. Administered $10 million business development budget. Reported directly to the CEO/COO, led a team of five Director-level executives, and interfaced with Board of Directors, Wall Street analysts, and strategic alliance partners.

Strategy & Leadership Successes

- Led the company's single most significant post-IPO strategic initiative—conceptualization, development, and execution of transformation of the company's infrastructure, business model, product offering, and marketing strategy—without negative impact on sales, operational performance, or customer service during execution.
- Shifted the business model and organizational structure—from a disconnected collection of resort properties—to a membership-based vacation sales company with an exclusive, points-based vacation product, and strong value proposition with single marketing message.

Business Development Results

- Credited with personal contributions to explosive growth—from $330 million in 1997 to $500 million in 1999—by spearheading the development and rollout of an innovative vacation ownership product and complementary offerings.
- Expanded market reach and brand recognition by initiating and leveraging relationships with high-profile strategic business partners—American Airlines, Time Warner, HSN, MemberWorks, and others in the travel, hospitality and marketing services industries.

Senior-Level Corporate Executive (addendum)

XYZ, Ltd., Lancaster, England   1994 to 1997
$65 Million, Privately Held Enterprise—One of Largest Vertically Integrated Vacation Ownership Companies in Europe—Specializing in Development and Management of Resorts, and Marketing and Sales of Timeshares and Travel Services

DIRECTOR—BUSINESS DEVELOPMENT (1995 to 1997)
CHIEF FINANCIAL OFFICER (1994 to 1995)

Held two key executive positions on the management team—both reporting to CEO (one of two principal shareholders)—following a major debt restructure, physical relocation, and preparation for sale. As CFO, managed all aspects of the corporate finance and administration functions (including treasury, tax, statutory reporting, and internal audit) for headquarters and 10+ overseas branches. Directed the preparation and analysis of financial statements, budgets, forecasts, desktop "dashboards," and other essential management reports. Hired, trained, mentored, and managed a team of 28 including three senior financial and accounting professionals.

As Director of Business Development, identified, created, and capitalized upon both innovative and traditional business opportunities. Conceived, developed, and managed strategic and tactical messaging, branding, marketing, sales, and relationship-building initiatives. Directed product development, positioning, and go-to-market strategies, and launched a series of breakthrough concepts and techniques—trial membership, incentive-driven referral program, customer/prospect profiling, direct-to-consumer sales, interactive multimedia presentations.

Strategy & Business Development Successes
- Key contributor to providing deep due diligence to ABC in its purchase of LMN Group—activities and relationships that led to recruitment to executive position with the acquiring company.
- Credited with personal contributions (strategy, finance, operations, business development)—to growth—from $40 million to $65 million—profitability—from 5% pre-tax margin in 1994 to 11% in 1997—and shareholder value—from $15 million to $55 million at sale of the company in mid-1997.

Finance & Operations Results
- Built and managed a best-in-class finance and accounting function. Managed the complete turnaround of the corporate finance organization to include new systems, technologies, processes, and personnel.
- Provided the executive team and stakeholders with comprehensive, meaningful decision support by restructuring virtually all financial reporting systems.

WXY Group, London, England   1987 to 1994
One of London's Largest Public Accounting and Business Consulting Practices—Professional Services for Entrepreneurial Public and Private Companies in Real Estate, VC Funding, Hospitality, and Leisure Travel Sectors

Rapidly Advancing Levels of Seniority to:
MANAGER—CORPORATE FINANCE & INVESTIGATIONS DEPARTMENT (1992 to 1994)

Managed client engagements involving deep due diligence for numerous acquisition and funding transactions. Provided a full range of advisory services and functions including creating/opining on corporate development strategies, authoring business plans, preparing projection models, and performing operational and financial assessments. Developed expertise in fraud and litigation support, debt workout, and internal audit. Interfaced with firm's Partners, investment bankers, private investors, senior-level corporate executives, board members, industry specialists, and regulatory officials.

Key Engagements
- **Debt Restructure**—Contributed to restructure of £100+ million debt with complex asset security position.
- **Fraud Investigation & Litigation**—Provided support on several high-profile engagements including collapse of a private financial services firm (represented WXY as the client) and a Formula One motor racing team.
- **Corporate Recovery**—Contributed to financial and operational turnaround of several hospitality and leisure firms.

EDUCATION & CREDENTIALS

British Chartered Accountant—ACA—(CPA equivalent), Institute of Chartered Accountants in England and Wales
G Mus (Hons)—Four year degree in Music (with honors), Royal Northern College of Music, Manchester, England
Training in Corporate Finance and Treasury, Association of Corporate Treasurers

PROFESSIONAL AFFILIATIONS

Institute of Chartered Accountants in England and Wales (ICAEW); American Resort Development Association (regular speaker and panelist at conventions) (ARDA); American Marketing Association (AMA); San Diego Chamber of Commerce; Association of Chartered Accountants in the U.S. (ACAUS); American Real Estate Society (ARES); and Financial Management Association (FMA)

DONALD T. THOMAS
donaldthomas@gmail.com

HIGHLIGHTS OF A CAREER IN EXCELLENCE
Addendum to Resume

EXCELLENCE IN CORPORATE STRATEGY & TURNAROUND
Managing Director—early-stage Internet start-up

Challenge	Revise corporate strategy and turnaround operational and financial performance of a venture capital-backed, early-stage start-up—fine arts and antiques dot-com.
Actions	Evaluated the original business plan against actual conditions and projected outcomes based on multiple scenarios. Created and executed a decisive strategy for "repackaging" the company's value proposition as an inventory and distribution solution to larger companies. Halted overspending, implemented strict financial controls, restructured operations, and re-engineered business processes.
Results	Provided investors with viable business strategies and alternatives, and at their direction, executed an exit strategy through the successful sale of the company for $10 million in stock. Provided investors with 660% ROI on their original investment/commitment.
Strengths	I am a turnaround specialist—I can rapidly assess a complex business situation, formulate a solution that meets overall commercial objectives (even if the solutions are a radical departure from initial direction), and inspire and gain buy-in for dynamic change.

EXCELLENCE IN STRATEGY & BUSINESS DEVELOPMENT
VP—Business Development, large resort development and sales company

Challenge	Lead high-profile, mission-critical strategic business initiative—characterized by COO as "betting the ranch"—to restructure and transform a $500 million resort and vacation development and sales company.
Actions	Developed and executed strategies, and planned and managed on virtually all cross-functional aspects of the business. Steered development of an appealing customer value proposition in an innovative product offering—"Club Main Attraction" a points-based vacation club—communicated through a clear, strong brand and marketing message. Partnered with legal counsel in structuring products that met state/federal regulatory guidelines. Built and led a team of top-performing strategic marketing professionals to execute rollout to 1,000+ person sales force.
Results	Exceeded expectations of founders/executive management and Wall Street analysts—rewarded in 1999 for exceptional corporate contributions by receipt of a specially created Award for Vision—in conceiving and driving innovation in corporate strategy, infrastructure, and product marketing.
Strengths	I am a true visionary and talented business leader who is always originating new concepts, innovating bold strategies, creating opportunities, and applying highly developed finance, marketing, business management, and people skills to take on huge challenges and overcome daunting challenges.

EXCELLENCE IN COST REDUCTION & PERFORMANCE IMPROVEMENT
CFO—large European, vertically integrated vacation ownership company

Challenge	Resolve serious financial and operational performance issues—increasingly high costs and productivity bottlenecks in the travel and reservations division.
Actions	Streamlined divisional operating processes, realigned key personnel, and updated and improved the payment processing and banking functions by establishing a relationship with a high-tech banking institution.
Results	Improved customer service while slashing invoicing and collection costs—from 10% to <5% and $5 million; and as volume grew to $25+ million, reduced the ratio even further—and created seamless connectivity in processes, communications and culture between the division and the rest of the organization.
Strengths	I am an expert in leveraging best practices, technologies, and relationships to enable and maintain inter-organizational cohesiveness and operational performance excellence.

EXCELLENCE IN DECISION SUPPORT

CFO—leading European resort developer

Challenge   Provide comprehensive, meaningful, and accurate decision support to the principals of a privately held, multisite resort development and sales enterprise.

Actions   Led complete restructure of the corporate finance and accounting organization, and all related systems, controls, processes, and technologies. Introduced sophisticated forecasting, analysis, and reporting tools, restructured the financial reports, refined the budgeting/variance analysis process, and implemented open-architecture accounting IT solutions/applications. Rebuilt, retrained, and mentored the 28-person finance and accounting team, and advised senior-level management in optimal utilization of new financial information.

Results   Created and led a top-notch finance and accounting organization that produced timely, precise, meaningful financial and operational data—executive decision support and departmental financial accountability credited with the company's realization of 65% improvement in profitability (despite zero revenue growth) within one year of implementing new corporate finance regime, and delivery of significant ROI in successful sale of the company two years later.

Strengths   I am valuable to any corporate executive team through my ability to provide mission-critical decision support, and I am proficient in building and leading best-in-class finance and accounting organizations.

EXCELLENCE IN STRATEGIC & TACTICAL BUSINESS DEVELOPMENT

Director of Business Development—European vacation ownership company

Challenge   Continue to grow revenue and market share despite dramatic changes in the European vacation ownership sector—new legislation impacting multiple areas of the business model (ban on down-payment at point of sale, expanded disclosure requirements, statutory cancellation period).

Actions   Went to senior sales executives with a new sales model—multimedia technology, new sales showroom environment, upgraded sales presentation and collaterals—and gained approval from shareholders for investing in the strategic and tactical innovations.

Results   Distinguished the company as an industry leader—first vacation ownership company (in both U.S. and U.K.) to utilize new technology-enabled sales/communication tools—a significant feature in sale of company. Maintained corporate revenue performance while reducing cancellation rates by 5%+.

Strengths   I am continuously devising ways to drive growth, operational performance, and profitability—despite any internal or external challenge. With acute understanding of the marketplace, I am able to create and execute business development strategies and tactics that put my company in front of the competition.

EXCELLENCE IN TURNAROUND & CHANGE

Consultant—international resort and vacation timeshare company

Challenge   Restore financial and operational health to a key strategic business unit—an SBU critical to the survival of the company—for an enterprise in post-Chapter 11 transition.

Actions   Contributed industry and business unit expertise (personally created, developed and exceeded performance objectives during period of 1997 through 1999) to a joint venture consulting engagement with ABC Partners (turnaround specialists). Evaluated existing operations and mapped-out a new strategy, organizational structure, business model (personal property vs. deeded real estate) and culture.

Results   Delivered the plan for putting in place a robust organizational structure with best-practices for risk management, inventory utilization, call center operations, program management, financial reporting, and member communications/satisfaction. Retained on extended contract to serve as Chief Architect (reporting to Interim CEO) to contribute cross-functional leadership to ongoing project phases. Received second extension (reported to permanent executive committee) to manage post-C11 integration of the U.S. and European programs. Combined annual cost savings of turnaround initiatives exceeded $5 million annually.

Strengths   In addition to industry expertise—resort and vacation timeshare—I bring the full complement of business and finance management qualifications. I am quick to identify and create solutions to complex business issues, and am proficient in managing large-scale, long-term, mission-critical projects.

SAMUEL HARRINGTON, Ph.D.

VA Dept. of Health & Human Services
Public Health Laboratories
6 Hazen Drive, Fairfax, VA 22033
Office: 800-555-5555
harringtons@dhhs.state.va.us

1012 South Street
Fairfax, VA 22033
Home: 571-555-5555
Cell: 571-555-5555
harringtonsam@aol.com

SENIOR EXECUTIVE—SCIENTIST
Chief Science Officer—Executive Director—Program Manager—Senior Scientist/Researcher
Biotechnology Enterprises—Molecular Research & Diagnostics Organizations

CAREER PROFILE & DISTINCTIONS

- Dynamic, entrepreneurial business professional with high-caliber general management qualifications ... strong orientations in finance and technology ... proven leadership talents. Led the startup of three biotechnology R&D organizations and turned around an existing test / surveillance laboratory.

- Accomplished senior-level scientist and recognized innovator in modern technical and managerial strategies, principles, methodologies, and processes for the biotech industry. Designed and developed numerous scientifically / commercially significant diagnostic reagents and assays.

- Professional experience spanning diverse clinical and technical settings; private biotech firms ... large R&D operations ... public health organizations ... hospitals ... academic facilities ... federally funded Homeland Security projects.

- Accustomed to, and effective in high-profile scientist executive roles ... managing large organizations ... overcoming complex business/technical challenges ... gaining respect from competitors and peers ... communicating complex concepts to technical and non-technical audiences ... maintaining impartiality in politically charged environments ... fostering consensus and generating cooperation from multicultural, multidisciplinary teams.

- Confident, assertive, diplomatic, and outgoing with exceptional communication, public speaking, and interpersonal relations skills. Multicultural, bilingual professional—speak fluent Arabic and English.

MANAGEMENT QUALIFICATIONS

Entrepreneurial Vision, Strategy, & Leadership	P&L and Operations Management
Financial Planning & Management	Budget Planning, Analysis, & Control
Program & Project Management	Process Design / Improvement—Business &
Technical	
Staff Training, Development, & Supervision	Technology Investments & Solutions
Team Building, Mentoring, & Leadership	Marketing, Communications, & Public Relations

AREAS OF EXPERTISE

Molecular Diagnostics R&D	Molecular-Based Surveillance
Disease Investigation & Management—Infectious & Genetic	DNA Fingerprinting & Gene Banking
Laboratory Management Quality Improvement & Assurance	Regulatory Affairs & Compliance—CLIA, CAP
Advanced Laboratory Procedures & Technologies	GLP, CQA, CQI
Homeland Security Strategies, Policies & Programs	Crisis / Emergency Preparedness & Response

PROFESSIONAL EXPERIENCE

State of Virginia, Fairfax, VA   1999 to Present

STATE MOLECULAR BIOLOGIST
Department of Health & Human Services, Public Health Laboratories (PHL)

Hold full P&L accountability for Virginia's only public health reference laboratory—infectious disease testing and surveillance services, bioterrorism detection, prevention, and response—serving the state's 1.2 million citizens. Manage all aspects of business operations (e.g., strategic planning, budgeting, financial reporting, staffing, workflow, administrative affairs, internal/external customer service, quality, regulatory reporting / affairs). Provide technical and managerial oversight to six primary areas of laboratory operations: test development, disease surveillance, disease outbreak investigations (including emerging infections, air-water-food-borne infections), and testing for biothreat organisms / bioterrorism. Manage $600K capital budget and $250K annual budget for operations. Lead a three-person management team and provide indirect supervision to seven technical and non-technical support employees.

DIRECTOR OF MOLECULAR DIAGNOSTICS—State of Virginia—*Continued:*

Management & Leadership Successes:

- Put the State of Virginia "on the map" in the U.S. biotech industry. Distinguished the facility as one of the best labs in the nation, and one of the first public health organizations to receive federal funding for bioterrorism testing and preparedness.

- Evolved a very basic laboratory operation into a dynamic scientific organization staffed with talented, highly trained professionals utilizing state-of-the-art technologies and contemporary methodologies to perform sophisticated testing and surveillance of emerging infections.

- Led an ambitious campaign to secure $600K+ investment in technology (state and federal sources). Achieved financial accountability and discipline throughout the organization in order to maximize ROI.

- Equipped the organization and prepared the staff to handle both routine and emerging infections (including potential bioterrorism organisms) despite the challenges of operating under serious financial and staff constraints.

- Converted the test development strategy from a successive to concurrent approach. Re-engineered laboratory processes and workflows enabling completion of 80,000+ tests in FY 2001/2002.

- Designed and led intensive training and career development programs—trained / qualified four professionals in advanced molecular testing—and provided team coaching and one-on-one mentoring.

- Served as an effective representative / spokesperson for the organization to internal and external parties—scientific community, state / federal agencies (CDC, FDA, USDA, other public health laboratories), regulatory officials, media, and the public—and continue to advocate on behalf of the MDX / PHL and its activities, budgets, personnel, and projects.

Clinical Projects & Achievements:

- Distinguished as the state's top-ranking science officer providing consulting, advisory, and leadership services on matters related to molecular diagnostics.

- Led the entire development cycle—design, validation, application, training, troubleshooting—of molecular diagnostics-based assays for rapid investigation, diagnosis, and surveillance of emerging / re-emerging infectious diseases including E. coli, salmonella, West Nile virus and Noro virus.

- Participated in validation of new rapid tests developed by CDC for BT organisms including anthrax, smallpox, and the emerging virus responsible for SARS.

Columbia University Medical Center (CUMC)—Mailman School of Public Health, New York, NY   1992 to 1998

PROGRAM COORDINATOR—DEVELOPMENT
Division of Molecular Diagnostics

Key member of a seven-person management team for a key division within this large, diverse health-care conglomerate—2nd largest medical center in New York and largest in northeastern area—comprised of several regional hospitals and specialty institutions (including Columbia Cancer Institute and Starzl Transplant Institute). Managed the business, clinical, and technology aspects of test development. Led a team of 13 full-time technologists.

Management Achievements:

- Established the MDX developmental laboratories from the ground up—lab was a model followed by other laboratories throughout the U.S.—and provided the vision and operational framework for accommodating emerging technologies and future expansion

- Contributed to planning, development, and control of annual budgets of nearly $1 million for operations—including $200K for capital equipment.

- Developed/presented formal training programs—one-month courses in lecture and wet lab formats—to physicians on topics related to emerging/advanced molecular diagnostics methodologies, technologies, and applications.

Clinical Projects & Achievements:

- Developed DNA fingerprinting method to distinguish between closely related isolates of *Legionella pneumophila*—causative pathogen for Legionnaire's Disease. Existence of this technique thwarted potential litigation (six-figure damage claim) by a former patient against the hospital.

- Developed test for identifying four most common gene mutations of Gaucher Disease among Ashkenazi Jewish populations. Delivered $110K+ per year in revenue from laboratory test fees

The Methodist Dallas Transplant Institute (MDTI), Dallas, TX   1995 to 1998

SCIENTIST/CONSULTANT

Contributed expertise in molecular diagnostics to a multidisciplinary team of professionals—immunology, molecular biology, genetics, cell biology, other disciplines—working clinical R&D activities for the oldest/largest comprehensive international organ transplant programs in the world (a division of the University of Texas Medical Center). Developed customized specialty reagents utilized in research at the Institute.

Clinical Projects & Key Accomplishments:

- Developed 2-hour assay—vs. existing test requiring 24+ hours—for detecting presence of low-level HCV in donated livers to be used in transplantation.

- Established custom oligonucleotide design and synthesis service. Generated $150K+ in annual revenue (commercial value exceeded $300K).

Applied Genetics Laboratories, Inc. (AGL), Melbourne, FL   1991 to 1992

PROJECT LEAD/STAFF SCIENTIST

Managed a five-year, $2.5 million project funded by the National Institute of Environmental Health Sciences (NIEHS) for R&D of early cancer detection/treatment methods. Provided technical and managerial oversight to all aspects of the project lifecycle. Tracked and controlled project budgets. Supervised four laboratory technologists.

Clinical Projects & Key Accomplishments:

- Designed and executed protocols for searching for TSGs in mice genome and detecting mutations enabling early diagnosis of cancer in humans.

- Participated in presenting annual project report to National Institute of Environmental Health Sciences in North Carolina.

Kuwait Institute for Scientific Research, Shwaikh, Kuwait   1985 to 1987

RESEARCH SPECIALIST
Department of Biotechnology

Established and managed Kuwait's first molecular genetics laboratory. Developed research strategies and managed projects. Provided consulting/advisory services on business and scientific issues. Built and led a team of 10 scientists, and hired/managed administrative support staff.

Research Projects & Key Accomplishments:

- Distinguished as the only molecular biologist in Kuwait, and independently started and managed mission statement, business/clinical strategy, business/laboratory operations, policy/procedure formation, budget, staff, equipment for this, the first molecular genetics laboratory in the country.

- Co-Principal Investigator on three-year, $480K+ project involving establishment of basic tools and methodologies for subsequent production of high-value compounds—single cell proteins—for use as animal feed supplements.

TEACHING EXPERIENCE

University of Virginia, Hampton, VA   2000 to Present

ADJUNCT ASSOCIATE PROFESSOR
Department of Microbiology

Served in a consulting role as a biotechnology subject-matter expert. Led presentations to faculty and graduate students on topics related to molecular diagnostics, public health, and bioterrorism. Provided advice on technical issues and made recommendations for academic/scientific programming.

Florida State University, Tallahassee, FL   1987 to 1991

RESEARCH ASSOCIATE

Supervised graduate students and taught undergraduate coursework in chemistry. Worked with senior scientists on projects.

TEACHING EXPERIENCE—*Continued:*

Kuwait University Faculty of Medicine, Jabriya, Kuwait   1985 to 1987

LECTURER

Provided classroom and laboratory instruction in biochemistry and molecular biology to undergraduate students. Led/participated in scientific research with focus on rheumatic fever.

EDUCATION

Ph.D.—Medical Biochemistry, West Virginia University, Morgantown, WV, 1983
MS—Biochemistry, Duquesne University, Pittsburgh, PA, 1979
B.Sc.—Biochemistry, Kuwait University, Khaldiya, Kuwait, 1977

PUBLICATIONS—*a partial list*

Samuel Harrington. Molecular Diagnostics of Infectious Diseases: State of the Technology. *Biotechnology Annual Review,* Elsevier Publishing Company (2000).

Samuel Harrington, Robert Lanning, David Cooper. Rapid detection of hepatitis C virus in plasma & liver biopsies by capillary electrophoresis. *Nucleic Acid Electrophoresis Springer Lab Manual,* Dietmar Tietz (ed), Springer-Verlag, Heidelberg (1998).

Samuel Harrington, William Pasculle, Robert Lanning, David McDevitt, David Cooper. Typing of *Legionella pneumophila* isolates by degenerate (D-RAPD fingerprinting. *Molecular and Cellular Probes,* 9 405-414 (1995).

John A. Barranger, Erin Rice, **Samuel Harrington,** Carol Sansieri, Theodore Mifflin, and David Cooper. Enzymatic and Molecular Diagnosis of Gaucher Disease. *Clinics in Laboratory Medicine,* 15 (4) 899-913 (1995).

Samuel Harrington, Robert W. Lanning and David L. Cooper. DNA Fingerprinting of Crude Bacterial Lysates using Degenerate RAPD Primers (D-RAPD). *PCR Methods and Applications.* 4 265-268 (1995).

Samuel Harrington, Carol A. Sansieri, David W. Kopp, David L. Cooper and John A. Barranger. A new diagnostic test for Gaucher Disease suitable for mass screening. *PCR Methods and Applications,* 4 (1) 1-5 (1994).

David L. Cooper, **Samuel Harrington.** Molecular Diagnosis: a primer and specific application to Gaucher disease. *Gaucher Clinical Perspectives,* 1 (3) 1-6 (1993).

PRESENTATIONS—*a partial list*

Samuel Harrington and Krista Marschner. "A new, two-hour test for *Bordetella pertussis* using the SmartCycler," 103rd General Meeting of the American Society for Microbiology (ASM), Washington, DC, May 2003.

Samuel Harrington. "Methods & Applications of DNA Fingerprinting Techniques," Five 1- and/or 2-week-long workshops presented at the University of Puerto Rico, 1997 through 2003.

Samuel Harrington and Denise Bolton. "Development of a duplex real time RT-PCR test for surveillance of West Nile and Eastern Equine Encephalitis viruses using the SmartCycler," 102nd General Meeting of the American Society for Microbiology (ASM), Salt Lake City, UT, May 2002.

D.K. Voloshin, A.W. Pasculle, S.P. Krystofiak, **S. Harrington** and E.J. Wing. "Nosocomial Legionnaire's disease: an explosive outbreak following interruption of hyperchlorination," Interscience Conference on Antimicrobial Agents and Chemotherapy, San Francisco, CA, October 1995.

S. Harrington. "Genetic identification technologies: PCR and DNA fingerprinting," Second UN-sponsored Conference on the Perspectives of Biotechnology in Arab Countries, Amman, Jordan, March 1993.

S. Harrington, G. L. Rosner, D. L. Cooper and J. A. Barranger. "A new PCR-based diagnostic test for Gaucher Disease (GD)," Amer. J. Hum. Genet. 53 (supplement) 1755, 1993.

Bahr, G., **Harrington, S.,** Yousof, A., Jarrar, I., Rotta, J., Majeed, H. and Behbehani, K. "Depressed lymphoprolypherative responses in vitro to different streptococcal epitopes in patients with chronic rheumatoid heart disease," Conference on Infectious Diseases in Developing Countries, Kuwait City, Kuwait, March 1987.

PROFESSIONAL AFFILIATIONS

Member, American Society for Microbiology—ASM
Consultant, INTOTA Corporation
Group

Member, Association for Molecular Pathology—AMP
Member, Council of Healthcare Advisors, Gerson Lehrman

SAMUEL HARRINGTON, Ph.D.

VA Dept. of Health & Human Services
Public Health Laboratories
6 Hazen Drive, Fairfax, VA 22033
Office: 800-555-5555
harringtons@dhhs.state.va.us

1012 South Street
Fairfax, VA 22033
Home: 571-555-5555
Cell: 571-555-5555
harringtonsam@aol.com

Leadership Addendum—Science & Management

Dr. Samuel Harrington brings exceptional value through the combination of his core management qualifications, leadership talents and scientific knowledge, proficiency, and experience. He continues to develop his cross-functional general management skills and remains on the cutting-edge of scientific advancements and contemporary topics in biotechnology.

BUSINESS MANAGEMENT & ORGANIZATIONAL LEADERSHIP
—Strategies, Initiatives, Contributions, & Successes—

Much more than a scientist, Dr. Harrington is a management professional who is experienced and successful in directing organizations, programs, projects, and teams. He brings strategic perspective, business acumen, sound judgment, and financial discipline to private and public organizations involved in the life sciences/biotechnology fields.

"His work ethic is exemplary and his professional demeanor a model for others to emulate."
David L. Cooper, Director, Division of Molecular Diagnostics, University of Virginia Medical Center

"The quality of Samuel's work is exceptional ... and he excels in this area [communications]."
Chief, VA Public Health Laboratories

Organizational Development & Leadership

Dr. Harrington has provided both technical and managerial leadership to scientific organizations, and over the course of this 20+-year career, he has:

- Established the Virginia Public Health Laboratory as an important participant/contributor in the national biotech industry.
- Led the complete organizational startup of the MDX developmental laboratory for the Division of Molecular Diagnostics at the University of Virginia Medical Center.
- Contributed the vision, technical expertise, and business management capabilities to create and direct Kuwait's first molecular genetics laboratory.

Business & Finance Management

Dr. Harrington's ability to achieve operational and financial performance objectives within the departments he leads has made significant contributions to the ROI, profitability, and value of the larger organizations. As demonstrated by his track record, Dr. Harrington takes personal responsibility for all general business, daily operations, and budgeting/cost control initiatives. For example, he has:

- Authored and executed the business plan for the MDX molecular development laboratory for the University of Virginia Medical Center (UVMC), and integrated it into the main organizational structure.
- Participated in planning, administering, and controlling the $1 million operating budget for the Division of Molecular Diagnostics at UVMC.
- Achieved all budgetary performance objectives and gained financial discipline within the Virginia PHL.

Laboratory Operations Management

With more than 20 years' of academic, research, and management work in science, Dr. Harrington is well-qualified in establishing, staffing, managing, and improving the performance of laboratory operations/organizations. For example:

- Manage all aspects of operations—including disease surveillance, disease outbreak investigations, test development, and testing for biothreat (BT) organisms—in a "best in class" public health laboratory.
- Established Virginia's first Microbial Gene (DNA) Bank.
- Modernized and improved performance in key operational areas—productivity, efficiency, personnel qualifications, quality, compliance—for the State of Virginia's PHL.

SAMUEL HARRINGTON, Ph.D.   Page Two

BIOTECHNOLOGY / BIOMEDICAL RESEARCH, DEVELOPMENT, & DIAGNOSTICS
—Projects, Activities, Contributions, & Achievements—

"[Samuel Harrington's] strengths [include]... scientific knowledge and technical expertise, quality of work, initiative, sense of humor, and ability to get along with people."

"[Dr. Harrington] set up an RT-PCR procedure for West Nile Virus which brought much praise to the PHL for its ability to quickly deal with a developing public health problem."

"[Dr. Harrington] has shown a great deal of initiative in learning about Virginia's infectious disease needs and developing molecular procedures for their detection and identification."
Chief, VA Public Health Laboratories

Dr. Harrington's career is focused on Infectious Disease, Molecular Diagnostics, and Genetic Disorders.

Molecular Diagnostics of Infectious Diseases

Dr. Harrington's work in molecular diagnostics of infectious diseases has involved extensive research, surveillance, testing, assay development, and publication. He is proficient in the utilization of sophisticated laboratory methodologies, techniques, and technologies including, but not limited to: DNA fingerprinting (PFGE, Ribo Printing, PCR-based fingerprinting – RAPD/AFLP); DNA/RNA sequencing; PCR (including Real Time, RT-PCR, multiplex); oligonucleotide primer/probe design and synthesis; Southern hybridization; molecular cloning; and recombinant DNA technologies.

- Developed a two-hour RT-PCR test for the detection of *B. pertussis* directly from crude clinical specimens, thereby eliminating the need for traditional labor-intensive, time-consuming specimen processing (DNA extraction) step. Laboratories across the U.S. (e.g. SC, OK, FL, others) and Europe (Germany and Spain) have requested permission to use this test in their laboratories, and a Canadian diagnostics company has expressed interest in participating with validation studies. Presented this work at the 103rd General Meeting of the American Society for Microbiology in Washington, D.C., May 2003.

- Developed and presented (at the 102nd General Meeting of the American Society for Microbiology in Salt Lake City, UT, May 2002) a duplex RT-PCR test for surveillance of West Nile and Eastern Equine Encephalitis viruses using SmartCycler.

- Developed and managed the design, validation, application, test, and troubleshooting of molecular diagnostics-based assays for rapid identification and surveillance of emerging infectious diseases for the State of New Virginia PHL.

- Distinguished the NH PHL as one of the first labs in the U.S. to participate in proficiency testing (RT-PCR) for SARS utilizing a RT-PCR test developed by the CDC—validated test is being performed routinely at VA PHL.

- Developed a RT-PCR test for the rapid detection of the food-borne pathogen Noro (Norwalk) virus from human stools using melt-curve analysis of the amplified product—several PHLs have requested permission to use this test in their facilities.

- RNA isolated from mosquito pools inhibits West Nile virus real-time RT-PCR. Presented findings at the 3rd International Conference on Emerging Infectious Diseases in Atlanta, Georgia in March 2002.

- Investigation of simultaneous outbreaks of *S. pneumoniae* and *H. influenzae* in major medical center. Presented abstract at the 6th Annual PulseNet Update Meeting in Ann Arbor, Michigan in April 2002.

- Molecular Diagnostics of Infectious Diseases: State of the Technology. Invited article summarizing emerging technologies and applications in the rapid diagnosis of disease. Published in *Biotechnology Annual Review*, Elsevier Publishing Company, 2000.

- Rapid detection of hepatitis C virus in plasma and liver biopsies by capillary electrophoresis. In: *Nucleic Acid Electrophoresis Springer Lab Manual*, 1998.

- Developed and co-presented an abstract entitled "Nosocomial Legionnaire's disease: An explosive outbreak following interruption of hyperchlorination," presented at the Interscience Conference on Antimicrobial Agents and Chemotherapy in San Francisco in October 1995.

- Co-developed "Depressed Lymphoprolypherative Responses *in vitro* to Different Streptococcal Epitopes in Patients with Chronic Rheumatoid Heart Disease," presented at the Conference on Infectious Diseases in Developing Countries held in Kuwait in March 1987.

Molecular Diagnostics of Genetic Diseases

Either independently or as a member of a team of multidisciplinary professionals, Dr. Harrington has conducted a wide range of scientific research/experimentation, developed mutation screening assays, written/published numerous articles, and delivered presentations covering a vast spectrum of areas related to genetic diseases.

- Developed mutation screening and detection assays for a number of genetic diseases such as breast cancer (BRCA-I mutation screening), Fanconi's anemia, Canavan's disease, Factor V Leiden, Fragile X syndrome, and Huntington's disease.
- Molecular Diagnosis: a primer and specific application to Gaucher disease. *Gaucher Clinical Perspectives* 1 (3) 1-6, 1993
- Phenotype, Genotype, and the treatment of Gaucher Disease. *Clinical Genetics.* 49 111-118, 1996.
- Enzymatic and Molecular Diagnosis of Gaucher Disease. *Clinics in Laboratory Medicine.* 15 (4) 899-913, 1995.
- A review of the molecular biology of glucocerebrosidase and the treatment of Gaucher disease," *Cytokines and Molecular Therapy*, 1995.1 149-163, 1995.
- A new diagnostic test for Gaucher Disease suitable for mass screening. *PCR Methods and Applications* 4 (1) 1-5, 1994.

BioSecurity

Dr. Harrington champions interest and involvement in the conduct of scientific research and development, especially diagnostic test development and validation, of organisms and pathogens potentially used in biological terrorism/warfare. His work makes him of significant value to organizations and programs involved in related medical practice and public health programs, actions, projects, and policies—to ultimately bridge the gap between public health specialists/organizations, the public, government agencies/intelligence community, and primary care providers.

In April 2003, the U.S. House of Representatives overwhelmingly approved President Bush's "Project Bioshield," solidifying national interest and commitment to preparedness against potential bioterrorism attack.

- Distinguished the Virginia Public Health Laboratory (VA PHL) as one of the first in the U.S. to be awarded funding for bioterrorism testing and preparedness.
- Established the MDX laboratory as the first PHL in the U.S. to use SmartCycler for the development and routine testing of emerging infections including BT organisms—enabling the laboratory to participate in validation studies with CDC and Lawrence Livermore National Laboratory in developing assays for BT organisms.
- Implemented and supervised internal proficiency testing—within CDC protocols—and personnel cross-training programs at the VA PHL.
- Initiated VA PHL's participation in PulseNet (National Molecular Sub-Typing Network for Food-Borne Disease Surveillance), a network of laboratories (including CDC, FDA, USDA, state and local PHLs) adhering to standardized microbial surveillance procedures using Pulsed Field Gel Electrophoresis (PFGE) in performing gene sub-typing—a membership of particular importance to being equipped to respond to potential bioterrorism threats/incidents.
- Adopted CDC-based anthrax testing procedures, facilitating VA PHL's selection as a testing beta site by the Lawrence Livermore National Laboratory.
- Led Virginia's participation in President Bush/CDC's strategy for immunizing public health workers and first responders against smallpox—including ensuring the capacity for testing for the vaccine strain of Smallpox and other related viruses.

DNA Fingerprinting & Gene Banking

- Established Virginia's first microbial DNA bank with 1,000+ DNA and RNA samples from various pathogens—food-borne pathogens, West Nile virus, hepatitis C virus, Noro virus isolates—each containing nucleic acids in one or more formats: highly purified genomic DNA or RNA, immobilized (aerosol-resistant) purified DNA, agorose DNA plugs (ready for PFGE analysis), and viable organism (whenever possible).
- Developed and presented several one- to two-week long workshops on methods and applications of DNA fingerprinting techniques at the University of Puerto Rico during the years of 1997 through 2003.

DNA Fingerprinting & Gene Banking—*Continued:*

- Developed a DNA fingerprinting method to distinguish between closely related isolates of *Legionella pneumophila*, the causative pathogen for Legionnaire's Disease—providing the only way to track the transmission of this pathogen from patients to hospital rooms/hospital rooms to patients. A six-figure liability suit against the University of Virginia Medical Center (University Hospital) was thwarted as a result of the availability of this technique.
- Coauthored an abstract on tDNA-PCR amplification of species-specific polymorphic bands in *plasmodium faciparum*, *plasmodium berghei* and *plasmodium yoelii* at the University of Puerto Rico in San Juan, 2001.
- Authored "Typing of *Legionella pneumophila* isolates by degenerate (D)-RAPD fingerprinting," published in *Molecular and Cellular Probes*, 1995.
- Coauthored and presented "Microsatellite Analysis (MSA) Using the Polymerase Chain Reaction (PCR) of Paraffin Embedded Material for Distinction of Tissues From Different Individuals," at the United States and Canadian Academy of Pathology (USCAP) Specialty Conference in Toronto, Canada in March 1995.
- Authored "DNA Fingerprinting of Crude Bacterial Lysates using Degenerate RAPD Primers (D-RAPD)," published in *PCR Methods and Applications*, 1995.
- Authored and presented "Genetic identification technologies: PCR and DNA fingerprinting" at 2nd UN-sponsored Conference on the Perspectives of Biotechnology in Arab Countries, held in Amman, Jordan in March 1993.

Other Biomedical Research

- Authored, "Prediction of biologic aggressiveness in colorectal cancer by p53/K-ras-2 topographic genotyping," published in *Molecular Diagnosis*, 1996.
- Authored, "Distribution and evolution of CTG repeats at the myotonin protein kinase gene in human populations," published in *Genome Research*, 1996.
- Authored "Loss of heterozygosity in spontaneous and chemically induced tumors of the B6C3F1 mouse," published in *Carcinogenesis*, 1994.
- Authored "Identification of allelic loss in liver tumors from the B6C3HF1 mouse," published in *Cell Biology Supplement*, 1992.
- Authored, "Antibody levels and in vitro lymphoproliferative responses to streptococcus pyogenes erythrogenic toxin A mitogen of patients with rheumatic fever," published in *Clinical Microbiology*, 1991.
- Authored, "Isolation and characterization of developmentally regulated sea urchin U2 snRNA genes," published in *Developmental Biology*, 1991.
- Authored, "The U1 snRNA gene repeat from the sea urchin (*Strongylocentrotus purpuratus*): The 70 kilobase tandem repeat ends directly 3' to the U1 gene," published in *Nuclear Acids Research*, 1991.
- Authored "A developmental switch in the sea urchin U1 RNA," published in *Developmental Biology*, 1989, and presented at the American Society for Biochemistry and Molecular Biology meeting held in San Francisco in January 1989.
- Authored, "Isolation and characterization of tandem repeated U6 genes from the sea urchin *Strongylocentrotus purpuratus*," published in *Biochemistry Biophysics*, 1994, and presented at the Developmental Biology of the Sea Urchin meeting in Woods Hole, MA (August 1988) and at the Annual Meeting of Florida Biochemists in Miami in February 1988.
- Authored, "Modified nucleosides and the chromatographic and aminoacylation behavior of tRNA[ile] from *Escherichia coli C6*," published in *Biochemistry Biophysics Acta*, 1988.

Special Reports

Once in a very long while a new idea comes along in the world of job-hunting. The Special Report is one of those ideas. It presents you as an expert in your field without overtly saying you are job-hunting, and as such gets the reader to create an initial impression of you that is very different from that of a typical job seeker. A special report is not for everyone, but if you really know your business and you like to write, this can be a very helpful tool to add to your job-hunting arsenal.

A Special Report has the appearance of a newspaper, newsletter, or trade magazine article that focuses on a commonly recognized challenge in your profession; but rather than mass publication, it is created by you to send directly to end users. You create it by using your professional knowledge and packaging it in a written document. Just about anyone in your field who receives one will read a well-written and properly edited special report, and at the end they'll get to read the resume of the person who created it. While a resume gets very little initial time investment, your report can have the reader building a respectful relationship with you even before they know you are available and looking. Special reports have titles like:

Computer Conversion: Plan it, Move on it, and Roll it out! Three simple things you can do that double the effectiveness of your school resource center

Research reveals little-used sales technique that dramatically improves product sales in financial investment market. Ten simple actions any FCM, BD, Bank, Prop Trading, and/ or Treasury Director can take to head off trouble at the pass Seven Secrets of the Successful Waitperson

Special reports all aim to help the reader solve problems, make money, save money, or save time. Think of them as departmental reports, position papers, or articles (whichever works best for you), where the goal is to give the reader some useful information they can actually use. This is why a special report is not for everyone. You have to know your stuff and enjoy the writing process, but as I always say, anyone can write so long as they don't have a so-called life! If this is you (at least the part about having an affinity for writing) read on; you will not only learn a new job-hunting technique you'll be contributing to your professional credibility and visibility in ways that reach well beyond this job hunt.In the space available here, I can't show you how to write short, job-hunting-oriented, nonfiction articles—a.k.a. Special Reports. Instead, I'll explain the basic structure and packaging and then refer you to a couple of additional resources.

What Goes into a Special Report?

- A benefit-oriented title
- An introduction

- The body copy usually in the form of "tips" or "mistakes to avoid"
- Author info (usually, your resume)
- A binding

The key to this Trojan horse approach is to include your resume with contact information in the author information section. If your resume isn't right for the job, you can use a biography that highlights information you feel is more relevant to the reader; in this instance you'll be able to cut and paste one of your broadcast letters without the salutation.

The proper length is up to you, and opinions differ. Some will tell you that special reports can be as long as you like, and I have seen some that run to 6,000 words (about ten pages). Personally, I think you should keep your report to between 600 and 1,000 words—in other words, about the length of a regular newspaper column (or the length of this section on what goes into special reports, which runs about 1,000 words). I say this for two reasons:

- Writing takes time away from the main thrust of your job-hunting activities, and you cannot allow this great secondary approach to affect your focus.
- You don't want to share everything you know about a particular subject on paper; you want to be able to continue the conversation in person with yet more information to share.

There is another benefit to this approach. Job offers usually go to the person who turns a one-sided examination of skills into a two-way conversation between professional colleagues. The nature of the special report goes a long way toward defining you as someone quite different from almost every other candidate.

If you look at the examples below and think that this might be a useful approach for your needs, but you feel you need more help, go to *www.salarynegotiations.com*, the website of longtime career consultant Jack Chapman, who developed the whole Special Report idea.

If you do try this as an additional approach for your job hunt, you will be able to re-use the fruits of your efforts. You can submit your article for publication to professional newsletters and magazines, and you can turn it into a presentation. In fact, your notes for the special report simultaneously form the outline of a business presentation. So even outside of the context of your job hunt, this approach of putting your professional expertise into a different delivery medium can have a significant impact on your professional visibility and credibility. Now look at these samples.

SPECIAL REPORT EXAMPLE #1: WAITRESS

BACKGROUND:

With NO experience directly as a waitress, Christine, a college freshman, got hired. She had only been a hostess at "23"—Michael Jordan's Restaurant near the University of North Carolina. She had observed waiters and waitresses, and she had definite ideas about what differentiated the satisfactory from the excellent. She wanted to "jump over" the menial waitress positions and get hired by an upscale, four-star restaurant (read: big tips!). This way, she positioned herself as an exceptional waitress who had the boss's viewpoint of the job.

TITLE: Christine's Four Keys to an Excellent Waitperson

EXCERPT FROM INTRODUCTION:

Excellent waiter, waitress? It's not all that complicated to be just a satisfactory waitperson. Practically anyone can write down an order and bring food to the table. Surprisingly, it's not all that hard to be an outstanding waitperson, either—but not everyone does it. I've put down my thoughts here on the 4 keys to excellence on the job as I see it. It will help you get an idea of my philosophy.

EXCERPT FROM RULES SECTION:

Key #3 There's always a way to get people what they want.

When you know that customers want more than just food, that they want a pleasant time as well, possibilities arise. As hostess at 23, waitstaff would often complain to me about customers ordering things not on the menu, or prepared a certain way. When, out of curiosity, I checked it out with the cooks, they almost always said, "No problem." So it was the waitperson creating a problem for a customer—that problem didn't exist! I find that if you put your mind to it, there's always a way to keep the customer satisfied.

OUTLINE OF THE REST OF THE REPORT:

Key #1: Remember that your job is not "things to do," but people to take care of.
Key #2: The friendlier you are, the friendlier the customers will be.
Key #3: There's always a way to get people what they want.
Key #4: It's a job for you, but it's a business for your boss. Summary
RESULTS: Christine leapfrogged into a fine-dining (and fine tipping) job.

SPECIAL REPORT EXAMPLE #2: SALESMAN

BACKGROUND:

Mike's success at sales came from meticulous attention to detail (read: boring!), but he turns that dull skill into a reason to be hired! His report shows how astoundingly elementary your report "rules" can be and still make an indelible impression. (His first rule is, "Answer the Phone.") He focused on software sales to financial investors, but this type of report could be applied to almost any type of sales. Mike also got the Hiring Decision Makers' attention in the cover letter by mentioning that theirs was one of the firms he called in his "secret shopper" research.

TITLE: Research Reveals Little-Used Sales Technique That Can Drama-tically Improve Sales [to the Financial Investment Market.]

EXCERPT FROM INTRODUCTION:

Recently I undertook a research project to determine how companies might improve their sales. I called several companies and said, "I would like to buy your software."

It was astonishing to me that from over twenty companies, I only reached someone knowledgeable about the product 14 percent of the time. Equally surprising was that only 28 percent of the organizations had someone return my call. Almost 40 percent didn't bother to send me any information. And even when they did, only 4 percent followed up with a phone call.

This confirmed my hunch. Just by applying a sales principle I've used for 18 years, namely follow-up consistency, any one of these firms could experience a dramatic increase in sales. Here is how consistent follow-up can be easily applied in five areas to increase sales. I'm embarrassed at how basic these actions are, but remember—only 14 percent of my calls reached a salesperson!

EXCERPT FROM RULES SECTION:

Follow-up Consistency Rule #1: ANSWER THE PHONE.

Having a dedicated line that is answered by a knowledgeable, helpful, friendly, live human being is essential in sales. No voice mail allowed! Not every line needs to be answered this way (although that's nice if you can afford it), but each and every call from potential customers must receive this follow-up consistency.

On one of my calls an operator informed me she could not take my name and address for information—that would have to be handled by a salesperson. She then informed me that she could not transfer me to a salesperson because they were all gone for the rest of the day. It was 11 A.M.! *QUESTION:* Have you called your own sales line recently? What happened next?

OUTLINE OF THE REST OF THE REPORT:

Rule #2: Return messages.
Rule #3: Send the materials.
Rule #4: Don't just call the prospect, get through.

Rule #5: Never discard the names of prospects. Summary **RESULTS: Mike got interviews with EVERY ONE of the 20 firms he had called as a "secret shopper." He got job offers from two of them.**

SPECIAL REPORT EXAMPLE #3: FINANCIAL INVESTMENT SERVICES CFO
BACKGROUND:
Scott was seeking a high six-figure CFO job in the investment field. Billion-dollar scandals at Enron, MCI WorldCom, and Tyco had just occurred so his report caught people's attention. His simple techniques to prevent these catastrophes were powerfully linked up with the war stories attached to each rule.

TITLE: How to Uncover Financial and Operational Trouble Before Your P&L Blows Up . . . Ten Simple Actions Any FCM, BD, Bank, Prop Trading, and/or Treasury Manager or Director Can Take to Head Off Trouble at the Pass

EXCERPT FROM INTRODUCTION:
When a company is in or about to be in trouble, there are *always* flashing yellow warning lights. The good news is that *problems rarely travel alone*. Usually they create a pattern of circumstances that aren't individually recognized as problems, but when the puzzle pieces are assembled—wham! It's an open invitation to red ink. It may be up to you to recognize enough of those pieces in time to stop the entire puzzle from being completed. For the past 20 years, as a troubleshooter CFO or COO at financial services firms, I've learned to read the signs. And what are some of those signs?

EXCERPT FROM RULES SECTION:
Rule #2: Pay attention to your checks after they're cashed and cleared.
How are they endorsed?
Your employees? The ones who can't trade because you won't let them? Why is one or more of their checks endorsed over to a third party or brokerage firm—is this a hidden trading account in their own name?
Your customer? Why are multiple checks for identical amounts drawn on a single customer's account and endorsed over to multiple third parties? Unregistered pool? What if one of those third parties is your employee in a position to allocate trades or initiate commission rate or brokerage rate changes in your computer system?
Your vendor? Why are checks always endorsed to the name of a company you don't recognize? Is it an innocent d/b/a or are you dealing with a middleman who is marking up goods or services you could get for less by going direct?

OUTLINE OF THE REST OF THE REPORT [FOUR SAMPLES OF THE TEN RULES):

Rule #1: Periodically, sort your name and address file. Look for dual-identity payments.

Rule #3: Review a month of original trade tickets, blotters, out-trade sheets. Slowly. It's worth it.

Rule #6: Use simple line graphs to compare periods. It's easy to be caught up in the day-to-day.

Rule #9: Regularly review IB/RR/AP/Broker/Trader Payouts. Without exception, the most consistent source of hidden losses is linked in some way to Payouts.

RESULTS: Scott's report opened doors to networking interviews with "heavy hitters" in his field, which led to his new job.

SPECIAL REPORT EXAMPLE #4: SHIPPING TERMINAL MANAGER

BACKGROUND:

Keith worked for Yellow Freight. Besides getting all the trucks loaded, unloaded, and on the road on time, he loved to catch cheaters—people collecting disability who weren't really disabled. His title is very intriguing and benefit-oriented.

TITLE: A Simple Way to Put a Couple Hundred Thousand Dollars Right to the Bottom Line: Watch People Who Aren't There, Make Sure Nothing Happens

EXCERPT FROM INTRODUCTION:

This report's title says that if you watch people who aren't there and make sure nothing happens, you can save money. I have found that a few simple techniques to watch people who are out because of injuries, and a few principles of safety to make sure that nothing (bad) happens, will put $200,000 or more to the bottom line each year.

EXCERPT FROM RULES SECTION:

Rule #1: Call at Odd Times

When I have a man out, I'll put in calls every once in a while ostensibly to get some information. "Where is that bill of lading?" "Truck #3 seems to be acting up, how did it run for you?" At 2:30 in the afternoon, or home at night. I'll remind them their doctor's appointment is tomorrow. They soon learn they will be caught if they aren't home.

This cuts costs because besides clipping the wings of the ones who are playing hooky, saving time off, or receiving disability payments, it also alerts the 80 percent with real injuries that if they ever want to fake it, that they'll have a hard time.

OUTLINE OF THE REST OF THE REPORT [FOUR SAMPLES OF THE RULES]:

Rule #2: [Watch people...] Make them come in to the facility.

Rule #3: [Watch people...] Call the Bluff of "Regular Offenders."

Rule #4: [Nothing happens...] Have safety meetings led by peers, not supervisors.

Rule #7: [Nothing happens...] Reward safety in teams to create peer pressure for safety.

RESULTS: The report was the focus of several telephone networking conversations, which led to interviews and a great job.

Making Your Resume Scannable

In today's electronic world, you need both a "keyword-conscious" paper resume that is scannable, and an electronic resume that can be sent via e-mail and is database-compatible. When you mail your resume to a company, it is a paper document. In order for a company to quickly and effectively transform your resume to an electronic format they scan, or digitize, it.

Here's what happens behind the scenes: A company receives your paper resume and they place it in a scanner that takes a picture of it. When you fax your resume to a company, the fax machine will act just like a scanner and create a file with a picture of your resume. A software program called OCR (optical character recognition) is then applied to that picture of your resume. The OCR software tries to identify parts of that picture that represent letters, numbers, and symbols. Knowing that recruiters and employers use this technology means that you must create your print resume to operate within the technical capabilities of the software. The software capability improves almost monthly, but that doesn't mean that every company always has the latest version of the best program, so we will err on the side of conservatism. Here are some general rules to follow to assure that your print resume is indeed scannable:

- Avoid paper with a dark or even medium color, a colored border, heavy watermark, or graining—plain white paper is best.
- Be circumspect about adding borders around a document or around a section of text in the resume. The OCR software could identify the outline as a single character and omit the entire content of that section.
- Do not use columns—when scanned, the order of words will be out of sequence and that could hurt the effectiveness of your keyword sections.
- Do not use fonts smaller than 10 point; 12 point is ideal. If the employer experiences difficulty in scanning your resume, you will not receive a polite phone call asking you to resubmit it.

When Should You Use a Scannable Resume?

Anytime you are mailing or faxing your resume to a company, assume that it will be scanned. Always use the "fine mode" setting when faxing your resume; this will result in better resolution and allows the OCR to optimize the digital conversion. Many companies do not print faxed resumes, but instead convert them directly to digital. Also, most PCs now come with standard software that allows the user to fax and receive documents without ever having to print them.

APPENDIX A
CAREER CONSULTANTS AND RESUME WRITING SERVICES

AS PART OF your job search, you might feel the need to look into getting extra help from a professional resume writer and/or a career counselor. A professional in the field might be able to help you develop a more polished layout or present a particularly complex background more effectively.

As in any other profession, there are practitioners at both ends of the performance scale. I am a strong believer in using the services of resume writers and career consultants who belong to their field's professional associations. They tend to be more committed, have more field experience, and have an all-around higher standard of performance, partly because their membership demonstrates their commitment to the field and partly from the ongoing educational programs that these associations offer to their members. The following is a list of career consultants and professional resume writers. All of these have contributed to the Knock 'em Dead books and are members of one or more of the above groups.

Martin Yate, Executive Career Strategist

E-mail: *martin@knockemdead.com*

Martin Yate, CPC

Typically works with C-level and C-level-bound professionals facing challenges in the areas of Job Search, Interviewing, and Career Strategy.

Phoenix Career Group

www.phoenixcareergroup.com

Debbie Ellis, CPRW, CRW

Serving career-minded professionals to senior executives, the Phoenix Career Group is a one-of-a-kind consortium of fifteen industry-leading professionals specializing in personal branding, resume writing, career management coaching, research, and distribution.

100PercentResumes

www.100percentresumes.com

Daniel J. Dorotik, Jr. NCRW

Global career development service specializing in the preparation of resumes, cover letters, and other associated career documents. In addition to traditional formats, prepares online-compatible documents for Internet-driven job searches.

A First Impression Resume Service

www.resumewriter.com

Debra O'Reilly CPRW, CEIP, JCTC, FRWC

Debra provides job-search and career-management tools for professionals, from entry level to executive. Areas of specialty include career transition and the unique challenges of military-to-civilian conversion.

A Resume For Today

www.aresumefortoday.com

Jean Cummings M.A.T., CPRW, CEIP, CPBS

Distills complex hightech careers into potent, memorable, and valuable personal brands. Provides resume writing and job search services to executives and managers seeking to advance their careers in high tech.

A Resume Solution

www.aresumesolution.com

Becky Erdelen

1716 Clark Lane

Barnhart MO 63012

(636) 464-4544

e-mail: *Becky@aresumesolution.com*

A Word's Worth Resume and Writing Service

www.keytosuccessresumes.com

Nina K. Ebert CPRW/CC

Serving clients since 1989, A Word's Worth is a full-service resume and cover letter development/career coaching company with a proven track record in opening doors to interviews.

A+ Career & Resume, LLC

www.careerandresume.com

Karen M. Silins CMRS, CCMC, CRW, CECC, CEIP, CTAC, CCA

Expertise includes career document development, career exploration and transition, assessments, job search methods, networking, interviewing, motivation, dressing for success, and career management strategies.

Abilities Enhanced

🖰 *www.abilitiesenhanced.com*
Meg Montford MCCC, CMF, CCM
Helps enable radical career change, as from
IT trainer to pharmaceutical sales rep and
technical writer to personal trainer. Career
coaching and resumes by a careers professional since 1986.

Advanced Resume Services

🖰 *www.resumeservices.com*
Michele Haffner CPRW, JCTC
Resumes, cover letters, target mailings,
interview coaching, and search strategy/
action plan development. Specialty is
mid- to senior-level professionals earning $75K+. Complimentary critique.
Over 10 years of experience. Guaranteed
satisfaction.

Advantage Resume & Career Services

🖰 *www.CuttingEdgeResumes.com*
Vivian VanLier CPRW, JCTC, CCMC,
CEIP, CPRC
Full-service resume writing and career coach-
ing serving clients throughout the U.S. and
internationally at all levels. Special expertise
in Entertainment, Management, Senior
Executives, and Creative and Financial
Careers.

Arnold-Smith Associates

🖰 *www.ResumesOS.com*
Arnold G. Boldt CPRW, JCTC
Offers comprehensive job search consulting services, including writing resumes
and cover letters; interview simulations;
career assessments and coaching; and

both electronic and direct-mail job search
campaigns.

A&E Consulting

🖰 *www.aspire-empower.com*
Laura Labovitch
45722 Wellesley Terrace #330
Sterling VA 20166
(703) 942-9390
Fax; (703) 406-0587
e-mail: *aspireempower@gmail.com*

A Successful Career

🖰 *www.ablueribbonresume.com*
Georgia Adamson
1096 N. Central Ave
San Jose CA 95128
(408) 244-6401
e-mail: *success@blueribbonresume.com*

Brandego LLC

🖰 *www.brandego.com*
Kirsten Dixson CPBS, JCTC
Creates Web Portfolios for executives,
careerists, authors, consultants, and speakers. Includes experts in branding, career
management, multimedia, copywriting,
blogging, and SEO to express your unique
value.

Career Directions, LLC

🖰 *www.careeredgecoach.com*
Louise Garver JCTC, CPRW, MCDP,
CEIP, CMP
Career Directions, LLC, is a full-service practice specializing in resume development, job-
search strategies, and career-coaching services
for sales and marketing executives and managers worldwide.

Career Ink

🖰 *www.careerink.com*

Roberta Gamza JCTC, JST, CEIP

Offering career marketing and communication strategy services that advance careers. Services include precisely crafted resumes and customized interview training sessions that persuade and motivate potential employers to action.

Career Marketing Techniques

🖰 *www.polishedresumes.com*

Diane Burns CPRW, CCMC, CPCC, CFJST, IJCTC, CEIP, CCM

A career coach and resume strategist who specializes in executive-level military conversion resumes and federal government applications. She is a careers industry international speaker and national author.

Career Solutions, LLC

🖰 *www.WritingResumes.com*

Maria E. Hebda CCMC, CPRW

A certified career professional, she helps people effectively market themselves to employers and position them as qualified candidates. Provides writing and coaching services in resume and cover letter development.

Career Trend

🖰 *www.careertrend.net*

Jacqui Barrett MRW, CPRW, CEIP

Collaborates with professionals and executives aspiring to ignite their careers or manage transition. The owner is among an elite group holding the Master Resume Writer designation via Career Masters Institute

Cheek & Cristantello Career Connections, LLC

🖰 *www.cheekandcristantello.com*

Freddie Cheek M.S. Ed., CCM, CPRW, CRW, CWDP

Resource for resume writing and interview coaching with twenty-five years' experience satisfying customers and getting results. Creates accomplishment-based resumes that help you achieve your career goals.

Confidentcareer.com

🖰 *www.confidentcareer.com*

Divya Gupta

(630) 364-1848

e-mail: *divya@confidentcareer.com*

Create Your Career

🖰 *www.careerist.com*

Joyce Fortier CCM, CCMC

Company collaborates with clients as a catalyst for optimum career success. Services include resume and cover letter services, and coaching services, including job search techniques, interview preparation, networking, and salary negotiation.

Creating Prints

🖰 *www.creatingprints.com*

Rosa Vargas

3799 Millenia

Orlando FL 32839

(407) 802-4962

e-mail: *Rvargas@creatingprints.com*

Dynamic Resume Solutions

🖰 *www.dynamicresumesolutions.com*

Darlene Dassy

14 Crestview Drive

Sinking Spring PA 19608
(610) 678-0147
e-mail: *Darlene@dynamicresumesolutions.com*

ekm Inspirations

🖰 *www.ekminspirations.com*
Norine T. Dagliano FJST, Certified DISC
Administrator
More than 18 years of comprehensive and
individualized career transition services,
working with professionals at all levels of
experience. Specializes in federal job search
assistance, assisting dislocated workers, and
career changers.

Executive Essentials

🖰 *www.career-management-coach.com*
Cindy Kraft CCMC, CCM, CPRW, JCTC
Prepares professionals and executives to outperform the competition. Top-notch marketing documents, a focused branding strategy,
and job search coaching result in a multifaceted, effective, and executable search plan.

Executive Power Coach

🖰 *www.ExecutivePowerCoach.com*
Deborah Wile Dib CPBS, CCM, CCMC,
NCRW, CPRW, CEIP, JCTC
Careers-industry leader helps very senior
executives stand out, get to the top, and stay
at the top. Executive brand development,
power resumes, and executive power coaching
services since 1989.

Guarneri Associates

🖰 *www.Resume-Magic.com*
Susan Guarneri NCC, NCCC, LPC, MCC,
CPRW, CCMC, CEIP, JCTC, CWPP

Comprehensive career services—from career
counseling and assessments to resumes and
cover letters—by full-service career professional
with top-notch credentials, twenty years of
experience, and satisfied customers.

Greenbrand

🖰 *www.1greenbrand.com*
Kevin Morris
168 SW Oakwood Court
Lake City FL 32024
(386) 623-5124
e-mail: *kmorris@lani.net*

JobWhiz

🖰 *www.JobWhiz.com*
Debra Feldman B.S., M.P.H.
Personally arranges confidential networking appointments delivering decision makers
inside target employers. Engineers campaign
strategy, innovates positioning, and defines
focus. Banishes barriers accelerating job
search progress. Relentless follow-up guarantees results.

The Loriel Group—CoachingROI: ResumeROI

🖰 *www.ResumeROI.com*
Lorie Lebert CPRW, IJCTC, CCMC
A full-service career management provider,
offering personalized, confidential support
and guidance; moving client careers forward
with focused customer service.

The McLean Group

Don Orlando MBA, CPRW, JCTC,
CCM, CCMC
Puts executives in control of the career they've
always deserved. Personal, on-demand support

that helps busy managers get paid what they are worth.

e-mail: *yourcareercoach@aol.com*

Mil-Roy Consultants

www.milroyconsultants.com

Nicole Miller CCM, CRW, IJCTC, CECC

Creates the extra edge needed for success through the innovative design of dynamic resumes and marketing tools that achieve results.

Partnering For Success, LLC

www.resumes4results.com

Cory Edwards CRW, CECC, CCMC

Resume writer and career coach currently achieving 98 percent success rate getting clients interviews. Specializing in all resumes, including federal, SES, postal, and private sector from entry-level to executive.

Resume Impressions

www.resumeimpressions.com

Melissa Kassler

540 West Union Street, Suite 4

Athens OH 45701

(740) 592-3993

Fax: (740) 592-1352

e-mail: *resume@frognet*

Resumes Etc

www.cnyresumes.com

Terrie Osborn

PO Box 454

Central Square NY 13036

(315) 676-3315

e-mail: *tosborn@twcny.rr.com*

Resumes for Less

www.ResumesForLess.com

Gwen Harrison

5847 North 9th Ave, Suite A113

Pensacola FL 32504-9312

(800) 706-2942

Fax: (800) 706-2942

e-mail: *resume@frognet*

ResumeRighter

www.ResumeRighter.com

Denise Larkin CPRW, CEIP

A mount-a-campaign, market-yourself, total-job-search support system. They promise to: Present your qualifications for best advantage, write an attention-grabbing cover letter, and coach you to ace your interview.

Resume Suite

www.resumesuite.com

Bonnie Kurka CPRW, JCTC, FJST

Career coach, resume writer, speaker, and trainer with more than 11 years' experience in the careers industry. Specializes in mid- to upper-level management, IT, military, and federal career fields.

The Resume Writer

www.theresumewriter.com

Patricia Traina-Duckers CPRW, CRW, CEIP, CFRWC, CWPP

Fully certified career service practice offering complete career search services, including personalized civilian/federal resume development, business correspondence, Web portfolios, bios, CVs, job search strategies, interview coaching, salary research, and more.

Tools for Transition

🖱 *www.toolsfortransition.com*
Irene Marshall
38750 Paseo Padre Parkway, #C1
Fremont CA 94536
(510) 790-9005
Fax: (510) 315-3132
e-mail: *irene@toolsfortransition.com*

Write Away Resume and Career Coaching

🖱 *www.writeawayresume.com*
Edie Rische NCRW, JCTC, ACCC
Creates targeted resumes and job search correspondence for clients in every vocation, and specializes in helping others discover their "Authentic Vocation," shift careers, and resolve issues using "QuantumShift" coaching.

APPENDIX B
INTERNET RESOURCES

THESE ARE REALLY Knock 'em Dead Internet resources, with links to Web sites in twenty-two job search and career-management categories.

You'll find the big job banks, profession specific sites for eighteen major industries, associations, entry level, executive, minority sites, and more. You'll discover tools that help you find companies, executives, and lost colleagues, plus sites that help you choose new career directions or find a super-qualified professional resume writer, job, or career coach. To save time, you can come to the Knockemdead.com website, where you can click on each of these resources and be connected directly—no more typing in endless URLs!

Association Sites

🖱 *www.ipl.org*
The Internet Public Library. Lots of great research services of potential use to your job search. This link takes you directly to an online directory of professional associations.

🖱 *www.weddles.com*
Peter Weddle's employment services site also offers a comprehensive online professional association directory.

Career and Job Coaches

🖱 *www.knockemdead.com*
Martin Yate CPC Executive Career Strategist
E-mail: *martin@knockemdead.com*
Martin typically works with C-level and C-level bound professionals facing challenges in the areas of Job Search, Interviewing, and Career Strategy.

🖱 *www.phoenixcareergroup.com*
A private, by invitation only, association of seasoned and credentialed coaches, of which I am a member. I know all the Phoenix consultants professionally, and I'm proud to know most of them personally; they're the finest you'll find.

🖱 *www.certifiedcareercoaches.com*
A website that features only certified career coaches.

🖱 *www.certifiedresumewriters.com*
A website that features only certified resume writers.

Career Assessments

🖱 *www.analyzemycareer.com*
A well-organized and comprehensive career choice online testing site.

🖱 *www.assessment.com*
A career choice test which matches your motivations against career directions. I've been using it for a number of years.

🖱 *www.crgleader.com*
Links to career planning and choice tools. The first free career choice test listed wasn't very helpful, but the site has other good resources.

🖱 *www.careerplanner.com*
Affordable RIASEC oriented career choice testing by an established online presence.

🖱 *www.careertest.us*
Allows you to take online career tests and get reports in minutes.

🖱 *www.college911.com*
Helps you find colleges based on your interests. No career choice tests; rather a site you might want to visit after you have a general sense of direction.

🖱 *www.livecareer.com*
Home page says it's free, and the free report is okay as far as it goes, which is not very far. To get a full report you will pay $25 and there are also premium options, but you don't know this until you have spent thirty minutes taking the test! Despite this sleight of hand, a good career choice test with comprehensive reports.

🖱 *www.princetonreview.com*
A $40 online test; this is a good solid test and the site is easy to navigate.

🖱 *www.rockportinstitute.com*
Excellent career choice tests for all ages. Although priced on a sliding scale dependent on income, they start at $1,500 for someone earning 40K a year or less.

🖰 *www.self-directed-search.com*
This is the famous SDS test developed by John Holland. An extremely well-regarded test, and at just $9.95 it's a great deal.

Career Choice and Management Sites

🖰 *www.acinet.org*
A site that offers career choice and advancement advice via testing for job seekers at all levels. Has good info on enhancing your professional credentials.

🖰 *www.phoenixcareergroup.com*
A premier site featuring deeply experienced and credentialed career counselors available for consultation on an hourly basis.

🖰 *www.quintcareers.com*
Career and job-search advice.
Excellent site for job search and career management advice. It's been around for years and is run by people who really care.

Career Transition

Military Transition

🖰 *www.destinygroup.com*
A great site for anyone transitioning out of the military. The number-one post-military careers site.

🖰 *www.corporategray.com*

🖰 *www.taonline.com*
Military transition assistance.

Other Transition

🖰 *www.careertransition.org*
For dancers once their joints go.

College and Entry Level Job Sites

🖰 *www.aleducation.com*
Directories and links for colleges and graduate schools, test prep, financial aid, and job search advice.

🖰 *www.aboutjobs.com*
Links and leads for student jobs, internships, recent grads, expats, and adventure seekers.

🖰 *www.aftercollege.com*
Internships and co-ops, part-time and entry level, Ph.D.s and post-docs, teaching jobs, plus alumni links.

🖰 *www.backdoorjobs.com*
Short-term and part-time adventure and dream jobs.

🖰 *www.blackcollegian.com*
Premier site for black college students and recent graduates; help and sensible advice in areas of concern for the young professional.

🖰 *www.campuscareercenter.com*
Job search, career guidance, and advice on networking for transition into the professional world.

🖰 *www.careerfair.com*
Career fair directory.

🖰 *www.collegecentral.com*
A networking site for graduates of small- and medium-size community colleges.

🖰 *www.collegegrad.com*
A comprehensive and well-thought-out site full of good information for the entry-level job seeker; probably the best in the entry-level field.

🖰 *www.collegejobboard.com*
A top job site for entry-level jobs in all fields.

🖰 *www.collegejournal.com*

Run by the *Wall Street Journal*, it's a savvy site for entry-level professionals, with lots of resources.

www.collegerecruiter.com
One of the highest traffic sites for students and recent grads with up to three years' experience. Well-established and comprehensive job site.

www.ednet.com
Reports on college aid, college selection, career guidance, and college strategy.

www.entryleveljobs.net
It's been around since 1999, and it does have jobs posted, though much is out of date.

www.graduatingengineer.com
A site for graduating engineers and computer careers.

www.internshipprograms.com
A good site if you are looking for an internship.

www.jobpostings.net
The online presence of one of the biggest college recruitment magazine publishers in North America; includes jobs across U.S. and Canada.

www.jobtrak.com
Now owned by Monster, it's their presence in the entry level job market.

www.jobweb.com
Owned and sponsored by the Association of Colleges and Employers. It's a great way to tap into the employers who consistently have entry level hiring needs.

www.snagajob.com
For part-time and hourly jobs.

College Placement and Alumni Networks

www.mcli.dist.maricopa.edu
Resource for community college URLs.

www.utexas.edu
Resource for locating college alumni groups.

Diversity Sites

janweb.icdi.wvu.edu
Job Accommodation Network: a portal site for people with disabilities.

www.bilingual-jobs.com
Like the name says: a site for bilingual jobs, in America and around the globe.

www.blackcollegian.com
Premier site for black college students and recent graduates; help and sensible advice in areas of concern for the young professional.

www.business-disability.com
Run by the National Business and Disability Council, job search through listings of member organizations, post resumes, career events, and internships.

www.bwni.com
Businesswomen's network.

www.christianjobs.com
Full-featured employment website focusing on employment within the Christian community.

www.diversitylink.com
Job site serving women, minorities, and other diversity talent.

www.eop.com
The online presence of the oldest diversity recruitment publisher in America. For women, members of minority groups, and people with disabilities.

www.experienceworks.org
Training and employment services for mature workers, 55 and older.

www.gaywork.com
A job site featuring a resume bank and job postings for gay men and women.

www.hirediversity.com
Links multicultural and bilingual professionals with both national and international industry sectors. Clients primarily consist of *Fortune* 1000 companies and government agencies.

www.imdiversity.com
Communities for African Americans, Asian Americans, Hispanic Americans, Native Americans, and women. No jobs or overt career advice, but lots of links for members of minority communities on issues that affect our lives.

www.latpro.com
The number-one employment source for Spanish- and Portuguese-speaking professionals in North and South America. The site can be viewed in English, Spanish, or Portuguese. Features both resume and job banks.

Executive Job Sites

www.netshare.com
Been around since before the Internet with tenured management; really understands and cares about the executive in transition. Job banks, resources, etc.

www.6figurejobs.com
Solid and well-respected site; includes job banks, resources, etc. A warning: Some of their career advice seems very nonspecific and geared to selling services.

www.careerjournal.com
Run by the *Wall Street Journal* with all the bells and whistles, this is an excellent executive transition site.

www.chiefmonster.com
Monster's site aimed at the executive area, though it's difficult to differentiate from the rest of the brand. Comprehensive job postings.

www.execunet.com
One of the top executive sites (along with Netshare, 6 Figure, and the *WSJ* site). Job banks and resources. Founder Dave Opton has been around a long time and runs a blog with interesting insights.

www.futurestep.com
Korn Ferry is the search firm behind the site and you can put your resume in their database.

www.spencerstuart.com
Executive site for eminent search firm Spencer Stuart. You can put your resume in their database.

www.theladders.com
Like pretty much all the executive sites, you pay for access. Good job board and aggressive marketing means this site has become a player in the space very quickly.

Finding Companies

flipdog.monster.com

www.corporateinformation.com
In addition to having an alphabetical listing of over 20,000 companies, you can also research a country's industry or research a U.S. state. Also, if you register with the site, it will allow you to load the company profile. Within the address

section, you will find a link to the company's
home page.

- *www.eliyon.com*
- *www.goleads.com*
- *www.google.com*
- *www.infospace.com*
- *www.searchbug.com*
- *www.superpages.com*
- *www.wetfeet.com*

General Job Sites

- *flipdog.monster.com*
- *hotjobs.yahoo.com*
- *www.4jobs.com*
- *www.americasjobbank.com*
- *www.bestjobsusa.com*
- *www.career.com*
- *www.careerboard.com*
- *www.careerbuilder.com*
- *www.careerhunters.com*
- *www.careermag.com*
- *www.careers.org*

Good one-stop site for job search resources.

- *www.careershop.com*
- *www.careersite.com*
- *www.directemployers.com*
- *www.employment911.com*
- *www.employmentguide.com*
- *www.employmentspot.com*
- *www.job-hunt.org*

Excellent site with sensible in-depth advice on
job search and career management issues.

- *www.job.com*
- *www.jobbankusa.com*
- *www.jobfind.com*
- *www.jobwarehouse.com*
- *www.jobweb.com*
- *www.localcareers.com*
- *www.mbajungle.com*

Site for current entry level-ish and future
MBAs.

- *www.monster.com*
- *www.nationjob.com*
- *www.net-temps.com*
- *www.quintcareers.com*

Diversity Job-Seeker Career, Employment, Job Resources

- *www.snagajob.com*
- *www.sologig.com*
- *www.summerjobs.com*
- *www.topusajobs.com*
- *www.truecareers.com*
- *www.vault.com*
- *www.wetfeet.com*
- *www.worklife.com*

Job Posting Spiders

- *www.indeed.com*
- *www.jobbankusa.com*
- *www.jobs.just-posted.com*
- *www.jobsearchengine.com*
- *www.jobsniper.com*
- *www.worktree.com*

International Sites

🖰 *www.ukjobsnet.co.uk*
UK Jobs Network: the easiest way to find vacancies throughout the United Kingdom.

🖰 *www.4icj.com*

🖰 *www.careerone.com.au*

🖰 *www.eurojobs.com*

🖰 *www.gojobsite.co.uk*

🖰 *www.jobpilot.com*

🖰 *www.jobsbazaar.com*

🖰 *www.jobserve.com*

🖰 *www.jobstreet.com*
Asia-Pacific's number-one job site.

🖰 *www.monster.ca*
Monster Canada

🖰 *www.monster.co.uk*
Monster UK: England's number-one job site.

🖰 *www.overseasjobs.com*

🖰 *www.reed.co.uk*

🖰 *www.seek.com.au*
Australia's number-one job site.

🖰 *www.stepstone.com*

🖰 *www.topjobs.co.uk*

🖰 *www.totaljobs.com*

🖰 *www.workopolis.com*
Canada's number-one job site.

Job Fairs

🖰 *www.careerfairs.com*
CareerFairs.com is the fastest one-stop Internet site for locating upcoming job fairs and employers. In some cases you can even find the specific positions you desire and the specific positions you are trying to fill.

🖰 *www.cfg-inc.com*
Career Fairs for all levels: Professional and General, Health Care, Technical, Salary, Hourly, and Entry to Senior Level.

🖰 *www.preferredjobs.com*

🖰 *www.psijobfair.com*

🖰 *www.skidmore.edu*

Networking Sites

network.monster.com

socialsoftware.weblogsinc.com
This blog maintains a comprehensive listing of hundreds of networking sites. If you want to check out all your networking options, this is the place to start.

🖰 *www.40plus.org*
Chapter contact information.

🖰 *www.alumni.net*

🖰 *www.distinctiveweb.com*

🖰 *www.eliyon.com*
Helps you find people and companies.

🖰 *www.execunet.com*
An extensive network of professionals with whom you can interact for advice, support, and even career enhancement through local networking meetings. To locate meetings near you (U.S. and the world), check under "Networking" on their website.

🖰 *www.fiveoclockclub.com*
National career-counseling network.

🖰 *www.fiveoclockclub.com*
Network with members and alumni database.

🖰 *www.rileyguide.com*

🖰 *www.ryze.com*

Helps people make connections and expand their networks. You can network to grow your business, build your career, and find a job. You can also join networks related to your industry for free.

🖱 *www.tribe.net*

🖱 *www.womans-net.com*

🖱 *www.linkedin.com*

Newspaper Sites

newsdirectory.com
Links to newspapers (global).

Profession Specific Sites

Advertising, Public Relations, and Graphic Arts

🖱 *www.adage.com*

🖱 *www.adweek.com*
Adweek Online

🖱 *www.amic.com*
Advertising Media Internet Center

🖱 *www.creativehotlist.com*

Communication Arts

🖱 *www.prweek.net*
pr week

Aerospace and Aviation

🖱 *www.aerojobs.com*

🖱 *www.avcrew.com*

🖱 *www.avjobs.com*

🖱 *www.spacejobs.com*

Agriculture and Horticulture

🖱 *www.agricareers.com*

🖱 *www.fishingjobs.com*

🖱 *www.hortjobs.com*

Broadcast, Communications, and Journalism

🖱 *www.b-roll.net*

🖱 *www.cpb.org*
Corporation for Public Broadcasting

🖱 *www.crew-net.com*

🖱 *www.journalismjobs.com*

🖱 *www.telecomcareers.net*

🖱 *www.womcom.org*
AWC Online

Business, Finance, and Accounting

🖱 *www.accounting.com*

🖱 *www.bankjobs.com*

🖱 *www.brokerhunter.com*

🖱 *www.businessfinancemag.com*

🖱 *www.careerbank.com*

🖱 *www.careerjournal.com*

🖱 *www.cfo.com*

🖱 *www.efinancialjobs.com*

🖱 *www.fei.org*

🖱 *www.financialjobs.com*

🖱 *www.jobsinthemoney.com*

Education

🖱 *www.aacc.nche.edu*
American Association of Community Colleges

🖱 *www.academic360.com*

🖱 *www.academiccareers.com*

🖱 *www.chronicle.com*

- www.higheredjobs.com
- www.petersons.com
- www.phds.org
- www.teacherjobs.com
- www.ujobbank.com
- www.wihe.com
Women in Higher Education

Engineering

- www.asme.org
- www.chemindustry.com
- www.engineeringcentral.com
- www.engineeringjobs.com
- www.engineerjobs.com
- www.enr.com
Engineering News Record Magazine
- www.graduatingengineer.com
- www.ieee.org
- www.mepatwork.com
- www.nsbe.org
National Society of Black Engineers
- www.nspe.org
National Society of Professional Engineers
- www.swe.org
Society of Women Engineers

Entertainment, TV, and Radio

- www.castingnet.com
- www.eej.com
Entertainment Employment Journal
- www.entertainmentcareers.net
- www.showbizjobs.com
- www.themeparkjobs.com

- www.tvandradiojobs.com
- www.tvjobs.com

Healthcare

- www.accessnurses.com
Travel nursing jobs
- www.allnurses.com
- www.dentsearch.com
- www.healthcaresource.com
- www.healthjobusa.com
- www.hirehealth.com
- www.jobscience.com
- www.mdjobsite.com
- www.medcareers.com
- www.nurses123.com
Nurses can use this site to find nursing jobs across the United States.
- www.nursetown.com
- www.nursing-jobs.us
Nursing jobs in the United States.
- www.nursingcenter.com
- www.nursingspectrum.com
- www.physemp.com

Human Resources

- www.hrjobnet.com
- www.hrworld.com
- www.jobs4hr.com
- www.shrm.org
- www.tcm.com

IT and MIS

- www.computerjobs.com
- www.computerjobsbank.com

- www.dice.com
- www.gjc.org
- www.mactalent.com
- www.tech-engine.com
- www.techemployment.com
- www.techies.com

Legal

- www.emplawyernet.com
- www.ihirelegal.com
- www.law.com
- www.legalstaff.com
- www.theblueline.com

Nonprofit

- www.execsearches.com
- www.idealist.org
- www.naswdc.org
- www.nonprofitcareer.com
- www.opportunityknocks.org

Real Estate

- www.realtor.org

Retail, Hospitality, and Customer Service

- www.allretailjobs.com
- www.chef2chef.net
- www.chefjobsnetwork.com
- www.coolworks.com
- www.hcareers.com
- www.leisurejobs.com
- www.resortjobs.com
- www.restaurantrecruit.com
- www.supermarketnews.com

Sales and Marketing

- www.careermarketplace.com
- www.jobs4sales.com
- www.marketingjobs.com
- www.marketingmanager.com
- www.marketingpower.com
- www.salesheads.com
- www.salesjobs.com

Science, Chemistry, Physics, and Biology

- www.biocareer.com
- www.biospace.com
- www.bioview.com
- www.bmn.com
- www.eco.org
- www.hirebio.com
- www.medzilla.com
- www.microbiologistjobs.com
- www.pharmacyweek.com

Recruiter Sites

- www.kellyservices.com
- www.kornferry.com
- www.manpower.com
- www.napsweb.org

A job seeker can search the online directory by state, specialty, or by individual. Be sure to check out the headhunters who are designated C.P.C.s—the few but the best.

- www.randstad.com
- www.recruitersonline.com
- www.rileyguide.com
- www.snelling.com

🖰 *www.spherion.com*

🖰 *www.staffingtoday.net*

Search the database by state, skills, and type
of services you need (temporary/permanent/
profession) and it will tell you about staffing
services companies in your area.

🖰 *www.therecruiternetwork.com*

Reference Checking

🖰 *www.allisontaylor.com*

Researching Companies

bls.gov

iws.ohiolink.edu
A place for getting started with company
research.

iws.ohiolink.edu
Helpful in understanding industry research.

newsdirectory.com

🖰 *www.competia.com*

🖰 *www.fuld.com*

🖰 *www.industrylink.com*

🖰 *www.learnwebskills.com*
A business research tutorial that presents a
step-by-step process for finding free company
and industry information on the web. This
online course will enable you to learn about
an industry, and locate company home pages.

🖰 *www.quintcareers.com*
The quintessential directory of company
career centers.

🖰 *www.quintcareers.com*
Guide to researching companies, industries,
and countries.

🖰 *www.thomasregister.com*

🖰 *www.vault.com*

Company research.

🖰 *www.vault.com*
Industry list.

🖰 *www.virtualpet.com*
Teaches you how to learn about an industry
or a specific company.

Resume Creation

Knockemdead.com
E-mail: *martin@knockemdead.com*

🖰 *www.phoenixcareergroup.com*

certifiedresumewriters.com

parw.com

Resume Distribution

🖰 *www.resumemachine.com*

Salary Research

🖰 *www.jobstar.org*

🖰 *www.salary.com*

🖰 *www.salaryexpert.com*

Telecommuting

🖰 *www.homeworkers.org*

🖰 *www.jobs-telecommuting.com*

🖰 *www.tdigest.com*

🖰 *www.tjobs.com*

Web Resumes/Portfolios

🖰 *www.brandego.com*

🖰 *www.qfolio.com*

INDEX